The
YEARBOOK
2003 EDITION

World Wrestling Entertainment™ Presents

The YEARBOOK 2003 EDITION

Michael McAvennie

POCKET BOOKS

New York   London   Toronto   Sydney   Singapore

ISBN: 0-7434-6373-0

First Pocket Books printing April 2003

10 9 8 7 6 5 4 3 2 1

POCKET and colophon are registered trademarks of Simon & Schuster, Inc.

Visit us on the World Wide Web
http://simonsays.com
http://www.wwe.com

Printed in the U.S.A.

For information regarding special discounts for bulk purchases, please contact Simon & Schuster Special Sales at 1-800-456-6798 or business@simonandschuster.com

Dedication

To my mom and dad,
for not sending me to bed when *All-Star Wrestling*
moved to Saturday nights at midnight.
And to my beautiful wife Áine,
who's been my all-star in making my dreams,
and this book, come true.

Chapter 1
Ready to "Rumble"
8

Chapter 2
A new (World) order
34

Chapter 3
'Mania Runs Wild
64

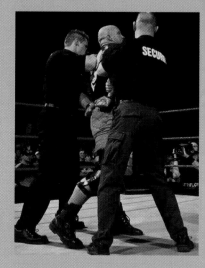

158
Chapter 7
Ruthless "Vengeance"

184
Chapter 8
Summer Slammed

218
Chapter 9
Sins "Unforgiven"

Chapter 4
Lashing Out

Chapter 5
Passing "Judgment"

Chapter 6
The Next Big "King"

98

116

136

250

286

320

Chapter 10
Tyrants Without Mercy

Chapter 11
"Survivor" of the Fittest

Chapter 12
The End

352 Acknowledgments

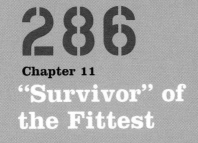

CONTENTS

JANUARY

Ready to "Rumble"

"I enjoy destroying lives.
It turns me on."
—WWE co-owner Vince McMahon,
regarding his upcoming
Royal Rumble match with Ric Flair.
(January 10 *SmackDown!*)

"This injury has taught me
that if you have the desire
to do it, you could come
back from just about any-
thing. How bad do you want
it? What sacrifices are you
willing to make? Seven
months with nothing to do
but rehab and train...live
like a hermit...every second
of it was worth it if I get
back in the ring and get back
to doing what I love to do."
—Triple H

The Superstars of World Wrestling Entertainment left 2001 behind with a furious *Vengeance*, and welcomed 2002 with a violent *Rumble*.

For the WWE's biggest and baddest, the key to winning the *Royal Rumble* was about desire. It was desire that saw "Hacksaw" Jim Duggan throw the One Man Gang over the top rope to become the winner of the first-ever *Rumble* in 1988, and it was desire fifteen years later that would inspire one man to stand alone in the ring and outlast twenty-nine human obstacles standing in the way of undisputed immortality at *WrestleMania X8*. Stone Cold Steve Austin, Undertaker, Kurt Angle ... *all* of the Superstars entered in *Royal Rumble 2002* had that desire to win. But first they would have to play The Game.

After 2001's foiled Invasion by the Alliance—an amalgam of two now-defunct organizations, World Championship Wrestling and Extreme Championship Wrestling—it was agreed to unify the WCW World Championship with the WWE Title at the Pay-Per-View *Vengeance*. It was there on December 9, 2001 that Chris Jericho achieved a life-long dream, defeating The Rock and Stone Cold Steve Austin on the same night to become the WWE's first-ever *Undisputed* Champion. Y2J would carry both belts into the New Year, and a staunch desire to *keep* them after the *Royal Rumble*.

Jericho's opponent for the January 20 PPV was determined at the first *SmackDown!* main event of the New Year, a No. 1 Contender's match between former five-time WCW World Champion Booker T and former six-time WWE, three-time WCW and *always* the *People's* Champion, The Rock. A loyal underling to WWE co-owner Vince McMahon of late, Booker prepped for his match by joining Boss Man in a beatdown of Stone Cold Steve Austin. Notwithstanding backstage interviewer Jonathan "Coach" Coachman's awful rendition of Barry Manilow's "Copacabana," it was The Rock who'd roll into Washington, D.C.'s MCI Center, overcoming interference from McMahon and Boss Man to deliver a Rock Bottom that nearly drove Booker through the canvas. That he and a returning Austin were laid out by the McMahon henchman after the match was moot; the Great One was headed for the big dance at the *Royal Rumble*.

Y2J didn't seem overly concerned; he'd beaten The Rock four times in 2001, a fact he conveniently reminded "best buddies" Test, Lance Storm and European Champion Christian while giving them presents simply for being the kind of friends "that will watch each others' backs." Besides, he had bigger concerns impacting him before the Pay-Per-View, starting with a DDT-styled Edgecution during January 3's Tag match against Rob Van Dam and Intercontinental Champion Edge. Though he'd crawl onto Edge for a three-count thanks to an Angle Slam assist from partner Kurt Angle, there was almost no climbing past the threat of going face-to-Stinkface with three hundred and fifty-pounder Rikishi on January 7 *Raw*. Narrowly avoiding the cheeky finisher due to one-sided officiating from referee Nick Patrick, Y2J resorted to an undisputed cheap shot, using one of the heavyweight belts on the Phat Man for a "larger than life" victory.

Fancying himself a "living legend" around which the entire world should revolve, Jericho's *Raw* arrogance toward WWE co-owner wrestling great Ric Flair, and the "chaw chewers" inside Dallas' American Airlines Arena earned the Nature Boy's legendary Figure-Four Leglock on January 14. A surprise attack from Flair's *Royal Rumble* opponent, fellow WWE proprietor Mr. Vince McMahon, spared Jericho from injury, though his impaired judgment in bragging backstage to Lance Storm and Christian quickly drew the ire of proud Texan Bradshaw, APA partner Faarooq and Rikishi. The Undisputed Champ would finally do more than talk during the back-and-forth Six-Man Tag match, catching Faarooq in a Breakdown maneuver and scoring the pin for his team.

Meanwhile, momentum seemed to be shifting The Rock's way. Putting aside their past differences (including their classic *WrestleMania XV* and *X-Seven* encounters), he and Stone Cold Steve Austin hoisted Steveweisers inside Madison Square Garden on January 7 to celebrate their *Raw* tag win over Boss Man and Booker T. Rock would enjoy even more MSG tag success January 10 *SmackDown!*, partnering Rob Van Dam against Test and *Royal Rumble* adversary Chris Jericho. RVD's Van Daminator kick and Five-Star Frog Splash from the top rope had outdone Test in their singles match three nights earlier, though they were still working out plenty of aggression as their battle spilled out into the crowd. With Rock and Jericho still in the ring, the Brahma Bull would use his knees to block a Y2J Lionsault off the ropes, then "pinebustered" the Undisputed Champion before turning him over with the sharpshooter, forcing Jericho to submit.

In a postmatch interview backstage, the Great One guaranteed the same result at the *Rumble*, since he had something "huge" waiting for the "larger than life" Y2J. It wasn't what "sick *freak*" interviewer Jonathan Coachman thought—Rock was going to take his size-fourteen boot, "… shove it up, pull it out, shove it *up*, pull it *out*, rub it all over Coach's face, 'cause he *likes* it, then take a big step back, turn it sideways and *shove it straight up Chris Jericho's candy ass!*"

> [**"It doesn't matter** who's going to win the *Royal Rumble*! The only thing undisputed is gonna be The Rock *leaving* the *Royal Rumble* as the Undisputed Champion!"**]

The people inside Louisiana's CenturyTel Center believed Rock could beat Jericho, as did several of the WWE Superstars who confronted him backstage at January 17 *SmackDown!* each warning him they'd prevail in the *Royal Rumble* and meet again at *WrestleMania X8*. But the People's Champ headed ringside with a message

LAST MEN STANDING

World Wrestling Entertainment's first *Royal Rumble* didn't start as a Pay-Per-View affair, instead airing live on USA Network in 1988. But the simple concept of throwing opponents over the top rope proved so popular it earned its annual January spot the following year. By 1993, winning the tournament became even more important to the entrants involved, since it automatically secured a WWE title opportunity against the Champion at that year's *WrestleMania*.

Over the years, some stipulations have changed, as has the size of the tournament. In 1992 it went from twenty combatants to thirty, when a then-vacated WWE title was up for grabs. The tournament remains as exciting as ever, especially for the winning participants whose names will always remain inside the squared circle. ∎

ROYAL RUMBLE WINNERS, 1988-2002

Winner (Entry Number)		Eliminated
"Hacksaw" Jim Duggan (13)	1988	Danny Davis (9), Nikolai Volkoff (12), One Man Gang (19)
Big John Studd (27)	1989	Akeem (23), Ted DiBiase (30)
Hulk Hogan (25)*	1990	Jimmy Snuka (17), Haku (14), Honky Tonk Man (24), Ultimate Warrior (21), Rick Rude (28), Mr. Perfect (29)
Hulk Hogan (24)	1991	Smash (15), Greg Valentine (3), Crush (20), Warlord (29), Tugboat (30), Brian Knobs (28), Earthquake (22)
Ric Flair (3)**	1992	British Bulldog (1), Texas Tornado (9), Big Boss Man (13), Sid Justice (29)
Yokozuna (27)	1993	Tatanka (19), Carlos Colon (24), Earthquake (23), Tito Santana (25), Owen Hart (28), Bob Backlund (2), Randy Savage (30)
Lex Luger (23) Bret Hart (27)***	1994	(By Luger:) Great Kabuki (22), Crush (13), Adam Bomb (30), Shawn Michaels (18) (By Hart:) Tenryu (24), Fatu (28)
Shawn Michaels (1)	1995	Duke "The Dumpster"Droese (4), Dr. Tom Prichard (7), Bushwhacker Luke (13), Jacob Blu (3), Bushwhacker Butch (18), Aldo Montoya (21), British Bulldog (2)
Shawn Michaels (18)	1996	Vader (13), Yokozuna (9),1-2-3 Kid (10), Jerry "the King" Lawler (4), Owen Hart (17), Issaac Yankem, D.D.S. (27), British Bulldog (29), Diesel (22)
Stone Cold Steve Austin (5)	1997	Phineas I. Godwinn (4), Bart Gunn (6), Jake "the Snake" Roberts (7), Marc Mero (16), Owen Hart (13), Savio Vega (19), Jesse James (20), Vader (28), Undertaker (30), Bret Hart (21)
Stone Cold Steve Austin (24)	1998	Marc Mero (13), 8-Ball (7), Thrasher (15), Kama Mustafa (23), Savio Vega (26), Chainz (29), The Rock (4)
Mr. McMahon (2)	1999	Stone Cold Steve Austin (1)
The Rock (24)	2000	Big Boss Man (9), Crash Holly (16), Al Snow (20), Big Show (26)
Stone Cold Steve Austin (24)	2001	Haku (29), Billy Gunn (28), Kane (6)

*Hulk Hogan was WWE World Heavyweight Champion when he won the *Royal Rumble 1990*.

**Ric Flair became the WWE World Heavyweight Champion after winning the *Royal Rumble 1992*.

***Both Lex Luger and Bret Hart went over the top rope simultaneously, and were named cowinners of the *Royal Rumble 1994*.

for them and any *other* tournament "winners" in the crowd (including a jabroni *SmackDown!* cameraman, a six-year-old in the front row, "a hot little mama" with a sign asking what Rock was doing after the show, the entire arena Section 108 and so on): *"It doesn't matter who's going to win the Royal Rumble!"* he yelled. "The only thing undisputed is gonna be The Rock *leaving* the *Royal Rumble* as the Undisputed Champion!"

> [**"This is *not* a joke! *I* am not a joke, and you will *not* look past me, you stupid son of a bitch!"**]

His entrance music suddenly filling the stadium, Jericho went ballistic on stage—he resented everyone's "foregone conclusion" that Rocky would beat him, as if he were merely "some kind of fluke champion, or transitional champion." It hurt to think he might be the most overlooked champion in WWE history, but he insisted that by *WrestleMania,* "I'll still *be* the champion!" Rock continued pressing Jericho's buttons, telling him that everyone just knew that he was better than him. "This is *not* a joke!" he screamed. "*I* am not a joke, and you will *not* look past me, you stupid son of a bitch!" Remaining composed as he approached Y2J, the Great One calmly replied, "The Rock is taking you very serious, Chris Jericho...*dead* serious, Chris Jericho...and cannot *wait* to whoop your candy ass at the *Royal Rumble.*" Looking straight at him, he added, "If you smell...what The Rock...is *cookin'.*"

Vincent Kennedy McMahon, *Time* magazine's "Person of the Year." *Almost.* The co-owner of World Wrestling Entertainment boasted on January 3 *SmackDown!* that he was a strong candidate for the accolade, second only to *another* "individual of great integrity," New York City's former Mayor Rudolph Giuliani. Like Giuliani, McMahon would be a "man of action" when it came to his primary New Year's resolution: "To embarrass Ric Flair at the *Royal Rumble.* To annihilate Ric Flair at the *Royal Rumble.* To beat Ric Flair beyond recognition at the *Royal Rumble!*"

Mr. McMahon's hatred for the former sixteen-time World Heavyweight Champion stemmed back to November 2001, when Flair publicly declared himself fifty percent owner of the WWE after purchasing its stocks from Shane and Stephanie, McMahon's estranged children and the foiled masterminds behind the Alliance. McMahon's backhanded business practices, topped by Flair's discovery of Vince's contract stating him as an owner/*wrestler,* would result in the Nature Boy challenging him to a match at the *Royal Rumble,* for which he'd offer some ring advice January 3. "You've got to *walk* that aisle!" Flair yelled

Mr. McMahon struts his stuff as "the Nature Boy."

in front of the MCI Center crowd. "You've got to *style and profile!* You've got to get your eyes poked out! You've got to get kicked in the balls! You've got to get your nose broken! Your eye cut! In other words, you've got to learn to *bleed, sweat,* and *pay* the price to be a *wrestler!*"

Vince's first installment—eight stitches to his left eye—came later that evening, after Flair punched him in the face for breaking up a three-count that would have given The Rock the No. 1 Contender's spot over Booker T. But McMahon would avenge the "unprovoked attack" four nights later on *Raw*—after airing an extraordinary video montage of "The Man's" career

Half-brothers at arms; D-Von, Bubba and Spike.

on the TitanTron, the billionaire ridiculed the moment, claiming, "Flair, I'm already The Man… and now I'm going to prove it." He then proceeded to mock the famous Nature Boy strut while wearing a Flair-like wig and one of his championship robes. Irate, the genuine article confronted Vince, who suddenly produced a lead pipe and cracked open Flair's skull. Pounding away and humiliating the concussed Flair, McMahon left the dirtiest player in the game lying in the ring, in a pool of his own blood.

"I want his family, and I want the whole world, to see what I do to Ric Flair," expressed a somewhat-deranged Mr. McMahon in a January 10 *SmackDown!* conversation with Jim Ross. "Flair will be humbled at the *Rumble…* and then Flair will *beg* me to buy his stock." Admitting to the *Raw* fans in Dallas on January 14 that he had been humbled, Flair pointed out that Vince wasn't the only WWE co-owner who knew how to abuse power, and changed the stipulations of their *Royal Rumble* match to a Street Fight. "No rules! No countouts! No

disqualifications!" he roared. "*Nothing* stops that match! We are going to fill our boots! We're going to *bleed,* we're going to *sweat,* and we're going to pay the price until *one* of us walks out a winner, *guaranteed!*"

Unfortunately, Flair's altercation with Chris Jericho minutes later would leave the Nature Boy open to a second lead-pipe attack from Mr. McMahon. As he and the Undisputed Champion celebrated over the fallen ring legend, Vince McMahon felt damn good; he may not have been *Time*'s 2001 "Person of the Year," but he was one step closer to being "The Man" at the *Royal Rumble.*

Desire comes in all shapes and sizes in the WWE. In the case of Tag Team Champions D-Von and Bubba Ray Dudley, their all-extreme demeanor and taste for wood placed the half-brothers atop the WWE Tag Team table…usually by putting their opponents *through* one. But the unlikely tandem of the Dudleyz' half brother Spike and *Sunday*

Some might say Chris Jericho is in a world of his own. But the fact is, for several months in early 2002, he *was*. At the *Vengeance* PPV in December 2001, Y2J became sports entertainment's first *Undisputed* Champion in over forty years, and the WWE's first ever, by unifying the organization's Heavyweight Championship with the defunct WCW World Championship. The WWE title (then recognized as the WWWF, or World Wide Wrestling Federation) was first held by "Nature Boy" Buddy Rogers in early 1963, the result of the organization's decision to split from the National Wrestling Alliance (NWA) and its recognized champion, legendary grappler Lou Thesz. With a proud history dating back to October 1948 and its first title holder, Orville Brown, the NWA World Heavyweight Championship would become the WCW World Title in 1991, recognizing "Nature Boy" Ric Flair as its first official champion in January of that year.

Six Superstars would wear the WWE Undisputed Championship,

OF TWO WORLD$

which would remain so until September 2, 2002, when *Raw* GM Eric Bischoff decided to reinstate the World Championship as its own entity again, and awarded it to Triple H. The WWE Championship, held by Brock Lesnar, remains on *SmackDown!* ∎

WORLD HEAVYWEIGHT CHAMPIONSHIP HISTORY

WON BY	DATE WON	WON BY	DATE WON
Ric Flair	1/11/91[1]	Kevin Nash	5/9/99
Lex Luger	1/14/91	Randy Savage	7/11/99
Sting	2/29/92	Hollywood Hulk Hogan	7/12/99
Big Van Vader	7/12/92	Sting	9/12/99
Ron Simmons (Faarooq)	8/2/92	Bret Hart	11/21/99[6]
Big Van Vader	12/20/92	Bret Hart	12/20/99[7]
Sting	3/11/93	Chris Benoit	1/16/00[8]
Big Van Vader	3/17/93	Sid Vicious	1/24/00
Ric Flair	12/27/93	Kevin Nash	1/25/00
Ric Flair	4/24/94[2]	Sid Vicious	1/25/00[9]
Hollywood Hulk Hogan	7/17/94	Jeff Jarrett	4/16/00[10]
The Giant (Big Show)	10/29/95[3]	Diamond Dallas Page	4/24/00
Randy Savage	11/26/95[4]	David Arquette	4/25/00[11]
Ric Flair	12/27/95	Jeff Jarrett	5/7/00
Randy Savage	1/22/96	Ric Flair	5/15/00
Ric Flair	2/11/96	Jeff Jarrett	5/22/00
The Giant (Big Show)	4/22/96	Kevin Nash	5/23/00
Hollywood Hulk Hogan	8/10/96	Ric Flair	5/29/00
Lex Luger	8/4/97	Jeff Jarrett	5/29/00[12]
Hollywood Hulk Hogan	8/9/97	Booker T	7/9/00[13]
Sting	12/28/97	Kevin Nash	8/28/00
Sting	2/22/98[5]	Booker T	9/17/00
Randy Savage	4/19/98	Vince Russo	9/25/00
Hollywood Hulk Hogan	4/20/98	Booker T	10/2/00
Bill Goldberg	7/6/98	Scott Steiner	11/26/00
Kevin Nash	12/27/98	Booker T	3/26/01
Hollywood Hulk Hogan	1/4/99	Kurt Angle	7/24/01[14]
Ric Flair	3/14/99	Booker T	7/30/01
Diamond Dallas Page	4/11/99	The Rock	8/19/01
Diamond Dallas Page	4/26/99	Chris Jericho	10/21/01
Sting	4/26/99	The Rock	11/5/01

WORLD TITLE HISTORY NOTES

[1] "Nature Boy" Ric Flair defeats Sting as the National Wrestling Alliance (NWA) Heavyweight Championship is now recognized as the World Championship Wrestling (WCW) Heavyweight title.

[2] Ric Flair recaptures the championship, made vacant after a double pinfall between him and Rick Steamboat a week earlier.

[3] The Giant wins the championship via DQ, made permissible by a contract stipulation. WCW later refuses to recognize the stipulation, and declares the title vacant.

[4] Randy Savage is the final man in a three-ring, sixty-man battle royal to win the World Championship.

[5] Sting recaptures the championship, declared vacant following a controversial ending in his December 29, 1997 match against Hollywood Hulk Hogan.

[6] Bret "Hitman" Hart wins a thirty-two-man tournament to capture the World title, declared vacant after previous champion Sting's October 24 assault on ring official Charles Robinson.

[7] Bret Hart vacates the championship twenty-four hours after a controversial match with Goldberg. Hart then defeats Goldberg to win the belt back later that night.

[8] Chris Benoit wins the World title vacated by the injured Bret Hart, then revacates the championship within twenty-four hours to join the WWE.

[9] Sid Vicious beats WCW Commissioner Kevin Nash for the World Championship, has it stripped away by Nash, then defeats Nash and Ron Harris to win it again in the same evening.

[10] Jeff Jarrett wins the World title one week after Eric Bischoff and Vince Russo declare all titles vacant in the "new and improved" WCW.

[11] Actor David Arquette defeats Eric Bischoff in a stipulation Tag match that awards him the championship. The belt is vacated May 1, 2000.

[12] One week after winning the championship, Kevin Nash presents it to Ric Flair, who loses it to Jeff Jarrett.

[13] Hollywood Hulk Hogan defeats Jeff Jarrett for the World Championship, but the victory isn't recognized by Vince Russo. Jarrett remains champion, only to lose the title to Booker T.

[14] Kurt Angle becomes the first WWE Superstar to win the World Heavyweight Championship.

WWE CHAMPIONSHIP HISTORY

WON BY	DATE WON	WON BY	DATE WON
Buddy Rogers	4/63[1]	Sycho Sid	11/17/96
Bruno Sammartino	5/17/63	Shawn Michaels	1/19/97
Ivan Koloff	1/18/71	Bret Hart	2/16/97
Pedro Morales	2/8/71	Sycho Sid	2/17/97
Stan Stasiak	12/1/73	Undertaker	3/23/97
Bruno Sammartino	12/10/73	Bret Hart	8/3/97
Billy Graham	4/30/77	Shawn Michaels	11/9/97[8]
Bob Backlund	2/20/78	Steve Austin	3/29/98
Antonio Inoki	11/30/79	Kane	6/28/98
Bob Backlund	12/12/79[2]	Steve Austin	6/29/98
Iron Sheik	12/26/83	The Rock	11/15/98[9]
Hollywood Hulk Hogan	1/23/84	Mankind	12/29/98
Andre the Giant	2/5/88[3]	The Rock	1/24/99
Randy Savage	3/27/88[4]	Mankind	1/26/99
Hollywood Hulk Hogan	4/2/89	The Rock	2/15/99
Ultimate Warrior	4/1/90	Steve Austin	3/28/99
Sgt. Slaughter	1/19/91	Undertaker	5/23/99
Hollywood Hulk Hogan	3/24/91	Steve Austin	6/28/99
Undertaker	11/27/91	Mankind	8/22/99
Hollywood Hulk Hogan	12/3/91	Triple H	8/23/99
Ric Flair	1/19/92[5]	Mr. McMahon	9/14/99
Randy Savage	4/5/92	Triple H	9/26/99[10]
Ric Flair	9/1/92	The Big Show	11/14/99
Bret Hart	10/12/92	Triple H	1/3/00
Yokozuna	4/4/93	The Rock	4/30/00
Hollywood Hulk Hogan	4/4/93[6]	Triple H	5/21/00
Yokozuna	6/13/93	The Rock	6/25/00
Bret Hart	3/20/94	Kurt Angle	10/22/00
Bob Backlund	11/23/94	The Rock	2/25/01
Diesel	11/26/94	Steve Austin	4/1/01
Bret Hart	11/19/95[7]	Kurt Angle	9/23/01
Shawn Michaels	3/31/96	Steve Austin	10/8/01

UNDISPUTED CHAMPIONSHIP HISTORY

WON BY	DATE WON	WON BY	DATE WON
Chris Jericho	12/9/01[1]	Undertaker	5/19/02
Triple H	3/17/02	The Rock	7/21/02
Hollywood Hulk Hogan	4/21/02	Brock Lesnar	8/25/02

WORLD HEAVYWEIGHT CHAMPIONSHIP		WWE CHAMPIONSHIP	
WON BY	DATE WON	WON BY	DATE WON
Triple H	9/2/02[2]	Kurt Angle	12/15/02
Shawn Michaels	11/17/02	Brock Lesnar	8/25/02[2]
Triple H	12/15/02	Big Show	11/17/02

WWE TITLE HISTORY NOTES

[1] Lou Thesz defeats Buddy Rogers January 24, 1963 for the National Wrestling Alliance Championship. WWE (then known as WWWF) promoters refuse to recognize the title change, and name Rogers their champion after breaking from NWA.

[2] Bob Backlund defeats Antonio Inoki in Tokyo December 6, 1979, but match is declared a no-contest due to interference from Tiger Jeet Singh. Inoki refuses the championship.

[3] Andre the Giant wins the Heavyweight title, then surrenders it to Ted DiBiase, prompting President Jack Tunney to declare the championship vacant.

[4] Randy Savage becomes champion after winning four matches in a tournament held at *WrestleMania IV*.

[5] Ric Flair wins the championship at the *Royal Rumble 1992*, one month after the title is made vacant following controversial wins for both Undertaker and Hulk Hogan over a one-week period.

[6] Yokozuna defeats Bret Hart at *WrestleMania IX*, then loses the title within minutes to Hulk Hogan.

[7] Shawn Michaels's knee injury vacates the title, which Bret Hart wins in a four-way contest.

[8] Bret Hart loses the championship to Shawn Michaels in the most controversial decision in sports entertainment history. Referee Earl Hebner calls for the bell after Michaels puts Hart in the sharpshooter.

[9] The Rock wins the title in a *Survivor Series* tournament, almost two months after a Triple-Threat match resulted in Stone Cold Steve Austin being pinned simultaneously by Kane and Undertaker, in effect vacating the championship.

[10] Triple H wins a Six-Way Challenge match, claiming the title made vacant one month before by previous champion and WWE owner Vince McMahon.

UNDISPUTED WWE CHAMPIONSHIP NOTES

[1] World Champion Chris Jericho defeats Champion Stone Cold Steve Austin at *Vengeance*, thereby unifying the two titles and forming the Undisputed Championship.

[2] Undisputed Champion Brock Lesnar's exclusive contract with *SmackDown!* prompts *Raw* General Manager Eric Bischoff to recognize the World Championship as a separate entity. Triple H represents the *Raw* brand as its champion.

Night Heat cohost Tazz—both known more for their toughness and heart than their size and strength—would shock the champs with a nontitle win at the end of 2001, then follow up with a near-upset for the belts during January 3's *SmackDown!* Instead, the underdogs had to settle for some under*wear,* pulling down the skirt of the Dudleyz' personal Diva, Stacy Keibler, before Bubba powerbombed Spike from the second rope for the one-two-three.

Going nose-to-chin backstage on January 7 *Raw,* the foursome agreed to another championship match, this time under Hardcore rules. It was a throwback to their ECW days, as was their conversation: "Beat us if you can," dared Bubba, to which Tazz replied, "Survive if we *let* you." Not surprisingly, the match proved just as extreme, though when the Dudleyz brought in a table to silence their opponents, it was Bubba who was struck speechless by a suggestive ring-apron pose Stacy had intended for Tazz. The thug from Red Hook suplexed Bubba, which Spike followed up with his Bulldog finisher, the Dudley Dog, through the table, pinning Bubba and winning the Tag Team titles.

Despite the monumental upset, no one believed Spike and Tazz could remain the champions. That included January 10 *SmackDown!* challengers Lance Storm and Christian, until a Tazzmission promptly choked out any misconceptions the European Champ had of them. Spike and Tazz showed even more resiliency moments after the match, fending off a sneak attack from D-Von and Bubba with a Dudley Dog and suplex respectively before hightailing it from the ring.

Inside New York's the World nightclub for January 13's *Sunday Night Heat,* Tazz told cohost Michael Cole that winning the Tag titles in Madison Square Garden was "a dream come true" for the Red Hook native. Spike added they had "no fear" about granting the Dudley Boyz a rematch at *Royal Rumble.* Meanwhile, D-Von and Bubba's misfortunes continued, eking a

win against WWE Hall of Famer Sgt. Slaughter and Perry Saturn that night (and only after the "has-been" Sarge was disqualified for literally belting them around with a strap). Bubba almost turned their luck around in a one-on-one with Spike during January 14 *Raw,* until Tazz broke up D-Von's flying headbutt off the top rope, allowing Spike to catch his half brother off-guard with the victory roll pin.

Since they couldn't gain momentum *inside* the ring, D-Von and Bubba chose to blindside the champions outside the CenturyTel Arena during January 17 *SmackDown!,* throwing Tazz inside a car trunk and injuring Spike's neck with a 3-D finisher onto the concrete ground. Leaving the scene of the crime, Bubba reiterated Tazz's January 7 comment to them, "At the *Rumble,* survive if *we* let you!"

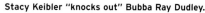

> "Survive if we *let* you."

Stacy Keibler "knocks out" Bubba Ray Dudley.

With the *Royal Rumble* looming closer, tension was in the air for many of its participants. Though whatever was in the air inside the bathroom during January 10 *SmackDown!*, Booker T *really* didn't like the smell of it. He'd dislike it even more when Rikishi came out of the stall and informed him they'd be squaring off that night. Booker held his own during the match, only to literally lose his lunch all over announcer Michael Cole after catching a Stinkface from the Phat Man!

Business as usual for Bradshaw and Faarooq.

The embarrassing incident hadn't gone unnoticed on January 14 *Raw*—inside the APA's office, Big Show turned a conversation with Faarooq and Bradshaw about kicking ass into a joke about Booker *licking* ass. Hardly appreciating being the butt of the joke, Booker would challenge Show to an ass-whooping that night. The ensuing contest went back and forth until Big Show's face hit an exposed turnbuckle, putting him out for the count and allowing Booker to stand tall over the giant.

With only three days to go before the *Royal Rumble*, Diamond Dallas Page was *not* entered in the tournament, and he didn't even have a spot on the WWE roster. But he was positive that would all change when he faced the Boss Man at January 17 *SmackDown!*; a victory would give him a job with the company. Some might have looked at having to face Mr. McMahon's henchman as a bad thing, but DDP saw it—not to mention every-

thing else—as a *good* thing. And he'd make the most of it, working his way out of a Boss Man slam to deliver the Diamond Cutter. As quick as one-two-three, DDP had become the WWE's latest employee, and the *Royal Rumble*'s latest entrant.

Billy Gunn and Chuck Palumbo were both enrolled in the *Royal Rumble*, but they were two Superstars who decided to share each other's desire…to wear more Tag Team gold. Both had the tools—Billy was an eight-time coholder of the WWE Tag Team titles (five of them as "Mr. Ass" with the New Age Outlaws), and Chuck was a three-time WCW Tag Team Champion. It was only a matter of time when these Superstars saw themselves on top.

Big Boss Man humbles Diamond Dallas Page.

The odd couple of Scotty 2 Hotty and Albert weren't among the Billy and Chuck devotees, having built up some singles *Heat* with them on January 6. Billy's Fame-Ass-er drove Scotty's face to the canvas for the win, then Billy serviced Chuck's victory by nailing

Tajiri — the Japanese Buzzsaw.

double-team him afterward would be ruined by The Hurricane, the superhero Superstar who the Japanese Buzzsaw had feuded with previously. Forming a *Raw* partnership on January 14, Hurricane and Tajiri made quite the dynamic duo, until Chuck caught Tajiri with a superkick that powered them to victory. The Buzzsaw would avoid that maneuver while facing Billy in singles action three nights later on *SmackDown!*, though Chuck's distraction was enough to set him up for the Fame-Ass-er and another loss.

Few are as desiring than the Divas of World Wrestling Entertainment, and not just in a physical sense. Their natural beauty, athletic talent and urge to excel made for much hot and heavy competition within both the Women's *and* Men's Divisions in 2002. And who better to ring in the New Year as Women's Champion than the Diva Internet fans voted as "Babe of the Year" for 2001, Trish Stratus.

Trish had come a long way from her days as the valet for "T & A" (Test and Albert) and the cohost of *WWE Excess.* She'd trained hard, transforming herself into a *fighting* Diva. Her determination paid off when she won the then-vacant Women's title in the Six-Pack Challenge at the *Survivor Series 2001*, going through past champions Ivory, Jacqueline, and Lita. Willing to take on all comers and deliver "Stratusfaction Guaranteed" to her fans, Trish answered a *Raw* challenge from rival and new *Excess* cohost Terri Runnels to compete in a wet T-shirt contest on January 7. A wet dream come true for *Raw* co-announcer Jerry "the King" Lawler and his cocked Super-Soaker gun, until the Women's Champion was assaulted from behind, then dealt a vicious DDT by former Alliance member Jazz.

A muscular female, Jazz debuted at the same *Survivor Series* match that saw Trish win the Women's title. However, Jazz was more interested in being a champion than a Diva, and made those feelings known to Lilian Garcia at January 3 *SmackDown!.* "I'm not like all these other bleach-blonde sluts who *sleep* their way to the top," she said. "I *fight* my way to the

Albert behind the unsuspecting official's back. There'd be payback when the two teams met on *Raw* the following night, including an Albert splash that induced Billy's painful landing into Chuck's groin and a Scotty Worm that just about turned off Billy. This time Chuck would rescue his partner from a three-count, allowing Billy to drop Scotty with the Fame-Ass-er for the victory.

Billy and Chuck's blossoming relationship would also help others connect on January 13 *Heat.* WWE Diva Torrie Wilson couldn't halt Chuck's ringside contribution to Billy's nontitle win over boyfriend and Cruiserweight Champion Tajiri. But their mood to

Billy tosses The Hurricane over and out.

top. Because I *can*. Because I *will*. And there's not one woman that can stop me!" Jazz backed up her words that evening in a match against The Hurricane's superhero sidekick Mighty Molly, driving her into the mat with a mighty brain buster for the easy victory.

Trish would get a better look at her attacker on *Raw* the following week, sitting at ringside while Jazz and Jacqueline fought over the No. 1 Contendership for the Women's title at the *Royal Rumble*. Jacqueline, herself a powerhouse and experienced grappler, fell to Jazz's well-executed fisherman's suplex, though Trish didn't hesitate about hooking up against her new *Royal Rumble* challenger when she tried intimidating the champion Diva after the match.

LEFT **Diva Terri instigates a wet T-shirt contest.**

RIGHT **A legdrop on Mighty Molly courtesy of Jazz.**

With the title shot already hers, Jazz took the escalating hostilities past the breaking point at January 17 *SmackDown!*, attacking Trish backstage and smashing a crate door down on her left hand. Walking away as Trish held her hand in agony, the smug antagonist told the champion she'd see her at the *Rumble*.

RVD goes Five Star on Kurt Angle.

Edge's star shined brightly throughout 2001—after a seventh go-round of Tag Team gold with brother Christian, he went on to win the *King of the Ring* tournament, then enjoyed a second, third, *and* fourth reign as Intercontinental Champion. It was a title he continued to hold going into 2002, despite dropping his first match of the New Year, a January 3 *SmackDown!* tag affair with Rob Van Dam against Undisputed Champ Chris Jericho and one-time friend Kurt Angle. Edge would successfully defend his crown with an Edgecution on Lance Storm at *Raw* the following week, only to get crowned on the runway moments afterward, courtesy of the brass knuckles of William Regal.

Regal made his intentions known from the TitanTron immediately following Edge's January 10 *SmackDown!* victory over Boss Man. He'd lost a title shot to Edge at *Vengeance* one month before, but now he was motivated by revenge more than desire, after a bloody Edgecution to a steel chair at the December 13 *SmackDown!* resulted in three separate surgeries to Regal's busted nose. "You gamble with the devil, and the devil *always* wins," Regal stated. "And unfortunately for *you*, sunshine, the devil has come to collect." Having *no* idea what Regal was talking about, Edge suggested a "novel" idea—"Speak English!" to which the Brit asked if the Intercontinental Champ was "man enough" to put his title up at *Royal Rumble*. Edge pointed out that *he* wasn't the guy stuffing things down his pants to win his matches, "But I guess you need those brass knuckles," he added, "because you *definitely* don't have a set of brass *balls!*" Edge accepted Regal's challenge, then added, "I hope that big schnoz is fully functioning, because you're gonna need it to smell me totally reeking of *awesomeness!*"

> **"I hope that big schnoz is fully functioning, because you're gonna need it to smell me totally reeking of *awesomeness!*"**

Unfortunately for Edge and partner Rob Van Dam, their January 14 *Raw* Tag match reeked of a setup by Regal, joined in his corner by Test. Though the official wouldn't find any brass knux on the Blackpool wrestler, both RVD and Edge discovered them soon enough; Regal had positioned the weapon under the ring *before* the bout, supplying a knockout blow to the champion's jaw for an easy pinfall. Van Dam didn't make it so simple for Regal in their *SmackDown!* singles contest three days later, keeping the Brit off-balance with the educated feet that made him a leading contender to win the *Royal Rumble*. But when the battle

Test puts the squeeze on RVD.

spilled outside, Regal found his "power of the punch" around the timekeeper's table, then grounded the high-flyer with a hard shot to pick up another win.

A frustrated Edge wouldn't pull any punches in his nontitle match with Test that night, nailing the big Canadian with an Edge-o-Matic, then a clothesline that sent both men sailing outside the ring. Regal came down to hammer Edge from behind, but the champ caught the Englishman, then smacked him around before trading Test's steel chair for a spear to his midsection. Yet just when it looked like Edge was in control, he suddenly lost it, unloading the chair on both men, then on the referee after he'd drawn the disqualification. It became obvious to the CenturyTel crowd that Edge's desire wasn't just to *Rumble* with Regal; he wanted to *obliterate* him.

The *Royal Rumble* meant something different for its thirty competitors. First-time entrants like Kurt Angle saw it as a chance to add another personal first to an already incredible resume. Seasoned veterans like Undertaker used it as an opportunity to remind the others who ran the yard. Past winners like Stone Cold Steve Austin looked at it as an opportunity to open up twenty-nine cans of whoop-ass. But all of them realized

RETURNING FAVORITES

The *Royal Rumble 2002* stood out from its predecessors for several reasons, among them being the return of four fan favorites to the WWE. While previous *Rumble*s have seen its share of one-time returnees and special guests (Drew Carey's *still* running away from Kane!), these Superstars' reinstatements were anything but once-only deals; they came back to fight their way to the top and stay there.

VAL VENIS: Quickly rising among the ranks following his 1998 debut, the towel-toting Superstar was a two-time Intercontinental Champion and European Champion whose high-flying "Money Shot" satisfied fans everywhere, particularly the ladies after his matches. Val was brainwashed into throwing in the towel and joining Steven Richards's "Right to Censor" in 2000, then disappeared when the faction disbanded in early 2001. Returning to *Royal Rumble* in January, the Big Valbowski threw in the towel this November and accepted the position as Eric Bishoff's chief of staff, and now goes by his given name Sean Morley.

THE GODFATHER: Pimpin' *ain't* easy...but it sure is fun for this conductor of the "Ho' Train" who adorns more than the gold earned by his hard-workin' female escorts. A former Intercontinental and Tag Team Champ, the Godfather's Death Valley Driver steamrolls his way past opponents who don't want to enjoy a good time with him and his luscious ladies. The "Right to Censor" changed his ways back in 2000, but after recognizing his duty to shake some booty, he returned to January's *Royal Rumble* before leaving the WWE in late 2002.

MR. PERFECT: The son of wrestler Larry "The Ax" Hennig and a two-decade veteran in the squared circle, Curt Hennig made his debut as "Mr. Perfect" in 1988, taking the name in reference to his amazing in-ring technical abilities. Hennig's Perfect-Plex would pin many adversaries during his years with the WWE, his cocky attitude supported by two WWE Intercontinental Championships. The Perfect One also developed into a superb manager, helping Hunter Hearst-Helmsley (Triple H) to his first Intercontinental title before leaving for the WCW in late 1996. Finishing second to then-WWE Champion Hulk Hogan in the *Royal Rumble 1990*, Hennig returned for a perfect *Royal Rumble* in 2002, remaining with the WWE until April of that year.

GOLDUST: Fans never forgot the name of the Golden One who premiered *In Your House* in October 1995. Joined by Marlena, then-wife Terri Runnels, the celluloid Superstar delivered Shattered Dreams to anyone who tried capturing his spotlight, and in the process was thrice awarded with the Intercontinental title. After a three-year hiatus, Goldust penned a spectacular sequel to his WWE career, nominating himself for the *Royal Rumble* in January. Today his eccentric personality continues to freak out tag partner Booker T as much as his opponents, though nothing has tarnished his desire to produce even more gold for his flamboyant attire. ∎

winning would catapult them to the main event at *WrestleMania X8,* and none of them would let that slip through their fingers.

It was desire that powered Undertaker to over a decade of destruction, and most recently the Hardcore Championship. The American Badass had annihilated everyone in his path during his month-long tenure when he faced an extraordinarily large challenge from Big Show. At seven feet, two inches and weighing five hundred pounds, the giant didn't show any fear of Undertaker, though some questioned if Deadman, Inc. felt likewise during their Hardcore title match on January 3 *SmackDown!.* Big Show dominated much of the contest, until an underhanded blow allowed Undertaker to cinch on his new Dragon Sleeper hold, giving the big man no choice but to tap out.

Before Triple H's anxiously awaited return on January 7 *Raw,* several of the Superstars who'd faced him in the ring were asked to comment. Undertaker only had one message for The Game, "Don't forget who runs the yard. At the *Royal Rumble,* when I win, I'll be the only dog standing in the middle of the ring."

Stone Cold Steve Austin had just one thing to say when it came to desire, the *Royal Rumble,* the return of Triple H, his ongoing battles with WWE co-owner Vince McMahon and just about any other topic in 2002, *"What?"*

The Texas Rattlesnake's latest catch phrase had done precisely that with fans—the four-letter word appeared on T-shirts and signs inside arenas everywhere, with crowds shouting it incessantly throughout every show. Not everyone liked it; gold medalist Kurt Angle hated it, and Mr. McMahon *despised* it. The "Person of the Year" didn't want to hear from the rude "What?" chanters in the MCI Center another minute, and ordered the lights inside the arena shut off. He threatened to keep the entire January 3 *SmackDown!* in total darkness…until Stone Cold's

The Texas Rattlesnake and his fans ask, "What?"

music hit. Vince screamed for the lights to be turned back on, but by then the Bionic Redneck was already standing behind him, screaming "What?" in his face and rallying the crowd against the *"Jackass* of the Year." Austin, like McMahon, had New Year's resolutions, and he sounded off each one of them to the billionaire, accompanied by a chorus of "What?" from the audience:

"At the beginning of the year, Stone Cold Steve Austin was gonna drink more beer!"

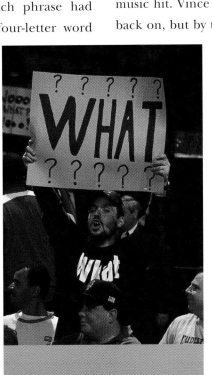

The most popular word.

"What?"

"Drink more whiskey!"

"What?"

"Drink more tequila!"

"What?"

"More vodka!"

"What?"

"More red wine."

"What?"

"And the biggest thing I said I was gonna do?"

"What?"

" 'Cause of what you've done the past couple of weeks?"

"What?"

"This year, the first time I laid my eyes on you …"

"What?"

" … I was gonna *knock you flat on your ass!"*

> **"I was gonna knock you flat on your ass!"**

Booker T and Boss Man would rescue the WWE co-owner, in the process busting Austin open with the microphone. Despite being taken to the hospital to remove microphone fragments lodged in his skull, the Rattlesnake would return later that night, following The Rock's victory over Booker T, only to catch another beat-down at their hands. But he'd tag up with the Great One for some *Raw* retribution on January 7, nailing Boss Man with the Stone Cold Stunner for the win, then started on one of his resolutions with a few Steveweisers.

Austin had other business to discuss with interviewer Michael Cole before his Tag match that night, including the much-anticipated return of Triple H, with whom he had a long history. "I'm not here to wish that man good luck," he said. "Stone Cold can't wait to look that man right in the eyes, face-to-face." The other matter was the *Royal Rumble,* "that match where you take a sonuvabitch and throw him over the top rope." Officially entering into the tournament, that was exactly the three-time *Rumble* winner's intent: counting off *twenty-nine* SOBs—each one followed by a "What?" from the crowd—he'd throw *all* of them over the top rope and advance to *WrestleMania!*

Kurt Angle's desire brought him Olympic gold back in 1996, and he carried that same passion into his rookie year with the WWE, winning *King of the Ring 2000* and the European, Hardcore, Intercontinental and WWE Heavyweight titles in a twelve-month span. Angle was instrumental in Vince McMahon putting an end to the Alliance Invasion at *Survivor Series 2001.* Kurt started 2002 strong with his and Chris Jericho's *SmackDown!* Tag victory over Edge and Rob Van Dam. So when Angle had an important announcement to make on January 7 *Raw,* why was everyone making such a big deal about Triple H? "Tonight is *my* night," he told Jonathan Coachman backstage. "It's true."

"Triple H tore his quad? Big deal! I tear my quadriceps *all* the time!" Angle complained to Christian backstage. "I tore it this morning. I'm fine. I'm here, I'm jumping around." And to hear Big Show, Tajiri and Torrie Wilson talk about Hunter "… like teenagers at a Ricky Martin concert" made him sick. Regardless, it was going to be Kurt Angle's night, and Triple H wasn't going to steal his thunder.

Stephanie McMahon-Helmsley was persona non grata at the January 3 *SmackDown!* in Washington, D.C. Her father Vince certainly wasn't about to invite her, and despite her insistence to a backstage staff member that she was a guest of WWE co-owner Ric Flair, her name didn't appear on the guest list. She couldn't even gain access from a family friend whose name was on the list, nor could she use her feminine charms to turn on the staff member, who revealed he was gay and was more impressed seeing Billy and Chuck enter the building. "If *they* ever came out with a calendar," he told her, "it would be *unbelievable!*"

Still, McMahons have an uncanny ability of getting their way. And when Ric Flair addressed the MCI

Center later that night, Stephanie would be at ringside, jumping a barrier and fighting off security guards until the Nature Boy invited her to speak her mind. Stephanie had no doubt that Flair would destroy her father in their *Royal Rumble* match. "In this ring, you *are* The Man," she said. "When it comes to *business...I'm* The Man." Slick Ric didn't take Stephanie or her business proposition seriously, strutting around the ring until she slapped him across the face. "You *need* me on your side," she warned, since she was bringing with her one of the WWE's crown jewels: her husband, Triple H. And if Flair wasn't on Stephanie's side when Hunter returned, "The Game will *really* begin."

Stephanie attempts to come to an arrangement with Ric Flair.

Triple H returns.

aw. January 7. Madison Square Garden. Twenty-two thousand fans. After an eight-month absence, The Game was on.

Few thought Hunter Hearst-Helmsley, Triple H, could return to the ring after the May 21, 2001 episode of *Raw,* when he'd torn his left quadriceps muscle from the bone. But it was Hunter's desire that made him one of the WWE's elite Superstars. It was his desire that pushed the badly injured Cerebral Assassin to finish that match. And it was his desire that spurred him on to endure months of torturous physical therapy.

"I. Am. The Game. And you can bet your ass *I'm back!*"

A five-minute standing ovation honored the returning Superstar as he entered the squared circle, but Triple H wasted no time when he finally spoke. "Just in case you've forgotten, let me tell you just who in the hell I am: *I. Am. The Game.* And you can bet your ass *I'm back!* And I'm the guy that tonight officially enters the *Royal Rumble!*"

Kurt Angle's entrance music started before the crowd could respond to Hunter's declaration, with the gold medalist making his way to the ring and telling Hunter his "big comeback" wasn't so impressive. "I won an Olympic gold medal with a *broken freakin' neck!*" he said, adding that he had an even bigger announcement to make: "I, Kurt Angle, will *also* enter the *Royal Rumble.*" His first ever, he noted, since "I was too busy pinning *your* ass to the mat" at last year's *Rumble.* "What do you think of *that?*"

Triple H answered with an explosive spear to Kurt's midsection, then drove the Olympian's face into the mat with a Pedigree moments later. If anyone else had doubts about The Game, he'd quickly silenced them as he stood over the unconscious Angle.

Mrs. McMahon-Helmsley walked tall at the January 10 *SmackDown!*, baring her backstage pass around Madison Square Garden as proudly as Kurt Angle wears his gold medals. She'd quickly add to an already exceptionally hot climate indoors, first telling Stone Cold's wife Debra that Hunter would kick the Rattlesnake's ass at the PPV. She next headed ringside and spelled it out for the fans: her husband was back in the WWE, and Stephanie's business savvy and brains would once again catapult him to the top, starting with the *Royal Rumble.* "I point my finger, and Triple H destroys," she warned. "And *nobody* in the WWE wants me pointing my finger in their direction."

Backstage with Lilian Garcia, Kurt Angle's finger was pointed not at "glory hound" Triple H, but at Austin—it was *his* catch phrase that urged the MSG attendees' nonstop "What?" chants after every sentence, driving him to distraction. Kurt decided to teach the

Kurt Angle has no sympathy for Triple H's injury.

Stone Cold Steve Austin opens up a can of whoop-ass on Kurt Angle.

Philips Arena
Atlanta, Georgia

2002 ROYAL RUMBLE

Triple H threw *Kurt Angle* over the top rope to win the tournament and become the No. 1 Contender at *WrestleMania X8*

UNDISPUTED CHAMPIONSHIP MATCH

Chris Jericho defeated *The Rock* via pinfall to retain the Undisputed title

OWNER VS. OWNER STREET FIGHT

Ric Flair defeated *Mr. McMahon* via pinfall

WOMEN'S CHAMPIONSHIP MATCH

Trish Stratus defeated *Jazz* via pinfall to retain the Women's title

INTERCONTINENTAL CHAMPIONSHIP MATCH

William Regal defeated *Edge* via pinfall to become the Intercontinental Champion

TAG TEAM CHAMPIONSHIP MATCH

Spike Dudley & Test defeated *the Dudley Boyz* (w/*Stacy Keibler*) to retain the Tag Team titles

JANUARY 20, 2002

Thirty men. One match. One winner. It was only January 20…but 2002 was already adding up to be quite a year in World Wrestling Entertainment.

The *Royal Rumble* kicked off from Atlanta's Philips Arena in extreme fashion, with WWE Tag Team Champions Tazz and Spike Dudley (sporting a neck collar after suffering a concrete-driven 3-D during the January 17 *SmackDown!*) defending the belts against previous champions the Dudley Boyz, accompanied by Stacy Keibler. Bubba Ray and D-Von's size and strength controlled the match early, but ever-durable Spike's two Dudley Dog Bulldogs on Bubba would eventually leave D-Von no choice but to tap out to the Red Hook thug's Tazzmission. Once again the Tag Champions had entered the ring as the underdogs, but it was the heavily favored challengers who left as "just another victim."

Tired of being on the receiving end of brass knuckles in recent weeks, Intercontinental Champ Edge was prepared to reacquaint William Regal's face with a steel chair, like he'd done on *SmackDown!* a month before. Though no chair entered into the contest, the match proved brutal enough, as both Superstars punished one another with suplexes, powerbombs and mat submission holds. Edge finally gained the upper hand with a spinning heel kick from the top rope, but as he went for the spear Regal used the ring official to absorb most of the impact. Regal pulled the brass knux from his trunks while the referee recovered, then used "the power of the punch" to clean Edge's clock, picking up the easy three-count and the Intercontinental Championship.

Jacqueline served as the special guest referee for the Women's title match between Jazz and Champion Trish Stratus, whose left hand was bandaged up as a result of the challenger's backstage attack only three days ago. Jazz quickly exploited the injury, pounding Trish as she tried to remove her jacket. From there, the Divas engaged in a series of pinning combinations and counters until Jazz again went for the injured hand, using the ropes for additional leverage. Jacqueline, who had no love for Jazz after losing the No. 1 Contender's spot to her less than a week before, would prove pivotal to the match, first arguing with the challenger over the use of the ropes, then delaying the count on a likely winning pinfall for Jazz. Trish would also establish herself as a tough champion, withstanding a powerful DDT to deliver a second Stratusfaction on Jazz and retain her title.

As Ric Flair promised, he and WWE co-owner Mr. McMahon would pay for their Street Fight in blood and sweat. The Nature Boy paid first outside the ring, where McMahon busted his head open after repeated shots from a street sign and garbage can. After grabbing a camera from Flair's daughter at ringside and taking a picture of himself with the crimsoned Nature Boy, McMahon threw him back in the ring, setting him up in his own figure-four. Flair countered, then low-blowed his business partner as he brought a lead pipe in the ring. From the outside floor, Ric smashed Vince's head with a monitor, then dragged him over to his daughter for some better quality photos. Back in the ring, Vince begged for mercy, but Flair showed none—after a second low blow, he nailed McMahon with the lead pipe, then enjoyed hearing the billionaire squeal as he tapped out to the figure-four!

It was Chris Jericho's hand in The Rock's face, telling him to "just bring it" to their Undisputed Championship match. Y2J gained the early advantage with a body press on the Great One, then removed a top turnbuckle before attempting the Walls of Jericho. The People's Champ fought out of it, then withstood a missile dropkick and reverse chin lock before mounting some offense, which Y2J quickly snuffed with a Bulldog and two Lionsaults off the second rope. Unable to pin the Brahma Bull, a frustrated Jericho got into a shoving match with referee Earl Hebner, which Rock capitalized on with a sharpshooter that made the Undisputed Champ tap out. But Lance Storm and Christian's sudden arrival distracted the official, buying Jericho time to catch Rock with his own Rock Bottom.

Following another kickout, the fight ventured outside, where Rock not only reversed Jericho's second Rock Bottom attempt on top of the Spanish announcer's table, but transferred the devastating move over to Jim Ross and Jerry Lawler's announcer's table! Back in the ring, a flying clothesline at Y2J would instead knock out the referee, allowing Jericho to nail the People's Champ with one of the two belts. Out came crooked ref Nick Patrick, who counted to two before Rock kicked out. The Brahma Bull then rolled Jericho up for a pin, but when Patrick refused to count, Rocky issued him the Rock Bottom, and a People's Elbow on Y2J. As Rock tried reviving Earl Hebner, Jericho delivered a low blow, then smashed him into the exposed turnbuckle and pinned him with his feet on the ropes to retain the Undisputed title!

It was Game Day for Triple H as the *Royal Rumble* tournament separated the contender from the pretenders. Rikishi (appearing in his eighth *Rumble*, the most by any active WWE wrestler) and Goldust kicked the tournament off, with a Superstar entering in two-minute intervals. The first victim sent over the top rope was No. 3 entry Boss Man, who might not have wanted to stay in after catching the Phat Man's Stinkface. Slugging it out on the outside

apron, Al Snow's (6) heads-up superkick eliminated Lance Storm (5), while Billy (7) snuck up and dumped Bradshaw (4) over.

Biking his way to ringside, Undertaker (8) started claiming his real estate, discharging Goldust, Snow, Rikishi and Billy in rapid succession. Out came Matt Hardy (9) with Lita, both of whom hadn't been seen in over a month. Fighting off their double-team effort, 'Taker tried suplexing Matt

Goldust at the *Royal Rumble*.

from the ring, until new entrant Jeff Hardy (10) raced down and made an incredible save from the outside. The Hardyz and Lita kept 'Taker reeling with the Twist of Fate and a Swanton Bomb, but a Poetry in Motion put Jeff in Dead Man's land, and he was sent flying outside the ring. Matt soon followed after a Last Ride in the ring center, and the Phenom stood alone in the yard again.

Fate, cruel as ever, next invited to the ring *Tough Enough* Champion Maven (11), making his WWE debut against the American Badass, who proceeded to make short work of him until the Hardyz interfered again. Undertaker fought them off, but in the process left himself open to a Maven dropkick that eliminated him! The rookie paid for the shocking feat in blood—'Taker re-entered the ring and beat him senseless, first with fists, then with a steel chair. Though Maven was never officially eliminated, he was hardly able to contest the match results after 'Taker took him backstage and fed him some popcorn—Hardcore-style, through the popcorn-machine glass!

Back inside the ring, Diamond Dallas Page (14) sent over Scotty 2 Hotty (12), then found himself on the outside after a double-team by European Champion Christian (13) and Chuck (15). The Godfather (16), accompanied by the bevy of beautiful women making up his escort service, took his sweet time entering the ring, though Christian and Chuck made sure he wasn't leaving long after they'd sent Albert (17) over. Stone Cold Steve Austin (19) "What?"-ed and whaled away on anything that moved, eliminating Christian, Chuck and Perry Saturn (18). Either bored waiting for the next competitor or looking to break the *Rumble* record of eliminating ten men (set by the Rattlesnake in 1997), Austin brought Christian, then Chuck back in for seconds before sending each of them over the ropes again. Val Venis (20) and Test's (21) *Rumble* campaigns would also be shortened by the Rattlesnake, Val taking an Austin clothesline over the rope while Test ate a Stunner before leaving.

The crowd erupted as Triple H (22) made his way to the ring and went right at it with Stone Cold. The two broke occasionally, first to turn The Hurricane (23) into Superman and send him flying after he tried chokeslamming the two men, then to put the bite on Faarooq (24) with a Stunner and a clothesline so they could get back to business uninterrupted. Mr. Perfect (25) and Kurt Angle (26) focused on Austin and Hunter respectively, while Kane (28) ended a Chokeslam standstill with Big Show (27) after *bodyslamming* the five hundred-pound giant over the top rope! But not even that amazing accomplishment could prevent the Big Red Machine from going over after a Stunner and Angle Slam. Rob Van Dam (29) came out and launched an aerial assault, only to be grounded by a Pedigree, then thrown to the outside floor by final entrant Booker T. Foolishly celebrating with a "Royal Spin-a-Roonie" in the ring, Booker went bouncing over the top after yet another Stone Cold Stunner. Angle would eliminate Austin as he tried to finish off Mr. Perfect, but the pissed-off Bionic Redneck re-entered the ring and laid out the last three finalists with a steel chair.

Angle's double-team miscue on Triple H resulted in a Perfect-Plex for the gold medalist, followed by The Game dumping the Perfect One to the outside. Angle and Hunter went toe-to-toe, trading vicious blows with one another until the Olympian sent the Cerebral Assassin over the top rope. Not realizing Hunter had pulled himself back in the ring before his feet touched the outside floor, Angle's error proved costly as Triple H clotheslined him over the top rope. Against all odds, The Game was back, and he was going to *WrestleMania X8!* ■

ROYAL RUMBLE 2002 BREAKDOWN

ENTRY	#	ELIMINATED
Rikishi	1	Boss Man
Goldust	2	Lance Storm
Boss Man	3	Bradshaw
Bradshaw	4	Goldust
Lance Storm	5	Al Snow
Al Snow	6	Rikishi
Billy	7	Billy
Undertaker	8	Jeff Hardy
Matt Hardy	9	Matt Hardy
Jeff Hardy	10	Undertaker
Maven	11	Maven
Scotty 2 Hotty	12	Scotty 2 Hotty
Christian	13	Diamond Dallas Page
DDP	14	Albert
Chuck	15	The Godfather
The Godfather	16	Christian
Albert	17	Chuck
Perry Saturn	18	Perry Saturn
Stone Cold Steve Austin	19	Val Venis
Val Venis	20	Test
Test	21	The Hurricane
Triple H	22	Faarooq
The Hurricane	23	Big Show
Faarooq	24	Kane
Mr. Perfect	25	Rob Van Dam
Kurt Angle	26	Booker T
Big Show	27	Stone Cold
Kane	28	Mr. Perfect
RVD	29	Kurt Angle
Booker T	30	

TRIPLE H

HEIGHT: **6'4"** WEIGHT: **260 lbs.**
OTHER NAMES: **The Game, The Cerebral Assassin**
FINISHING MOVE: **Pedigree**
CAREER HIGHLIGHTS: **World Champion (2); WWE Champion (5); World Champion; Intercontinental Champion (4); Tag Team Champion; European Champion (2); King of the Ring 1997; Royal Rumble 2002**
2002 HIGHLIGHTS: **Returning after an eight-month absence to win the Royal Rumble 2002; defeating Chris Jericho for the Undisputed Championship at WrestleMania X8; separating from wife Stephanie McMahon-Helmsley; being declared World Champion on Raw; competing in Elimination Chamber World title match at Survivor Series; defeating Shawn Michaels for the World at Armageddon.**

"rude" fans a lesson by kicking the Bionic Redneck's butt in the *SmackDown!* main event. That the crowd switched briefly to a round of "You suck!" during Angle's entrance music was of no consolation to him; of even less comfort was a brawler like Austin matching the gold medalist in straightforward wrestling techniques. With his match going south, Kurt opted likewise with a shot between Austin's legs, leaving Stone Cold open to a moonsault and ankle lock. The Rattlesnake struck back, countering an Angle Slam with the Stunner, but the match ended abruptly when Kane entered the ring and delivered a Chokeslam on Austin. For a moment, it looked like Kane and Angle were allies...until the Big Red Machine Chokeslammed the gold medalist!

Both out for the count, Austin and Angle's matchup had evolved into a preview of the *Royal Rumble,* as Big Show next made his way to the ring and cut Kane down to size. Then appeared Triple H, who ended the consecutive Chokeslams with a kick to the Big Show's groin and a Pedigree to the canvas. The Game stood ready as Undertaker's music hit, and the Dead Man stood in front of the *SmackDown!* TitanTron. But 'Taker chose simply to stare at Hunter, then head backstage; he'd pick the time and place to fight...and it would be on *his* terms.

Hearing both Kane and Big Show had officially entered themselves in the *Royal Rumble,* a visibly annoyed Kurt Angle challenged the Big Red Machine to a match on January 14 *Raw.* Kane almost won *Royal Rumble 2001,* and he'd establish himself as a favorite in the 2002 tournament three nights later with an impressive win in a Handicap Over the Top Rope match. But Angle reminded Michael Cole backstage that he was the only man to ever make Kane submit in a match. This time he planned to break the "big red freak's" ankle, "and it's very difficult throwing twenty-nine other wrestlers over the top rope with a broken

Kane grabs Big Show by the throat.

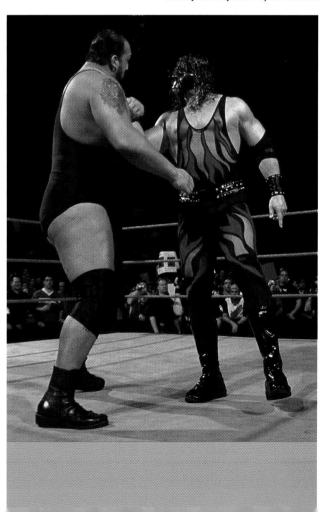

Austin's business with Triple H is interrupted by Undertaker and a chair.

ankle." Unlike their previous encounter, Kane would break the ankle lock, even putting Angle himself in the hold and making him tap out. Unfortunately, the referee went down moments before, giving Kurt time to recover and reverse the maneuver into a pinfall, using the ropes for leverage and the victory.

"Uh-uhh! Triple H is gonna do a lot of things in his life, but the one thing he'll **never** do is throw Stone Cold Steve Austin over the top rope!"

Stephanie McMahon-Helmsley thought having The Game in her pocket gave her the leverage she needed, and the right to do whatever she wanted. But when Hunter began chewing her out for starting an argument-turned-catfight backstage with Debra Austin, Stephanie said Debra was the instigator saying Stone

Cold would kick his ass at *Royal Rumble*. Meanwhile, Austin told Michael Cole and the "What?" faithful in Dallas the story of a *Royal Rumble* battle plan he came up with in a bar that would make his posterior harder to kick. By drinking lots of beer, developing a beer belly and filling up on burgers, he'd lower his center of gravity and make it difficult to throw him over the top rope. And if Triple H thought he'd win the tournament, "*Uh-uhh!* Triple H is gonna do a lot of things in his life," he explained, "but the one thing he'll *never* do is throw Stone Cold Steve Austin over the top rope!"

Addressing the American Airlines Arena crowd later that night, Triple H went over his own "Game plan." He'd spent the past eight months "going through hell" so he could make it to *WrestleMania X8* and compete for the Undisputed title, "the one thing that says beyond a shadow of a doubt, you are the best that there is." And if getting there meant having to throw Austin and twenty-eight other Superstars over the top rope at the *Royal Rumble,* then so be it. "That might sound a little bit cocky," he admitted, "but like the song says, 'It ain't bragging if you can back it up.' And I *can* back up every single word I say, because I am The Game, and I am that damn good!"

Deciding to find out for himself, Austin headed ringside. But as the two started trading punches and countering each other's finishers, Undertaker showed up and clobbered both Superstars with a steel chair. Triple H and Austin could trash-talk all they wanted; with just two swings the American Badass had made his own statement about winning the *Royal Rumble.*

Ironically, Triple H's first match since his return would be to partner with Austin on January 17 *SmackDown!*. Despite a stint as Tag Team Champions

in 2001 prior to Hunter's injury, plus eliminating a potential powder keg by barring their respective spouses from ringside, both men had a hard time being on the same page against Kurt Angle and Booker T, especially with the *Rumble* only three days away. But Angle and Booker were also caught up in their own power trips while planning their match strategy backstage, and when the bell signaled the end of the match, it was the Rattlesnake and the Cerebral Assassin coming out on top, finishing Booker with a Stunner *and* a Pedigree. Triple H and Stone Cold squared off to pick up where they left off on *Raw,* only to be interrupted once again by Undertaker's music. Staring down all four Superstars in the ring, the Hardcore Champion didn't need to tell them that he was going to win *Royal Rumble.* He was just going to *show* them.

Superstar ★ profile

CHRIS JERICHO

HEIGHT: 6'
WEIGHT: 231 lbs.
OTHER NAMES: Y2J, King of the World
FINISHING MOVES: Walls of Jericho; Lionsault
CAREER HIGHLIGHTS: First Undisputed Champion; WCW Champion (2); Intercontinental Champion (4); European Champion; Hardcore Champion; Tag Team Champion (3); WCW TV Champion; WCW Cruiserweight Champion
2002 HIGHLIGHTS: Going to *WrestleMania X8* as the first-ever Undisputed Champion; defeating Rob Van Dam for the Intercontinental title; defeating Kane and The Hurricane to become a World Tag Team Champion (with Christian) on October 14 *Raw*; competing in the Elimination Chamber World title match at *Survivor Series.*

2

FEBRUARY

"This right here is the future of wrestling! You can call this the 'New World Order' of wrestling! Not only are we gonna take over the whole wrestling business...we will destroy everything in our path!"
—Hulk Hogan, joined by Scott Hall and Kevin Nash at WCW's *Bash At The Beach* (July 7, 1996)

"Heaven has no rage like love to hatred turned,
Nor hell a fury like a woman scorned."
—William Congreve's *The Mourning Bride*

A new (World) order

Vince McMahon saw *No Way Out* for World Wrestling Entertainment—it was going to die on February 17, 2002. And the creator and co-owner would be its murderer.

Twenty-four hours after making his business partner tap out in their blood-filled Street Fight at the *Royal Rumble*, a jubilant Nature Boy "Woooo!"-ed and walked that aisle into "Flair Country"—Greenville, South Carolina's BI-LO Center—for the January 21 *Raw*. WWE co-owner Ric Flair enjoyed that his *Rumble* win had changed the expression "To be The Man, you've got to *beat* The Man," to "To be The Man, you've got to beat *Vince McMahon*!" Flair celebrated, showing his daughter's *Rumble* photos on the TitanTron, especially enjoying the shot of a bloody, battered McMahon. The laughing ceased, however, as the bandaged billionaire made his way to the ring, not to fight Flair, but to get one thing straight. "If I lost at the *Royal Rumble*, then I wasn't the only one," he said. "You see, Ric... *you lost, too*. Every WWE Superstar *lost* at the *Royal Rumble*. Every WWE fan *lost* at

Mr. McMahon announces a New World Order.

the *Royal Rumble*. Because I'm about to do something that even *I* will regret."

McMahon's cryptic warning turned downright eerie at the January 24 *SmackDown!*, where Vince spent the evening talking to himself in a darkened room. Looking completely unhinged by his *Rumble* loss, McMahon was convinced Flair's assumption of leadership had given the WWE a "terminal cancer" from which it would slowly die. Though it pained him to do it, he saw no alternative. "I'm *not* going to let Ric Flair kill what I created," he proclaimed, "because *I'm* going to kill it. I'm going to *kill* it! I'm going to kill my creation! I'm going to inject the WWE with a lethal dose of *poison*! If anybody's going to kill my creation, *I'm* going to do it! *Me...*," said McMahon, turning around in his chair, which revealed all in a nearby mirror, "...And the *nWo!*"

THE NWO

SCOTT HALL: *Hey, yo.* When it came to being the bad guy in the squared circle, this six feet, six inch native of Miami, Florida, didn't just sing it. He'd *bring* it. Joining the WWE as Razor Ramon in 1992, Hall cut down opponents with the Razor's Edge, a crucifix powerbomb that made him the first four-time Intercontinental Champion in WWE history. Jumping ship in 1996, Hall and Kevin Nash were the Outsiders who stormed the WCW and founded the New World Order with Hollywood Hulk Hogan, developing the faction into the single most dominant force in that promotion. During his tenure at WCW, Hall wore WCW Tag Team gold five times (four with Nash, once with The Giant, aka Big Show), won the WCW U.S. title twice and captured the WCW TV title. Returning to the WWE with fellow nWo "4-Lifers" Nash and Hogan at *No Way Out* in February 2002, Hall remained with the organization until May of that year.

KEVIN NASH: At six feet, eleven inches and three hundred twenty-five pounds, "Big Sexy" was destined for Heavyweight gold. Within a year of joining the WWE in 1993 as Shawn Michaels's bodyguard Diesel, the big man went on to win the Intercontinental, Tag Team and WWE Championships, the last of which he'd hold for an entire year, the longest WWE title reign of the past decade. Much like they had in the WWE, Nash and his jackknife powerbomb dominated the WCW—in addition to being a seven-time coholder of the WCW Tag titles (four with Hall), he won the WCW World Championship five times, most notably against Bill Goldberg at *Starrcade* in 1998, ending the former NFL player's undefeated streak at 173 wins. Nash joined nWo brothers Hall and Hollywood Hulk Hogan in returning to the WWE at February's *No Way Out,* and resumed his dominance within the company until a severe quadriceps tear sidelined him in early June. He has since sworn to return in 2003 and pick up where he left off.

HOLLYWOOD HULK HOGAN: Undoubtedly, the man, the myth, the legend that revolutionized professional wrestling. Since winning his first of six WWE Heavyweight Championships in January 1984, Hulk Hogan and *Hulkamania* ran wild *everywhere*—television, movies, Pay-Per-Views and, most importantly, the squared circle, where his twenty-four-inch pythons "Hulked up" and squashed every threat. Hogan took his signature big boot and legdrop over to World Championship Wrestling back in 1994, where he'd achieve much of the same mat success (including six separate reigns as World Heavyweight Champion). But something had changed; he stopped "saying the prayers" and "taking the vitamins," and became embittered and angry. At 1996's *Bash at the Beach*, Hogan turned "Hollywood," revealing himself as the third man in Hall and Nash's New World Order that terrorized, and eventually helped destroy, WCW.

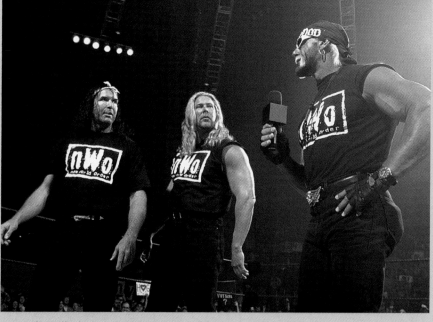

When Vince McMahon decided Ric Flair was wresting control of the WWE out of his hands, the billionaire decided to bring in Hogan, Hall and Nash and kill his own creation. A month-long reign of terror rampaged throughout the company. During *WrestleMania X8*'s epic "Icon vs. Icon" match against The Rock, Hogan realized his *Hulkamaniacs* never abandoned him. Choosing to abandon his nWo ways and focus on cementing his already immortal status in the WWE, Hogan has since enjoyed a run as the Undisputed WWE Champion, as well as his first-ever Tag Team title with Edge, a devout *Hulkamaniac* since childhood. Once again, "The Hulkster rules, brother!" ∎

Hollywood Hulk Hogan. Scott Hall. Kevin Nash. Ric Flair had witnessed firsthand how their "New World Order" helped World Championship Wrestling rise to the top of the sports entertainment industry in 1996. He'd also seen the faction ravage the company from within, until WCW became the dead, lifeless husk that Shane McMahon purchased five years later. That was more than enough of a reason for Flair to appeal to Vince on January 28 *Raw*, from the ring in Richmond, Virginia's Coliseum. He'd speak from his heart while airing on the TitanTron a "Desire" video history of World Wrestling Entertainment—this was the company Vince's father, Vince McMahon Sr., had the vision to start. The same company Vince McMahon had the vision to build into "the greatest sports entertainment company in the world."

[
"I want my company back...and I want you out."
]

"If I've done something so wrong in the last three months that you would bring those people here, then I owe you a huge apology," Flair said, imploring McMahon to tell him how to heal the problem. The billionaire's terms were simple: "I want my company back...and I want *you out*." He'd give Flair a few days to "do the right thing" and sell all WWE stock to him ("at the price you paid for it," he emphasized), but if his answer was no, "Then the poison of the nWo will flow through the WWE's veins, wiping out everything in its path." And the only solace McMahon would take is that he'd see Flair, every WWE Superstar and WWE fan in the world in hell, "because on the nWo killing fields, *I'll* be the last to *survive!*"

For the good of the industry, it was an offer the Nature Boy couldn't refuse. And on *SmackDown!* three nights later, in an emotional speech from the Norfolk

Stone Cold confronts his "twin" Will Sasso from *MADtv*.

Before the Texas Rattlesnake headed for *No Way Out*, he enjoyed stomping a mudhole in *MADtv* funnyman Will Sasso at the February 7 *SmackDown!* so much, he headed out to California and taped an episode of the syndicated variety show. Featured segments of the episode, which aired February 16, included: Stone Cold singing about his feelings to the audience, until his rendition of "Can't Touch This" incurs the dancing wrath of "M.C. Hammer" (Aries Spears); "Fightin' Ron" (Michael McDonald) itchin' for a trailer-park slobberknocker when his girl (Mo Collins) puts the move on his Bionic Redneck buddy; Austin and his "family" (including "adopted son" Frank Caliendo) getting in the Louie Anderson-garbed Sasso's face again while facing "Mike Tyson" (Aries Spears) and his family of lawyers during "Celebrity Family Feud"; and "Tony Little" (Austin) working alongside "Stone Cold" (Sasso) to promote the cardboard-powered "Ultimate Push-Up Machine." Fortunately for Sasso, he was funny enough this time to avoid another Stone Cold ass-whooping! ■

Scope Arena, a tearful Ric Flair bid farewell and thanks to fans everywhere. "I was proud to be a professional wrestler, and proud to be a part of your lives." But Mr. McMahon decided to rub it in; Flair was going to say good-bye on *his* terms and sign the documents inside the ring. "Perception is not always reality," he explained, and though Flair may be perceived as one of the ring's all-time greats, "in reality, the Ric Flairs of the world, when they are pitted against the Vince McMahons, the Vince McMahons *always* win."

Flair stood over the documents, pen in hand, as the crowd begged him not to sign. But there was no begging when Stone Cold Steve Austin came down and interrupted the proceedings. "If you think Ric Flair should take this contract, tear it into pieces and tell Vince McMahon and the nWo to go to hell, gimme a '*Hell, yeah!*'" The fans obliged, as did Flair, who tore up the contract while Stone Cold signed a Stunner over to a near-maniacal McMahon!

From Las Vegas' Thomas and Mack Center, Mr. McMahon called Flair out to the ring for February 4 *Raw*, demanding to know why "the lying SOB" reneged on his word. Flair knew what was at stake; did he do it because he's selfish? Because he listened to Stone Cold? Why? Flair's answer: "The fans." Vince couldn't grasp it. "They don't know what's good for them, and obviously you don't have any idea what's good for the WWE." As the members of the New World Order came up on the TitanTron, McMahon declared that Hogan, Hall and Nash were on their way to the February 17 Pay-Per-View. And if anyone got *in* their way, "I guaran-damn-tee there will be *no way out!*"

The spectrum of competition in the WWE has always been extensive, but it seemed especially so in the Tag Team Division of late. Unlikely Champions Tazz and Spike Dudley had retained the

Ric Flair and Stone Cold share Steveweisers over the fallen Vince McMahon.

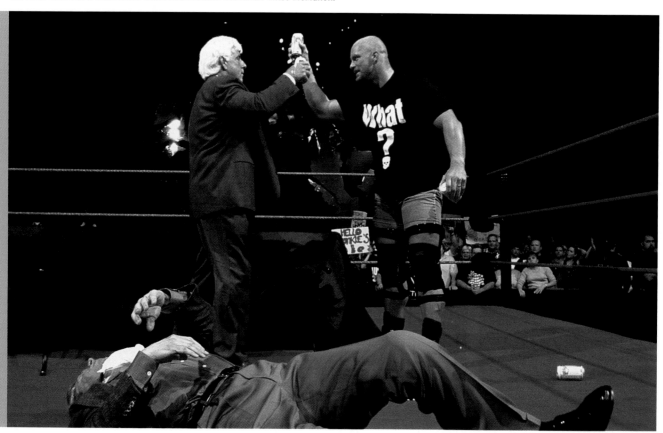

belts against the Dudley Boyz at the *Royal Rumble,* but instead of finally earning the respect of their peers, it just made the smaller tandem bigger targets. As a result, the division would be faced with "Tag Team Turmoil" at *No Way Out.*

Spike (sporting a neck collar after the Dudleyz' outside attack January 17) and Tazz first slugged it out with the Dudleyz and partner Booker T in a *Raw* Six-Man Tag match on January 21, with the win supplied by tag ally Rob Van Dam's Five-Star Frog Splash on Bubba. Scotty 2 Hotty and Albert turned it up against the Champs at January 24 *SmackDown!*—Scotty's Worm chop on Tazz might even have resulted in a title change, if not for Spike's last-second save and a Dudley Dog on Albert that set Scotty up for a Tazzmission.

Booker T runs into Bradshaw's big boot.

Two guys *not* thinking about the Tag Team Championships during the January 21 *Raw* were the APA's Faarooq and Bradshaw; they were too busy drinking in New York's the World nightclub, celebrating the return of The Godfather and his ladies to the WWE. Hearing about the "self-serving, egomaniac, lying, backstabbing sons of bitches" that call themselves the nWo was a sobering thought they'd call to Ric Flair's attention a week later, but the Nature Boy encouraged them to continue on with their everyday business while he sorted things out with Mr. McMahon.

In the APA's case, "everyday business" meant drinking beer, playing cards and beating people up, and they'd comply on all counts at January 31 *SmackDown!*, enjoying an evening of suds and poker with *Rollerball* stars LL Cool J, Chris Klein and Rebecca Romijn-Stamos until Booker T barged in. Griping to LL Cool J about not being invited to the film's premiere, or why a five-time WCW World Champion like him wasn't the lead in the movie, Booker challenged the APA to a match so he could

show the actor/rapper "...who the *real* star is around here, sucka." Begging to pair with him was Test, who had a different motive—"I just want to impress Rebecca," he said. "Once she sees me in action, she won't be able to resist taking the Test." The big Canadian didn't look too impressive when Bradshaw's Clothesline from Hell almost took his head off, or when he was pinned to the canvas for the three-count. Not that Romijn-Stamos or her *Rollerball* costars cared by that point; they were too busy partying in the ring with the APA.

Having spent the past several years together as a tag team, one could understand why Faarooq and Bradshaw would be tight. Then there was Billy and Chuck, a new team that for all appearances just seemed...*tight.* Uncomfortably tight. Almost *too* tight for their fellow Superstars' liking. Even Kane was disturbed by them, particularly when they tried offering him some *Raw* fashion tips on January 21 with a big headband sporting his name. Put off by the Big Red Machine's hostility, Billy and Chuck pounced on Kane, beating him down and sending the message that their feelings were not to be trampled on.

Big Show works over Billy and Chuck.

dishing out some pain after watching the tandem give chocolates to one another prior to their St. Valentine's Day match on *SmackDown!* The contest would leave a bitter taste in Faarooq's mouth after Chuck smacked him with a heavy object from their confections, allowing Billy to cover him for the win.

Not all tag teams play so well together, even if they look great on paper; much like no one had expected Spike and Tazz to beat the Dudleyz for the championship, *everyone* predicted a long title reign for Kane and Big Show after *Vengeance* in 2001. Instead, they became a prime example of how power, size and mutual respect don't always equate to Tag Team gold.

No one could argue with the results Billy and Chuck produced in the ring, though not for lack of trying. They'd come up with a huge upset over Kane and Big Show later that evening, then sizzle at the January 27 *Sunday Night Heat* with a Fame-Ass-er win over Crash Holly and Funaki. And backstage at January 24 *SmackDown!*, it suddenly smacked Billy harder than his pat on Chuck's ass—why not just become Tag Team Champions? "Who's got more tools to be Tag Team Champions than *us?*" he asked. "*Look* at the headbands, the cool red stuff…who's more manly than *us?*" Divas Torrie Wilson and Stacy Keibler would have something to say about that when the boys showed them their prototype calendar at February 4 *Raw*, but they'd settle up with them later, *after* they took the Tag Team belts from Tazz and Spike that night.

Billy and Chuck were defeated by the Champs *and* the APA in a Three-Team Elimination match, thanks mostly to an outside assist from Bradshaw that allowed Spike to Bulldog Billy. Clearly, the APA didn't like Billy and Chuck's overt ways, and were sweet on

> [**"*Look* at the headbands, the cool red stuff…who's more manly than *us?*"**]

The two giants were first at odds with one another as they headed to the *Royal Rumble*, which ultimately saw the Big Red Machine bodyslam Big Show over the top rope. Even Show admitted backstage on January 21 *Raw* that Kane's feat had impressed him, though respectfully added, "Next time, it'll be a different story." It wouldn't be long before that story had a chance to unfold, as a backstage attack on Kane moments later resulted in the behemoths pairing together against

Billy and Chuck. Kane went to finish Billy off with a top-rope clothesline, until Show's sudden weight on the ropes dislodged him to the outside floor. Billy caught Show with a Fame-Ass-er, while Chuck held down the giant's leg to ensure the pinfall.

Similar circumstances occurred during a Tag Team Tables match against the Dudley Boyz on January 24 *SmackDown!*, in which Big Show inadvertently whipped Bubba Ray into Kane, causing him to fall though a table on the outside floor and end the match. A swarm of officials struggled to keep Big Show and Kane from coming to blows following the loss, but it was inevitable the two would collide at January 28 *Raw*, during which the Big Red Machine withstood a massive Chokeslam to the mat, then caught Show with a big boot and Chokeslam of his own for the victory. The conflict between them subsided around this point, perhaps because both realized that the ring just wasn't big enough for the two of them.

Booker T and Test, on the other hand, didn't look like a natural fit, but their contrasting ring styles actually made them potent WCW World Tag Team Champions for a brief period in November 2001. And following Test's February 10 *Heat* singles win over Spike Dudley, coupled by Booker's February 11 *Raw* triumph over Tazz (with an outside assist from Test), it's not surprising the duo liked their chances when they were granted a title shot at *No Way Out*. Booker would even refuse his partner's ringside assistance while facing Spike on

February 14 *SmackDown!*, only to discover what many other adversaries had learned about the Tag Champs—it's not the size of the dog in a fight, but the size of the fight in a dog. Rolling Booker's top-rope superplex into a small package for the win, Spike sent a message to Booker that he and Tazz were more than ready to fight at the Pay-Per-View.

Lance Storm and European Champion Christian were something of a mystery—they established themselves as a cohesive unit, though both continued looking for individual success. Neither found any during the January 27 *Heat*—a week after The Godfather offended the ever-serious Storm by promoting his legitimate escort service on *Raw*'s "sacred ground," he disgraced the Canadian party pooper in the ring with a legitimate ass-whooping win. Meanwhile, Christian's inability to cover new WWE employee Diamond Dallas Page drove the European Champ to the point of a near tantrum, which the positive-minded Page exploited into a Diamond Cutter for a nontitle win. Things didn't improve much when Storm and Christian teamed on *Raw* the next evening against The Godfather and "positively satisfied" customer DDP, who'd mark Storm as the next Diamond Cutter recipient.

Working separately over the next few weeks would prove to be, in DDP terms, "a good thing" for Storm. He'd ground the heroic Hurricane on February 3 *Heat* with a superkick to the head, then cinch a Canadian Maple Leaf half crab on Cruiserweight

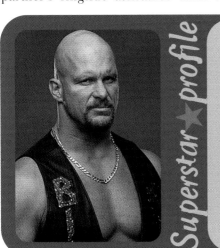

Superstar ★ profile

STONE COLD STEVE AUSTIN

HEIGHT: **6'2"**
WEIGHT: **252 lbs.**
OTHER NAMES: **Texas Rattlesnake, Bionic Redneck**
FINISHING MOVE: **Stone Cold Stunner**
CAREER HIGHLIGHTS: **WWE Champion (6); Intercontinental Champion (2); Tag Team Champion (4);** *King of the Ring 1996*; *Royal Rumble 1997, 1998, 2001*; **WCW TV Champion (2); WCW U.S. Champion (2); WCW Tag Team Champion**
2002 HIGHLIGHTS: **Competing against Champion Chris Jericho for the Undisputed title at** *No Way Out*; **terrorizing Scott Hall and the nWo at February 21** *SmackDown!*; **defeating Hall at** *WrestleMania X8*; **being a free agent in the first-ever WWE Draft (later signing with** *Raw*); **departed from WWE in June.**

Christian's sleeper hold wears down DDP.

Tag Champions at the grandaddy of all sports entertainment, *WrestleMania!*

Despite Trish Stratus's literally single-handed victory at *Royal Rumble,* the powerful Diva Jazz wasn't going anywhere until she got what she came for. That was the WWE Women's Championship, though it might have looked like Trish's arm during their nontitle *SmackDown!* encounter on January 24, in which Jazz leveraged herself on the ropes to intensify an already painful armbar submission hold. And with no reason to care about drawing the disqualification, she put the exclamation point on her attack with a hardcore DDT.

Hardly the sociable type, Jazz was further agitated by Billy and Chuck's backstage grunts and groans on January 28 *Raw,* but even she had to admit their rigorous *stretching* exercises paid off dividends during their Intergender Six-Man Tag match against Trish and the APA. Otherwise, Chuck might not have been "loose" enough to powerbomb his way out of the corner, where Trish sat on top of him! Their conflict still unresolved, the champion Diva decided to put her title up at February 4 *Raw,* and gave her challenger everything she had. However, it wouldn't be enough this time—Jazz back-suplexed Trish as she went for the Stratusfaction, then delivered a crushing fisherman's suplex to earn the three-count, and the Women's title.

Trish and Jazz weren't the only Divas waging war that week. Catty calendar comments posed by Billy and Chuck set up a "posedown" competition against Torrie Wilson and Stacy Keibler at February 7 *SmackDown!*. Referee Jerry "the King" Lawler made no secret where his allegiances lay, nor did the sold-out Staples Center audience that voted against Billy and Chuck's "manly" poses and declared Torrie and Stacy

Champion Tajiri for a nontitle submission a week later. Christian's increasing emotional regression, however, sent his career on a downward spiral, costing him the European title at January 31 *SmackDown!* when DDP countered his Unprettier with the Diamond Cutter. He lost it again on February 10 *Heat,* when even a steel chair wouldn't keep Kane down (though the Big Red Machine calmed him with a Chokeslam to the mat), then once more during the February 11 *Raw,* where his histrionics foolishly positioned him into an RVD Five-Star Frog Splash.

The only time Christian's fits did him any good was on February 11 *SmackDown!,* when he and Lance Storm lobbied WWE co-owner Ric Flair for a Tag Team Championship match at *No Way Out.* They didn't get one, nor did the Dudley Boyz, who also demanded a match. Booker T and Test were already meeting Spike and Tazz at the PPV, but Flair decided that Storm and Christian, the Dudleyz, the APA, Scotty 2 Hotty and Albert, Billy and Chuck and the returning Hardy Boyz would all participate in a "Tag Team Turmoil" match, eliminating one another until only one team remained. And that team would face the

During a Mixed Tag Team, Trish finds herself in the wrong place.

"When the final curtain is lowered and the end credits roll... he will remember the name and never forget...*Goldust*."

who promised, "When the final curtain is lowered and the end credits roll, he will remember the drama, he will remember the passion and above all else, he will remember the name and never forget...*Goldust*."

One name Edge couldn't forget was William Regal, whose so-called "power of the punch" stole his Intercontinental Championship belt at *Royal Rumble*. He looked to rectify that on *Raw* the following night, and might have if not for unscrupulous referee Nick Patrick, who "failed" to notice the brass knuckles that were kicked out of the Brit's hand, then disqualified Edge when he used them on Regal. Snapping over the bogus decision, Edge knocked Patrick out with the knux, then took out three other officials who came in to quell the situation. The assaults resulted in a temporary suspension for the usually good-natured Superstar, though if Regal was expecting an Edge-free evening at the January 24 *SmackDown!*, he was sorely mistaken.

Jazz after defeating Trish Stratus for the Women's Championship.

the winners. But jealousy would rear its ugly head when Stacy thought Torrie was hogging the spotlight, and the King soon found himself in the ideal compromising position of coming between the battling beauties. The girls laced up for a Bikini match on February 11 *Raw*, though Torrie wouldn't find the end result suitable, as the Duchess of Dudleyville who avoided her shoulder block, then rolled her up for the pinfall victory.

Just when he thought he was out, the WWE pulled Goldust back in. In a "Shattered Dreams" production on January 21 *Raw*, the Golden One proclaimed that after three years, his time had come for "the biggest, most spectacular comeback ever witnessed," although that meant dimming the one star that shined brighter than his. Who that star was remained a mystery to all but Goldust,

Regal William pummels Edge, keeping the Intercontinental title.

After Rob Van Dam's Five-Star Frog Splash made surprisingly short work of the new Intercontinental Champ in a nontitle contest, Edge rushed in and speared Regal, then escaped into the crowd before security could restrain him.

RVD's *SmackDown!* win over Regal earned him an automatic Intercontinental title bid at January 28 *Raw*, during which he again owned the champion, until a deliberate low blow made it high time for the ref to DQ Regal. It was Van Dam's turn to vent some postmatch frustration on the Brit, though he was interrupted by D-Von and Bubba Ray Dudley, who sought payback for the prior week's Six-Man Tag defeat. Racing down for the save, Edge joined RVD in a Dudley-directed aerial assault to the outside floor, though he'd soon feel the power of the punch again when Regal caught him coming off the top rope. Van Dam would quickly follow him into oblivion after a Dudley 3-D drove him face-first into the canvas.

"They like you. They really, *really* like you," quoted the Golden One in his next filmic presentation at the

January 28 *Raw*. Edging ever closer to that rising star, he warned, "Here's lookin' at you, kid, because one day, you'll look back on all this period and remember how happy you were. How life was simple back then, before the pain, before the suffering and before your life was forever altered by the name you will never forget …*Goldust.*"

William Regal allegedly had no desire to alter the outcome of the Dudley Boyz' match with Edge and RVD on January 31; he only wanted to provide *SmackDown!* commentary with Michael Cole and the King. Not taking any chances, the ring official searched him for concealed objects. Had the King known, he might have offered to search Duchess of Dudleyville Stacy Keibler, who sat herself down on Regal's lap during the match. Meanwhile, both sides went at each other heavily—RVD's Five-Star on D-Von was offset by a Bubbabomb, which in turn was met with an Edge spear. Reaching into the back of Stacy's pants, Regal produced the brass knux and headed toward the ring to clobber Edge, only to get hammered himself when Edge ducked a Bubba Ray charge that caught the Brit by mistake. The Edgecution on Bubba quickly followed, giving Edge the one-two-three, and the unconscious Regal a whopping headache to recover from.

The February 4 *Raw* started off bumpy for William Regal; his title was on the line against Rikishi, and he wanted no part of the Banzai drop the Phat Man wrought on Boss Man during January 24 *SmackDown!* Regal tried keeping Rikishi off his vertical base throughout the match...and regretfully succeeded when the three hundred fifty-pounder squashed down on top of him! Barely avoiding the Banzai, Regal went for the brass, only to taste some knuckles from Edge, whose run-in gave the Intercontinental Champ another DQ win. This time, however, the smell of victory was a pungent one for Regal, whose prominent proboscis was mired deeply in a Stinkface!

Later that evening, Bubba Ray Dudley went up against RVD in singles competition...which in Dudleyville means "double- or triple-teaming when the ref isn't looking." This time, however, the official caught D-Von going for the top-rope headbutt, and sent him and Stacy back to the dressing room. Bubba still gave a good fight, though eventually fell victim to the Five-Star Frog Splash. RVD's in-ring celebration was cut short when Goldust suddenly appeared on the TitanTron, singing "When You Wish Upon a Star" and congratulating Van Dam. "*You* are the rising star," he revealed. "But unfortunately for you, your dreams

" Here's lookin' at you, kid, because one day, you'll look back on all this period and remember how happy you were. How life was simple back then, before the pain, before the suffering and before your life was forever altered by the name you will never forget...*Goldust*."

Rikishi sends Regal to the ropes.

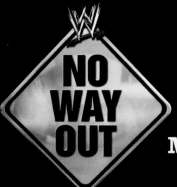

NO WAY OUT

Bradley Center Milwaukee, WI

UNDISPUTED CHAMPIONSHIP MATCH

Chris Jericho defeated *Stone Cold Steve Austin*
via pinfall to retain the Undisputed title

NO. 1 CONTENDER'S MATCH

Kurt Angle defeated *Triple H* via pinfall
to become the No. 1 Contender at *WrestleMania X8*

The Rock defeated *Undertaker* via pinfall

**INTERCONTINENTAL CHAMPIONSHIP
BRASS KNUCKLES ON A POLE MATCH**

William Regal defeated *Edge* via pinfall
to retain the WWE Intercontinental title

TAG TEAM CHAMPIONSHIP MATCH

Tazz & Spike Dudley defeated *Booker T & Test*
to retain the WWE Tag Team titles

Rob Van Dam defeated *Goldust* via pinfall

TAG TEAM TURMOIL

Christian & Lance Storm defeated *Scotty 2 Hotty
& Albert* via pinfall; *Hardy Boyz (w/Lita)* defeated
Christian & Lance Storm via pinfall; *Hardy Boyz*
defeated *Dudley Boyz (w/Stacy Keibler)* via pinfall;
Billy & Chuck defeated *Hardy Boyz* via pinfall;
APA defeated *Billy & Chuck* via pinfall to become
the No. 1 Contenders at *WrestleMania X8*

FEBRUARY 17, 2002

After weeks of ominous speculation, fearful allusions and distasteful allegations, the wait was over. The New World Order opened *No Way Out* to assure the Bradley Center fans and World Wrestling Entertainment that its arrival in the company *wasn't* a Black and White issue. "Big Sexy" Kevin Nash asserted they weren't "poison, cancer" or "company-killing bastards," like their reputation suggested. Scott Hall described themselves as "marks" —fans—who wanted some autographs, maybe a few beers with the boys, but "we don't want any trouble." Hollywood Hulk Hogan guaranteed, "We aren't here to kill the WWE. We're here to make it *better*." Grateful to WWE co-owner Mr. McMahon for giving them that chance, they asked fans everywhere and the Superstars to do the same.

Scotty 2 Hotty and Albert turned it up from the onset of the elimination-style "Tag Team Turmoil" match, until Lance Storm disrupted Scotty's Worm, setting him up for an Unprettier win by tag partner Christian. Far less prettier to watch was the crybaby's temper tantrum after the Hardy Boyz advanced, thanks to Matt's Twist of Fate and Jeff's Swanton Bomb for the three-count on Storm. The Hardyz also survived a next-round onslaught from the Dudley Boyz, with Lita and Jeff handling Stacy and Bubba Ray while Matt countered a reverse DDT and rolled D-Von up for the win. The frustrated Dudleyz vented to Jeff with a 3-D on the outside floor, leaving Matt outnumbered by Chuck's superkick and Billy's Fame-Ass-er. The APA was the last team in, and the last one standing after Bradshaw's Clothesline from Hell on Billy gave him and Faarooq a shot at the Tag Team titles at *WrestleMania X8*.

Goldust and Rob Van Dam spent the early stages of their contest on the outside, working the ring apron and barricades into each other's arsenal. Both men were on top of their contrasting games, with the Bizarre One's psychological edge often successful at keeping RVD grounded on the canvas. But a stayed Curtain Call eventually opened Goldust up to serious hang time with the Five-Star Frog Splash, and the evening's victory belonged to the Whole Dam Show.

At a combined weight of three hundred ninety-eight pounds, Tazz and Spike Dudley entered the evening's title match against Booker T and Test as the lightest Tag Team champs in WWE history...and that's exactly how they'd leave. It wasn't easy—Spike was tossed like a salad for much of the fight before hitting Booker with a modified Dudley Dog. Test almost pinned Tazz late in the match, then got into a shoving match with Jack Doan when the referee caught him using the ropes for leverage. Unfortunately for Test, he was pushed right into a Tazzmission and forced to tap out.

A pair of brass knuckles would determine the Intercontinental title in a special stipulation match between current champion William Regal and Edge...though it *wouldn't* be the pair suspended high atop a pole in one corner of the ring. Edge, his ribs still hurting from a prior encounter with the knuckle dusters, looked to make Regal bleed even before the bell sounded the start of the match. But it was the angry Brit who drew first blood, working away at Edge's midsection and putting him in the Regal Stretch. Regal soon grabbed hold of the weapon on the pole, then dropped them after Edge superplexed him from the top rope. Edge recovered the knux from the outside floor, only to get his clock cleaned by Regal, who surprised him with the spare pair stashed in his trunks to retain the title.

Earlier that night, Undertaker interrupted Michael Cole's interview with Ric Flair to warn the WWE co-owner to stop concerning himself about the crap Hall, Nash and Hogan were selling the fans, and to start worrying about who had their eye on *him*. The Rock, meanwhile, promised Jonathan "Coach" Coachman *and the millions* of his fans that Undertaker was, in fact, a "Dead Man walking" into their *No Way Out* match. Their encounter

Guest ref Stephanie insures there's *no way out*.

quickly reached Jim Ross's slobberknocker status as both men exchanged blows throughout the arena. Back inside the ring, the American Badass, frustrated when his Chokeslam couldn't finish off the People's Champ, grabbed a steel pipe from his motorcycle and threw the protesting official into the outside steel steps. Flair raced down, staggering 'Taker with several chops before falling to the big boot, while Rock recovered and pinebustered the re-entering Phenom, then put him in the sharpshooter. Vince McMahon also charged ringside, sacrificing his jaw to some right hands from the Great One so 'Taker could regain the advantage. But as the Dead Man went for the Tombstone, Flair smacked him with the pipe, sending him reeling into a Rock Bottom that gave Rock the victory.

The Game—and his *WrestleMania* Undisputed title shot—were up against it, especially with estranged wife Stephanie McMahon (now sans the "Helmsley") as the guest referee for his match with Kurt Angle, who was confident that he'd make himself "Triple H's daddy" in the ring. It seemed that way in the early stages, with the princess quick-counting her husband and cheering Kurt until his missed clothesline knocked her senseless to the outside. Referee Tim White took over calling the match, though Angle soon dropped him and caught the Cerebral Assassin with the Angle Slam as Stephanie returned to make the count. Triple H kicked out, then escaped the ankle lock by pushing Kurt into Stephanie, knocking her loopy again.

Drilling Angle with the Pedigree would have ended the match, if not for Stephanie's elbow on White that broke the three-count. As The Game set her up for a Pedigree, Angle nailed him from behind with two chair shots, then added an unnecessary Angle Slam to score the pinfall. It

was an exuberant gold medalist informing a Bradley Center parking attendant outside to tell anyone looking for him that he was off to *WrestleMania*.

Throughout the evening, Superstars' opinion of the nWo members were evident—The Rock told them what to do with a camera after Hogan asked for a photo for his son, then muttered a disparaging remark. Earlier, Stone Cold Steve Austin not only told them he wasn't thirsty when they offered him beer, but he took their six-pack of Steveweisers and tossed them to the side before walking off. The Rattlesnake didn't expect to see them again that night; he was too focused on trying to take the Undisputed title from Champion Chris Jericho. And he got off to a good start, delivering a slew of suplexes and knife-edge chops to wear Y2J down. Jericho shifted the momentum after landing a low blow, then brought in the championship belt when he couldn't finish the Bionic Redneck with a Bulldog and two Lionsaults. Both Superstars used the gold against each other—Austin with a spinebuster, a Break-down from Jericho—though neither man could capitalize.

The referee went down for a second time in the match, just before Austin made Y2J tap out to his own Walls of Jericho. Stone Cold followed up with a Stunner that would have sewn up the Undisputed Championship, until the nWo rushed in and pummeled Austin. A Stunner by Hall left the Rattlesnake down and out while Y2J slowly rolled onto him for the three-count to retain the title. The nWo continued beating on Stone Cold after the match, with Hall dishing out another Stunner that finished off any fight remaining in Austin. Breaking out the spray cans, Hogan helped Nash hold the beaten Rattlesnake down while Hall branded him, spray painting the letters "nWo" on his back and signaling a New World Order was making its mark in the WWE. ■

"The Whole Dam Show" splashes down on Bubba Ray.

won't come true. They're about to be *shattered,* courtesy of the one man whose name you will never forget... *Goldust.*" Without warning, the Golden One surprised Van Dam, setting him up in the corner for a kick to the "golden globes" before delivering a hard neckbreaker to the canvas as his "Curtain Call."

While Goldust didn't make any personal appearances on February 7 *SmackDown!,* Van Dam's recuperative abilities had him partner with Edge and Rikishi in a Six-Man Tag contest against Regal and the Dudleyz. The match looked well in hand as RVD's Rolling Thunder came down on D-Von, Edge speared Regal and Rikishi Stinkfaced Bubba. But the Dudleyz' experience as one of the greatest tag teams in sports entertainment was the difference maker, nailing the Phat Man with the 3-D and picking up the three-count. D-Von and Bubba then aided Regal with a triple-team on Edge, holding the young Superstar on the ramp while the Intercontinental Champion caught him in the breadbasket with the brass knuckles. This time, however, the damage was serious, leaving Edge bleeding from the mouth and in need of medical attention.

It was learned on *Raw* the following week that Edge suffered badly injured ribs from Regal's cheap shot, and the injury proved costly in a nontitle loss to Undisputed Champion Chris Jericho. Meanwhile, RVD decided to tarnish Goldust's possible victory over Rikishi that night with a top-rope kick to the chest. The Phat Man didn't seem to mind that he'd been DQ'd in the process, instead passing on any hard feelings to the Golden One. There'd be no retaliation when RVD added another "W" to his column against Christian that evening, though Goldust would appear on the TitanTron afterward, where he announced a "feature presentation" between them would occur at *No Way Out.*

Val Venis literally had a heart-on for his *SmackDown!* Valentine's Day bout with William Regal, though the Big Valbowski wouldn't be doing much after the match when the Intercontinental Champion supplied "the power of the punch." For that matter, neither would Coach, who received a poor reaction from the Brit regarding a just-announced "Brass Knuckles on a Pole" Championship match between him and Edge at the February 17 PPV. Still recuperating from his injured ribs, Edge decided not to wait the three days, spearing Regal and pounding away at him on the stage until a horde of officials broke it up. As for Goldust, his Curtain Call Cruiserweight Champ Tajiri provided a winning performance, but his attempted "Shattered Dreams" on Torrie Wilson ended with a rude awakening from an RVD Five-Star Frog Splash. At *No Way Out,* Goldust was going to learn that he couldn't cancel "The Whole Dam Show" *that* easily.

> **"But unfortunately for you, your dreams *won't* come true. They're about to be *shattered*, courtesy of the one man whose name you will never forget...*Goldust.*"**

"It's twenty-four hours after the *Royal Rumble*...and guess who is *still* the Undisputed Champion of the World!"

For anyone in the BI-LO Center not listening, Chris Jericho clarified the rhetorical question—he had successfully defended his title against The Rock, and now he demanded the fans in Greenville clap their "filthy hands" for him at January 21 *Raw.* "I have done what no other man has ever done," he boasted. "I have beaten every WWE Superstar there is to beat, and I have *earned* the right to become the Undisputed Champion, dammit!"

The only man applauding Y2J's "load of crap" was Triple H, winner of the *Royal Rumble 2002,* who pointed out there was *one* man Jericho had never beaten, and he was headed to *WrestleMania X8* to meet the Undisputed Champion. Which prompted The Game to ask, "Will *you* be there?" Hunter explained that Chris had another two months to prove to the world that his reign wasn't a fluke. "And if you make it to *WrestleMania* as the Undisputed Champion," he added, "unfortunately for you…it will be *time to play The Game.*"

Coming out to his entrance music (which the audience often kept in tune to with "You suck!"), Kurt Angle, as usual, had a complaint. He could accept Triple H keeping his feet from hitting the outside floor at the *Rumble,* but to attack the gold medalist *from behind,* and without any warning? Kurt headed ringside to confront Hunter "man-to-man," which fast turned into a two-on-one when Jericho joined in the attack. But The Rock just as quickly evened the sides, racing down and clearing the ring of Angle and Jericho.

The Cerebral Assassin visited Rock's locker room afterward—he didn't want a savior, least of all one of his greatest adversaries, with whom he'd been involved in some of the most memorable title matches in WWE history. The People's Champ couldn't figure

The Rock lays a smack down on Kurt Angle.

out Hunter's rage. "You won the *Royal Rumble!* You're going to *WrestleMania!*" he said. "Go eat some ice cream! Drink a protein shake! Make yourself a ham 'n' cheese sammich! Go do *something…*but *don't* be angry!" The two saved their mutual hostilities for their tag opponents that evening, during which the Great One ducked a ring bell that caught the freshly Pedigreed Angle, then chimed in with a Rock Bottom on Y2J that suitably avenged his *Royal Rumble* loss.

Kurt's ears weren't the only ones ringing; before the match, Stephanie McMahon-Helmsley harped on Triple H about his locker-room chat with the Brahma Bull, and why he wouldn't "kick The Rock's ass" like she instructed. She wasn't thrilled with her husband's response, "When are you going to realize that the whole world does not revolve around what *you* want? Why don't you make a

Triple H is caught in the Walls of Jericho, to Kurt Angle's glee.

contribution right now to my sanity, and do the one thing you never seem to be able to do: *shut up.*"

There was *no* quieting Stone Cold Steve Austin on January 21. He had a *Raw* story to share with the "What?" chanters in Greenville, he *had* to deliver what announcer Jim Ross called "a *Perfect* chair shot to the cranium" of Mr. Perfect, who at the time was wrestling Val Venis, so *he* got a Stunner. It *wasn't* the story of a mountaineer named Jed…though that didn't stop the Bionic Redneck from treating everyone to the entire opening to *The Beverly Hillbillies* theme. No, Stone Cold's story dealt with bad news and good news. The bad news was that after all his beer- and whiskey-drinking, taco- and enchilada-eating training for the *Royal Rumble*, after all the push-ups, pull-ups and sit-ups ("Okay, I didn't really do the sit-ups," he confessed), he'd been "hoodwinked!"

"*What?*"

"Bamboozled!"

"*What?*"

"Flabbergasted!"

"*What?*"

"Eliminated!"

The good news: he was officially entering himself in *Royal Rumble 2003. Bad* news: he wasn't going to *Wrestle-*

> "Why don't you make a contribution right now to my sanity and do the one thing you never seem to be able to do: *shut up.*"

Mania X8 to face the Champ. *Good* news: "Stone Cold Steve Austin is goin' to *WrestleMania* to whip *somebody's* ass!"

Austin was in for better news at January 24 *SmackDown!*, learning he could conceivably go to *WrestleMania* as the Undisputed Champion. He, Booker T, Rock and Kurt Angle would compete in two qualifying matches that evening, with the winner of each contest squaring off on *Raw* to determine the No. 1 Contender for the Undisputed Championship at *No Way Out*. Despite hurting his knee, Austin countered a Stunner from Booker with one of "Stone Cold" quality to grab the victory in his qualifier. But the Rattlesnake suffered more damage backstage afterward, when Angle served his head *with* a silver platter, then inflicted more punishment to his bad wheel with the ankle lock.

During the same broadcast, rumors of *marital* pains within the McMahon-Helmsley household were circulating, and supported after Stephanie first threw hot coffee at the well-intentioned Lilian Garcia, then intimated to her increasingly distant husband that his prosperity in the WWE was due to marrying into Vince McMahon's family. "Your father is an *asshole*," Triple H snapped, reminding her how Vince likened him to "a racehorse with a broken leg" after his quadriceps injury. As for marrying Stephanie, "I married you in *spite* of your last name. The McMahon name has done *nothing* for me." Hurt, the princess said maybe her father was right; maybe Hunter *wasn't* good enough for her. Leaving the room, The Game retaliated, "Maybe everybody else was right about *you*." Interviewer Sharmell Sullivan knew better than to press Hunter about the argument, though European Champion Christian would pick a rotten time to bond. "From one guy to another, I feel for you," he said, moments before feeling a brutal beating from Triple H.

A Brahma Bull size-fourteen boot found the Coach's candy ass after making him dance the People's Charleston *in* Charleston—The Rock had something

[
"Your father is an *asshole*... I married you in *spite* of your last name."
]

to say before his qualifying match with Angle. He realized the *Royal Rumble* was "a night of the unexpected," citing among other things *Tough Enough* Champion Maven eliminating Undertaker. But he'd "guaran-damn-*tee*" the people that once he beat Angle, then laid the smack down on Chris Jericho ("The biggest monkey's anus walking God's green Earth!") at *No Way Out*, he'd make it "The Rock's *WrestleMania*" come March! Unfortunately, he'd have to find another way—guest match commentator Y2J pulled the referee out of the ring just as Angle tapped out to Rocky's sharpshooter, while Undertaker surprised the Brahma Bull with a Chokeslam to the canvas, giving the gold medalist an easy victory.

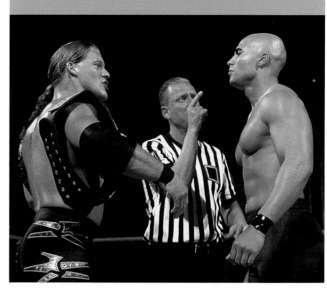

The confident champion confronts Maven.

Though eager to watch Angle and Austin "beat the hell out of each other" on January 28 *Raw*, Jericho first wanted to show everyone in Richmond that he was "a *fighting* champion." And he assured Michael Cole that pitting his title against the rookie Maven had *nothing* to do with feeling his big *Royal Rumble* win was overshadowed by what "the kid from *Tough Enough*" did at the PPV. Expecting to dispense "an undisputed beating," Jericho was unpleasantly surprised when Maven took the fight to him—he'd slam the champion's head into the ringside steps, evade a Walls of Jericho and slingshot Chris into the very turnbuckle he exposed. Experience eventually won out, however with Y2J rolling into the Walls of Jericho for the submission win. Maven wouldn't escape so lucky—Undertaker entered the ring, put on some gloves and beat the holy hell out of the newcomer, then helped him to a ringside seat... across his throat!

At great risk to his teeth, Jonathan "Coach" Coachman approached the Hardcore Champion for some comments backstage. The fact was, Maven took advantage of Undertaker's "generosity to give the kid ring time" at the *Rumble*. "Now he's got to live with the consequences. He paid at the *Rumble*. He paid tonight. And he's gonna continue to pay for it until I decide he's paid up." And bringing up Undertaker's business on *SmackDown!* might have been "a big joke" to The Rock, but no one heard him laughing when the Dead Man cost him an Undisputed title shot last week. "I don't sing and I don't dance… and I *don't* get disrespected. What happened to The Rock last week will continue to happen every time he disrespects me."

It's true, it's true…Undertaker doesn't dance, though Stone Cold was looking to do a number on Kurt Angle after last week's *SmackDown!* assault. Angle was *counting* on it, hoping the Bionic Redneck's temper would get him disqualified in their No. 1 Contender's match. But the Rattlesnake wouldn't bite, restraining himself when Angle threw a chair in the ring and dared Austin to use it. Unfortunately, it was Stone Cold tasting cold steel moments after he was shoved into the referee, while Kurt savored victory with the Angle Slam and pinfall. Or so he thought—learning Austin's foot was on the bottom rope made him irate, though Stone Cold quickly calmed him with a Stunner for the three-count. Having earned himself the title shot at *No Way Out,* Austin celebrated with a

Steveweiser in one hand, and another Stunner on a charging Y2J!

While Stone Cold focused on the Undisputed title, Stephanie McMahon-Helmsley blamed WWE co-owner Ric Flair for troubling her husband with a match against Booker T, only to learn her vindictive father was responsible, probably because of what Triple H called him on *SmackDown!* Hunter didn't care; he planned on kicking Booker's ass regardless, and *without* his wife's proposed presence at ringside. The Cerebral Assassin controlled much of the contest until Christian came down and reverse-DDT'd him on the outside floor, in retaliation for the *SmackDown!* beating. Further distracted upon seeing Stephanie race to the ring apron and slapping the European Champion, Triple H tried protecting her by clobbering Christian off the apron…then inadvertently did the same to Stephanie when Booker nailed him in the back. Grabbing a handful of tights, Booker rolled Hunter up for the one-two-three upset!

Triple H seethed as he made his way up the ramp and to the dressing room, with Stephanie apologizing

Triple H tries to choke out Booker T.

every step of the way. Slamming the dressing room door in her face, she kept pleading with him from the hallway, yelling, *"I love you!"* Finally, he opened the door…then gave Stephanie her bags and belongings before slamming it shut again!

Despite the ugly incident, the Billion-Dollar Princess remained closed-minded about her marriage during a taped interview with Jim Ross for the January 31 *SmackDown!* Describing herself as "the epitome of a career woman" whose past successes attributed to Triple H's four WWE Championship reigns, Stephanie tearfully added that while Hunter's reaction to her *Raw* mistake had hurt her feelings, "I forgive him. That's what marriage is all about. That's what *love* is all about." She resented J.R.'s queries regarding the couple's fidelity toward each other. "There's no other woman out there like me," she stated, "and certainly no other woman who's as good in bed as I am. So, no, it doesn't concern me at all." As to the "problems" everyone witnessed over the past several weeks, "You can take your remarks and your questions from all the fans, and you can *shove* them." But the talk did give Stephanie an idea, one that would prove to the entire world "just how much Triple H loves me…and how *perfect* our marriage is!"

The princess was in good company with other deluded individuals that night—regardless of his humiliating *Raw* cut-down at the hands of Stone Cold, Chris Jericho's "larger than life" attitude continued to swell. Following a low blow and Breakdown on Tag Team Co-Champion Tazz for a nontitle singles win, the Undisputed Champion put guest referee Jacqueline in the Walls of Jericho when she begrudgingly raised his hand in victory. Kurt Angle's ego was pretty bruised—on top of losing the No.1 Contender's match to Austin—just who the hell was Lilian Garcia to remind him he didn't win the *Royal Rumble*? "That was *my Royal Rumble*," he insisted, "and it was my only chance of winning it on my first try. I will *never* forgive Triple H for that." In fact, Kurt decided that when he and Undertaker took on Triple H and The Rock later that

night, "I plan on going *Olympic* on his ass. Oh, it's true."

Kurt had a chance to back his words up when the bell sounded, but elected Undertaker to start the match…*until* Triple H's back was turned. Rock soon went toe-to-toe with the Hardcore Champion, exchanging fists, countering finishers and converting a Chokeslam to a DDT that left both sprawled on the canvas. Angle and Triple H tagged in, and before long The Game connected with the Pedigree, only for 'Taker to break up the subsequent pinfall with a chair shot. Rock and Triple H got the "W" via DQ, though the fight continued in and outside the ring; the Brahma Bull Rock Bottomed Undertaker through the *SmackDown!* announcer's table, while Angle slapped the ankle lock on the dazed Triple H, first in the ring and then toward the ramp, and refused to relinquish the hold until he was satisfied he'd broken The Game's ankle.

Approaching Undertaker backstage—prior to his February 4 *Raw* Tag match with Y2J against The Rock

> **"The Rock disrespected me, so tonight…I'm gonna teach him the word 'respect.'"**

and Stone Cold—Michael Cole asked for his reaction to being Rock Bottomed last week. Instead, the Hardcore Champion drew a fearful reaction from Cole, which is how he liked it. "Fear and respect go hand in hand," he said. "The Rock disrespected me, so tonight…I'm gonna teach him the word 'respect.' " The Brahma Bull had his own announcement, telling the Coach, "At *No Way Out*, 'Dead Man walking' is gonna walk right into going *one-on-one* with the Great One!" It didn't matter what 'Taker's reasons were for his recent actions, "The Rock doesn't answer to you. The Rock is not *Undertaker's* Champion. No-no-no-no-*no*. The Rock is the *People's* Champion!" And there was no way the Phenom would change that, *or* stop him from belting out a verse to his favorite song for the sellout crowd, "Viva Rock Vegas!"

Jericho's "assurance" of having Undertaker's back sounded good backstage, even if it was the Dead Man backing the "living legend" throughout the tag contest. He first rescued him from Austin's Walls of Jericho, then pulled the referee from the ring when a Stone Cold Stunner allowed Rock to cover the Undisputed Champion. And with the official still down while a Rock Bottom laid out Jericho, 'Taker produced a lead pipe from his motorcycle and smacked it over Rock's head! A barely conscious Y2J rolled on top of the *un*conscious Brahma Bull, getting the three-count before Austin could rush in for the save.

T riple H could consider himself fortunate he was able to walk to the ring when *Raw* opened on February 4, but "Mr. Gold Medalist" Kurt Angle made two very big mistakes when he tried to break his ankle on *SmackDown!*: "One, you didn't get the job done. And two, you screwed with the wrong guy." Calling for Angle to get his ass kicked in the ring, The Game had to settle for Booker T, who came out onstage and talked trash about his *Raw* "victory" over Hunter last week. Booker wasn't saying much after the Cerebral Assassin delivered a Pedigree, but their rematch was interrupted when Angle charged in and flattened Hunter with an Angle Slam. Minutes later, an irate Triple H found Angle coming out of Mr. McMahon's backstage office, only to be restrained by two policeman watching the door. Kurt had some good news for Triple H— they were going to have "a little match" at *No Way Out*, which suited Hunter just fine

until Angle added, "Oh, and your *WrestleMania* title shot is going to be up for grabs."

Amazingly enough, The Game's night got a whole lot more interesting when Stephanie later called him to the ring and made her huge announcement after her *SmackDown!* conversation with Jim Ross, who'd had an epiphany. "It seems like we're fighting all the time and not communicating," she explained. "I realize that there's only *one* way to prove our love for each other, and that's in one week, live on *Raw…that we renew our wedding vows!*" She'd waited to tell Hunter until *Raw* came to Las Vegas, the city where they first were married.

The Game's face said it all, but his words punctuated it, "You want us to renew our wedding vows? To stand in front of you and the world, and express our love for each other?" The princess' face looked hopeful as she said, "Yes…" then crushed when Triple H emphatically replied, *"No."*

Stephanie became distraught; Hunter *had* to do it for her, which angered him even more. *"Why* do I have to do it? Because you're the 'Billion-Dollar Princess'? Because you're Stephanie McMahon? Because you

The *un*-happy couple *before* Stephanie tells Hunter about the baby.

always get your way? Because everything in our lives is about *you?*" He started exiting the ring until Stephanie, crying, blurted out, *"It's because I'm pregnant!"* She didn't want to tell everyone, but she knew how much the two of them had wanted to be parents. "That's why we need to renew our wedding vows," she sobbed. "So we can be a family all together." Triple H stood silent in the ring…then hugged and kissed Mrs. McMahon-Helmsley, elated over the news. Their problems didn't matter anymore, and he'd gladly honor his princess' wish, for themselves and for the baby.

The Rock's kid gloves were off when he kicked off *SmackDown!* in Los Angeles' sold-out Staples Center on February 7. After his lead pipe assault on *Raw* three nights before, the Great One didn't care if Undertaker had a match with Maven that night; he wanted him one-on-one there and now. Booker T, like he'd done with Triple H on *Raw,* interrupted—having played The Game *twice* now, he decided to make an example of the Brahma Bull. Rock saw it as a chance for Booker to become a leading man. "We've got the lights, we've got the cameras, we've got the action! You come on in—the name of the movie's gonna be *The Rock Whoopin' Your Candy Ass All Over L.A.!*" The predictable happy ending—Rock putting Booker's spine on the pine, then landing the People's Elbow for the three-count—drew rave reviews from the fans.

Meanwhile, advance word on Maven's Hardcore title match with Undertaker didn't sound too good. Nevertheless, *Tough Enough* mentor Al Snow was proud of his former student for issuing the challenge, and offered some valuable advice, "If things go really bad, I've got the car running, it's gassed up. I'll get you out of there as quick as I can…and we'll get you off to the hospital." It certainly looked like a trip was in order; the rookie was busted open shortly after the bell

sounded, and not even his teacher's ringside assistance… and a trashcan, *and* the ring bell…could save him. But as the Hardcore Champion started "Takin' Care of Business" with his Dragon Sleeper, The Rock jolted the Phenom with a steel chair to the head, then a Rock Bottom to the mat! Barely cognizant himself, Maven slowly covered the down-and-out Dead Man for the three-count, and in what had to rank as the biggest upset of 2002, he defeated Undertaker for the WWE Hardcore Championship!

Before leaving the Staples Center, the People's Champion made one thing clear to the Coach; he and Undertaker weren't even. That would have to wait until *No Way Out.* Suddenly, it was the American Badass' turn to attack—after chokeslamming the Great One onto the hood of a limousine, he put him on top of the vehicle and delivered a devastating Tombstone piledriver! "No, Rock," said the Dead Man on top of the car, "we *ain't* even."

> **"We've got the lights, we've got the cameras, we've got the action! You come on in—the name of the movie's gonna be *The Rock Whoopin' Your Candy Ass All Over L.A.!*"**

No one at February 7 *SmackDown!* was surprised to hear Chris Jericho crow about his unprecedented *sixth* victory over The Rock on *Raw* three nights ago, then complain how "the losers on Hollywood Boulevard" still didn't respect him or believe he could beat Stone Cold Steve Austin at *No Way Out.* They were surprised, however, to hear him order the "coward" Rattlesnake to come out and fight, and *stunned* to see *MADtv* comedian Will Sasso dressed as a beefy Stone Cold and avoid an undisputed beatdown by telling Jericho he's the better man! But the last laugh would go to the real Austin, who'd physically eject Y2J from the ring as he tried to blindside him. Turning his attention to the fear-frozen Sasso, Stone

Cold offered him a Steveweiser so long as he agreed to certain conditions. "Now…you're not gonna do this again."

"*What?*"

"Promise?"

"*What?*"

"Cross your heart?"

"*What?*"

"Hope to die?"

"*What?*"

"Stick a thousand needles?"

"*What?*"

"In your little eye?"

A relieved Sasso agreed, but Stone Cold still Stunned him.

Backstage, WWE co-owner Ric Flair decided to add to the Undisputed Champion's fun by having him play The Game later that night, as a nontitle sneak

"Uncle" Kurt Angle with "Triple H, Jr."

peak of the *WrestleMania* main event. Triple H, meanwhile, was doing something he hadn't done for a long time: he was *smiling*. Stephanie's physician, Dr. Richards, came by and added to the couple's newfound bundle of joy—Stephanie was eight weeks along, and the baby was developing beautifully. While looking at a sonogram photo of their child, Stephanie beamed that they were going to be "a happy family."

The good feeling wouldn't last long, thanks to "Uncle Kurt," who entered the ring with a baby carriage and triumphantly informed the fans, "Look who's going to *WrestleMania*." But even while guaranteeing he'd take away Hunter's title shot at *No Way Out*, the medalist confessed to being blown away by Stephanie's *Raw* announcement. "I never felt sorry for a baby before," he said, "but imagine having to go through life with *Triple H* as your father. Wow…even as a *fetus*, the kid is smarter than his dad." Uncle Kurt also didn't need a sonogram photo to tell him what the baby would look like, he produced from the carriage "Triple H Jr.," a stuffed baby gorilla wearing a big paper nose, and tried feeding it baby bananas. Admittedly, it *was* funny;

even Triple H looked amused as he stepped into the ring…then laid Angle out with a right hand and slammed the baby carriage onto him! Kurt made a beeline for the *SmackDown!* ramp, realizing that messing with Hunter's family was no game to *The* Game.

The father-to-be next visited his hated father-in-law Vince McMahon backstage, but it wasn't to confront him about putting Hunter's *WrestleMania* title shot at risk at *No Way Out*. Instead, he asked Vince to put aside his differences with Stephanie. "She has a soft spot in her heart for the *bastard* who raised her," he explained and, asked Vince to walk her down the aisle when they renewed their wedding vows. But that would be *it*, he warned. "You will never, *ever* get anywhere near my child…*Grandpa*."

McMahon said he'd consider it…then informed his son-in-law that the evening's bout against Jericho was now a Handicap match that also featured Kurt Angle. Triple H would put up a courageous fight, but the double-team effort and Angle Slam onto a steel chair soon proved too much for him. But even more alarming was mother-to-be Stephanie coming down to help her husband, only to be menaced by Y2J. Fearing her safety, Triple H attacked Angle and Jericho with the chair, but as he and Stephanie hugged in the ring, Kurt knocked down Hunter, who landed on top of his pregnant wife! Stephanie motioned she was okay, but the brief scare was yet one more thing for which Triple H would owe Kurt Angle.

Being a fan favorite for over a decade still entitled Undertaker to expect respect from audiences everywhere, including Arkansas State University's Convocation Center, the site of February 11 *Raw*. Recognizing the "hillbilly" fans' cheers as appreciation for "the man who finally shut The Rock's mouth," the Dead Man noted that what he did on *SmackDown!* wasn't going to stop there. "I ain't no Aretha Franklin, and I won't be singin' it," he said. "I will continue to beat the word 'respect' into The Rock until he sings, 'R-E-S-P-E-C-T. 'Taker, that is what you mean to me.' "

The American Badass was suddenly cut off by the Nature Boy's entrance music and the "Woooo!" howls filling the arena. Ric Flair came out to let 'Taker know that whatever respect he'd built over the past decade disappeared the moment he gave The Rock a grade-one concussion and serious neck injury. Not appreciating the comments from the fifty percent owner of the WWE, 'Taker warned, "When the *real* owner gives me the word…I'm gonna bust your ass." But Slick Ric had some bad news for him: not only was The Rock going to bring "everything he has for the Dead Man" at *No Way Out*, but Undertaker was first going to have a one-on-one that night against Stone Cold Steve Austin.

Though he was, "Nervous! Petrified! Horrified!" to hear Jonesboro was a *dry* county, Stone Cold hit the liquor store and loaded up on alcohol before *Raw*. Now he was "jacked up" that he and the Arkansas fans were "gonna disrespect all over the Dead Man's ass!" And with "alcohol to drink and a man's ass to whip," he just bottom-lined in his interview with Coach what he'd do at *No Way Out:* "The Undisputed titles are

comin' with Stone Cold Steve Austin! Why? *'Cause Stone Cold said so!"*

The brief comments were enough to concern Y2J, who used one of those belts on Edge's injured ribs for a cheap win earlier that evening. That's why he decided to waylay the Bionic Redneck as he made his way down the ramp for his match, making him easy pickings for Undertaker. Austin's resolve and a late-rallying Lou Thesz Press would keep him in the contest, though his desperation Stunner to counter 'Taker's Tombstone left him in no shape to fend off a second Y2J ambush. Stone Cold was awarded the match via disqualification, yet he'd pay dearly as Jericho assaulted him with one of the championship belts, then with the very beer cooler Austin filled with Steveweisers beforehand.

Kurt Angle had something to say about Triple H's big night, so he kept his match with The Godfather short (fortunately, Godfather headed ringside with his escorts, who assisted him back up the ramp moments after he'd tapped out to the gold medalist's ankle lock). He thought Stephanie could do "a lot better," but he offered The Game his own personal vow. "I, Kurt Angle, hereby take this match at *No Way Out,* to kick your butt, to make you tap, to take your *WrestleMania* title shot and to go on to become the Undisputed Champion. In sickness and in health, as long as we both shall live. Amen."

Flair shows no fear of the "Dead Man walking."

Chris Jericho adds insult to victory over Edge.

The medalist wasn't going to ruin the special occasion, though. Triple H had promised Stephanie he wasn't going to get in a fight with Angle or anyone else, and even gave her a special ring that he wanted her to have. Then, with only minutes to go before the ceremony, Vince McMahon approached his daughter. "I'm not going to forget the fact that you tried to put me out of business, and I'm not going to forget the fact that you said you wanted to watch me die," he told her. "But I *will* forgive…because I know that, down deep, you're a McMahon. And no matter what, you're Daddy's little girl. So, yes, I will walk you down the aisle." Truly, it was a perfect night for Stephanie.

Triple H also was in for a surprise that evening, but it wasn't nearly as pleasant. On his way to get Stephanie's ring, Hunter bumped into Flair's right-hand man, retired ring great Arn Anderson, who had a package addressed for Hunter. Arn later visited Hunter as he was getting ready for the ceremony, to inform him that WWE CEO Linda McMahon had contacted Flair's office and was looking for The Game. Triple H called his

mother-in-law, who explained that inside the package was a videotape that proved Stephanie's doctor was an actor. Watching the tape on a VCR and thinking he and Stephanie were conned, Hunter became outraged, then heartbroken as Linda revealed, "Stephanie's been *lying* to you. She was *never* pregnant."

No matter what anyone thinks, World Wrestling Entertainment knows how to throw a lovely wedding. Flowers and a white carpet ran the length of the ramp and up to the ring, where the vows would be exchanged. Coming out to his theme music first, Triple H was decked out in full tuxedo and smiling, despite the news he'd learned only minutes before. Next came Stephanie, dressed in white, her arm draped around her father as he proudly walked his princess down the aisle. Though Vince wasn't thrilled with the swine-loving "What?" chanters of Jonesboro, he gave his daughter over to Hunter, and the ritual was underway. Stephanie started with her vows, "Hunter, I take thee as my husband, again. And I wanted to do it in front of the entire world because I want to share how I felt about you since the first moment I laid eyes on you, and how I feel about you right now. Your smile lights up my heart, your touch makes me feel safe and secure, and your words give me encouragement. And when I speak, I know that you're truly listening, because you're the only one who ever really hears me. And Hunter, I believe we were really destined to be together, because I really feel blessed. And no other words could sum up how I feel, besides 'I love you.' "

Triple H, still smiling, then exchanged his feelings with his bride. "God, that was so beautiful, Steph. I, too, want to stand here in front of the world, and tell you how I feel about you. Tell you how I felt about you since the moment I saw you, and tell you how I feel about you *right now*. Y'see, Steph, we've been together for a little over two years, and sure, we've had our ups and our downs. But despite all of that…last week…when you told me that I was gonna be a father…it was the greatest moment in my life. The emotion that I felt was unbelievable. And since that day, I've looked at you in a different way. When I look at you, I see you not just as my loving wife, but I see you as the mother of my child. When your wife is pregnant, you love her more. And today, standing here in front of the world, in this ring, after hearing the beautiful words that you say, I see you in a different light again. I see you not as my loving wife, not as the mother of my child. Stephanie, as I look

> **"As I look into your eyes tonight, I see you for what you *truly* are…*a no-good lying bitch!*"**

into your eyes tonight, I see you for what you *truly* are…*a no-good lying bitch!*"

Stephanie reeled back in disbelief as Triple H's hostility exploded on her. "Steph, I have done some pretty bad things in my life. I admit it—I'm an asshole. But even *I* wouldn't go this low. You *disgust* me! You care about nothing but yourself! You never gave a crap about us! It was always about *you!* Well, you don't have to worry about 'us' any longer, because as of this moment, Stephanie, our marriage…it's *over!* We… are…*through!*"

The sellout crowd raised the roof as The Game brought Stephanie's world—plus the wedding decorations—crashing down around her, in the process reducing her to tears and giving his father-in-law a well-deserved Pedigree in the ring. Her tears turned to anger as she started yelling at Hunter, who piefaced her down to the mat, then removed and threw down his wedding band. Huddling over her fallen father, Stephanie screamed at Triple H as he made his way up the ramp, her face hideously twisted and registering pure hatred for the man that was her husband.

Stephanie and Hunter prepare to renew their wedding vows.

Pushed to the breaking point, Triple H snaps.

Needless to say, with the threat of the nWo looming and a triple main event at *No Way Out* in just three days' time, the February 14 *SmackDown!* in Little Rock's AllTel Arena promised *several* massacres on St. Valentine's Day (plus a two-for-one sale with The Godfather's Escort Service!). That included Chris Jericho, whose *Raw* attack on Stone Cold had even Ric Flair fearing for the Undisputed Champ's safety. "When Stone Cold gets here," he cautioned, "he's gonna tear you up and the building down." Y2J wasn't scared, though he'd have reason to be when the WWE co-owner decided the "fearless" champion should face Kane in a nontitle bout that night. Another reason followed shortly thereafter, when a contemplative Austin publicly confessed to being a drug addict. "My drug of choice being the WWE Championship," he explained. "Like a drug, I *need*

that championship. I *want* that championship. I've got to *have* that championship. I do not want to *live* without the World Wrestling Entertainment Championship! You heard me—I said I've got to have that sonuvabitch!"

Jericho might not be able to just say no; for the rest of the nervous champ's evening, revenge was a beer best served Stone Cold, starting in Y2J's backstage room, where he'd find Austin waiting for him with some brewskis. The Rattlesnake made Jericho pick one up and started a toast, then knocked it out of his hands. "Any time I want—*BAM!*—your ass is *mine*," he warned, then left. Austin next appeared as Jericho made his way to the ring for his match with Kane, making the Undisputed Champion anxious enough to flee into the crowd on two separate occasions. The Big Red Machine stopped him both times, but he wouldn't be able to stop Y2J from ultimately cleaning

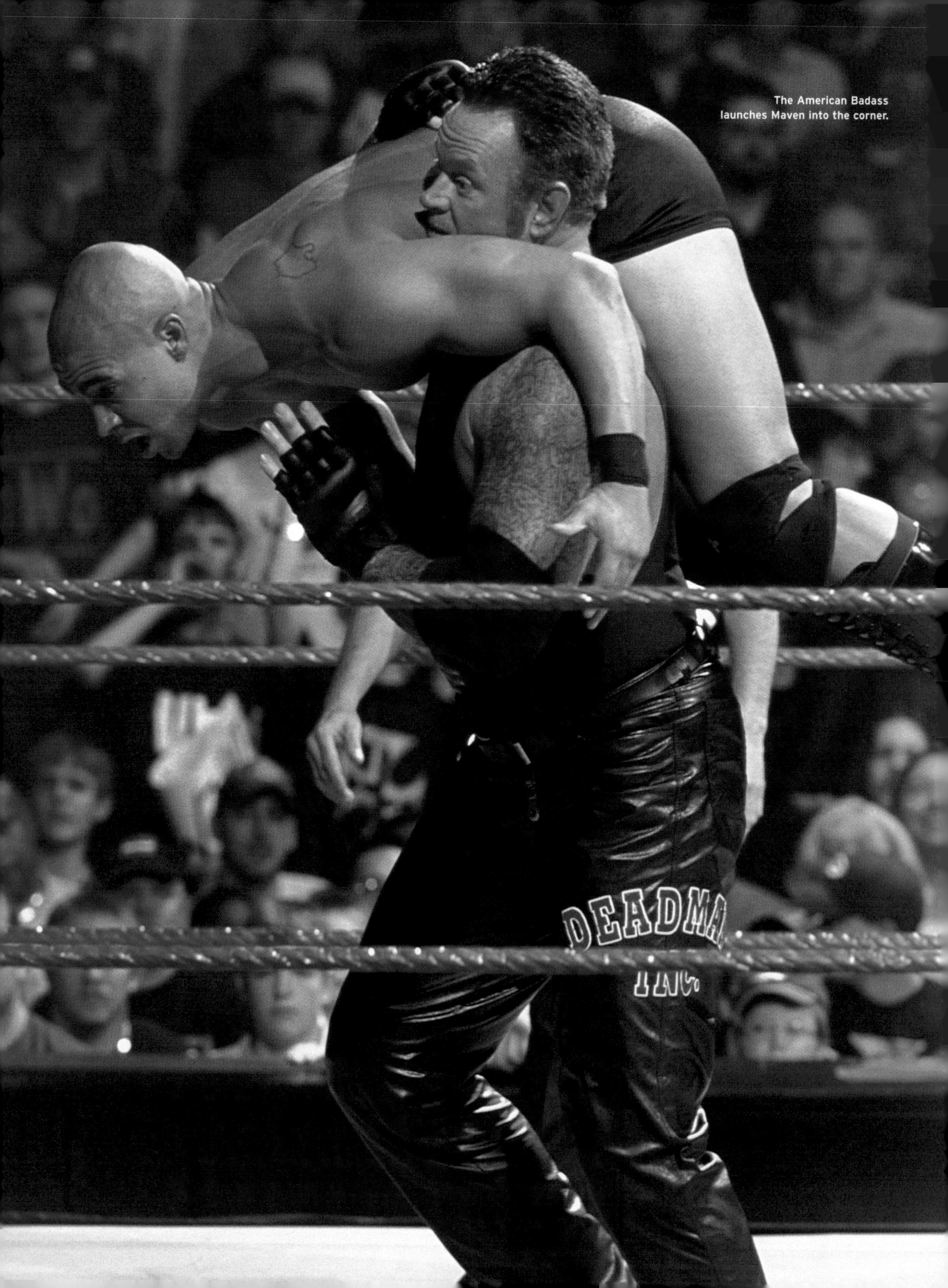

The American Badass launches Maven into the corner.

his clock with one of the undisputed belts, drawing himself a DQ. Austin suddenly darted towards the ring, where he'd cap off a hellacious Y2J beatdown with a Stunner that nearly took the Undisputed Champion's head off. Austin's bottom line on the matter: "Chris Jericho, you got *No Way Out!*"

Vince McMahon accompanied Stephanie to the ring when *SmackDown!* opened that evening; he wouldn't abandon his little girl in her time of need. "Stephanie lied," he admitted to the crowd, "but she didn't do anything that all of you don't do each and every single day." As for Triple H, he committed "a cardinal sin" when he struck McMahon's daughter down, "a sin for which you will eternally pay." Stephanie took hold of the mic and blamed her lies on her soon-to-be *ex*-husband, for being inattentive and not paying her enough respect. Since kicking him out of their house, she'd destroyed or burned everything he owned, and made a vow "to make your life a living hell." And before *SmackDown!* ended that night, the vengeful princess promised she'd have "a special, sweet Stephanie Valentine's Day Surprise" for The Game.

[
"I want you to rip Triple H apart, limb from limb. I want you to bring me his *heart!*"
]

Frighteningly enough, that surprise *wasn't* the Tag Team match Vince had sanctioned, pitting Kurt Angle and Undertaker against Triple H and new Hardcore Champion Maven. 'Taker was certainly up for it, telling the McMahons backstage that things had gotten quiet since The Rock wasn't around, though if he showed up at *No Way Out,* "It's gonna be quiet around here for a *long* time." Stephanie's plan for Kurt and 'Taker was plain and simple: "I want you to rip Triple H apart,

limb from limb," and seeing as it was St. Valentine's Day, "I want you to bring me his *heart!*"

The Game's back was certainly up against it as he approached the ring later that night, and it didn't help that his woefully inexperienced tag partner was already getting pounded on by the Dead Man. The rookie once again proved himself a fighter, dropkicking Angle from the top rope to buy Hunter time to recover from an Undertaker assault, but he paid dearly for the assist when the American Badass launched him outside the ring, then gave him a bone-jarring Last Ride through the *SmackDown!* announcer's table. Despite the odds, Triple H soon gained the upper hand, setting 'Taker up for the Pedigree, but the match would come to an abrupt end when the gold medalist smashed a chair across Hunter's back.

The Cerebral Assassin could hardly feel like the winner of the contest with Angle and Undertaker continuing to beat him, and not even an intervention from Ric Flair could put a stop to it. 'Taker laid the Nature Boy out with a boot to the face, then set him up for the Last Ride before being stopped by Flair's business partner. "I want Ric Flair to be able to make it to *No Way Out,*" yelled Mr. McMahon, joined at ringside by his daughter, "because it's *Ric Flair's* fault that the nWo is going to inject poison in the veins of the WWE!" As for the helpless Triple H, Stephanie divulged her big surprise before he took another Olympic chair shot, "When you face Kurt Angle and your *WrestleMania* title shot is on the line, 'baby'…*I'm* going to be the guest referee!" Four weeks ago, Triple H asked Chris Jericho if he could make it to *WrestleMania X8* as the Undisputed Champion; now it looked all but certain that it was "Game Over."

3
MARCH

'Mania Runs Wild

The gold medalist was going to face the Undisputed Champion. The Game wasn't. The Texas Rattlesnake went to jail. The People's Champ went to the hospital. The Dead Man wanted blood. The Nature Boy wanted to set things right. The Undisputed Champion wanted to know who the hell his opponent was. And with the nWo around, the WWE was going straight to hell. And there was still twenty-seven days to go before WrestleMania X8.

After four hundred fifty-five episodes, the February 18 Raw in Chicago's Allstate Arena offered two of the WWE's finest hours, as wrestling's past met with its future, existing story lines built toward their epic conclusions and World Wrestling Entertainment headed toward its showcase of the immortals—the Super Bowl of sports entertainment, WrestleMania. Regarded by many as the founding event of Pay-Per-View television, WrestleMania has been a cultural institution since it premiered March 31, 1985. It was WrestleMania where Hulkamania first reached worldwide proportions, then ran wild two years later as a record-breaking crowd of 93,173 fans witnessed Hogan lift Andre the Giant and deliver the "Slam Heard 'Round the World." WrestleMania VI saw the "Ultimate Challenge" take place between Hogan and the Ultimate Warrior, in a contest still regarded as one of the greatest ever. WrestleMania XII endured a grueling Iron Man match that lasted over sixty minutes, with Shawn Michaels eventually winning his first WWE Championship. WrestleMania 13 brought a Texas Rattlesnake to bloody prominence in a Submission match against Bret "Hitman" Hart, and served as the first WrestleMania for a "People's Rookie." And after the events of February 18, WrestleMania X8 promised to outdo all of them.

Stone Cold Steve Austin was really pissed off in the ring as Raw opened in Chicago's Allstate Arena on February 18. With steel chair in hand, he called out Scott Hall, Kevin Nash and Hollywood Hulk Hogan, the nWo "chicken-shits" who cost Austin undisputed gold at No Way Out. "I will whip every one of your asses!" he yelled at the unholy trio as they came out onstage, discussed their course of action…and left. Not satisfied, the Bionic Redneck sat himself in the ring with his cooler full of Steveweisers and declared himself on strike "till I get a piece of that nWo ass!"

Instead, out came Kurt Angle, accompanied by a group of security guards, off-duty policemen courtesy of WWE co-owner Mr. McMahon. "If somebody's going to take up valuable airtime, it should be…I dunno… somebody who's *going* for the title at *WrestleMania*," Angle said, earning some well-thrown Steveweisers as he headed ringside with the guards and demanded Austin to leave. "It's *my* time now, and if there's one thing I can't stand, it's a crybaby!"

Austin flipped off Kurt as he entered the ring to make his big announcement: "I, Kurt Angle, hereby having beat Triple H at *No Way Out*, for the record, will go to *WrestleMania* and become the Undisputed Champion, because if anybody deserves it, it's *me*." The coiled Rattlesnake suddenly struck, pounding away on the gold medalist until the guards handcuffed him and put him in a squad car out back. Scott Hall and the nWo came up to the car, talking trash at Austin as the vehicle headed for the precinct.

Backstage, Stephanie McMahon and Angle were patting each other's backs. The medalist appreciated Stephanie for being a tremendously "fair and impartial" guest referee for his *No Way Out* match with her estranged husband, Triple H, while she congratulated Kurt for having Stone Cold jailed, and for beating The Game "clean." WWE co-owner Ric Flair suddenly joined the mutual admiration society; his business partner's "absolute genius" of sanctioning last night's contest for the *WrestleMania* title shot had inspired him to

make the same match on *Raw* that night! Angle and Triple H would go at it again, and if the princess interfered, The Game would get the automatic win!

[**"There's only one thing I've got to say to you WWE fans: *you can kiss my ass!*"**]

The Rock challenges Hogan to headline one more *WrestleMania*.

Austin's arrest and the main event news already had the *Raw* crowd pumped when Hollywood Hulk Hogan made his way to the ring, solo this time. Despite his wayward turn to nWo colors, the fans chanted "Hogan! Hogan!" in respect for his illustrious accomplishments in the red and yellow. "It feels great to be back in this ring, in the WWE," he said, fondly reminiscing their history together—fighting Russians, facing monsters, slamming the "seven-hundred-pound" Andre the Giant at *WrestleMania III*—before he about-faced the crowd. "But…something happened. And then you people *turned* on me."

Hogan's tone shifted from sentimental to embittered as he recalled how fans one day stopped respecting him, then drove him from the WWE like Chicago had done with Michael Jordan. "Now that I'm back—thanks to Mr. Vince McMahon—there's only one thing I've got to say to you WWE fans: *you can kiss my ass!*" Seeing himself as the icon responsible for putting the WWE on the map, he laid it out straight for his so-called supporters, "I'm the biggest star, past or present, in the wrestling world today, and there'll *never* be a bigger star in the wrestling business than Hollywood Hulk Hogan."

The Allstate Arena audience exploded as the Great One's music sounded; finally, The Rock had come back to Chicago, home to what would be considered the most electrifying encounter in sports-entertainment history. The two men locked eyes as Rock circled Hollywood, asking if he really thought the people drove him out of the WWE. Hogan started answering when Rock blared, *"It doesn't matter what you think!"*

Anger seethed from the Brahma Bull's words; it wasn't the people that drove Hogan away. "They *loved* you!" he yelled. "They *believed* in you! And dammit, *The Rock* believed in *you! You* know what happened? It was years after years *after years*...of you eating the vitamins, saying the prayers, ripping your T-shirt off, running wild on everyone—'What'cha gonna *do* when *Hulkamania* runs wild over *you?*' The Rock'll *tell* you what the people did: after all that, the people ran to the toilet, pulled their pants down and took one big Hulka-*crap* every time you opened your mouth!" Though he gave Hogan his due as a legend and an icon, all of his talk about main-eventing *WrestleMania*s prompted the People's Champion to ask, "Well, Hulk Hogan...how do you feel about headlining one more *WrestleMania* with *The Rock?*"

["Well, Hulk Hogan...how do you feel about headlining one more *WrestleMania* with *The Rock?*"]

The reaction was so immense both Superstars couldn't help but pause and look around. "Rocky!" and "Hogan!" chants competed for crowd dominance until Hogan, finally turning his attention back to the Great One, said, "They've got a phrase for guys like you. It's called 'flavor of the month.' " Having faced a *lot* of them throughout his career, Hogan stuck his finger into Rock's chest and asked, "What makes you think that you're even in my league? What makes you think that you're even *close* to being as big a star as I am? What makes you—"

A hand in Hogan's face silenced him. "Yes...or *no?*" The Rock painted a picture for him: their contest

THE ROCK

HEIGHT: **6'5"** WEIGHT: **275 lbs.**
OTHER NAMES: **The People's Champion, Brahma Bull, The Great One**
FINISHING MOVES: **Rock Bottom; People's Elbow**
CAREER HIGHLIGHTS: **Undisputed Champion; WWE Champion (7); Intercontinental Champion (2); Tag Team Champion (5); WCW Champion (2); Royal Rumble 2000 winner**
2002 HIGHLIGHTS: **Defeating Hollywood Hulk Hogan in an "Icon vs. Icon" match at *WrestleMania X8*; his first lead role in the box-office hit *The Scorpion King*; defeating Undertaker and Kurt Angle in a Triple-Threat match for the Undisputed Championship at *Vengeance*; losing the Undisputed title to "The Next Big Thing" Brock Lesnar at *SummerSlam*.**

would be *the* fantasy matchup no one dreamed possible, one that would transcend their industry and "determine who will go down in history as being the absolute best, *ever.*" Realizing the decision may not be for himself or Hogan to make, Rock asked the audience, "At *Wrestle-Mania*...do you people want to see the immortal Hulk Hogan go one-on-one with the Great One?" He didn't need to mimic the Hulkster's classic hand-wave-to-the-ear; the response was already defeaning. Again Rock asked, "Yes...or *no?*"

"Yes," was Hogan's reply, and again the fans erupted. "It will be a *pleasure* to kick your ass at *WrestleMania.*" As the two shook hands to seal the deal, Hogan said, "Good luck," then pulled Rock closer and added, "You're gonna *need* it." But as Hogan started to leave, the Brahma Bull, not relinquishing the handshake, drew him back and offered, "Not as much as *you... brother,*" then Rock Bottomed Hulk Hogan in the center of the ring!

The matter should have ended there, until the day of *WrestleMania X8*, but it didn't. Hall and Nash surprised Rock at the top of the stage, then beat him back down to the ring where Hogan, using his thick "Hollywood" weight belt, whipped him repeatedly. Hall contributed the Razor's Edge finisher he used to cut down opponents in his WWE days as Razor Ramon, while Nash followed with the Jackknife Powerbomb maneuver that once "Diesel"-fueled the WWE Championship. The duo then held the helpless Brahma Bull as Hogan, wielding a toolbox hammer he took from under the ring, cracked it over the back of his skull! Following up with an unnecessary legdrop and mocking pinfall, Hollywood broke out the spray cans and "branded" Rock's exposed back with the words "nWo 2 sweet."

With paramedics stretchering the unconscious Rock into an ambulance, again the matter *should* have ended there. Again, the nWo *wouldn't* end it, using a car and a truck to box in the emergency vehicle as it left the arena. The medics were sent running as Hall and Nash bashed the ambulance windshield and chained its back doors, while Hogan climbed behind the wheel of a semi, then drove it repeatedly into the emergency vehicle until it was smashed beyond recognition. The nWo members were already gone by the time rescue services arrived, and the threat of a fuel leak forced away the *Raw* cameras, leaving announcers Jim Ross, Jerry "the King" Lawler and everyone inside the Allstate Arena wondering about The Rock's condition. Even the girls who escorted The Godfather down to ringside for his match with Booker T couldn't help but talk about it, which in turn distracted their boss long enough for Booker to catch him with a side kick and get the win. For a time, it appeared the fantasy matchup scheduled to become reality at *WrestleMania* would be shelved.

Backstage, Kurt Angle answered Michael Cole's question honestly; after hearing "the worst news of the year," he wasn't sure if he could concentrate on his No. 1 Contender's match. "It's shocking," he said. "Ric Flair making this match after I *beat* Triple H last night? Give me a break!" Disbelieving his ears, Cole clarified himself; he'd meant the nWo's attack on The Rock. Kurt looked like he was still waiting to hear the bad news, then answered, "Oh. Well...yeah, I feel bad. I feel horrible for The Rock...but at least *he* didn't have a title shot at *WrestleMania. I* did." But the gold medalist promised he'd end the night on a good note for every-one: he would defeat The Game and win back his *WrestleMania* title shot.

Anxious to find out who he'd face at *WrestleMania* next month, Undisputed Champion Chris Jericho joined J.R. and the King on commentary for the *Raw* main event. As fate would have it, Triple H and Angle's battle would spill out toward the announcer's table, with the gold medalist jawing in Y2J's direction. As the referee restrained Jericho from factoring into the contest, Angle used the distraction to nail The Game with one of the Undisputed Championship belts. Showing tremendous resiliency, Hunter kicked out of a two-count, then withstood two ankle lock attempts before he'd finally Pedigree Angle for the victory. Winning back his *WrestleMania* title shot almost twenty-four hours after losing it, Triple H immediately directed his eyes toward Jericho, now standing on the announcer's table, and toward the Undisputed Championship.

Stephanie promises Jericho victory at **WrestleMania.**

On February 21 *SmackDown!*, Stephanie confronted Ric Flair in his office backstage at Rockford, Illinois' MetroCentre, and held him responsible for making her life "a living hell." She left the office even more agitated when Triple H entered and told Flair, "It's like they say, 'Life's a bitch. Then you *marry* one.' " Before Hunter's scheduled match with Undertaker, she brought her grievances to ringside, insisting her husband would win the Undisputed title at *WrestleMania* "over my dead body." Out came Chris Jericho, who in months past would have associated her comment toward her virtue and price point, but his elevated "living legend" status helped him since realize she was "a brilliant, calculating, conniving genius." Knowing better than to argue with him, Stephanie instead proposed a business partnership that would make them "an unstoppable force" at *WrestleMania.* "Who knows Triple H better than *I* do?"

> **"It's like they say, 'Life's a bitch. Then you *marry* one.'"**

she said. "I know his strengths, and most importantly, I know his *weaknesses.*" Jericho loved the idea, "I say 'Triple H's worst nightmare just came true." The two shook on it.

Seeing the duo united at ringside for his match with the Dead Man must have been difficult for The Game to swallow, which is probably why he spat out a drink of water all over them. Stephanie followed Jericho and Hunter as they fought their way into the ring, then caught her husband off-guard with a slap to the face. Y2J saved his new partner from a Pedigree, only to get knocked back to the outside floor. Suddenly, Undertaker's music sounded, and the Phenom rode his bike down to the ring, where Triple H greeted him with a right hand that knocked him off the apron. Deciding to fight another day, the American Badass got back on his bike and rode up the ramp, while The Game remained the sole player in the ring.

Jericho and Stephanie engineered some *Raw* retaliation on the TitanTron from the Dunkin Donuts Center in Providence, Rhode Island, on February 25. Claiming what he did to Triple H on May 21, 2001 was far worse than ever defeating him in the ring, the Undisputed Champ aired footage from the match where Hunter tore his quad muscle, an injury made even worse when Y2J followed it up with

SkyDome
Toronto, Ontario, Canada

UNDISPUTED CHAMPIONSHIP MATCH

Triple H defeated **Chris Jericho** (w/Stephanie McMahon) via pinfall to become the Undisputed Champion

TRIPLE-THREAT WOMEN'S CHAMPIONSHIP MATCH

Jazz defeated **Trish Stratus** and **Lita**, pinning Lita to retain the Women's title

ICON VS. ICON MATCH

The Rock defeated **Hollywood Hulk Hogan** via pinfall

FOUR-CORNER TAG TEAM CHAMPIONSHIP ELIMINATION MATCH

Dudley Boyz (w/Stacy Keibler) eliminated **APA**; **Hardy Boyz** eliminated **Dudley Boyz**; **Billy & Chuck** eliminated **Hardy Boyz** to retain the Tag Team titles

Stone Cold Steve Austin defeated **Scott Hall** (w/Kevin Nash)

Edge defeated **Booker T** via pinfall

NO DISQUALIFICATION MATCH

Undertaker defeated **Ric Flair** via pinfall

Kurt Angle defeated **Kane** via pinfall

HARDCORE CHAMPIONSHIP MATCH

Spike Dudley pinned **Maven**; **The Hurricane** pinned **Spike Dudley**; **Molly Holly** pinned **The Hurricane**; **Christian** pinned **Molly Holly**; **Maven** pinned **Christian** to become the Hardcore Champion

EUROPEAN CHAMPIONSHIP MATCH

Diamond Dallas Page defeated **Christian** via pinfall to retain the European title

INTERCONTINENTAL CHAMPIONSHIP MATCH

Rob Van Dam defeated **William Regal** via pinfall to become the Intercontinental Champion

---

The Undisputed Champion came to make his mark and be remembered as one of the greats. The challenger tortured himself for ten months to recapture what appeared forever lost to him. Wrestling's past was there to cement his spot as the Babe Ruth of wrestling. All of the WWE Superstars had a chance to shine on the grandest stage of them all. The time had come for *WrestleMania X8*.

Establishing a new Toronto SkyDome attendance record of 68,237 fans, the second largest crowd in WWE history (surpassing *WrestleMania X-Seven*'s 67,925 fans in Houston's Reliant Astrodome, and preceded only by *WrestleMania III*'s 93,173 attending Michigan's Pontiac Silverdome), World Wrestling Entertainment kicked off the biggest show of 2002 with recording group Saliva and their hit "Superstar." No competitor was better suited than Rob Van Dam to head to the ring and start the first match; after a career of performing mostly in gym halls, Van Dam looked to make the most of his *WrestleMania* debut, and wasted no time in doing so against Intercontinental Champion William Regal. Launching a strong offensive campaign early, RVD disarmed Regal of his "power of the punch," kicking the brass knuckles from his hand and to the outside floor. Regal, bleeding from the mouth, took control after dodging Van Dam's top-rope finisher, hitting a full nelson slam that dropped the challenger on his head. Recovering the knuckle dusters from the outside, the Brit was thwarted when the referee took them out of his hand...until he pulled another set from his trunks. Van Dam caught Regal with a heel kick before he could use them, however, then mounted the top rope and executed the Five-Star Frog Splash to win the Intercontinental title.

Christian told Lilian Garcia backstage that now he was back to his winning ways, being ready to reclaim his title wasn't a good thing for current strapholder Diamond Dallas Page; it was a *bad* thing. The Canadian's newfound positive outlook didn't win any fans (especially since he now declared himself a resident of Tampa, Florida) as he immediately went to work on Page. DDP built back momentum after converting Christian's top-rope maneuver into a powerbomb, but his attempt to counter the Unprettier with the Diamond Cutter resulted in a reverse DDT. Unable to get a three-count, Christian restrained himself from throwing a hissy fit, only to get caught with the Diamond Cutter. DDP picked up the win to retain his title, then grabbed a mic and told Christian he was proud of him for not losing his temper in front of *sixty-eight thousand fans in the SkyDome,* and the *bazillions* watching from home. DDP headed into the crowd, while Christian exploded in the middle of the ring.

For Hardcore Champion Maven, his first *WrestleMania* was truly nothing like he could have ever expected. He was defending his title against Goldust, whose array of gold weapons included a golden shovel that caught the rookie in the throat, but it was Spike Dudley—capitalizing on the title's 24/7 rule—who ran in and scored the pinfall to win the belt! Spike was clearly not celebrating with a victory lap as Goldust, Maven and Crash Holly chased him to the back. While recording artists Drowning Pool performed their hit song "Tear Away" to a video highlighting the evening's Undisputed title match, Crash and Spike whaled on each other backstage, until Al Snow, with a ref in the passenger's seat, almost drove into them with a golf cart! Snow missed, while Spike broke away from Crash…only to get nailed by The Hurricane, who swept into him on a rope, pinned him to win the Hardcore title, then blew out of there!

"Big Red, White and Blue Machine" Kurt Angle came out to a rousing chorus of "You suck!" First he wanted to let the SkyDome audience know something before he faced Kane: he *earned* his 1996 Olympic medals the old-fashioned way, not "by whining and complaining until someone gave it to him" like Canada's gold medal figure skaters! Kane's pyro entrance shut him up, but before the bell could signal the start of the match, Angle *used* it on the Big Red Machine's head! Kane eventually battled his way back into the match, almost scoring a Chokeslam victory until the gold medalist's hand draped the bottom rope. Kurt grabbed at Kane's mask, leaving him open to the Angle Slam and ankle lock, but the Big Red Machine swung around and floored his opponent with an awesome Enziguri. As Kane went for a top-rope clothesline, it was Angle's turn to amaze, pulling the big man down with the belly-to-belly suplex. Kurt tried for another Angle Slam, which Kane converted into another Chokeslam until Angle countered with a rollup, using the ropes for leverage to score an impressive pinfall victory.

Backstage, Hurricane sought shelter from his Hardcore adversaries, hiding in what he soon discovered was the dressing room for The Godfather's escorts! Not knowing what evil lurked in the heart of the man hiding behind a screen partition, the scantily clad ladies screamed for The Godfather, forcing Hurricane to Hurri-speed his way out of the room.

Having collected so many vital statistics in over a decade of destruction, one often-overlooked figure in the Dead Man's body of work was that he'd *never* been defeated in nine previous *WrestleMania* appearances. But Ric Flair wasn't keeping score as he headed into his

No Disqualification contest with Undertaker. The dirtiest player in the game took the Phenom outside and over the announcer's table, then drew first blood in the ring with a series of punches to 'Taker's jaw. Undertaker returned the favor with a size sixteen to the Nature Boy's face and the big soup bones to his head. Following a devastating top-rope superplex to the canvas, Undertaker went back up to go "old school" with the rope walk and chop, but Flair yanked him off the turnbuckle. The Nature Boy soon gained the momentum after beating Undertaker to his bike and pulling out a steel pipe, then used the equalizer repeatedly across the Phenom's skull.

Both men were a bloody mess as the action returned to the ring—'Taker set Flair up for the chokeslam, but the Nature Boy went south of the border, with a low blow that raised the roof off the SkyDome. Flair then latched on the figure-four, but Undertaker powered his way out with a hand to Flair's throat and the chokeslam. He was almost beside himself when Flair kicked out of the cover, then drilled by a spinebuster from a charging Arn Anderson. Kicking out of a cover, 'Taker bloodied Anderson up and cinched on the Dragon Sleeper, until Flair nailed him across the back with a steel chair. The Dead Man dropped the Nature Boy with another kick to the head, but when he couldn't hitch him up for the Last Ride, he drove Flair down for good with a frightening Tombstone to the mat. Undertaker's *WrestleMania* record remained unblemished, though he could hardly say he felt that way as he staggered out of the ring.

Sporting a pair of glasses backstage, Booker T insisted to Michael Cole he was going to make smart guy Edge the spokesman for the book *I Just Got My Ass Kicked at WrestleMania by the Five-Time WCW Champion!* The Toronto native wasn't digging that, nor did he appreciate a missile dropkick that kept him reeling. After a hurracanrana in the corner turned the tables, Edge followed up with a top-rope spinning heel kick. Booker regained the advantage with a side kick that launched him into the Spin-a-Roonie, but he was unable to keep Edge down even after a powerful scissors kick. Edge recovered in time to spear Booker, which propelled him into an "Edge-a-Roonie," then delivered the Edgecution for a big victory in front of his hometown fans.

Catching up with a very wary Hurricane backstage, Jonathan Coachman questioned his "unbecoming" actions around The Godfather's escorts. Offended by the insinuation, the hero insisted he was no "Hurri-perve"; he was a Hurri-Hardcore Champion! Sidekick Mighty Molly arrived and urged they head for the Hurri-Cycle, but as he started off, she unloaded a Hurri-hellacious shot to his Hurri-cranium with a frying pan! Pinning him for the one-two-three, Mighty Molly was the new Hardcore Champ!

Icon vs. Icon; Rock and Hogan vie for wrestling immortality.

Next up was the Texas Rattlesnake and the Bad Guy, accompanied to the ring by fellow nWo brother Kevin Nash. Stone Cold Steve Austin started off strong with the Lou Thesz Press and a series of hard rights to Scott Hall, until an Irish whip to the turnbuckle and some cheap shots from Big Sexy outside took the wind out of his sails. Hall controlled the match until Austin surprised him with the Stunner, but again Nash involved himself in the match, throwing the referee outside to the floor and entering the ring to pound on the Rattlesnake. Hall returned to the ring with a steel chair while Big Sexy kept Austin in a full nelson, but a Stone Cold kick between Nash's legs opened both men up for some Stunners with extra stink. After interrupting a second referee's count with an elbow to the head, Austin nailed Nash to the outside, then countered a Razor's Edge with a back body over the top rope.

Several officials ran down and forced Nash to the back, while Hall and Austin continued fighting around the ring. Back inside, Hall blocked the Stunner and delivered one of his own, then tried again when he couldn't get the pin. But it was the Rattlesnake striking back lightning quick, catching Hall with a Stunner, then another before the Bad Guy could hit the floor. Austin got the three, then broke out the Canadian Molson Steveweisers and toasted the SkyDome crowd!

Saliva performed the Dudley Boyz' new entrance music "Turn the Tables" as Bubba Ray and D-Von, accompanied by Duchess of Dudleyville Stacy Keibler, headed ringside for the Four-Corner match. But no one was singing after the APA's Faarooq and Bradshaw, Matt and Jeff Hardy, and Tag Champs Billy and Chuck made their way out. The APA alternated beating down Billy and Chuck, but upon sending a Clothesline from Hell to Billy, Bradshaw got laid out by the Dudleyz' 3-D, eliminating him and Faarooq. The Dudleyz set up a table on the outside floor while the Hardy Boyz double-teamed Chuck, until Jeff delivered first a Whisper in the Wind to D-Von, then a slap on the ass, a kiss on the lips and a push off the ring skirt for Stacy. The Dudleyz hammered away at Jeff for a while, until Billy disrupted the flying headbutt off the top rope, sending D-Von to the outside and through the table. Matt caught Bubba with the Twist of Fate, and Jeff finished him off with the Swanton Bomb for the three-count.

With Billy and Chuck and the Hardyz remaining, the match quickly got out of hand—Jeff Swantoned Chuck, though Billy caught him with a Fame-Ass-er. Chuck only got a two-count as Matt was knocked to the outside by Billy, who grabbed one of the tag belts and used it on Jeff to keep him down. Billy and Chuck may not have looked so good to each other after the rough-and-tumble contest, but they were still the champs.

New Hardcore Champ Mighty Molly was on the move backstage, looking behind her every step of the way. Which is probably why she didn't catch half the door closing in front of her until it was too late. Emerging from behind the door was Christian, who pinned Molly and became the new Hardcore Champion!

Earlier in the evening, The Rock busted the Coach's stones over his "sick freak"-like prayers, then swore to Hollywood Hulk Hogan that while seventy thousand strong chanted their names during their "Icon vs. Icon" match, he would feel the People's Elbow, and smell what The Rock is cookin'. Hall and Nash, remaining backstage after Austin's win, had other plans for the Great One, until Hogan approached and asked them *not* to interfere. He wanted to fight this match on his own. He didn't realize it until he headed toward the ring, but Hogan was *not* alone; he easily had half of the sixty-eight thousand fans cheering his name. Coming out to an equally thunderous pop from the sellout crowd, The Rock walked down the aisle, entered the ring and stood face-to-face with Hogan, as sport entertainment's most important match ever was about to get underway.

The two icons locked up in the center of the ring several times, with Hogan's twenty-four-inch pythons shoving the Brahma Bull down to the canvas in each instance and inviting Rock to "just bring it." The Great One soon did, catching Hogan with a flying clothesline, then mounting some offense while Hollywood tried catching his breath outside the ring. Back inside, the People's Champ attempted a Rock Bottom, but Hogan countered with an elbow and a series of blows to regain the advantage. Softening him up with an abdominal stretch, Hogan rolled up Rock, but couldn't get the three. Fists flew from both directions until Hogan threw Rock over the top rope. Both men continued exchanging punches on the outside, with Rock soon drawing boos from the increasingly pro-Hogan crowd as he went for a chair. The referee stopped the Brahma Bull, who walked into a clothesline by Hogan.

Taking it back in the ring, Hogan sidestepped Rock coming off the ropes, resulting in the referee getting his lights dimmed. The People's Champ placed some spine on the pine, then put Hogan in the sharpshooter. Hogan's incredible body strength powered him to the ropes, but he started tapping when Rocky pulled him back to the center. With the official still down, Rock released the hold and tried reviving him, then walked into a low blow and a Rock Bottom from Hogan! The

Brahma Bull barely kicked out, while Hogan started using the heavyweight belt on his back. Moments later, Rock caught him with a DDT and returned the belt shots (again to the crowd's disapproval), softening him up for a Rock Bottom to the mat. Amazingly, Hogan kicked out and Hulked up, unloading his powerful fists on the Great One before nailing him with the big boot and the legdrop! Rock stunned Hogan by refusing to stay down, and when Hollywood went for another legdrop, Rock would dodge it and deliver not one, but *two* more Rock Bottoms. The People's Champ removed his elbow pad, threw it into the decidedly mixed crowd and gave Hogan the People's Elbow, picking up perhaps the most electrifying victory in sports entertainment.

For a moment, the two icons stared each other down again, leaving people to wonder if the fight would continue. Instead, Hogan extended a hand, and The Rock accepted before leaving the ring. Suddenly, Hall and Nash came down, irate that Hogan had not only lost to The Rock, but congratulated him in doing so. Without warning, the two turned on Hogan, beating him down in the ring until the People's Champ returned and helped the Hulkster clean house. Hall and Nash retreated, but as a grateful Hogan started exiting the ring, Rock pulled him back inside, motioning for him to start posing for the crowd. Both men won on this night; The Rock won the match, and bragging rights for the moment. Hollywood Hulk Hogan had won back his *Hulkamaniacs*, including the one leaving the ring with him, and in the process won the very immortality he'd sought.

The Triple-Threat Women's Championship match proved fast and furious, with challengers Lita and native favorite Trish Stratus going to work early on Women's Champ Jazz. But the Diva double team wouldn't last long—Trish Bulldogged Lita, who'd soon put Jazz in a Twist of Fate originally intended for Trish. Lita then stopped short on a Stratusfaction, propelling Trish into the turnbuckle and outside the ring. But as Lita headed up top to finish off Jazz, Trish dislodged her footing on the ropes, allowing Jazz to climb up and catch Lita with the fisherman's suplex for the win.

Christian was ecstatic as he successfully made his way out of the SkyDome with the Hardcore Championship. But as he threw his bags in the trunk of a cab, he was thrown off-guard by Maven, who rolled him up for the three-count, won the title *and* took off in his taxi, leaving Christian behind to throw his second temper tantrum for the evening.

It was time for recording artist Drowning Pool to play The Game's entrance music as the final match of *WrestleMania X8* got underway. Triple H's left leg was heavily bandaged due to Undisputed Champion Chris Jericho's sledgehammer attack earlier in the week, an

Triple H becomes Undisputed Champion.

injury both Jericho and Stephanie McMahon would exploit throughout the contest. Forced to work on only one leg put Hunter behind the eight ball early, leaving him prone to Y2J's attacks inside and outside the ring. But the Cerebral Assassin worked smart, taking Jericho's legs out wherever possible. Breaking up a figure-four on Jericho earned Stephanie a hairpull up to the ring apron, then a spear from her business partner after Hunter moved. But The Game spent too much time on his wife, allowing Y2J to catch him with a missile dropkick before he could Pedigree her.

Jericho went back to Triple H's injured quad, ramming it into the ring post before latching a figure-four around it. The Game fought back valiantly, but the injured leg worsened with every step. Sending Hunter back to the outside floor, Y2J attempted the Walls of Jericho on top of the announcer's table. Hunter countered and went for the Pedigree, until the Undisputed Champion back body-dropped him through the Spanish announcer's table! Jericho rolled Hunter back inside and executed a Lionsault, but couldn't get the pin. He turned him around for the Walls of Jericho, yet Triple H still wouldn't quit, reaching the ropes to break the hold. Stephanie distracted the ref while her business partner grabbed a chair from the outside, but The Game kicked it back in his face, then DDT'd him onto the cold steel.

Stephanie entered the ring and tried using the chair, but as she argued with the referee for trying to stop her, she came face-to-face with her husband, who finally delivered a long-awaited Pedigree on her! While the official rolled Stephanie outside, Jericho caught Hunter inside the ring with the chair, yet could only get another two-count. Frustrated, Y2J tried to Pedigree Hunter, who instead slingshotted Jericho into the corner. Jericho landed on the second rope and jumped toward Triple H, who kicked him in the gut and caught him in the Pedigree! Rolling Jericho up for the three-count, Triple H had defied the pundits who told him it was Game Over, and captured the Undisputed Championship! ■

the Walls of Jericho on the *Raw* announcer's table. "I beat one-two-three-four-five-six-seven-eight—*eight months out of your career!*" Jericho boasted, noting it was time that could have been better spent elsewhere than "in hell" rehabbing. Perhaps his marriage wouldn't have fallen apart if he'd given his wife the attention she deserved, "...and maybe instead of poor Stephanie having to *lie*, you might have been man enough to get her pregnant on your own, for *real!*"

[
"When it came to the bedroom, 'The Game' always came up a bit *short*."
]

"Oh, I don't know about that," she scoffed. "When it came to the bedroom, 'The Game' always came up a little bit *short*."

Triple H walked down to the ring with a few observations of his own, looking Stephanie over and suggesting, "Maybe it wasn't so much The Game that was short; maybe it was that the field I was playing on was just too damn *big*." He then challenged Y2J to a match that night, "just for the hell of it." Jericho didn't even have to put the belts on the line. Before he could answer, Kurt Angle came out to the stage with news for all of them; after being "robbed" of his *WrestleMania* title shot, Mr. McMahon made it up to him with a chance at the Undisputed title for later that evening! "And Steph," he assured her, "after I beat Chris Jericho, I will be more than happy to make you my business partner when I face your soon-to-be *ex*-husband at *WrestleMania!*"

Stephanie might have considered the job change when Angle gained the advantage late in the match. Jericho's last-ditch Enziguri kick sent him to the outside floor, where the gold medalist's suddenly recurring problem Kane came through the crowd and clean-pressed Kurt back inside the ring. Jericho nailed the distracted Angle with the Breakdown to escape with

The Big Red Machine whips Y2J into the ropes.

the victory, while Kurt escaped through the crowd to avoid the Big Red Machine and a solid steel chair!

If ignorance is bliss, then Jericho might have been happier not attending Boston's Fleet Center for the February 28 *SmackDown!* He had to partner with Angle against whom he just defended his title, in a Tag match against a big red freak and the man he'd face at *WrestleMania*. Even worse, his new business partner, Stephanie, was giving Jericho a hard time backstage about picking up the wrong brand of hand lotion! She explained tersely that she breaks out in hives with the wrong lotion, and she needed to be kept happy if she was going to help Jericho beat Triple H at

Caged heat: Triple H Pedigrees Angle.

the main event (translation: it was in his best interest to just go to the store and get the right lotion). She'd have plenty of 'tude to spare when she entered her estranged spouse's locker room soon after, telling him his slanderous *Raw* comments toward her "private parts" were uncalled for, and that his lawyer was being "completely unreasonable" about their settlement. Hunter thought splitting everything fifty-fifty was a fair deal. But the princess begged to differ; she wanted fifty percent of what he made already, "and fifty percent of everything you earn from this day forward until you *die*. And I'll get it, because I *always* get what I want."

That said, one had to wonder what Stephanie wanted during that evening's Tag match that would urge her to hit Kane with a chair. If it was to make the Big Red Machine so mad that he'd hammer Angle with the chair *she* brought in, in turn setting Kurt up for a Pedigree that cost him and Jericho the match, then she succeeded in spades. Angle, on the other hand,

was thrilled that Mr. McMahon put him and The Game in a Steel Cage match for March 4 *Raw*, from the Frank Erwin Center in Austin, Texas. The gold medalist told Jonathan "Coach" Coachman backstage that Hunter was too busy worrying about his *WrestleMania* match "that you *don't* deserve," when he should be worrying about Kurt. "I am more dangerous than you can possibly imagine," he explained. "Think about it, Triple H; I'm a man with *nothing* to lose."

At this point, Hunter literally dumped off a box of Stephanie's belongings onto her office floor, among them her "Pristine Mist" hand lotion, which she started rubbing all over herself, not realizing The Game had changed the lotion on her...until she broke out in hives. Despite Kurt's "poker face" and claims the blemishes weren't noticeable, the blotchy princess ordered him to tear her husband apart in their match. Ultimately, she'd have to take hand in the act herself, after Triple H Pedigreed Angle and made his way toward the referee opening the cage door. Racing to the ring, she knocked the referee into the cage and slammed the door into The Game's head, busting him open. She wasn't much help to Kurt when she tried giving him a chair in the cage, only for Hunter to get hold of it first and DDT Angle's head onto it. With the match pretty much won, the Cerebral Assassin started climbing his way to the top of the cage, until Stephanie herself entered the ring and nailed him with the chair, causing The Game's leg to become tangled in the ropes while she pulled Angle to the outside floor for the victory.

> **"The robe is half mine and it should only be worn by a *champion*."**

The treachery just added layers to Triple H and Stephanie's ongoing battles backstage at San Antonio's Freeman Coliseum for the March 7 *SmackDown!* Hunter promised the beloved Corvette she got for her Sweet Sixteen birthday would be delivered there later, then became visibly upset when she refused to part with his bulldog Lucy. He understood the agreement was to split everything fifty-fifty, but he asked, "Isn't *one* bitch in the house enough?" Chris Jericho, showing up backstage with Stephanie's water, was also getting annoyed with doing so many chores for the demanding princess, who reminded him how she cost Triple H

the Steel Cage match on *Raw*, and that's precisely who Chris needed in his corner for *WrestleMania*. Besides, she had a present for him—The Game's very first ring robe, given to him by his mentor, Killer Kowalski. "The robe is half mine," she said, "and it should only be worn by a *champion*."

An ecstatic Y2J wore the robe for that evening's nontitle match with the Big Red Machine, who almost fashioned an impressive Chokeslam victory when Stephanie distracted the referee. Kurt Angle rushed in and Angle Slammed Kane, allowing Jericho to Lionsault off the second rope for the three-count. Kane chased after Angle while the princess started helping Jericho into his new robe, until the Cerebral Assassin attacked and put a beating on the champion. Jericho rescued Stephanie from another Pedigree attempt, though both were furious to see Triple H in the ring not only with his robe, but also holding the Undisputed Championship belts high. Minutes later, the Coach tried talking with her backstage, but she wasn't in the mood; she had a long drive ahead of her. That drive, however, promised to be a lot more difficult when she saw literally *half* of her Corvette sitting in the garage! "*You* said that everything is split fifty-fifty,"

LAYIN' THE SMACKDOWN! IN ASIA

World Wrestling Entertainment took great steps in firmly establishing itself as the *world*wide leader in sports entertainment when the company announced it was conducting several international tours for 2002. The first, known as Asia's *SmackDown!* Tour, was a three-city house show journey that ran in early March. Over forty thousand fans attended the three sold-out events, which took place in the Yokohama Arena in Tokyo, Japan, on March 1, the Indoor Stadium in Singapore on March 3, and the Putra Stadium in Kuala Lumpur, Malaysia, on March 4. ∎

laughed Hunter as he gave the hysterically sobbing Stephanie the keys. "I just wasn't sure *which* half you wanted."

With only six days to go before *WrestleMania*, Triple H wouldn't be laughing by the end of March 11 *Raw*. Backstage at Detroit, Michigan's Joe Louis Arena, Stephanie brought his dog Lucy, only to tell Hunter she obtained a judge's court order that gave her sole custody until the divorce proceeding. "So who's the bitch now?" she said triumphantly. In truth, she *hated* the bulldog, as did Y2J when he first saw her, though both agreed it was a great idea to screw with The Game's mind before the Pay-Per-View. But when Lucy's "accident" in the backstage room resulted in Jericho having to walk the dog outside, he decided to just tie her to the door handle of a limousine...the same one he'd enter minutes later when the princess told him to get some air freshener for the office. The driver backed up the limo until they heard a noise; Jericho got out of the car, realizing they had just run over The Game's dog.

Lucy survived, but Stephanie was convinced she was a dead woman. Attempting to save herself, the panicked princess headed ringside to let Hunter know that what happened to his dog was "a complete accident." Triple H was past the point of listening, however, as he entered the ring and set her up for the Pedigree. Suddenly, Jericho ran in with a sledgehammer, then used it on Triple H's surgically repaired left leg! After hitting the thigh with the weapon a second time, Y2J headed back up the ramp with Stephanie, both pleased with themselves, while The Game clutched his leg, writhing in total agony around the ring. Jericho added one more cheap shot as officials got Hunter to the top of the ramp, but the damage had already been done; from all appearances, Triple H had torn his quadriceps muscle again.

The fans in Cleveland's Gund Arena were prepared for the worst when Triple H had an announcement to make on March 14

SmackDown!. Stephanie and Jericho were almost euphoric backstage; seeing Hunter go down three nights ago was déjà vu for the princess, and the prospect of him having to drop out of *WrestleMania* and retire from the WWE was "like music" to her ears. As Triple H noticeably limped his way down to the ring later that night, it seemed all but certain The Game was about to play her tune.

"I stand in this ring tonight to make an unfortunate announcement," he said, "but that announcement is

[**"To me, it's about pain. And pain is just temporary...but *The Game is forever*."**]

unfortunate for *Chris Jericho*. Because you see, Chris Jericho did *not* get the job done!" The crowd erupted into cheers as The Game relayed that Y2J had failed to take him out of the business ten months ago, and he'd failed again on *Raw* three nights ago, because he was there and he was feeling one hundred percent. Triple H wanted Jericho to realize something: "To me, it's about pain. And pain is just temporary...but *The Game is forever*. I will go to *WrestleMania* and in the main event, I will kick Chris Jericho's ass and I will become the Undisputed Champion!"

Y2J's entrance music cut Hunter short, as he and Stephanie came out to the *SmackDown!* stage. Like Triple H had done to him the night after *Royal Rumble*, Jericho mockingly clapped over a "great performance," but he had a hard time believing Hunter was "one hundred percent ready" to face the "living legend" at *WrestleMania*. Stephanie revealed she'd spoken with Dr. Andrews, who operated on The Game's torn quad ten months ago, and consulted with the surgeon who looked over Hunter's leg following *Raw*. "According to Dr. Andrews, your quadriceps is *barely* holding together," she gloated, explaining the wires connecting his muscle were weakened by the sledgehammer to the point where "one false move, one misstep, and one of those wires can *snap.*" Hunter had two options: he could let the quad heal for a month, or he could risk it all by facing Jericho at *WrestleMania*. But if he made that one miscalculation, Stephanie warned, *"You will never be able to wrestle again."*

Triple H admitted his wife was right; his repaired quad was indeed "holding on by a thread." But he didn't care, swearing, "When I leave *WrestleMania,* whether I am walking or I have to get rolled out of that arena, I *will* leave as the Undisputed Champion!" Y2J, frustrated by Hunter's resolve, charged the ring, only to be clotheslined toward the *SmackDown!* announcer's table. The Cerebral Assassin pulled up lame on his way to the outside floor, where Stephanie kicked away at his injured leg. Hunter set her up for

the Pedigree on the announcer's table, until Jericho smacked him in the leg with one of the championship belts, then climbed onto the table and put him in the Walls of Jericho. Though he wouldn't finish off Triple H that night, Chris Jericho and Stephanie McMahon were certain that *WrestleMania X8* would be time to *end* The Game.

Ric Flair didn't want to be a wrestler anymore; certainly not full time, anyway. But the Nature Boy stuck his nose in Undertaker's business, costing him his *No Way Out* contest against The Rock, so on the February 18 *Raw* the Dead Man walked into Flair's office with every intention of beating him down. Then 'Taker came up with another idea, "On the grandest stage of them all, I want your ass in the ring at *WrestleMania,*" he said. "We're going to see

Stephanie gloats as Y2J holds Triple H in the Walls of Jericho.

what kind of man you are, because I'm going to beat you down for the world to see." Flair refused; he would have been up for it ten years ago, but he was now concentrating on being the fifty-percent owner of World Wrestling Entertainment. Not liking the answer, 'Taker replied, "Let's see what I can do to change your mind," and left.

While Flair talked with righthand man—and best friend—Arn Anderson backstage during the February 21 *SmackDown!,* the Phenom paid him another visit. Undertaker asked him again if they were going to dance at *WrestleMania.* Again, Flair refused. "That's just like you, to be a coward like that," 'Taker sneered, then added it would be the last no he'd accept from the Nature Boy. Come *Raw* the following week, "something tells me your answer's gonna be yes."

It was almost immediately after Jazz's postmatch pummeling of Might Molly on February 25 *Raw* that Undertaker started the process of changing Flair's mind. Arn Anderson and several WWE officials were helping the injured Molly to the back when Deadman, Inc. headed toward the ring, then suddenly assaulted Anderson, busting him open instantly. Anderson, known as "The Enforcer" among Flair's Four Horsemen in their WCW days, was no pushover, but the retired ring great was helpless as the American Badass rolled him into the ring and beat him senseless. "I told Ric Flair that I wasn't going to accept no for an answer again," warned 'Taker before knocking out the crimsoned

Undertaker drives a knee into Hardcore Champ Maven.

Anderson. "So this is on *his* head." When Flair arrived at the arena later that evening, after celebrating his birthday, he wouldn't stay long; turning ghost white as WWE official Earl Hebner told him about Anderson, he got back in his limousine and headed for the hospital.

The Phenom was sitting backstage at *SmackDown!* three nights later, enjoying a videotape of his *Raw* work, when Flair approached. The Nature Boy was seething, then looked stupefied when Undertaker asked, "So… we on for *WrestleMania?*" Flair promised him an answer later that evening, though the Dead Man decided that rather than just sit around, he'd settle some unresolved

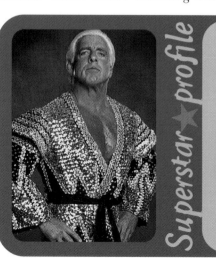

Superstar ★ profile

RIC FLAIR

HEIGHT: 6'1" WEIGHT: 243 lbs.
OTHER NAMES: Nature Boy
FINISHING MOVE: Figure Four Leglock
CAREER HIGHLIGHTS: NWA Mid-Atlantic Tag Team Champion (3); NWA Mid-Atlantic Heavyweight (4); NWA Mid-Atlantic TV Champion (2); NWA World Tag Team Champion (3); NWA Missouri Heavyweight Champion; NWA/WCW United States Heavyweight Championship (6); NWA/WCW World Heavyweight Champion (14); WWE World Heavyweight Champion (2)
2002 HIGHLIGHTS: Beating Mr. McMahon at the *Royal Rumble;* fighting Undertaker in front of sixty-eight thousand fans at *WrestleMania X8;* losing ownership of *Raw* to Mr. McMahon on June 10 *Raw.*

issues with Maven, the rookie who defeated him for the Hardcore Championship (with a heavy assist from The Rock). The greenhorn had just defended his title against Goldust when Undertaker rode down and hammered him into a corner. Al Snow raced in and took up the fight for his former student, though it wasn't long before the Dead Man caught the *Tough Enough* teacher with the Dragon Sleeper. Suddenly, it was Flair "takin' care of business," grabbing the lead pipe from 'Taker's bike and beating the hell out of the Phenom. His answer regarding *WrestleMania* was still no, "But if you ever touch a friend of mine again, I will show you *why* I am the dirtiest player in the game!" Flair punctuated his warning with the pipe to 'Taker's skull one last time before leaving the ring.

Though Undertaker took the beating, a strangely elated Vince McMahon kicked off "Fan Appreciation Night" on *Raw* the following week with the news his business partner would *not* be in attendance, "due to circumstances beyond Mr. Flair's control." The reason behind Flair's absence soon became painfully clear to the fans when Undertaker came out to address the crowd. He told them he had no desire to "victimize" Arn Anderson, but the blood was on Flair's hands for refusing to meet him at *WrestleMania*. And since the Nature Boy still wouldn't accept, the American Badass needed "to push the envelope a little further," and showed on the TitanTron a visit he paid Flair's oldest son David that morning, at the WWE's developmental facility in Stamford, Connecticut. The brutal footage documented the American Badass beating David to a bloody pulp inside a bathroom, then giving the elder Flair a message. "I told you I wasn't going to take no for an answer," he said. "You've got what I want…and all it is, is a *yes*."

The heinous act was the final straw for Flair, who marched toward the ring when Undertaker wouldn't open his locker-room door at the March 7 *SmackDown!*

"I am going to *hurt* you, Dead Man!"

In front of the sellout crowd in San Antonio, Flair told the Dead Man about how he'd realized a dream when he came to the WWE five months ago, "I was no longer a wrestler. I was an owner." Mr. McMahon pushed him to one more fight at the *Royal Rumble*, but being an owner was what he wanted to focus on. He almost accepted Undertaker's challenge after the attack on Arn Anderson, but it was his best friend who'd convinced him not to. But when he attacked Flair's son, his choice was clear. "Goddamn it, as of tonight, I'm a wrestler again!" he said. "Undertaker, you have got the Nature Boy at *WrestleMania!* I am going to *hurt* you, Dead Man!"

Coming out to the stage, a perplexed Undertaker shocked Flair once again when he said he wasn't sure if he still wanted to fight him at the PPV. Though 'Taker would give him an answer later, he had the audacity to tell Flair, "I'm willing to let bygones be bygones," he said, "be the bigger man and forgive you for everything that you've put me through." After "Takin' Care of Business" with a Dragon Sleeper on Maven to defeat him and Al Snow in that evening's Handicap match, the American Badass

Undertaker won't take no.

announced he would fight Flair, provided he "...walk down to the ring, get down on his hands and knees, and *beg* me for the match." There wouldn't be much begging from Flair, who ran down and went toe-to-toe with the Phenom, their fight spilling out into the crowd. Unfortunately, weeks of pent-up rage got the better of the Nature Boy, and a right fist intended for the American Badass instead caught a fan. Though it was an accident, the fan pressed charges, and as San Antonio police arrested the truly apologetic Flair backstage, the Dead Man watched from a distance and laughed.

The incident provided much cannon fodder for co-owner Vince McMahon, who during the March 11 *Raw* called an emergency meeting between the WWE board of directors in the Stamford, Connecticut, headquarters. There, McMahon declared the WWE was in "a state of emergency," and that Ric Flair's acquisition of fifty percent of the company was causing the WWE to operate "like a ship without a rudder, still very much afloat." McMahon further cited the fan assault at *SmackDown!* as a "humiliating" testament of Flair not being "in the right emotional state of mind," and asked the board for a unanimous vote that only one of them be given absolute authority and power over the WWE. After deliberating, CEO Linda McMahon asked Flair if he intended to go through with his *WrestleMania* match against Undertaker. When he answered yes, she declared the board had, "No alternative but to grant Mr. McMahon a unanimous vote of confidence with full authority to act." However, the board reserved the right to review the decision immediately following *WrestleMania*.

Flair agreed to the board's decision, and apologized for his recent actions embarrassing the board members and their respective families. But after having watched his best friend massacred, his *son* beaten to a pulp, he explained, "I too, have a family, and I have responsibilities. And my main responsibility is to protect my family." Flair could accept the temporary suspension, "But no one in this room will ever strip me of my pride. More than that, no one in this room will ever strip me of the name Flair. And more than *that*, at *WrestleMania*, I *will* even the score with Undertaker...*at any cost* to myself."

With the board's vote of confidence at *SmackDown!* March 14, Mr. McMahon informed Flair backstage that since he was "just now another WWE Superstar," he was giving Flair the night off. He didn't want to risk the Nature Boy's safety and welfare, especially since Vince also decided his *WrestleMania* match would be a No Disqualification contest, "when I personally want to watch Undertaker rip you limb from limb." Vince then offered *David* Flair "the opportunity of a life-time" that night—a match against Undertaker! David declined, but Vince "persuaded" the youngster that he really had no choice. The Gund Arena audience expected a bloodbath as the

> **"I personally want to watch Undertaker rip you limb from limb."**

The American Badass shows David Flair just why he's earned that name.

Dead Man held the ring ropes open for his sacrificial lamb to walk through, though it was Undertaker soon being slaughtered by the Nature Boy and a steel chair. And Ric Flair was going to make sure he realized that at their No DQ match for *WrestleMania,* everything was fair game for the *dirtiest* player in the game!

It was a spare set of knuckle dusters that preserved William Regal's Intercontinental Championship at *No Way Out*'s Brass Knuckles on a Pole match against Edge. But no amount of brass—or *Coldust*—would help him withstand Edge's standing reverse figure-four (come to be known as a "Figure-Four Edgelock"), giving the young Superstar and Rob Van Dam a *Raw* Tag match win on February 18. It also looked like Rikishi would "back that ass up" into the title at February 24 *Sunday Night Heat,* though Regal's often picked-on nose somehow endured the Stinkface long enough for the Brit to find his "power of the punch" and get the win.

Regal provided his own *Raw* analysis while J.R. and King called the following night's Triple-Threat match between Van Dam, Big Show and Lance Storm that determined the No. 1 Contender for the Intercontiental Title at *WrestleMania.* The champion rallied for Storm as "a scientific wonder in the ring," and the preferred adversary for his crown, but was as vocally unimpressed by a steel-chaired Van Daminator kick to Big Show that set RVD up for a winning Five-Star Frog Splash. "How pathetic," Regal said, disgusted. "The *least* qualified is the man who's going to *WrestleMania.* He's a waste of my bloody time and energy." He didn't have much respect for Big Show, either, though the giant made more than a lasting impression during their *SmackDown!* nontitle contest on February 28—the southpaw was on the mat when he caught Show square on the jaw with the brass knux. Unfortunately, Regal's momentum off the ropes caused the unconscious five-hundred-pounder to fall directly on top of the Intercontinental Champion! Not even the "jaws of life" could free a pinned Regal before the referee counted to three!

Meanwhile, Van Dam continued his preparations to become the fourth-ever WWE Superstar to win the Intercontinental Championship in his *WrestleMania* debut. He'd produce back-to-back victories in hard-fought contests with last week's Triple-Threat contender Lance Storm, riding the Five-Star at the March 3 *Heat,* then again in a *Raw* rematch the next evening. Seeing RVD come up with the one-two-three once too often prompted Regal to join Michael Cole and the King at the *SmackDown!* table on March 7, allegedly to scout his *WrestleMania* adversary in a Hardcore title match against then-new Champion Goldust. Van Dam knew better when he saw the Brit get up from his chair, and took him out with a baseball slide to the outside floor. But when it appeared RVD had the Hardcore title won after nailing Goldust with a gold trashcan lid, an apron shot from Regal caught him off-guard, helping the Golden One to a quick rollup pinfall.

A master counter-style wrestler, Regal was already a formidable opponent for a high-flyer like Van Dam, though he'd insist at the March 10 *Heat* there was really no match. Being "unrelenting, sadistic and most importantly of all, *English*" already made him better than a laid-back Superstar who was "lazy and weak," like all of his fans. And come *WrestleMania,* "R-V-D" could point his thumbs at his head all he wanted, because Regal knew "two thumbs in the air is certainly no threat to *my* power of the punch." But Van Dam wasn't using his thumbs on the Blackpool wrestler or the Dudley Boyz in a Six-Man Tag match on March 11 *Raw;* it was his educated feet and Five-Star on Regal that gave him and the Hardy Boyz an impressive win. Regal got even at *SmackDown!* three nights later, disrupting Van Dam on the ropes long enough for Kurt Angle to suplex him and cinch on the ankle lock for the win. But he'd pay for the interference with a bone-jarring Chokeslam from Angle's *WrestleMania* opponent, Kane, whose save ensured that RVD and the Intercontinental Champion started on even ground for the Pay-Per-View in three days' time.

BEING FAN AXXESS-IBLE

Before *WrestleMania X8* rocked Toronto's SkyDome Arena, the WWE and its Superstars spent March 14 to 16 with their fans in downtown Toronto's Automotive Building at the National Trade Centre at Exhibition Place. The three-day festival, WWE Fan *Axxess*, is a time-honored tradition since *WrestleMania X* in 1994.

At WWE Fan *Axxess*, WWE enthusiasts from around the world get a chance to meet their favorite WWE Superstars; visit the WWE Hall of Fame—a virtual museum of wrestling history; are offered Superstar photograph opportunities and autograph sessions; and can take part in interactive attractions (fantasy play-by-play, video games, etc.), demonstrations, Q&A's with WWE Superstars and exhibits. In addition to this year's *Axxess* weekend raising over ninety thousand dollars (Canadian) for the Canadian Special Olympics and the Make-A-Wish Foundation through the generosity of the fans, the *Toronto Sun*, Home Game and Wal-Mart. The WWE has always seen the event as a way to say "thank you" to its audience, and to prolong the all-too-brief *WrestleMania* moments. ■

Since first arriving in the WWE at 1997's *In Your House: Badd Blood*, Kane has done most of his talking inside the ring. The seven-foot, three hundred twenty-five-pound brother of Undertaker has been successful at shutting up many of his adversaries. The former champion made an example out of Mr. Perfect on the February 18 *Raw*, when the Perfect One saw linebacker Brian Urlacher in the crowd and described the Chicago Bears' great NFL season to his WWE opponents: *im*perfect. Mr. Perfect wasn't saying much after a Chokeslam from the Big Red Machine, though, much to Urlacher and the Allstate Arena's appreciation.

Then there's Kurt Angle, another former WWE Champion who'd undoubtedly win a gold medal if making ill-timed comments were an Olympic event. It was his comments on February 21 *SmackDown!* that helped ignite his on-again, off-again feud with Kane, when the gold medalist—frustrated he'd lost his *WrestleMania* title shot to Triple H—open-challenged anyone "stupid enough" to face him in a match "so I can show them the definition of pain!" The Big Red Machine obliged, though Kurt quickly turned in his dictionary for a steel chair, giving Kane the DQ win. Their battle not only continued, but intensified to the outside floor, where Kurt German-suplexed Kane through the *SmackDown!* announcer's table, then onto the broken pieces. He grabbed the timekeeper's chair (suplexing the timekeeper for good measure), then used it to smash away at Kane's ankle repeatedly before slapping on the ankle lock.

Several days passed before Kane returned the pain at the February 25 *Raw*, but he'd hurt Angle in a much more sensitive spot—damaging his psyche and costing him his Undisputed Championship match against Chris Jericho. Three nights later on *SmackDown!*, he'd hit the Olympian with the same chair Stephanie used on him, allowing partner Triple H to Pedigree Kurt with little resistance. The win in Boston's Fleet Center might have been a little sweeter than most for Kane, since it was there he provided a classic *WrestleMania XIV* moment and Tombstoned retired baseball great Pete Rose in the middle of the ring. But after spoiling a likely nontitle win over Y2J one week later, Angle arranged a not-so-memorable moment for the Big Red Machine—as their battle continued out to the parking lot, Kurt knocked the big man senseless with a metal lighting case, slammed a steel garage door across his back and delivered a chair shot to the head that nearly bent the chair frame in half.

The vicious attack resulted in Kane not making it to the Joe Louis Arena for March 11 *Raw*, though the gold medalist *was* there to address "...a topic I know you fans in Detroit are familiar with: crime." Specifically, robbery, and more precisely, being robbed of his *WrestleMania* title shot two weeks ago, when "that big, burned moron Kane *had* to interfere" and cost Kurt the Undisputed title match against Y2J. Bragging how the Big Red Machine was taught a lesson at *SmackDown!* by "the Big *Red, White and Blue* Machine," Angle had another announcement: since he wasn't going to *WrestleMania* as the champion, he'd been given Mr. McMahon's approval to face Kane at the big event, where he promised, "I'll make that whole childhood burning thing seem like a paper cut!"

Despite giving up considerable size and mass—Angle had already beaten Kane on several occasions—the gold medalist Angle Slammed Big Show that night, giving him and Booker T the tag win over the giant and Edge. However, Kurt might have added too much fuel on the fire that already burned inside Kane, who seemed to have the inside track on one of Angle's "three I's" when he returned to March 14 *SmackDown!*. The gold medalist certainly wasn't showing much intensity when he saw the Big Red Machine charge to ringside. He already hadn't demonstrated

[**"I'll make that whole childhood burning thing seem like a paper cut!"**]

much integrity when he took advantage of William Regal's interference to defeat Rob Van Dam. But Kurt Angle did illustrate loads of intelligence bolting out of the ring while Regal took a massive Chokeslam in his place. And if he was going to beat a very focused Kane at *WrestleMania*, Kurt would need to become even smarter, *fast*

Anyone who's ever seen the classic film *It's A Mad, Mad, Mad, Mad World* might have an idea as to how the WWE Hardcore Championship works. Everyone has their eyes on the prize held by the champion; anyone can get it *anywhere* and *at any time*, thanks to the 24/7 rule, and *anything* one can put their hands on can be used as a weapon and everything is fair. What tends to occur is a near-madcap runaround throughout arenas by challengers trying to catch the defending strapholder off-guard. That runaround understandably calmed during Undertaker's several-month reign, but when The Rock helped young rookie Maven defeat the American Badass for the title at February 7 *SmackDown!*, hardcore madness ensued anew.

Maven's first title defense came against Goldust at February 28 *SmackDown!*, and though he took his share of lumps, he'd make good use of a fire extinguisher the Bizarre One brought in to score the schoolboy rollup. But after a beating from Undertaker required Maven to be taken backstage and attended to, Goldust

Big Show clotheslines both Kurt Angle and Booker T.

took advantage of the situation and pinned him to become the new Hardcore Champion.

After talking trash with Lilian Garcia about being "the Hardcore man of them all," it seemed somehow appropriate that Goldust smacked a trashcan lid over Tazz's head to defend his Hardcore crown on *Raw* March 4. He seemed better prepared at *SmackDown!* three nights later, furnishing only gold-colored trash-cans, lids and chairs against former Hardcore Champ Rob Van Dam. The determining factor in retaining the belt, however, was a Gold Gloves-style punch from William Regal on the outside apron.

Goldust's Hardcore luck ran out on March 11 *Raw*, when Al Snow picked up the three-count after driving the Bizarre One down onto a trashcan with the Snow Plow. Not yet ready for his Hardcore finale, Goldust tried to capture the belt again on *SmackDown!* on March 14, during Snow's title match against Big Show. And when all was said and done, the new Hardcore Champion was…*Maven*. He ran into the ring as Show dumped Goldust to the outside floor, dropkicked the giant over the top rope (shades of *Royal Rumble*) and pinned the fallen Snow for the victory. Less than three months since his WWE debut, Maven was a two-time Hardcore Champion, and he was going to *WrestleMania!*

The "Tag Team Turmoil" that took place at *No Way Out* ended with Bradshaw and Faarooq capturing the No. 1 Contender's spot for the Tag titles at *WrestleMania*. But it didn't end the turmoil that continued throughout the division, especially after Champions Spike Dudley and Tazz dropped their titles to Billy and Chuck at February 21 *SmackDown!*. After countering a Dudley Dog Bulldog and throwing Spike into Chuck's superkick, Billy caught the runt of the Dudley litter with the Fame-Ass-er to win the championship. It was a very emotional celebration in the ring, to say the least, and a revealing backstage interview with Lilian Garcia—Billy told Chuck he was the best partner he's ever had, while Chuck credited his better half's "personality, beautiful physique and most of all, that fun-loving attitude" as the keys to their success. Bradshaw and Faarooq came by to offer their congratulations as well and some advice: "Get

Goldust retains the Hardcore Championship against Rob Van Dam.

Hardyz are Poetry in Motion against Chuck.

used to bein' close," said Bradshaw, " 'cause come *Wrestle-Mania*, you two can kiss each other's ass—and those belts—good-bye!"

Having won WWE Tag Team gold five times (and the WCW tag titles once), Matt and Jeff Hardy made a formidable first title defense for Billy and Chuck at February 25 *Raw*. They were also on a win streak, with ever-Xtreme Jeff's Swanton Bomb landing a February 18 *Raw* victory against Lance Storm and Christian, followed by a Six-Man Tag win with Rob Van Dam against Storm and the Dudley Boyz at February 21 *SmackDown!*. Their luck would run out, however, when Chuck's superkick on Jeff enabled Billy to get on top for the three-count, preserving their first time together... as champions.

[**"Get used to bein' close, 'cause come *WrestleMania*, you two can kiss each other's ass—and those belts—good-bye!!"**]

The twosome next showed a spiteful side that evening, setting up Faarooq and Bradshaw with an invite to the Friendly Tap, a Rhode Island bar that offered everything the APA lives for: beer. The suds were flowing when they entered the establishment, though the brawlers became more than a bit alarmed finding out it was "Men's Night" and having drag queens asking them to dance! Catching them with their pants down (figuratively speaking), Billy and Chuck attacked, serving Faarooq a beer bottle to the skull while putting Bradshaw's head through the glass of a pinball machine. The result was another first for Billy and Chuck, and perhaps anyone in the WWE—they won a barroom brawl against the APA!

Given a shot at the tag team belts on February 28 *SmackDown!*, Faarooq and Bradshaw seemed more intent on reciprocating the *Raw* beating they took. Yet it was the champs escaping with another win as Billy, seeing Faarooq bent over after catching Chuck with a spinebuster, took advantage and hit him with the Fame-Ass-er. It wasn't until the March 10 *Heat* when Bradshaw gained some personal satisfaction for himself and his partner, nailing Chuck with a Clothesline from Hell for the win, while Faarooq floored Billy on the outside.

While Billy and Chuck and the APA went at it, the long-standing feud between the Hardyz and the Dudley Boyz continued. Matt, Jeff and Lita first dropped an Intergender Six-Man Tag contest to Bubba Ray, D-Von and WWE Women's Champion Jazz (subbing for an "injured" Stacy Keibler) at February 25 *SmackDown!*, though the "2Xtreme" team found *Raw* success on March 11, when partner RVD's Five-Star rode high over Intercontinental Champ William Regal and the Dudleyz.

Since both the Hardyz and the Dudleyz were involved in two of the most impressive Tag title bouts in *WrestleMania* history (a Triangle Ladder match in 2000, and the "Tables, Ladders and Chairs II" contest the following year), it seemed only fitting that they be included in the championship match for *WrestleMania X8*. As a result, the contest was changed to a Four-Corner match at the PPV, done elimination style. As a preview to the contest, Jeff Hardy, Billy, Bubba Ray and Bradshaw squared off for a *SmackDown!* Four-Corner match on March 14, with their partners (plus Lita and Stacy) choosing to remain at ringside. The match itself made for some interesting teamwork—including the Dudleyz' trademark "Wassup?" flying headbutt, as performed by Bradshaw and Jeff—though it was Chuck's outside interference of Jeff's Swanton Bomb that quickly built into a melee among

the four teams. Billy took advantage of the confusion, putting his feet on the ropes to pin Jeff, then hurried up the runway with Chuck while the other teams continued fighting one another. And with eight men in the ring and fighting for the straps at *WrestleMania*, the championship match promised even more tag turmoil than *No Way Out*.

The Women's Division was proving as tumultuous as the Tag Team competition as it headed toward *WrestleMania*. New Women's Champion Jazz would have two Divas worthy of contention to her crown: Trish Stratus and Lita, both former champions, and both determined to be on top of the heap again. Lita's high-flying maneuvers made her the most daring Diva, and a valuable ringside asset to the Hardy Boyz. Trish's resolve and ring adaptability made her an explosive threat, one that could pull out a win at any time.

Jazz didn't exhibit any of those characteristics, nor did she need to. The Women's Champion had power, technique and aggression combined, a dangerous combination that fueled her past Trish for the title on February 4, then again made itself painfully evident to Mighty Molly on February 25 *Raw*. Despite scoring the win with her fisherman's suplex, Jazz DDT'd Molly to the mat so hard she needed WWE officials to help her out of the ring. It also sent a statement to the Divas in the back that she was firmly in charge.

Stacy Keibler, the Duchess of Dudleyville, is hardly any kind of ring technician, but she knows how to manipulate a situation to her benefit. She was supposed to join the Dudleyz in a *SmackDown!* Intergender Six-Man Tag match against the Hardy Boyz and Lita on February 28, only to come up lame due to "a difficult photo shoot" earlier that day. Jazz took her place for the match, and clearly dominated Lita throughout portions of the contest. Lita mounted a late offense and prepped the champion for a Twist of Fate, until a big boot from Stacy broke it up and gave Jazz an opening for the fisherman's suplex and the win.

Lita and Trish put the double team on Jazz.

With her broken left hand still taped, Trish looked to regain the Women's title at March 4 *Raw*. But her dislike for Jazz was so great she eventually lost her temper, her top and ultimately the match via disqualification when she refused to break the STF submission hold even after Jazz reached the ropes. Trish could take comfort in the fact that her performance proved the Women's Champion wasn't invincible. Lita, meanwhile, scored a quick victory with a spinning belly-to-back sit-out slam on Stacy at *SmackDown!* on March 7, then made her aspirations to become the next Women's Champion known in a postmatch ringside interview with Lilian Garcia. A cheap shot from Stacy resulted in Lita re-entering the ring and delivering a Twist of Fate and top-rope moonsault to the leggy Diva, but she was soon grounded in a surprise attack by Jazz, then planted hard into the canvas with the DDT.

A Triple-Threat Women's Championship match for *WrestleMania* was announced at March 11 *Raw*, the same night contenders Trish and Lita were teaming up against the champion and Stacy. The two Divas made a solid tag team as they double-teamed Jazz in the match, but Trish's aggressive nature again proved costly after Jazz ducked a kick that caught Lita. Stacy took Trish to the outside floor while Jazz scored the rollup victory. At the March 14 *SmackDown!*, Trish apologized to Lita in the locker room for the accident, but Lita assured her that there wouldn't be any "accidents" at the March 17 Pay-Per-View. "Whether I have to go through Jazz or I have to go through you, I'm walking out of *WrestleMania* as the next WWE Women's Champion." Push suddenly came to shove, as Trish and Lita started pounding away at each other, requiring a number of officials to pull them apart. However the two Divas felt about the Women's Champion, it was obvious they'd have more than enough hostility to go around at *WrestleMania*.

Edge didn't win the Intercontinental Championship back at *No Way Out*, though he seemed to resolve his recent anger issues after putting William Regal down with his Figure-Four

Edgelock during their *Raw* Tag match on February 18. He'd follow up with a nice singles win against his brother Christian at *SmackDown!* three nights later, where the new submission move again proved successful. Having also come up short at *No Way Out* in his Tag Championship bid with Test, Booker T got back on the winning track in singles competition, derailing first The Godfather with a side kick at the February 18 *Raw*, then Val Venis during the February 24 *Sunday Night Heat*.

Booker's greatest challenge to date came at February 25 *Raw*, though it wasn't in the ring; he was reading a "Learn Japanese" book backstage. Hearing some representatives from a Japanese hair treatment company were looking for a spokesperson, he wanted to brush up on his verbal skills, since he figured he'd already look good to them later that night in his match with Rikishi. One close-up he made sure to avoid was the Phat Man's Stinkface, using the referee as his stand-in while he got up and took Rikishi down with a winning side kick.

Wanting to show he'd make an ideal writer as well a spokesperson, Booker read off one of his own scripts to Tajiri and Torrie Wilson backstage at February 28 *SmackDown!*. He didn't appreciate hearing the Cruiserweight Champion's comments that the offensive script made fun of other people's hair "when your hair is crap." Booker didn't care; he thought he had the job locked up, especially after picking up another win that night against Scotty 2 Hotty. Unfortunately, he was about ready to pull his own hair out after the match, when the company representatives appeared on the TitanTron and announced their new spokesperson, Edge!

Learning Tajiri played a big role in helping Edge land the job prompted Booker to challenge the Japanese Buzzsaw to a nontitle match on March 7 *SmackDown!*. The Cruiserweight Champion fought valiantly, but Booker's size and strength proved dominant early and often, leading him to a fairly easy victory. After celebrating the win with a Spin-a-Roonie, Booker decided to dish out more punishment to the Cruiser-

THE STRONG MAN
RETURNS

After a lengthy hiatus, World's Strongest Man Mark Henry returned to World Wrestling Entertainment after taking first place in the Arnold Strong Man competition, a contest tied in with Arnold Schwarzenegger's annual Arnold Classic Fitness Weekend. The event, held February 22 to 23 in 2002, drew over seventy thousand visitors to Columbus, Ohio's Veterans Memorial Auditorium. Henry, a two-time Olympic powerlifter, deadlifted eight hundred eighty-five pounds; clean-and-jerked the "Apollon's Wheel" (a three hundred sixty-six-pound barbell with a 1.93-inch bar that doesn't rotate); lifted a pair of logs bolted together that weigh between one hundred sixty-five to one hundred eighty-five apiece, and walk up a fifteen-meter ramp in a thirty-second time period; pushed a two-and-a-half ton Hummer fifteen meters (with the air let out of the tires for good measure); and then *lifted* the Hummer for a single repetition. The six feet, one inch, three hundred eighty-pounder from Silsbee, TX, made his official return to the WWE in April, and currently resides with the *SmackDown!* brand. ■

---

weight Champ, until Edge raced in and speared him, then played the part of a "hand spokesperson" and mocked the Spin-a-Roonie!

The crowd in Detroit's Joe Louis Arena thought Booker had come around when he confronted Kurt Angle in the ring on March 11 *Raw*—he was sick of hearing Kurt's comments about the fans' stupidity. "These people in the arena right here," he said, "they're *beyond* stupid! They're brain-dead!" Booker complained that the fans were the reason why he didn't have a title shot, an endorsement deal or even an opponent for *WrestleMania* ("You damn *skippy* it ain't right, homie!" said Kurt in sympathy), until Edge came out onstage and corrected him. "Didn't you hear? You already have a title. You're officially the *dumbest* man in the entire company!" Citing Booker's recent performance on the TV show *The Weakest Link* as evidence, Edge found it strange that "someone with the word 'book' in his name has apparently never *read* one." As for Booker needing an opponent for *WrestleMania*, "You're looking at him. Now can you dig *that*, sucka?"

Booker was up for that idea, as well as a Tag match later that evening that saw Angle (who earlier performed what Edge laughingly described as "the first-ever *Dork-a-Roonie*") slap on the ankle lock on Edge's partner Big Show for the win. Edge paired with Tajiri at *SmackDown!* three nights later against Booker and his usual tag partner Test, and despite hitting the Edgecution on the big man, it was Booker scoring the win over Edge with the side kick. Booker had Test hold Edge while he performed a Spin-a-Roonie, then knocked out the young Superstar with another kick to the head.

> [**"These people in the arena right here, they're *beyond* stupid! They're brain-dead!"**]

At the rate Christian was going, he *wasn't* heading to *WrestleMania*. He couldn't buy a win in recent weeks, and his temper tantrums grew exceedingly worse with every match. Lance Storm couldn't calm his fit in the middle of a *Raw* Tag match against the Hardy Boyz on February

18, leaving him open to a Litacanrana and Swanton Bomb that got the three-count. Even his opening pyro fizzled as he headed ringside against Edge for February 21 *SmackDown!*. And when he fell to a Figure-Four Edgelock, that was the last straw. "I guess you're expecting me to throw a temper tantrum," he told the MetroCentre crowd. "Well, I'm *not* going to cry. I'll do you one better. As of right now…*I quit!*"

Clearly, Christian needed positive reinforcement. And there was no one more positive than the man who beat him for his European Championship, Diamond Dallas Page. DDP prevented Christian from signing his resignation papers at *Raw* the following week, explaining that his losing streak came from harboring negative energy. "The only way you're going to get where you want to go is to harness that energy into something *positive*."

Based alone on the extensive smile techniques required, the next few weeks proved difficult; at the February 28 *SmackDown!*, one fan asked why Christian was such a loser, to which he responded, "If you want to find a loser, why not find *your dad?*" He offered *Raw* advice on March 4 to a family member on the phone regarding Grandma Edna. ("Pull the damn plug! The faster she goes, the faster I cash in! *Cha-ching*!") And he didn't want to follow DDP into the crowd during March 10 *Heat*, after Page defended his title with a Diamond Cutter to Lance Storm.

Finally, all of Christian's hard work at being positive paid off on March 11 *Raw*. Billy and Chuck's snide backstage remarks about him and Page being "those kind of people"—losers—spurred Christian to challenge "Ass Man" Billy to a match. Though he'd suffer an outburst during the match, DDP kept him calm from the outside floor, then added an assist with a Diamond Cutter to Billy while the referee was distracted. Picking up the three-count and a much sought-after win, Christian threw another tantrum, this time one of jubilance. But as Page pointed to the crowd in celebration, Christian came up from behind and gave him a reverse DDT! He then positively pounded DDP before giving him the Unprettier and leaving. Now that he was back on

his winning ways, he didn't need Page anymore. And he was *positive* he could win back the European title from him at *WrestleMania*.

The legend returns.

The lethal poison of the New World Order struck the WWE's veins early; within twenty-four hours of determining the outcome of an Undisputed Championship match, the faction had put the People's Champion in the hospital. Even Vince McMahon, the man responsible for injecting the poison into his own company, supposedly found the group's actions on February 18 *Raw* "absolutely reprehensible." Though one could say the same regarding the co-owner's videotaped statement for February 21 *SmackDown!*, and his proposed course of action to ensure "all parties will be satisfied by the punishment the nWo will receive"—that being community service—and "to insist that the nWo publicly apologizes to The Rock and to all of the fans."

The Academy Awards wouldn't be awarded for another month, but it was a safe bet in the office pool that evening's "heartfelt apology" of Kevin Nash, Scott Hall and Hollywood Hulk Hogan wouldn't garner any acting nominations. From a prepared statement (courtesy of McMahon's attorneys), the trio read off each of their "regrets" for attacking The Rock in dead, monotone voices. When the paper passed over to Hogan, he thanked first the D.A.'s office for accepting a lesser charge, "even though The Rock assaulted me first," then McMahon for his understanding, love and support. "On a personal note, Rock, I ask for your forgiveness. For, Rock, I forgave you for attacking me first, and because I am truly, truly sorry." Hogan's tone suddenly changed as he stopped reading and said, "But trust me, 'icon,' and believe in my heart, 'People's Champ'... I'm *not* going to be sorry for what I do to you at *WrestleMania*."

No statement could prepare the New World Order for what happened next, as Stone Cold Steve Austin, fresh from his evening in the Chicago stir, drove his

> **"I'm *not* going to be sorry for what I do to you at *WrestleMania*."**

pickup truck into the MetroCentre and up to the ring! He quickly introduced Hogan and Nash to his tire iron before chasing down Hall and beating him senseless to the ground, then jumped back in his truck and put it in reverse, seemingly to run Hall down! Grabbing their "4-Life" brother, the nWo members made it to their limo out back...only to discover their ride had four flat tires and the word "WHAT?" spray-painted across it.

With the extremely pissed-off Rattlesnake right behind them, the nWo had no choice but to run and hide, though in the process the injured Hall fell behind and became separated from them. Austin

wasn't worried—he found him, and kept him heavily taped and gagged to a chair while wheeling him around the arena throughout the evening. Austin stopped every few minutes to lay in a few shots, taunt Hall over a few Steveweisers and put him through a mental wringer, but the bottom line at every stop: "You do *not* mess with Stone Cold Steve Austin!" Hogan and Nash hid at first, then looked for their missing comrade, eventually tracking him down inside a fenced maintenance area. They learned, too late, that Stone Cold put Hall there as bait, so he could again introduce them to his "little friend"—the tire iron. Austin bashed away at Hogan and Nash, then locked them inside the maintenance area and joked, "There's no way out, get it? There's '*No Way Out*'!"

Minutes later, Austin loaded the already battered and beaten Hall into his truck and back to the ring, where he unloaded some more on the nWo member. Bringing in his cooler of Steveweisers, the Bionic Redneck helped him to a few beer cans to the head, then had the Rockford audience participate in an ass-whooping: "I'm..."

"*What?*"

"...gonna kick this sonuvabitch's ass..."

"*What?*"

"...every time..."

"*What?*"

"...you say 'What?'!"

The "What?" chants piled on, as did the beating, until finally Austin offered Hall a Steveweiser. Not in any shape to refuse, Hall accepted it...then took a Stone Cold Stunner to chase it down! The Rattlesnake topped the night off in nWo fashion, grabbing some spray cans and, at the crowd's vocal behest, spray-painted on the "4-Lifer's" back "3:16." Translation: Stone Cold Steve Austin just branded Scott Hall's ass!

A very serious New World Order opened February 25 *Raw*, with several issues to address. Hogan directed his attention toward The Rock, hearing his injuries were more severe than originally reported, and that the People's Champ was supposed to show up in

Providence. "And when you do, we're going face-to-face." Nash had words for only the disrespectful fans, "You are looking at three of the biggest stars in the history of wrestling. The nWo expects to be *treated* like it!" Then Hall took the mic, and recalled his ordeal of being tortured "like an animal" at the hands of Stone Cold. "Austin, I am not an animal," he said. "I'm a man, and I'm *all* man. The question is…are *you* a man?" Hall threw down a challenge to meet the Rattlesnake one-on-one, "but not tonight." He wanted to embarrass and humiliate him at the biggest show on earth, and if Austin agreed, "We'll call a little truce until *WrestleMania.* Either way, Stone Cold…you're *screwed.*"

> **"I am not an animal. I'm a man, and I'm *all* man. The question is…are *you* a man?"**

Hogan's "face-to-face" with The Rock that evening consisted of a backstage locker-room confrontation with a life-sized standee of the People's Champ. Hollywood explained to "Rock" that his popularity was a fad that would eventually be forgotten. "Legends don't grow on trees, Rock," he said. "I should know; I *am* one." Hogan then used his weight belt to knock down the standee, promising the "Brahma Bull" that when it came to being an icon, "at *WrestleMania,* you're going to find out the difference between a wannabe and the real thing…*brother.*"

Meanwhile, Austin wasn't interested in any truce—"Does it look like I *want* to stop?" was among Austin's varied "What?" responses to Michael Cole backstage—but he would accept the challenge to face the "big, fat jackass" Scott Hall at *WrestleMania.* The Rattlesnake wouldn't be surprised seeing the jackass come down to the ring later that night, moments after Austin landed the Stunner to end his match with Mr. Perfect. He also didn't care that the nWo member had a wheelbarrow filled with cement blocks; he just headed to the outside floor and started whaling on Hall. But the one-on-one soon became a mugging as Nash and Hogan attacked, beating down Stone Cold long enough to hold his legs against the ring post, where Hall smashed a cement block over his right knee!

Stone Cold's blood-curdling screams had created fearful speculation his knee had been destroyed, but the Bionic Redneck was back in the ring three nights later for *SmackDown!,* wearing a hunting flak jacket and holding a chair that *wasn't* for resting the heavily taped-up knee. As the nWo came out and motioned toward the ring, Austin warned he might go down, "but I'll damn sure take one of you sonuvabitches with me!" Hogan decided to return backstage; his buddies could handle the banged-up "gimp," and since The Rock was out again, he had a video tribute to finish about himself being "the *true* icon of the WWE." Hall told the "white-trash, beer-guzzling redneck" the *Raw* attack was just the beginning of Austin "being treated like an animal, and at *WrestleMania,* you'll go *down,* then *out.*" The Black and White started laughing as Stone Cold ditched the chair and limped his way up the ramp… then turned yellow when he pulled out a gun! The weapon fired off a net that ensnared Nash, while the Rattlesnake hammered away at Hall, until a cheap kick to his bad leg slowed him down enough for them to escape. Nevertheless, Austin's message was clear: he wasn't the hunted; he was the *hunter.*

Unfortunately, the bad knee and three-on-one odds would prove too much for Austin on March 4 *Raw.* His match against Booker T was fierce but brief when the nWo attacked, overwhelming the defiant Rattlesnake and busting his head open with a wrench. As the trio started leaving, Hall decided to get in a few more shots on the bloodied Austin, then capped off the beatdown with one last touch: a Stone Cold Stunner!

With Austin gone for the rest of the evening, the Black and White decided one of them should find

The Rock shows Kevin Nash his new order.

some entertainment in the ring. Eventually getting the nod, Hall warned the audience that in his mind, he'd consider his randomly selected opponent to be Stone Cold. The unlucky victim turned out to be Spike Dudley, whose grit and determination were, as always, admirable, but just no match against the especially brutal Hall that evening. Hogan and Nash would also contribute some shots from the outside floor to the runt of the Dudley litter, softening him up enough for Hall to get the "hard-fought" win with a Razor's Edge.

The games would come to an end at March 7 *Smack-Down!,* as the People's Champ made his triumphant return to the ring. And The Rock had a confession to make to the ecstatic Freeman Coliseum crowd; he was *happy* when he first heard the nWo was coming to the WWE. While everyone worried about the "poison" being injected into the WWE, "I was thinking about one thing only: The Rock, Hulk Hogan, *WrestleMania.*" Then, when Hogan accepted his challenge, Rock admitted he'd made a mistake. "I was so obsessed with what Hulk Hogan *was,*" he said, "I forgot about what Hulk Hogan is: a jaded, self-centered, bitter *son of a bitch!*" But Hogan made an even bigger mistake—he didn't finish the Brahma Bull when he had the chance.

"So The Rock says this...*brother*...Why don't you try and finish off The Rock tonight?"

Approaching the stage with his nWo brothers, Hogan told the People's Champ he'd wait until Rock was one hundred percent at *WrestleMania*. "I don't want you having any excuses when I beat you." Rock wasn't buying what Hogan was selling, "Who would have ever thought that the man with twenty-four-inch pythons would have *half-inch testicles?*" The comment got Hogan's dander up, but his fellow "4-Lifers" held him back. Taking the microphone, Hall said Hollywood may be "... too nice of a guy to take advantage of The Rock while he's crippled," but *he* wasn't. "You want some? Don't sing it. *Bring* it." The Rock told "Chico" they were on, but warned Hogan, "Don't get too comfortable, because once The Rock is done with Hall, get ready... your candy ass is *next!*"

The Great One wasn't offering any excuses when he squared against Hall later that night, but the taped ribs on his left side only supported rumors of injuries more severe than he let on. Though The Rock started strong with a spinebuster and sharpshooter, Hogan and Nash's ringside arrival distracted him long enough for their nWo brother to gain the advantage. Hall focused his attack on the taped area, exploited further when Hogan pulled Rock to the outside and worked the ribs over. But the Brahma Bull's fortitude proved stronger than ever, powering him to a Rock Bottom on Hall, teeing off on Nash as he entered the ring, and going face-to-face with Hogan. The two stared each other down, only to have it broken up by Hall and Nash. But as the triple-team beating started, Stone Cold raced down and helped clear the ring of the Black and White.

As Hogan, Hall and Nash headed up the ramp, out came Mr. McMahon, extremely unhappy that Austin had disrupted things once again. "Since you and The Rock want the nWo so bad," he said, "that's what you'll get." McMahon declared the March 11 *Raw* would be "a pre-*WrestleMania* celebration," in which Rock and Austin would face all three members of the nWo in a Handicap match!

With six days to go before the biggest Pay-Per-View event of the year, Hogan had goose bumps, and Hall had Rattlesnake skin on his mind. Nash had his sights on the present, "It's the first time the nWo is in a WWE ring. The most important thing is *tonight,* we have to make sure this Handicap match goes down in history." And it was a match of historic proportions, one that saw both sides put their bodies on the line. The confrontation everyone waited for wouldn't happen until late in the match, and when Hogan and Rock finally squared off against each other, Nash's shot from behind gave Hollywood the advantage over the Great One. Austin duked it out with Hall and Nash on the outside, while Hogan delivered the classic big boot to the Brahma Bull, then came off the ropes and dropped the leg for a clean three-count. Hollywood Hulk Hogan had defeated The Rock.

The nWo celebrated Hogan's shocking win with another triple-team beating on the Rattlesnake, with Hall once again delivering Stone Cold his own Stunner. But Austin wasn't going to let that change what he had planned for his nWo opponent at *WrestleMania*; at March 14 *SmackDown!,* he started going over his game plan with Jonathan "Coach" Coachman backstage when the nWo's music cut him off. Hall was in the ring, trying to goad the Rattlesnake, who watched from the Titan-Tron. "You don't have to hide in the back like some kind of cockroach," he said. "I hear—from *you*—that you're the toughest SOB in the WWE. *Prove* it." As Stone Cold disappeared from the TitanTron screen and his music hit, Hall faced the entrance and geared up for a fight. But his plan went awry—thinking Austin had come out on stage, Kevin Nash stormed out with a chair, only to discover it was a WWE official. Hall, still watching the stage area, never saw the Rattlesnake coming through the crowd and entering the far side of the ring. Austin opened a big fat can of whoop-ass on the "4-Lifer," then topped it off with a Stunner before heading back into the crowd. He'd had the last say on Scott Hall that night, and he intended to deliver the bottom line at *WrestleMania X8.*

Hollywood Hulk Hogan, meanwhile, had some things to tell Cleveland's Gund Arena fans about his upcoming "Icon vs. Icon" match with the Great One. For years, he'd watched and heard every "next big thing" step into the ring and threaten to "kill *Hulkamania*," citing Roddy Piper, Ultimate Warrior and Andre the Giant. "But Andre, like everybody else, failed," he said. "They all fell victim to the exact same thing The Rock fell victim to last Monday night." And the People's Champ would fall victim once more at *WrestleMania*. "After I beat you, Rock, one-two-three in the middle of the ring, you're going to realize that you're *ordinary*. You're *common*. Just like everyone else."

Hogan showed the match footage several times before he was interrupted by The Rock, who conceded Hogan his victory at *Raw*, but he needed to make something clear, "Unlike every other man you faced, The Rock could care *less* about 'killing *Hulkamania*.'" As far as the People's Champ was concerned, *Hulkamania* was a fantasy, but *WrestleMania* was *reality*. "Hogan, you can beat The Rock in a tag. You can take a hammer to the back of The Rock's head. But there is no way—and The Rock means *no way*—that The Rock is *not* going to walk into the biggest match *ever*, and *not* whoop your candy ass, one-two-three."

It was Hogan's turn to give the Great One his due—he wasn't exactly a "flavor of the month," and he was as responsible for making their contest "the biggest match in the history of this industry." That said, he had only one more question to ask, "Whatcha gonna do, Rock, when the biggest icon this industry has ever seen puts you down at *WrestleMania?* Whatcha gonna do when the biggest icon in the history of wrestling *runs wild on you?*"

The Rock slowly made his way to the ring, entered and told Hogan exactly what he intended to do. "It goes like this, Hulk Hogan…at *WrestleMania*, The Rock is going to put an end to your legend, and go down in history as being the best *ever*. But until then, The Rock will take his vitamins. But if I were you, I would say my prayers. If you smell…what The Rock… is cookin'."

HARDY AND HIGH-BROW

The WWE was all over the TV set in the weeks leading up to *WrestleMania*, most notably on the NBC series *Fear Factor* and *The Weakest Link*. The *Fear Factor* episode that aired February 25 featured Matt and Jeff Hardy, Lita, Test, Molly and Jacqueline, each of whom competed for a fifty thousand-dollar purse to be donated to the charity of their choice. Stunts included the "Helicopter Climb" from the bottom rung of a rope ladder dangling over the waters of the Pacific Ocean (ironically, Jeff fell, and Lita's time was the slowest among the Divas); drinking from the "Blender of Fear," a concoction of ground-up pig brains with ingredients labeled on three dice, including pig intestine, durian, animal fat, rooster testes, cow eyes, veal brain, spleen, cod liver oil, bile and fish sauce (Molly gagged, while Test passed on the rooster testicles); and the "Pole Hopper," which required walking atop six poles, under rain and ice conditions, and moving three flags from the shortest to the highest pole. Jacqueline tried to accomplish the feat, but was forced to "convince" host Joe Rogan she wanted to quit, while Matt completed the task after seven minutes. Fear was not a factor for winner Matt Hardy, who played on behalf of the American Cancer Society.

While perhaps not as frightening as *Fear Factor*, *The Weakest Link* had its moments on March 10. Contestants included Kane (in costume and mask), Terri, Bubba Ray Dudley, D-Von Dudley, Edge, Jerry "the King" Lawler, Debra and Stone Cold Steve Austin. Edge was the first to go despite only getting one question wrong. In round two, Stone Cold gave the wrong answer to "one hundred times eleven," so the obvious choice was to vote out *D-Von*. Answering the most questions correctly for four consecutive rounds, Bubba became the tie-breaking vote that nixed Debra (since Austin wouldn't do it to his wife), then Terri. Host Anne Robinson showed no fear in giving Stone Cold the bottom line in the fifth round—he *was* the weakest link. Austin took his nameplate and held it in front of her before leaving. The King bowed more gracefully in the next round, while Kane and Bubba Ray went all the way to sudden death (figures). Kane got his question right, Bubba didn't and St. Jude's Children Hospital became the recipient of $83,500, courtesy of the Big Red Machine. ∎

APRIL
4

back lash
(bak-lash) n. 1. a sudden or violent recoil.
2. a violent and usually hostile reaction to some event.
—*Oxford American Dictionary*

Lashing Out

It's a given—the actions at every *WrestleMania* elicit positive and negative reactions that create a "backlash" throughout the WWE. The effects are so strong and long-lasting that in 1999 World Wrestling Entertainment decided the post-*WrestleMania* house show tour should become its own Pay-Per-View event, and so *Backlash* was born.

Since its inaugural year, *Backlash* has hosted its share of historic moments—in 1999, Mankind and Big Show cranked up the heat in a Boiler Room match, while Stone Cold Steve Austin successfully defended his WWE Championship against The Rock in a classic post-*WrestleMania XV* rematch. At *Backlash* one year later, the Rattlesnake would help the Great One defeat then-Champion Triple H and earn his fifth WWE title. In 2001, Shane McMahon was the "Last Man Standing" after dropping an elbow on Big Show—from *forty feet up!*—while Champion Austin and The Game defeated Undertaker and Kane for the WWE Tag Team belts.

The *Backlash* that followed *WrestleMania X8*, however, was perhaps the most significant in its four-year PPV history. On April 21, 2002, a month-long chain of events culminated with *Hulkamania* soaring to new heights in a WWE that had been irrevocably split into two separate entities.

The recoil began March 18 on *Raw*, in Montreal's Molson Centre, where the crowd of seventeen thousand-plus focused on the TitanTron while World Wrestling Entertainment CEO Linda McMahon made a monumental live announcement from WWE Headquarters in Stamford, Connecticut. Explaining that the ongoing feud between WWE co-owners Vince McMahon and Ric Flair had become "a liability to the company's continued growth," Linda and the board of directors decided to form a *brand extension* that would split the WWE and its respective talent in two—Flair would have total control and authority over *Raw,* while Mr. McMahon would be granted the same for *SmackDown!* In addition, a draft would take place on *Raw* in one week's time, and with the exception of the Undisputed Champion and Women's Champion—whose services would be available to everyone—each co-owner would have the opportunity to *handpick* the WWE Superstars they wanted *exclusive* to their brand!

Flair and McMahon catch wind of the Draft.

Linda described the board's decision as "an exciting adventure" for World Wrestling Entertainment, one that would turn McMahon and Flair's bitter competition into "...a *positive,* for the better of our company, and for our Superstars. But most importantly, for *you,* the fans." The sentiment wasn't shared by her husband, who bitterly warned

everyone they would miss "the man who created *Monday Night Raw,*" especially with "a miserable failure" like Ric Flair now in charge.

The Nature Boy strutted down the aisle and into the ring, where he promised Vince *Raw* would continue "without *your* miserable ass!" A coin toss determined the first draft pick would go to Mr. McMahon, who told Flair to get accustomed to the feeling—"Starting this Monday, and each and every week thereafter...*I win. You lose.*"

Amazingly, the draft announcement wasn't the evening's only historic event. Only twenty-four hours after their match at *WrestleMania X8,* The Rock and Hollywood Hulk Hogan joined forces against the nWo's Scott Hall and Kevin Nash, who turned on Hogan for losing sight of the group's plan to destroy the WWE one by one, starting with Stone Cold Steve Austin. The icons were victorious in the ensuing Tag match via countout, but the nWo drew next blood at Ottawa's Corel Centre on the March 21 *SmackDown!* Ignoring Vince McMahon's heeding backstage to take the night off and consider becoming his first-round pick, Hogan aided The Rock after a DQ win over Kevin Nash left the Great One open to attack. But the arrival of new nWo member, X-Pac, shifted the tide back in the nWo's favor—Rock was powerbombed through the broadcasters' desk, while several chair-shots to the head left Hogan a bloody mess in the ring.

A Handicap match with Hall, Nash and X-Pac stacked the odds against Hogan and Rock on the

> **"Starting this Monday, and each and every week thereafter... I win. You lose."**

March 25 *Raw,* until Kane's sudden ringside arrival put the nWo on notice—they *weren't* going to run roughshod over the WWE! The Big Red Machine's actions inferred a major change in his demeanor, one that further manifested itself inside the locker room of Philadelphia's First Union Center on the March 28 *SmackDown!* A startled Rock and

X-Pac helps fellow nWo member Kevin Nash give Hogan a proper send-off.

Hogan watched Kane ask the nWo, "Whatcha gonna *do* when the millions…and the *millions* of The Rock's fans, twenty thousand *Hulkmaniacs* and twenty thousand Kanenites *run wild on you?!*"

Kane backed up his words at that night's Six-Man Tag Team match, delivering a devastating Chokeslam to X-Pac for the one-two-three. Unfortunately, X-Pac and the nWo would have the last word—and Kane's mask—in Phoenix's America West Arena, as their vicious backstage assault on the April 8 *Raw* would put the big man out of commission for the next several months.

F eeling the physical backlash of his fierce *WrestleMania* title match with Chris Jericho, a battered and bruised Triple H headed down the *Raw* runway in the Molson Centre on March 18, carrying the belts that represented the Undisputed Championship. After ten months of wondering whether he could successfully come back from his career-threatening quadriceps injury, Hunter's victory proved to both Y2J and himself that "I *am* The Game, and apparently, I *am* that damn good!"

Taking issue with the champ's claim, Stephanie McMahon came out and challenged her soon-to-be ex-husband to a rematch against Y2J on next week's *Raw.* Hunter granted the match on the condition that *she* team up with Jericho as part of a Handicap match. Furthermore, if he were to pin Stephanie in the ring, she would have to *leave* the WWE!

Backed into a corner, the Billion-Dollar Princess accepted the Cerebral Assassin's challenge…though she'd play this game by *her* rules. During the March 21 *SmackDown!,* Stephanie had her father change the bout to a Triple-Threat match, meaning if "Daddy's little

The Bryce Joyce Center at Penn State University was the site for World Wrestling Entertainment's historic first-ever Draft, which took place March 25 on *Raw*. WWE co-owners Ric Flair and Vince McMahon would each draft ten Superstars that night, with the remaining Superstars to be divided via a lottery on the WWE website immediately following the show. The only Draft exemptions were champions Triple H and Jazz; Chris Jericho and Stephanie McMahon, who were part of that evening's Triple-Threat Undisputed title match; and Stone Cold Steve Austin, whose contract included a free-agent clause, giving the Rattlesnake the option to sign with the WWE owner of his choice.

Mr. McMahon's first-round pick was a *Rock*-solid choice for *SmackDown!*...though the Great One wasn't entirely thrilled about working for the WWE co-owner, given their history together. Vince warned his new *SmackDown!* employee that he brought The Rock and Hulk Hogan into this world, "and I can damn sure take you *out* of it!" The Brahma Bull made it crystal clear that *the people* had made The Rock, then urged those people in the Bryce Joyce Center audience to tell Mr. McMahon *exactly* what they thought of him!

A disappointed Kurt Angle might have been sharing similar thoughts about his boss that night—feeling *he* deserved to be Vince's first choice, Kurt pressured the *SmackDown!* owner to make the gold medalist his second-round pick. This would allow Ric Flair to complete the second of two shocking *Raw* picks: Undertaker and the New World Order!

What was Flair thinking? Undertaker had left the Nature Boy bloody and defeated in "a *WrestleMania* moment" just two weeks before, and McMahon had brought in the nWo—whose members were entered into the Draft as a single entity—to destroy the Flair-poisoned WWE. The dirtiest player in the game, however, was also one of the sharpest businessmen—Slick Ric realized that drafting the Dead Man and the nWo not only gave him a formidable *Raw* lineup, but it would completely frustrate and throw Vince off his own game plans.

For the rest of the show, the two owners went back and forth, at times making their Superstar selections with an almost chesslike approach. When the smoke cleared, the Draft and subsequent lottery had divided tag partners, friends and brothers, and created mixed feelings for everyone throughout the company. The WWE, for all intents and purposes, had been split right down the middle! ■

THE DRAFT

WWF DRAFT RESULTS—MARCH 25, 2002

RAW	#	SMACKDOWN!
UNDERTAKER	1	THE ROCK
nWo	2	KURT ANGLE
KANE	3	CHRIS BENOIT
ROB VAN DAM (Intercontinental Champion)	4	HOLLYWOOD HULK HOGAN
BOOKER T	5	BILLY & CHUCK (Tag Team Champions)
BIG SHOW	6	EDGE
BUBBA RAY DUDLEY	7	RIKISHI
BROCK LESNAR	8	D-VON DUDLEY
WILLIAM REGAL (European Champion)	9	MARK HENRY
LITA	10	MAVEN (Hardcore Champion)

WWE LOTTERY PICKS—MARCH 25, 2002

RAW	#	SMACKDOWN!
BRADSHAW	11	BILLY KIDMAN
STEVEN RICHARDS	12	TAJIRI (Cruiserweight Champion)
MATT HARDY	13	CHRIS JERICHO
RAVEN	14	IVORY
JEFF HARDY	15	ALBERT
MR. PERFECT	16	HURRICANE
SPIKE DUDLEY	17	AL SNOW
D'LO BROWN	18	LANCE STORM
SHAWN STASIAK	19	DIAMOND DALLAS PAGE
TERRI	20	TORRIE WILSON
JACQUELINE	21	SCOTTY 2 HOTTY
GOLDUST	22	STACY KEIBLER
TRISH STRATUS	23	CHRISTIAN
JUSTIN CREDIBLE	24	TEST
BOSS MAN	25	FAAROOQ
TOMMY DREAMER	26	TAZZ
CRASH HOLLY	27	HARDCORE HOLLY
MOLLY HOLLY	28	THE BIG VALBOWSKI
NO PICK—SIDE HAS 30	29	SATURN
NO PICK—SIDE HAS 30	30	NO PICK—SIDE HAS 30

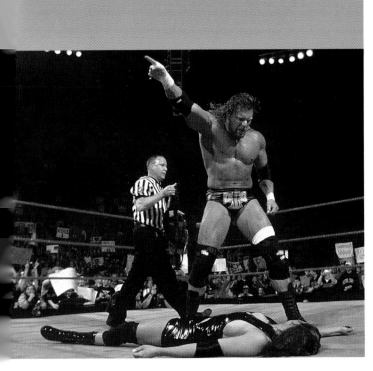

The game is over Stephanie McMahon.

chant good-bye to the fallen princess, whom security dragged kicking and screaming from Penn State's Bryce Joyce Center. For Stephanie McMahon, it truly was "Game Over"!

With the first-ever WWE Draft now in the history books, a new era for World Wrestling Entertainment began with the April 1 edition of *Raw*. The show's set, logos and music emphasized an exciting new look under the direction of Ric Flair, who planned to further style and profile at the Pepsi Arena by presenting Champion Triple H with a new Undisputed Championship belt and signing free agent Stone Cold Steve Austin exclusively to the *Raw* brand.

Slick Ric's plans didn't sit well with Mr. McMahon, who showed up uninvited on *Raw* to sign Stone Cold to an exclusive *SmackDown!* contract. Flair had Big Show physically escort Mr. McMahon out of the arena, but when Austin later arrived and told Flair to let Vince back into the building, the crowd wondered if the Bionic Redneck had already decided whose dotted line he planned on signing.

Business literally picked up at the end of the show as Flair and McMahon presented their exclusive brand

girl" were to pin *either* Hunter or Jericho, she would become the Undisputed Champion! Unfortunately for Stephanie, her visions of WWE gold around her waist ended in that match, when Triple H caught her with a bone-shattering spinebuster and scored the pinfall. Hunter encouraged the crowd to wave and

A Stone Cold Stunner delivered to Austin's now former boss, Vince McMahon.

contracts to Austin. Mr. McMahon told Flair he was about to lose again to a man whose "intellectual sperm fertilized the egg that became sports entertainment," and who first introduced Stone Cold to the world. To the crowd's chorus of "What?" Austin said he didn't give a rat's ass about Vince's intellectual sperm...though he *did* realize how successful he'd been under the billionaire, and agreed to sign his contract!

McMahon suddenly felt the bite of the Texas Rattlesnake, however, who told the *SmackDown!* owner, "April Fools," and gave him the Stone Cold

Ric Flair tries to "Woo!" Stone Cold Steve Austin into *Raw*.

Stunner! Austin signed Flair's *Raw* contract while a jubilant Nature Boy popped open some Steveweisers for a toast...only to become the recipient of a Stunner as well!

Ric Flair got what he wanted. Now he had to live with Austin on *Raw*, plus six feet, ten inches of trouble called Undertaker, who was still pissed off that he'd been drafted by the Nature Boy. The Red Devil also accused Flair of further disrespecting him by presenting a new Undisputed Championship belt to Triple H, someone Undertaker had beaten in all of their prior encounters, including a violent matchup at last year's *WrestleMania*.

Out came The Game, who stared down the Dead Man and said their previous matches didn't matter,

Undertaker challenges Triple H's Undisputed Championship.

"That was then. This is *now*." 'Taker told Triple H to put his money where his mouth was by putting up his Undisputed title at *Backlash*. Hunter accepted, and Flair was more than happy to sanction the match.

There was just one catch; the board of directors had previously established that the WWE owner who won the coin toss for the first draft pick would get to name the No. 1 Contender at *Backlash*. This meant Vince McMahon would sanction the title match, *not* Ric Flair.

The Nature Boy would regret his mistake when an irate Undertaker confronted him in Phoenix's America West Arena on April 8 *Raw*. Calling Flair "a liar and a no-good son of a bitch," The American Badass said it was time for another *WrestleMania* moment, but *Raw*'s newest acquisition came down the ring and got up in Undertaker's grill. To a round of "What?" chants, Stone Cold asked what made 'Taker a Dead Man, and why *he* was more worthy of the No. 1 Contender spot. He then checked his imaginary watch and said it was time for Flair to make up his mind.

Ric Flair didn't become a sixteen-time World Heavyweight Champion by letting people walk all over him, so he set the record straight with both WWE Superstars—he was in charge of *Raw* now, and if Stone Cold, Undertaker or any other wrestler put their

> **If Stone Cold, Undertaker or any other wrestler put their hands on him again, there would be hell to pay!**

hands on him again, there would be hell to pay! Flair would make good on his threat later that evening, suspending Kevin Nash while admonishing the nWo for its brutal backstage assault on Kane.

That said, Flair ruled there would be *two* No. 1 Contender's matches that night, to determine who would face the Undisputed Champion after *Backlash*—Undertaker would take on Intercontinental Champion Rob Van Dam in a non-title match, while the Rattlesnake would square off against the nWo's Scott Hall. Both men would win their respective matches with the help of outside interference, in Austin's case with an assist

from the Nature Boy himself. Unfortunately, the only thanks Flair got for his efforts was another Stone Cold Stunner!

At the campus of Texas A&M University a week later, Flair admitted he wanted nothing more than to see Stone Cold kick Undertaker's ass at *Backlash*, but Austin's repeated assaults prompted the *Raw* owner to fine the Rattlesnake five thousand dollars. Furthermore, to ensure that neither Austin nor Undertaker would push him around, Flair declared *himself* the guest referee for their match at *Backlash!*

Ownership may demand respect, but as Ric Flair, Vince McMahon and all WWE champions would often discover throughout 2002, such respect doesn't come easily, and is forgotten quickly. Take new Intercontinental Champion Rob Van Dam, for instance. Becoming only the fourth Superstar in World Wrestling Entertainment history to capture a title in their *WrestleMania* debut, RVD was

Eddie Guerrero gets the drop on Rob Van Dam.

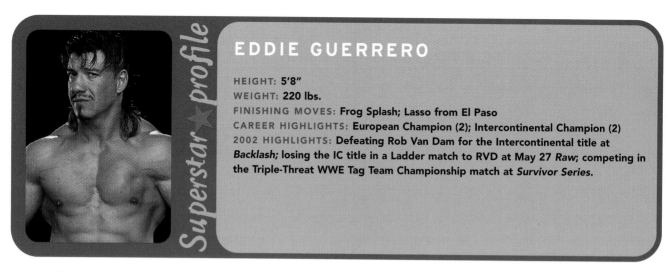

EDDIE GUERRERO

HEIGHT: **5'8"**
WEIGHT: **220 lbs.**
FINISHING MOVES: **Frog Splash; Lasso from El Paso**
CAREER HIGHLIGHTS: **European Champion (2); Intercontinental Champion (2)**
2002 HIGHLIGHTS: **Defeating Rob Van Dam for the Intercontinental title at** *Backlash;* **losing the IC title in a Ladder match to RVD at May 27** *Raw;* **competing in the Triple-Threat WWE Tag Team Championship match at** *Survivor Series.*

fast establishing himself as one of a kind in the company. Not buying into "The Whole Dam Show," however, was Eddie Guerrero, whose return to April 1 *Raw* literally made quite the splash on Van Dam. Insisting RVD's success came from *his* finishing maneuver, Latino Heat continued interfering in Van Dam's matches up till *Backlash,* where he intended to take the Intercontinental belt he thought was rightfully his.

Then there was William Regal, who lost the Intercontinental title to RVD at *WrestleMania X8,* but quickly snatched up the European Championship when he used his trademark bass knuckles to positively kayo Diamond Dallas Page on the March 25 *Smack-Down!* The power of the punch reigned supreme until the April 8 *Raw,* when challenger Spike Dudley—who already pulled off a royal nontitle upset against Regal one week earlier—crowned the Brit with his own brass knux to become European Champion.

Newcomers to the WWE may find respect even harder to come by...unless you're a

six-foot, four-inch, two hundred ninety-five-pound former NCAA Heavyweight Wrestling Champion like Brock Lesnar. "The Next Big Thing" made his auspicious debut the night after *WrestleMania X8,* interrupting a bout between then-Hardcore Champion Raven, *Tough Enough* teacher Al Snow and Spike Dudley and demolishing them within instants. Perhaps even more frightening than Lesnar's massive frame, however, was the man cheering him from ringside—Paul Heyman!

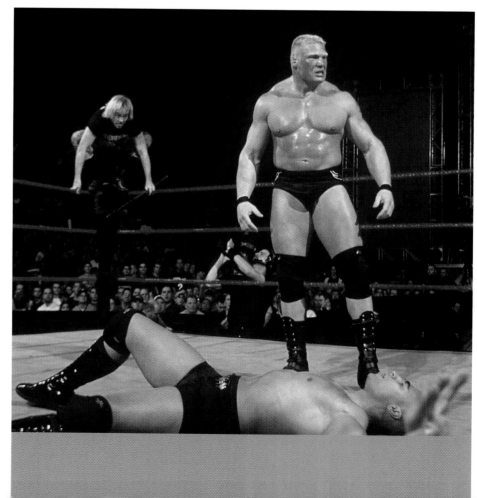

Brock Lesnar debuts, unfortunately for Maven and Spike Dudley.

Impressed by the young prospect, both Vince McMahon and Ric Flair vied for Lesnar at the Draft, with Flair succeeding in making him the eighth-round selection for *Raw*. At the Pepsi Arena on April 1, Lesnar made the Hardy Boyz *his* next pick, pummeling Matt with several power moves, then catching Jeff in mid-Hurracanrana and planting him with a triple power-bomb! The Hardyz would retaliate in Phoenix a week later with several chair shots to the head of the former NCAA Champion, though it was painfully obvious they'd need a *lot* more if they wanted to take Lesnar down.

"When you're with Brock Lesnar, you can do anything you damn well please!"

"When you're with Brock Lesnar, you can do anything you damn well please!" was a statement Heyman intended to prove in Lita's locker room at the April 15 *Raw*, after Matt Hardy was named Lesnar's opponent at *Backlash*. Twirling one of her thongs on his finger, Heyman explained that Brock could play nice with Matt at *Backlash*, or he could play rough. "It all depends on how nice *you* play…with *me*."

Lita slapped the smirk off the hyena's face and forced him to leave. But Heyman returned during the Hardyz' match with Goldust and Booker T, where from the top of the *Raw* set he started pulling thongs and other belongings from Lita's personal travel bag! Before Matt Hardy could reach Heyman, Brock Lesnar came out and demolished the Superstar with a spinning facebuster on the solid steel stage! Matt would require medical attention, and Jeff would now have to face Lesnar at *Backlash*.

If the Hardy Boyz had one thing in their favor, it was that they could still rely on each other as partners after the March 25 Draft. The same

Bubba Ray proves Dudleyville produces champions.

couldn't be said about other legendary WWE tag teams like the Dudley Boyz or the APA, now divided by the brand extension. Bubba Ray Dudley abated his separation anxiety on April 1 *Raw* by landing the Bubbabomb on Raven and finding Hardcore gold. Brother D-Von, meanwhile, found comfort of a different sort on *SmackDown!*…from the man above. Of course, that term could also apply to Vince McMahon, who agreed to be D-Von's benefactor in his cause of testifying against sinners.

D-Von obviously hadn't gotten around to Faarooq yet, who was busy taking bets from *SmackDown!* Superstars over feats of strength performed by "the World's Strongest Man" (winner of the Arnold Strongman Challenge in February), Mark Henry. The

Kemper Arena
Kansas City, MO

UNDISPUTED CHAMPIONSHIP MATCH

Hollywood Hulk Hogan defeated *Triple H* via pinfall to become the Undisputed Champion

TAG TEAM MATCH

Billy & Chuck (w/Rico) defeated *Al Snow & Maven* via pinfall to retain the WWE Tag Team titles

NO. 1 CONTENDER'S MATCH

Undertaker defeated *Stone Cold Steve Austin* via pinfall to become the No. 1 Contender at *Judgment Day*

INTERCONTINENTAL CHAMPIONSHIP MATCH

Eddie Guerrero defeated *Rob Van Dam* via pinfall to become the Intercontinental Champion

Kurt Angle defeated *Edge* via pinfall

Brock Lesnar defeated *Jeff Hardy* when the referee stopped the match

WOMEN'S CHAMPIONSHIP MATCH

Jazz defeated *Trish Stratus* via submission to retain the Women's title

Scott Hall (w/X-Pac) defeated *Bradshaw (w/Faarooq)*

CRUISERWEIGHT CHAMPIONSHIP MATCH

Tajiri (w/Torrie Wilson) defeated *Billy Kidman* via pinfall to become the Cruiserweight Champion

---

The climb was long and perilous. For Triple H, it was ten months of grueling physical therapy from a potentially career-ending injury, with self-doubt threatening to dislodge him at any moment. For Hollywood Hulk Hogan, it had been nine years before he'd find his way again, with his reborn *Hulkamaniacs* acting as his compass. Two men would meet at the top of the mountain at *Backlash* on April 21. Only one could stay there.

The Pay-Per-View opened in spectacular high-flying fashion with WWE Cruiserweight Champion Billy Kidman defending his title against Tajiri, accompanied by geisha-clad Torrie Wilson. Both Superstars relied heavily on their speed and agility throughout the match, though a powerbomb would give Kidman the near-pinfall, while Tajiri used a "mist" opportunity to blind his opponent and regain the Cruiserweight title.

Bradshaw's match with Scott Hall was intended as a one-on-one competition, but as fellow "4-Lifer" X-Pac joined Hall at ringside, the Big Texan found old APA partner Faarooq in his corner. Bradshaw pounded on the nWo veteran throughout most of the contest, almost decapitating him with a Clothesline from Hell. Unfortunately, X-Pac distracted the smashmouth wrestler long enough for Hall to land a low blow and win with the schoolboy rollup.

Trish Stratus looked to retake the Women's title from Jazz, but the Diva hadn't counted on hurting her back from a sneak attack by "pure and wholesome" Molly Holly just prior to the match. Despite a gutsy effort against the champion, the injured Trish had no choice but to tap out after Jazz put her in an agonizing crossface hold.

At least Trish could take comfort in that she was able to tap out, something Jeff Hardy *couldn't* do against Brock Lesnar. The young daredevil used the entire ring to keep "The Next Big Thing" off-balance, but Lesnar shrugged everything off, including a Swanton Bomb, before systematically taking Jeff apart with a spinning facebuster and powerbomb. Realizing the near-unconscious Team Xtreme star couldn't continue, the referee mercifully stopped the fight and declared Lesnar the victor.

The Kemper Arena crowd may think "Angle sucks," but it had to credit both the gold medalist and Edge for a first-rate match that had featured everything from dropkicks to flapjacks, clotheslines to sleeper holds, and suplexes to crossbodies. Neither Superstar could gain the clear advantage, though, and when even Kurt's

Angle Slam *and* ankle lock couldn't finish Edge off, the frustrated gold medalist resorted to a steel chair…only to inadvertently hit *himself* with it! (It's true! It's true!) Experience would be the deciding factor in this match, as a missed spear left Edge open for a second Angle Slam, giving Kurt the hard-fought pinfall victory.

Latino Heat met educated feet as Eddie Guerrero took on Intercontinental Champ Rob Van Dam in a title match that could have logged frequent flyer miles. Although the wrestlers generated much of their offense from the top rope, fans were floored by the outcome as Guerrero grounded RVD with a neckbreaker onto the Intercontinental belt! An unnecessary Five-Star Frog Splash provided the icing on the cake, and Eddie Guerrero walked out of *Backlash* as the new Intercontinental Champion.

The No. 1 Contender's match between Undertaker and Stone Cold Steve Austin was the perfect showcase for why both WWE Superstars were worthy of a shot at the Undisputed Championship…and why guest referee Ric Flair should *really* keep himself out of striped shirts. Beating the hell out of each other in and out of the ring, Austin and 'Taker's virtual stalemate wouldn't be decided by the nWo's unexpected arrival at ringside, a Stone Cold Stunner or an Undertaker Chokeslam, but by the Nature Boy's slow counts and "*Rawness*" as a referee. Flair wouldn't see Undertaker hit Austin with a steel chair, and he counted to three without noticing the Rattlesnake's foot was on the bottom rope. The mistake (or *was* it?) cost Stone Cold the match, and made Undertaker the No. 1 Contender at *Judgment Day!*

For a while it appeared as if Al Snow and Maven were more than tough enough to take the WWE Tag Team belts from Billy and Chuck—a drop toehold from Snow dropped Chuck right on top of Billy's "guns," while stylist Rico's misplaced spinning heel kick was *so* not en vogue with the defending champs' game plans. Fortunately, Chuck was able to fashion a bone-crunching kick to young Maven's jaw, and covered the rookie for the three-count.

Enough controversy had surrounded Hollywood Hulk Hogan on his way to the Undisputed Championship

match at *Backlash*. It was time to play The Game, and the icon would prove he could still do so with the best of the best, Triple H. The two Superstars struggled for control early, exchanging glares and flexing muscles in some old-fashioned ring psychology. The Cerebral Assassin soon zeroed in on Hogan's left knee brace—ironic when one considers the major surgery done on his left quad less than a year ago—but Hogan worked through the tremendous pain, reversing the momentum against Hunter with his patented boot to the face and legdrop.

That might have been the decider right there, if not for Chris Jericho, who earlier in the evening told the

Al Snow clotheslines Chuck.

Kemper Arena crowd he was leaving since he wasn't scheduled for a match. Y2J cracked a steel chair over Hogan's skull, but was forcefully driven away from ringside when Triple H delivered a facebuster. It appeared to be "Game Over" for the Hulkster as Hunter landed with the Pedigree, until Undertaker broke up the ref's three-count and clocked Hunter with the chair! Hogan punched the Dead Man out of the ring, then scored a second huge legdrop on Triple H, this time successfully covering him for the win. As "Voodoo Chile" filled the arena, Hulk Hogan found himself sitting on top of the mountain; for the sixth time in his already legendary career, he had become the champion! ■

Trish Stratus unloads on Molly Holly.

former APA member hadn't wagered on Test being such a sore loser over the bets, but it didn't stop him from collecting his pound of flesh from the big man. On *Raw*, Bradshaw was putting himself at odds with the nWo after its members staked a claim over the old APA office and sneak-attacked Kane backstage. Bradshaw promised to provide Scott Hall with an especially painful *Backlash*, courtesy of a Clothesline from Hell!

Other than the Hardy Boyz, the only tag team to remain intact after the Draft was Billy and Chuck, whose status as WWE Tag Team Champions ensured being drafted as one. Feeling their position on top required constant peak conditioning, the duo brought in stylist Rico Costantino, who from ringside would get in many Superstars' hairs. The threesome took a little too much off the top when their cutting remarks to young Maven on the April 11 *SmackDown!* got Al Snow's dander up. From there, the *Tough Enough* teacher and student would cause several bad hair days for Billy, Chuck and Rico, both in individual and tag competition, and they looked to make some permanent changes by taking the WWE Tag Team belts at the upcoming Pay-Per-View.

How had the Draft affected the WWE Divas? As Jazz put it at New York's the World on March 25, being WWE Women's Champion made her "the *only* bitch on both shows." The others had to fight harder for airtime. This included the woman Jazz defeated for the title in February, Trish Stratus, whose cover of the *Divas 2002* magazine made Terri jealous enough to pick a fight with her on *Raw*. Stratusfaction was guaranteed on Terri during a combination Bikini/Paddle on a Pole match, though it was Trish who fell victim to a paddle across the head from Molly Holly.

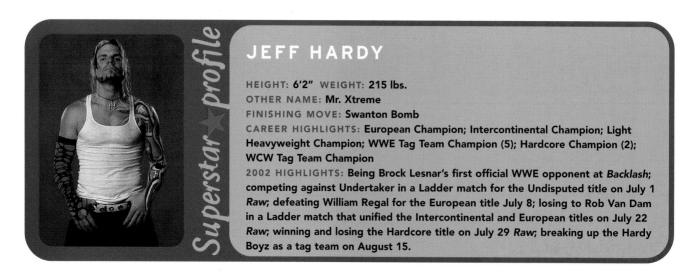

Superstar ★ profile

JEFF HARDY

HEIGHT: **6'2"** WEIGHT: **215 lbs.**
OTHER NAME: **Mr. Xtreme**
FINISHING MOVE: **Swanton Bomb**
CAREER HIGHLIGHTS: **European Champion; Intercontinental Champion; Light Heavyweight Champion; WWE Tag Team Champion (5); Hardcore Champion (2); WCW Tag Team Champion**
2002 HIGHLIGHTS: **Being Brock Lesnar's first official WWE opponent at *Backlash*; competing against Undertaker in a Ladder match for the Undisputed title on July 1 *Raw*; defeating William Regal for the European title July 8; losing to Rob Van Dam in a Ladder match that unified the Intercontinental and European titles on July 22 *Raw*; winning and losing the Hardcore title on July 29 *Raw*; breaking up the Hardy Boyz as a tag team on August 15.**

On The Record:

FORCEABLE ENTRY

Smackdown Records assaulted music and retail stores "Across the Nation" with the March 26 release of *WWE Forceable Entry*, a "One of a Kind" assortment of eighteen WWE Superstar entrance themes interpreted by the hottest names in rock 'n' roll today. Featuring tracks from Drowning Pool, Creed, Limp Bizkit, Kid Rock, Marilyn Manson, Rob Zombie, Disturbed and Cypress Hill, *Forceable Entry* immediately lived up to its name on sales charts, "Rollin' " as high as No. 3 on the *Billboard* Top 200 and showing strong "Legs" throughout 2002. ■

Tired of her superhero sidekick role, Molly dyed her hair chocolate brown and declared herself the best female wrestler in the ring, as well as the most beautiful, pure and wholesome Diva in the WWE. Trish decided it was time to put Molly in "a position she obviously wasn't acquainted with—flat on her back!" That's precisely what happened when the two locked up on April 15 *Raw*, and the pinfall win gave Trish a shot at reclaiming the WWE Women's Championship at *Backlash!*

After being on the receiving end of some Dudley Boyz wood a few weeks earlier, Stacy Keibler decided to table her ringside work for an entirely different position on *SmackDown!* She offered her services to Vince McMahon, telling him his "intellectual sperm" fascinated her and that she liked the way he talked. McMahon, in turn, liked the way the leggy Diva walked, and discussed the possibility of her becoming his personal assistant. Dressed in her old Ms. Hancock outfit from her WCW days, Stacy "applied" for the job at the Tuscon Convention Center on April 11, and showed the *SmackDown!* owner her qualifications with a table dance that had Vince falling out of his chair! Needless to say, the job was hers...and the benefits were *all* his!

Diva Torrie Wilson also made the cut on *SmackDown!*, along with boyfriend and WWE Cruiserweight Champion Tajiri. While in Rochester, New York for the April 4 show, she was reunited backstage with her friend Billy Kidman, who had a title match with Tajiri that

evening. Wishing one another well, the two friends hugged...until Tajiri came out and blew the innocent get-together out of proportion. During the match, Torrie suspected Kidman might use the Cruiserweight belt against her boyfriend, so she moved the title from where Tajiri placed it at ringside, not realizing *he* had actually intended to use it. The mistake would cost Tajiri the match, and the Cruiserweight Championship.

In the weeks that followed, opponents like The Hurricane would feel the new cutting-edge anger of the Japanese Buzzsaw, while Torrie was subjected to repeated intense verbal and mental abuse, and forced to cover up her beautiful physique head-to-toe in a

Stacy Keibler auditions to become Mr. McMahon's personal assistant.

THE PEOPLE'S KING

He's been the Undisputed Intercontinental Champion, the Tag Team Champion, the WCW Heavyweight Champion and the WWE Champion. More than ever, he remains the People's Champion. And in April 2002, The Rock added one more title to his incredible résumé: Box-Office Champion!

The Scorpion King premiered in theaters nationwide on April 19 and immediately laid the smack down on the competition, earning $36.2 million in its first weekend at the box office and becoming the highest-grossing April opening of any film in motion picture history. The successful prequel to the blockbusters *The Mummy* and *The Mummy Returns* (where Rock first played the Akkadian assassin Mathayus) dug up over one hundred million dollars domestically.

Powered by *The Scorpion King*'s rave reviews and worldwide box office, Hollywood definitely smells what The Rock is cookin'. Having just wrapped up his latest starring vehicle, the Universal action comedy *Hell Dorado*, as well as a cameo in *Terminator 3*, he's currently negotiating with several major studios about his next project, one rumored to be a live-action *Johnny Bravo*. But the most electrifying man in *all* of entertainment, sports or otherwise, has no desire to hang up his wrestling boots any time soon. It doesn't matter what The Rock's next movie will be; for now, he's more than content to put the Rock Bottom on some candy asses in the WWE! ■

geisha outfit! Unable to watch his friend be degraded any further, new Cruiserweight Champion Billy Kidman thought it was time to teach Tajiri some manners, starting with a surprise missile dropkick during the April 11 *SmackDown!,* and hopefully ending at the Cruiserweight title rematch scheduled for *Backlash.*

With Stone Cold and Undertaker vying for the title shot after *Backlash,* who would Vince McMahon name as Triple H's opponent at the Pay-Per-View? The question quickly turned into heated debate between Kurt Angle and Chris Jericho on the April 4 *SmackDown!* Angle pointed out he was a gold medalist, adored by children and senior citizens everywhere, and he'd defeated Triple H more than anyone else in the WWE. Y2J felt he deserved the shot since it was Stephanie McMahon who lost the Triple-Threat match, and he was determined to prove he wasn't the "has-been" people started calling him.

Out came The Rock, who pointed out that *no one* other than he had been in as many big matches with The Game, so no one deserved the title match more...except for maybe *one* man. The crowd started chanting that Superstar's name, and the People's Champion declared that since *SmackDown!* would now and forever be known as "the People's Show," then the people would tell Angle and Jericho who they wanted at *Backlash*—Hollywood Hulk Hogan!

Vince McMahon told interviewer Marc Loyd he knew what the people wanted better than the people did, though he did confirm that Hogan would be the No. 1 Contender at *Backlash.* Jericho was beside himself over the news, calling Rock "a stupid son of a bitch." And he

The Rock latches Jericho in the sharpshooter.

asked, "What has Hogan ever done in this business?" Rather than answer such a stupid question, Rock did all his talking in the ring that night, landing a Rock Bottom on Y2J for the win.

Triple H told the Rochester fans he didn't care who he faced at *Backlash.* As far as the Undisputed Champion was concerned, he'd deal with Undertaker once he went through Hogan...and he *would* go through Hogan, despite being a little sad that he'd now have to hurt someone he looked up to his whole life. "Make no mistake," Hunter told Hogan in the ring, "I will not hesitate. Not for one second." No longer was he

"Whatcha gonna do when *Hulkamania* runs wild on *you*?!"

"The Immortal" Hulk Hogan, but "an obstacle" for The Game to run down.

Hogan thought it couldn't get any bigger than the first *WrestleMania*, when he and Mr. T defeated Paul Orndorff and "Rowdy" Roddy Piper, or when he slammed Andre the Giant at *WrestleMania III*, or even *WrestleMania X8*, when the fans resurrected *Hulkamania* during his match with The Rock. He added that whenever experts say *Hulkamania* is dead, it rises up again, and it would do so once more at *Backlash*. All that was left was for Hogan to ask Hunter, "Whatcha gonna do when *Hulkamania* runs wild on *you*?!"

Despite their mutual respect for each other, the two Superstars didn't need any outside influences to goad them into locking up...which was reason enough for Kurt Angle and Chris Jericho to get involved. On the April 11 *SmackDown!*, Kurt expressed to "What?"-chanting Tuscon Convention Center fans his disappointment that Mr. McMahon had "gone mental" and made it Hogan-Game at the Pay-Per-View. "*I* beat Russians and Iranians in the Olympics a *heck* of a lot tougher than Nikolai Volkoff and the Iron freakin' Shiek!" Even worse, with Undertaker and Austin fighting for the No. 1 Contender's spot at *Backlash*, Angle wouldn't get a title shot any time soon.

Edge came out onstage to help his one-time friend. Reminding Kurt his gold medal win *was* inspiring and uplifting, "...but most importantly, it was *six years ago!*" Edge offered Kurt a chance to get out of the past and

Hollywood Hulk Hogan challenges Triple H for the Undisputed title.

settle their own personal feud of late at *Backlash*. Having been the butt of Edge's jokes in recent weeks—including one particularly embarrassing moment where the backs of several oversized photographs he gave Angle to hold said things like "I have no testicles"—the gold medalist said it would be an honor to kick the ass of the "snot-nosed punk." Edge followed up with something he said Kurt didn't hear very often—"It's a date!"—then urged the fans to show their appreciation of everything Angle said by chanting, "You suck!"

While Angle seethed back in the locker room, Y2J offered to beat the hell out of Edge later that night; in exchange, he and Kurt would form a pact to watch each other's backs against Edge, Hogan and Triple H. Angle accepted Jericho's offer. If there was one thing he couldn't stand, it was "a loud-mouth Canadian with blond hair who dresses like a rock star!"...*except* for the Ayatollah of Rock and Rollah, of course.

The collaboration proved effective in the two weeks before the Pay-Per-View. Angle and Jericho first teamed up to give Y2J a cheap win over Edge, then later doubled up on The Game during his nontitle match with Angle. Hogan came down to make the save, despite Hunter's earlier warning that he didn't want help from anyone, *especially* the challenger to his title. After Hunter reiterated his position and Hogan turned away to leave the ring, Angle pushed Triple H into him. Thinking The Game had just sucker-punched him, Hogan retaliated with the big boot and legdrop, only then to be laid out by the real culprits responsible.

On the April 18 *SmackDown!*, Hogan and Triple H tried putting their differences aside for a Tag Team match against Jericho and Angle in Houston's Compaq Center. During the match, however, Hogan accidentally nailed the Cerebral Assassin with a chair intended for Angle. Edge came down and chased Kurt away while Hogan planted the legdrop on Jericho, but Hunter broke up the pinfall and connected with a steel chair on top of the Hulkster's skull! Holding his Undisputed Championship title over the unconscious Hogan, The Game was on at *Backlash!*

Before his Undisputed Championship match with Triple H at *Backlash*, Hollywood Hulk Hogan had already made five incredible journeys to the top of the mountain known as the WWE. Here's a recap on the history of *Hulkamania:*

JANUARY 23, 1984: *Hulkamania* is born in New York's Madison Square Garden. The sellout crowd roars as Hulk Hogan drops the leg on the Iron Sheik and captures the Heavyweight title, beginning a championship reign that lasts four years.

APRIL 2, 1989: The Mega-Powers explode at *WrestleMania V*, inside Atlantic City's Trump Plaza Hotel and Casino. But not even the madness of Champion Randy Savage can stop Hogan from "Hulking up" in front of 20,369 fans and reclaiming the title from the Macho Man. *Ooohh yeaahh, brother!*

MARCH 24, 1991: Patriotism runs wild in the wake of the Persian Gulf War, as 16,158 spectators inside the Los Angeles Sports Arena witness a bloodied Hulk Hogan defeat the traitorous Sgt. Slaughter. Bringing home the gold for the red, white and blue, the Hulkster lives up to his theme song and establishes himself as a "Real American!"

DECEMBER 3, 1991: Not even a Phenom like Undertaker can make *Hulkamania* rest in peace. In front of a sold-out crowd in San Antonio, Hulk Hogan "urns" his fourth championship at *Tuesday in Texas*. Hogan and Undertaker would next meet for the title at *Judgment Day*, over a decade later.

APRIL 4, 1993: Las Vegas' Caesars Palace hosts the world's largest toga party, and an event for the ages with *WrestleMania IX*. Despite an eye injury, Hulk Hogan hits the jackpot in his second match of the day, becoming champion for a record fifth time by overcoming the Sumo giant Yokozuna in a mere *twenty-three seconds!* It would be Hogan's final *WrestleMania* and title reign until April 2002. ■

HULK STILL RULES!

MAY 5

"I hope the dream never ends...that I never have to wake up to reality again. Every night, I turn on the news... and when I see what's going on in the world, reality sucks. When I'm in the ring, I'm in my own fantasy world, and I hope it never ends."
—Hollywood Hulk Hogan
Montreal's Molson Centre, May 16 *SmackDown!*

Passing "Judgment"

At *Backlash, Hulkamania* once again became the dominant force in World Wrestling Entertainment. But the Red Devil who played a hand in Hollywood Hulk Hogan's upset victory over Triple H sought to collect payment at the next WWE Pay-Per-View, *Judgment Day*...and his price was the Undisputed Championship.

Using a blown call by guest referee Ric Flair to steal the No. 1 Contender's spot from Stone Cold Steve Austin at *Backlash,* Undertaker then sabotaged The Game's title defense against Hogan. On the April 22 *Raw,* Undertaker promised the patrons inside St. Louis' Savvis Center he would become "judge, jury and executioner of *Hulkamania*" at *Judgment Day,* and take the coveted belt from an icon he considered past his prime. Hogan admitted he might not have defeated Triple H without Undertaker's uninvited assist, but cautioned the Phenom not to underestimate his *Hulkamaniacs*—

The Big Evil passes judgment on Hogan.

it was they who gave birth to the dream eighteen years ago, and they *would* run wild on him at *Judgment Day*!

Undertaker wasn't running—in fact, he made good on a promise to beat Hogan "like the bitch that you are" at the April 29 *Raw* in Buffalo's HSBC Arena, during the champ's nontitle match with William Regal. Using Hogan's own weight belt to lacerate his skull and choke him out, 'Taker then delivered a bone-crunching Choke-slam to punctuate his message!

The Dead Man failed to realize, however, that this *wasn't* the same Hogan he fought for the title at *Tuesday in Texas* eleven years ago.

ROAD TO INSURREXTION

World Wrestling Entertainment's second international tour in 2002 took the organization to Europe—specifically Germany, Scotland and England—May 1 to 4, concluding in Wembley, England, for the U.K. Pay-Per-View *Insurrextion*. The first leg took the WWE Superstars to Cologne, Germany, May 1. Ten thousand fans packed the Kolnarena to witness the Hardcore title switch from Steven Richards to Tommy Dreamer to Goldust to Steven Richards; they then saw Stone Cold Steve Austin drop the Stunner on Undertaker.

The following night in Glasgow's Scottish Exhibition & Convention Centre was the first live WWE event in Scotland in over a decade. Every member of the sell-out crowd of 8,316 cheered on Nature Boy Ric Flair as he latched the Figure-Four Leglock on William Regal to give himself and tag partner Triple H the win over the disgruntled Brit and the American Badass. It was on that night that Shawn Stasiak won Hardcore gold *twice*, in a Four-Man Championship match that also featured Crash Holly, Justin Credible and previous Champion Steven Richards, all of whom took the championship in a one-minute period before Richards escaped with the Hardcore title again.

Trish Stratus provided "Stratusfaction, Guaranteed" for nearly twelve thousand fans inside Birmingham, England's NEC Arena on May 3, as she delivered the Bulldog finisher that gave her and *extremely* Stratusfied tag partner Jerry "the King" Lawler the victory over Molly Holly and Mr. Perfect. The WWE then held its second annual "Eve of *Insurrextion*" Charity Dinner for the Make-A-Wish Foundation. Money was raised with the help of over three hundred of the WWE's sponsors, licensees and friends. By the time the May 4 PPV event in London came to its spectacular conclusion, the WWE had successfully made leaps and bounds in furthering international relations for years to come. ■

This Hogan had a mean streak that reared its ugly head on May 6 *Raw* at the Hartford Civic Center, where he ran over 'Taker's forty thousand-dollar bike with a semi! The irate Undertaker retaliated a week later by taking Hogan's bike for a ride inside Toronto's Air Canada Centre... with the Undisputed Champion hogtied to the back! Colliding into a stack of metal rods, Hogan writhed on the floor in agony, while a laughing Undertaker said he'd see him at *Judgment Day* in six days.

Limping down the *SmackDown!* ramp at the Molson Centre on May 16, the Hulkster was moved to tears by the crowd's thunderous chants of "Hogan! Hogan!" He thanked the Montreal fans for helping him realize dreams he hoped would never end, only to be interrupted by brand owner Mr. McMahon. Adding insult to Hogan's injuries, McMahon proclaimed, *"Hulkamania sucks!"*, and he explained what the icon's famous colors *really* stood for—"The red represents the blood you'll shed at *Judgment Day*, and the yellow represents the cowardly streak that runs down your back!"

Then Vince stupidly slapped Hogan, which sparked a fire in the Undisputed Champion that had dwindled on *Raw* earlier that week. Giving the *SmackDown!* owner *two* massive legdrops, Hogan decided that win or lose at the Pay-Per-View, *Hulkamania* would live forever!

McMahon's questionable decision-making might have been a result of his preoccupation with soon-to-be former son-in-law Triple H. Although now exclusive to *SmackDown!*, The Game showed up on the April 22 *Raw* looking for the Red Devil who cost him the title. The Cerebral Assassin busted Undertaker open with a TV monitor, then brutalized him backstage with a sledgehammer until St. Louis' Finest had no choice but to cart him away in handcuffs.

Triple H's arrest proved costly at the April 25 *SmackDown!*, when Mr. McMahon stopped Hogan from offering "a criminal" an Undisputed Championship rematch in Illinois' Peoria Civic Center. And since Hunter never offered a proper rematch to Chris Jericho after beating him for the title at *WrestleMania X8*,

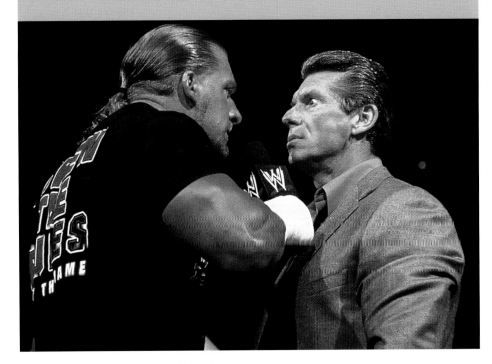

Triple H provokes the "wrinkled-up old man."

The incident prompted a swift response on the May 9 *SmackDown!* Accompanied by his "personal assistant" Stacy Keibler, Vince McMahon notified the sellout crowd at Connecticut's Arena in Harbor Yard that The Game would start playing by new rules, or "there's going to be hell to pay." Triple H confronted McMahon, asking, "Is *everything* that comes out of your mouth complete bullshit?" That included his threats, and how "a wrinkled-up old man with bad breath and a bad toupee" can satisfy a twenty-year-old Diva who's another Anna Nicole Smith, "waiting for the billionaire to kick the bucket so she can collect the cash! And if you get in my face anymore," he warned McMahon, "I'll *speed up* the process."

Vince decreed (in the interest of fairness, of course) the two Superstars compete for the opportunity to face Hogan on next week's *SmackDown!* Triple H would almost Pedigree his way to victory in their match, until Undertaker's sudden arrival enabled Y2J to roll Hunter up for the pin.

The Game and the Dead Man were scheduled to settle their differences at *Insurrextion,* the May 4 PPV at England's Wembley Arena, but Jericho worried their feud might erupt two days early, during his *SmackDown!* title contest with "Hollywood Hulk *Has-Been*" in Pittsburgh's Mellon Arena. Vince McMahon assured Y2J that any interference in the main event would be "career suicide" for Triple H or any unscheduled *Raw* wrestler.

Unfortunately for Jericho, the threat didn't stop Hunter from joining Michael Cole and Tazz on ringside commentary, nor did it prevent Undertaker's music from sounding minutes later, prompting an irate Jericho to look toward the entranceway. The latter interruption, however, was a diversion arranged by Triple H, one that allowed Hogan to schoolboy Y2J from behind for the one-two-three!

> "Is **everything** that comes out of your mouth complete bullshit?"

Hunter didn't get the chance—jumped and rendered helpless by Test, Christian, Lance Storm, Hardcore Holly and Reverend D-Von, he was busted open with a steel chair by Chris Jericho. As Y2J locked on the Walls of Jericho, McMahon screamed in Triple H's bloodied face that at *Judgment Day,* "you really *are* going to hell— *Hell in the Cell!"*

Meanwhile, Ric Flair's officiating screwups at *Backlash* had intensified his *personal* hell with Stone Cold Steve Austin on the following night's *Raw.* Explaining how the nWo's presence at an already

Wembley Arena
London, England

Triple H defeated **Undertaker** via pinfall

Stone Cold Steve Austin defeated **Big Show** via pinfall

EUROPEAN CHAMPIONSHIP MATCH

Spike Dudley defeated **William Regal** via pinfall to retain the European title

Hardy Boyz defeated **Shawn Stasiak & Brock Lesnar (w/Paul Heyman)** via pinfall

HARDCORE CHAMPIONSHIP MATCH

Booker T defeated **Steven Richards** via pinfall; **Crash Holly** defeated **Booker T** via pinfall; **Booker T** defeated **Crash Holly** via pinfall; **Steven Richards** defeated **Booker T** via pinfall to become Hardcore Champion

X-Pac defeated **Bradshaw** via pinfall

DIVAS TAG TEAM MATCH

Trish Stratus & Jacqueline defeated Women's Champion **Jazz & Molly Holly** via pinfall

INTERCONTINENTAL CHAMPIONSHIP MATCH

Rob Van Dam defeated **Eddie Guerrero** via disqualification; Guerrero retains the Intercontinental title

---

MAY 4, 2002

Insurrextion capped off what was truly a phenomenal European tour for World Wrestling Entertainment, and the sold-out Wembley Arena showed their appreciation as the uprising began! Rob Van Dam was out to reclaim the WWE Intercontinental title he lost to Eddie Guerrero at *Backlash* two weeks ago, but Latino Heat wasn't willing to give it up. RVD controlled the match early with moonsaults off the apron and top rope, until Guerrero focused on grounding Mr. Pay-Per-View. Van Dam soon regained momentum with a superkick and monkey flip from the corner, but a missed Five-Star Frog Splash worried Guerrero enough to bring his Intercontinental title into the ring. When the referee tried to stop him, Guerrero nailed him with the belt and drew a disqualification. Van Dam didn't walk out with the championship, but he cooled off Latino Heat moments later with a Five-Star on top of his belt!

Molly Holly declared to Terri backstage that she and Women's Champ Jazz would achieve "a victory for morality" against Trish Stratus and Jacqueline, and that the U.K. was full of "sleaze and trash" who'd look at such smut. Terri told her they had *two* problems...and *showed* them! Trish and Jacqueline showed them, too...but in the ring. With their *fists*. Virginlike Molly and Jazz (dubbed the "female Mike Tyson" by J.R.) practically double-teamed their way through the match, until Trish came in and broke up Jazz's half crab on Jacqueline. All four Divas were in the ring then, with Jacqueline and Trish delivering double the Stratusfaction, then getting a double pinfall for the win! As Jerry "the King" Lawler called it, a "victory for morality was now a victory for the puppies!"

X-Pac, twirling the Kane mask in hand, told nWo brother Scott Hall backstage that if he couldn't beat Bradshaw, "I'm never coming back to this lousy country again!" That said, the Wembley fans cheered louder as the big Texan pounded away at the "4-Lifer," until he rammed Bradshaw's head into an exposed turnbuckle, busting him open. Bradshaw recovered with pure power—a powerbomb from the corner, a powerslam to the canvas and a power clothesline from the top rope—but Hall's sudden arrival on the outside bought X-Pac time to catch Bradshaw with the low blow and X-Factor for the win.

The crowd gave Booker T a huge pop as he took on newly crowned Hardcore Champ Steven Richards and threw in the traditional Hardcore weapons from under the ring—trashcans, lids and whatnot—while Richards threw them *out* the other side. He didn't catch the serving tray until Booker served it across his head! The hard-fought contest was anyone's match until Booker caught Richards with a trashcan, then missile-dropkicked him from the top rope. Folding Richards up like an accordion with the Book End, Booker got the one-two-three and became the new Hardcore Champion! But he was too exhausted to kick out of a surprise rollup from Crash Holly, who utilized the 24/7 Hardcore rule and became the new champion. Crash thought about commemorating with a "Crash-a-Roonie" until Booker nailed him with the scissors kick and won the title again! Fending off a table attack from Tommy Dreamer and Justin Credible, Booker celebrated with the Spin-a-Roonie…until a low-blow from Jazz allowed Steven Richards to put him through the table and become the new Hardcore Champion!

Agent Paul Heyman didn't want Shawn Stasiak on Brock Lesnar's side when they took on the Hardy Boyz, so his instructions were specific: do *not* tag in. Leave it all to The Next Big Thing. Sure enough, Stasiak ran in to start the match, and Team Xtreme did a number on him, until Lesnar saved him from a Poetry in Motion and tagged himself in. Brock manhandled Matt, but when he missed a shoulder block into the ring post, Planet Stasiak heard the voices and tagged himself in. Moments later, Matt's Twist of Fate and Jeff's Swanton Bomb tagged him *out* for the three-count. Irate, Lesnar came back in and decimated the Hardyz with his swinging facebuster, then turned on his own partner and delivered a spinning powerbomb that sent Planet Stasiak into another orbit.

William Regal told the Coach that his own countrymen—"underachieving dossers with their divvy children"—disgusted him, but facing Spike Dudley in London would allow him to put the European Championship around his waist and provide "a ray of sunshine to their miserable lives." Too bad he wouldn't offer any relief for the runt of the Dudley litter, who turned his ankle and needed to be helped backstage. Regal instead threw Spike back in the ring and tortured him, choosing on some occasions not to pin him. Regal's arrogance cost him, however, when Spike surprised him with an inside cradle for the pinfall victory. Livid, the Brit pulled the brass knux from his trunks and "congratulated" the European Champ across the face, then left the ring.

Raw owner Ric Flair, wearing pinstripes to everyone's surprise, came out and thanked the audience in England for being such great fans. He declared himself "the second referee" on the outside, to ensure there'd be no nWo interference for Stone Cold's match with Big Show. Out came the Rattlesnake, who received a tremendous reaction from the "What?" chanters in the Wembley. Show played immovable object at first, but Austin soon proved an irresistible force that wouldn't be pushed around. The Bionic Redneck kept trying to take the giant's pins out from underneath, but Big Show wouldn't stay down, and continued to slap him around.

Finally mounting steady offense after a series of head-butts to Show's nose broke a bearhug, Stone Cold ducked a clothesline that took out the referee, then hit the Stunner on the big man. Suddenly, X-Pac and Hall ran down, preventing second referee Flair from finishing the three-count and forcing him to chase them backstage. Big Show recovered and caught Austin by the throat, then held him for nWo member Kevin Nash, who appeared from the crowd with a set of nunchucks. Austin caught him with a kick and the Stunner, then delivered two more on Big Show to keep him down for a three-count. Austin celebrated in the ring with some Steveweisers while Flair returned and tried joining in the celebration. But as both men downed a brewski, Austin downed the *Raw* owner with a Stunner!

Triple H gets pay back and the win.

Earlier in the evening, Undertaker told the "Coach" he intended to give opponent Triple H the same savage beating he'd given Undisputed Champion Hollywood Hulk Hogan on April 29 *Raw*. And if Hunter had thoughts of revenge against Big Evil for costing him the Undisputed title, "those thoughts…will *rest…in peace.*" Though The Game wasn't part of the *Raw* brand, he'd been granted special dispensation to face the Dead Man, and he wouldn't let it go to waste. The two exchanged fists from the onset, with Hunter in control early until the American Badass snapped his neck off the top rope, then followed with a painful legdrop off the ring apron.

Hunter whipped Undertaker into the ropes at such a velocity the top rope broke, but the Dead Man recovered quickly, and the two Superstars continued trading blows. The Cerebral Assassin gained momentum with two neck-breakers and a spinebuster, then lost it as Undertaker threw him into the corner where the top rope had broken. The Phenom next connected with a jarring Chokeslam, but was shocked when The Game kicked out. He brought in a chair to finish him off, though Hunter caught him square in the face with a kick to the steel. It looked like the match was over as 'Taker dropped Hunter onto the top turnbuckle, but Triple H recovered with a high knee to the Dead Man's face, then a Pedigree to grab the victory! Any further thoughts of *Insurrextion* on Undertaker's part would have to wait another day; for now, The Game continued on! ■

intense contender's match had gotten to him, then providing TitanTron footage that supported his claim of not seeing Austin's foot on the rope, Flair owned up, "I blew the call, and that's something I'll have to live with a long time." The Rattlesnake wasn't interested; he simply hissed, "When you screwed Stone Cold, you made the single biggest mistake of your life!" He then showed Flair some *personal* footage in the form of a middle finger!

Big Show's betrayal of Austin initiates him into the nWo.

Promising to make things right, Flair booked a match that night for Austin and Bradshaw to take on the nWo's Scott Hall and X-Pac. But when Bradshaw was later discovered unconscious backstage, the Nature Boy named Big Show as Stone Cold's new partner. It appeared to be a great plan until late in the match, when the seven-foot, two-inch, five hundred-pounder gave the Bionic Redneck a Show-stopping Chokeslam and established himself as the newest member of the New World Order!

The Buffalo crowd would hear "the story of a bald-headed SOB named Stone Cold," who demanded a match with the traitorous Big Show on April 29 *Raw*. Spinning his own yarn about Big Show being overseas on a promotional tour, Slick Ric booked Austin and Bradshaw against Hall and X-Pac instead, and appointed himself guest referee. Flair's officiating was like a page taken right out of *Backlash*, though this ending read better for Austin, who pinned X-Pac despite Hall putting his Stunned partner's foot on the rope before the three-count.

> **"When you screwed Stone Cold, you made the single biggest mistake of your life!"**

The story took a drastic turn at the May 6 *Raw* in Connecticut, in a Six-Man Tag Team match that pitted Flair, Bradshaw and Austin against Big Show, Hall and X-Pac. Hall had earlier warned of a surprise that would forever change the WWE, and several items Flair amassed—including the injured Kane's mask and an APA hat—suggested that Bradshaw had joined the nWo. But as the Rattlesnake executed a show-finishing Stunner, it was *Ric Flair* laying Austin out with a steel chair! Wrapping his signature Figure-Four Leglock around a helpless Austin, Flair declared he and Big Show had a date with Stone Cold in a Handicap match at *Judgment Day!*

In front of a hostile "What?"-chanting Toronto crowd on May 13, Flair explained how he tried being Austin's friend, "…but all I ever got for it were Stunners." Before he'd make Stone Cold bleed at the upcoming PPV, he put his *Raw* power to use that evening—first by dismissing Scott Hall for not getting the job done for the nWo, then by booking himself in a No DQ Championship match with Hollywood Hulk Hogan.

The two legends took it to one another in their match, with Bradshaw assisting Hogan at ringside against nWo interference. A low blow soon gave the dirtiest player in the game the upper hand, but his claim to the Undisputed Championship fell short when Stone Cold raced down and Stunned Flair, buying Hogan time to hit the legdrop and get the win.

A vengeful Flair first sanctioned Bradshaw to a Handicap match with X-Pac and Big Show, then ordered Austin to face a yet-to-be-named new member of the nWo in a Lumberjack match. Despite a good showing, Big Show's size and constant double-teaming would ultimately prove too much for Bradshaw. For the main event, handpicked lumberjacks like Goldust, Eddie Guerrero and Brock Lesnar would rough up Stone Cold at ringside while Flair named his new nWo member: Booker T! Amazingly, Stone Cold withstood Booker's scissors kick (*and* his Spin-a-Roonie) to score the one-two-three, but Arn Anderson's blindside attack on Austin would enforce an in-ring celebration that evening for Ric Flair and the nWo.

Although he took to the assignment very quickly, Booker T appeared genuinely surprised by his nWo nod at the Lumberjack match, as did Goldust. Booker's nomination disrupted what he thought was a potentially lethal weapon in the tag team circuit, as demonstrated in an impressive

Hollywood Hulk Hogan takes it to the Nature Boy.

Booker T finds Goldust's interest in him too weird for words.

Raw win on April 22 over Bubba Ray and Spike Dudley. But even during their first collaborative efforts—including an…*interesting* movie review where the Superstars inserted themselves into a scene from The Rock's hit film *The Scorpion King*—it was always clear the Bookerman thought they were too much of an odd couple, and that Goldust was a freak.

When his continued indecent proposals to work together cost Booker T several matches in the ensuing weeks, Goldust was forced to "disguise" himself and track his chosen one to a 7-Eleven in Hartford. Unfortunately, he also tarnished that reunion when he asked for a drink of Booker's Slurpee in exchange for a bite of his wiener! Booker went mental and said it was over between them…or so he'd think.

Rob Van Dam may have dropped his WWE Intercontinental Championship to Eddie Guerrero at *Backlash,* but the following night's *Raw* proved their rivalry was anything *but* over. Latino Heat had failed to burn RVD

in his match with Mr. Perfect, though he succeeded in provoking Van Dam on a new campaign to recapture the Intercontinental belt. Mr. Monday Night would earn an impressive, though ultimately disappointing DQ win over the new champ at *Insurrextion* on May 4, then tagged with Jeff Hardy two nights later in Hartford, putting the Five-Star Frog Splash on Guerrero and Booker T.

Latino Heat generated a semihot streak against other challengers to his title—he put Tommy Dreamer into Slumberland with a brain buster and Frog Splash on May 12 *Sunday Night Heat,* then took "Planet Stasiak" out of his orbit on the May 13 *Raw.* But it was after that latter contest when RVD's educated feet once again embarrassed the Champion. With thumbs pointed at himself, the "One of a Kind" wrestler then incited the Toronto crowd to remind Guerrero who he was facing at *Judgment Day;* "Rob! Van! Dam!"

Another vendetta that only intensified after *Backlash* was the one between Brock Lesnar and Hardy Boyz

Matt and Jeff. Matt went after The Next Big Thing on *Raw* April 22 to avenge Jeff's serious beating at the PPV, but Lesnar's vicious facebuster and power-bomb achieved the same results from a night earlier—Matt tasted canvas, and the ref called for the bell.

Lesnar pummeled space cadet Shawn Stasiak during the next two *Raw*s—though *tag teamed* with him between the beatings in a losing effort to the Hardyz at *Insurrextion*—before focusing on Jeff and Matt in a Handicap match on May 13. The former NCAA Champion dominated early, but Team Xtreme's Poetry in Motion worried manager Paul Heyman enough to break up a pin count and get his boy disqualified. Heyman demanded a rematch with the Hardyz at *Judgment Day,* and further sweetened the deal by saying *he'd* tag with Lesnar. Shutting Heyman's mouth in the ring was too good an opportunity to pass up, so Matt and Jeff gladly accepted.

Brock Lesnar makes easy work of Matt Hardy.

The Hardcore Championship's 24/7 rule often keeps things interesting around World Wrestling Entertainment…especially when it affects the status of other WWE titles. Women's Champion Jazz set her sights on Bubba Ray Dudley's Hardcore gold on the April 29 *Raw,* but it was Steven Richards who'd run in and nail the Bubba-Tough Superstar with some wood to win the belt! Jazz walked into the match, but ran off with a new champion who screamed like a girl, *"I'm hardcore! I'm hardcore!"*

Richards's and Dudley's title rematch in Hartford on May 6 came during Jazz's No Disqualification match with Trish Stratus for the *Women's* Championship. A Steven-kick ruined Trish's Women's title bid, but Dudley's Bubbabomb on Richards helped him win back Hardcore gold…for a few moments, anyway. Subsequent run-ins resulted in several seconds-long Hardcore reigns for Raven, Justin Credible, Crash…and *Trish,* who pinned Crash after Bubba nailed him with a garbage can! Her

Bubba goes hardcore on Steven Richards.

Gaylord Entertainment Center Nashville, TN

UNDISPUTED CHAMPIONSHIP MATCH

Undertaker defeated *Hollywood Hulk Hogan* via pinfall to win the Undisputed Title

TAG TEAM CHAMPIONSHIP MATCH

Rikishi & Rico defeated *Billy & Chuck* via pinfall to win the Tag Team titles

HELL IN THE CELL

Triple H defeated *Chris Jericho* via pinfall

HAIR VS. HAIR MATCH

Edge defeated *Kurt Angle* via pinfall

HANDICAP MATCH

Stone Cold Steve Austin defeated *Ric Flair & Big Show* via pinfall

Brock Lesnar & Paul Heyman defeated *Hardy Boyz* via pinfall

WOMEN'S CHAMPIONSHIP MATCH

Trish Stratus (w/Bubba Ray Dudley) defeated *Stacy Keibler (w/D-Von & Deacon Batista)* via pinfall to retain the Women's title

INTERCONTINENTAL CHAMPIONSHIP MATCH

Eddie Guerrero defeated *Rob Van Dam* via pinfall to retain the Intercontinental title

MAY 19, 2002

Judgment Day was indeed a day of reckoning for the WWE and its Superstars in the sold-out Gaylord Entertainment Center. And its repercussions were felt throughout the summer of 2002.

In a rematch of the Frog Splashes from last month's *Backlash*, Rob Van Dam was off to a flying start (as usual) with a split-legged moonsault off the top rope and a series of kicks that kept Intercontinental Champion Eddie Guerrero reeling. Focusing on Latino Heat's back, The Whole Dam Show unloaded his whole damn arsenal, including a painful surfboard submission and the Rolling Thunder. Crafty veteran Guerrero disrupted RVD's Five-Star Frog Splash attempt with a top-rope powerbomb from the corner, then sabotaged his own finisher by wasting too much time heading up and being cocky. Van Dam moved just as Latino Heat splashed down, though Guerrero followed suit after Mr. Pay-Per-View went Five-Star again. The match was ultimately decided not by aerial tactics, but through a common backslide pin and Guerrero's egregious use of the ropes for leverage.

SmackDown! owner Vince McMahon joined Reverend D-Von, Deacon Batista and Stacy Keibler in prayer backstage prior to her Women's title match against Champion Trish Stratus. Bubba Ray Dudley was in Trish's corner for ring support, though Trish wouldn't need help to handle Stacy. The champion's ring experience and a neckbreaker gave her an early advantage, while Stacy's trip to the outside floor gave Bubba a good laugh. Stacy responded with a slap to his face, and while the ref tried breaking up the outside action, Batista came in and slammed Trish to the canvas! Stacy could only produce a two-count from the cheap shot, but when Batista tried interfering again moments later, Trish hit him with a baseball slide, then found Stratusfaction in Bulldogging Stacy for the victory.

After the match, Bubba Ray and D-Von found themselves in the ring together for the first time since the Dudley Boyz were split up by the WWE Draft. A friendly moment between them was interrupted by a charging Batista, who Bubba quickly sent back outside. Without warning, D-Von attacked his own half-brother, and soon had Batista set up a table. Bubba fought them off until Batista nailed him with the steel collection box, and the holy men planted him through the table in an ungodly fashion.

It wasn't that much of a stretch for the Hardy Boyz to realize they wouldn't see much of Brock Lesnar's tag partner, Paul Heyman, in the ring. Their only chance was to keep double-teaming The Next Big Thing, and after taking their share of punishment, succeeded with a

Poetry in Motion that knocked Lesnar out of the ring. The Hardyz provided more "poetry" for Heyman, and almost scored the upset when Brock caught Matt off the top rope and tripped over his agent! But Lesnar quickly recovered, and after delivering the devastating side slam, allowed the anxious Heyman to cover Jeff for the one-two-three! The agent's unbeaten streak remains at one to this day.

During a backstage interview, new nWo member Booker T told Marc Loyd he was a professional who was down with being part of the faction…and he was up for getting to know the hottie standing nearby. Asking her if she wanted his autograph, the Book was very excited when she gave him a card and said she had a special place for him to sign.

Earlier that evening, Vince had visited Raw owner Ric Flair's office, where he shook hands with Arn Anderson, then the Nature Boy himself. Their feud seemingly ended now (though neither man obviously liked hugging each other moments later), Flair told Vince he and Big Show were going to get "no-good son of a bitch" Stone Cold Steve Austin "under control" in their Handicap match. Easier said than done—before the match even officially started, both men had a hard time ganging on the Rattlesnake, made more difficult when Stone Cold put a Figure-Four on Show first, then Flair himself! With Flair's instruction, the five hundred-pounder dropped himself directly on top of Austin's legs, setting him up for the Nature Boy's Figure-Four. Austin countered at first with an inside cradle, then reversed a second attempt before Show broke it up. Stone Cold paid him back with a second-rope Lou Thesz Press moments later, then nailed Flair with a spinebuster. The giant grabbed Austin by the neck, only to get downed first by a Stunner, then by X-Pac, who ran down from backstage and nailed him with a kick intended for the Rattlesnake. Stone Cold then Stunned X-Pac and Flair, pinning the Raw owner for the win.

More than pride was at stake as Edge and Kurt Angle locked up for their "Hair vs. Hair" match, with a barber's chair sitting by the stage in wait for the loser. Much like last month's Backlash confrontation, both men pulled out all the stops, unveiling virtually every move they had at their disposal. The Gold Medalist tried wearing his adversary down, until Edge belly-to-belly-suplexed him and followed up with an aerial assault, including a top-rope plancha to the outside floor and a missile dropkick off the ropes. Edge soon went for a spear, but nailed the ref as Kurt dodged it. Angle soon delivered one of his own, then followed up with the Angle Slam and an ankle lock. Edge countered with an Enziguri, but Kurt went back and slapped it on again. Unable to reach the ropes, Edge surprised the medalist by shoving him into them

and rolling him up for the one-two-three! Angle, refusing to let himself be shaved bald, attacked Edge after the match, barely escaping the barber's chair and going on the run backstage a while, until he Hardcored Edge with a trashcan lid. Angle promised the fans would see "a freakin' haircut" as he dragged the young Superstar to the barber's chair, but Edge fought back, countering an Angle Slam with a sleeper hold that put Kurt out, making it that much easier to cut off all his hair. Edge then introduced a new chant for the fans to sing to Kurt, changing "You suck!" to "You're bald!"

Meanwhile, Booker T was looking to score a win of his own, with the lady he met earlier. The two hooked up in a hotel room, where the woman wanted to engage in some high-risk maneuvers in the dark. The lights went out, and Booker heard sweet nothings like "Leave the nWo, and return to Goldust." The Bizarre One had climbed into bed with the Book, and he was asking him to do the same! A very freaked out—and turned off—Booker left the room.

Next up was a game even The Game didn't look forward to, as he and Chris Jericho entered two tons of steel and were locked into "Hell in the Cell." Hunter's prior "hell" experience gave him the early advantage on the outside floor, tossing Jericho into the Cell structure repeatedly. Y2J, his arm bleeding, avoided a piledriver onto the ring steps by slingshotting the Cerebral Assassin into the Cell. Jericho then bloodied Triple H's face, alternating between a ladder he grabbed from underneath the ring and the cage, until Hunter retaliated with a chair shot that knocked the ladder into Y2J. Jericho soon brought the ring steps into the ring, but the Cerebral Assassin front-toehelded him into the steps face first. Charging toward Hunter, Y2J missed and blasted referee Tim White into the cage, knocking him unconscious. Frustrated that White couldn't count a pinfall attempt on Triple H moments later, Jericho took the downed ref and busted him open on the cage.

While WWE officials used a bolt cutter on the Cell lock to rescue White, The Game kicked a chair into Y2J's face, then produced his sledghammer from under the ring and smashed it into Jericho's face. Slowly exiting the Cell, a crimson-masked Y2J bounced Triple H's head off the Spanish announcer's table, then tried for a Pedigree on top of it, but The Game reversed the move into a DDT that sent both of them crashing through the table! Y2J recovered quicker than even he expected, climbing up the Cell as Triple H reached under the other announcer's table and produced a barbwire two-by-four! Hunter brought it with him as he climbed up after Jericho, who grabbed the weapon as he reached the top and nailed the Cerebral Assassin's back several times. An official climbed up top while Jericho hooked The Game in the

Jericho suffers the painful reality of Hell in the Cell.

Walls of Jericho. Hunter threw him off, then landed the low blow as Y2J again grabbed the two-by-four. Following a failed Pedigree attempt, Triple H used the weapon to soften Jericho up as he hit his finisher on top of the Cell, and won the hellacious battle.

Billy and Chuck had no idea who Rikishi's mystery partner was for their Tag Team title defense, though neither did the Phat Man, thanks to the stipulations Mr. McMahon set last week on *SmackDown!* It was no wonder all of them would be surprised to discover it was the champs' stylist, Rico! Realizing it was Vince's revenge for catching a Stinkface in December 2001, Rikishi was on his own, but held his own until Billy and Chuck's double-teaming eventually overwhelmed him. The Phat Man appeared about done as Chuck held him for Rico, who inadvertently nailed Chuck after Rikishi ducked the shot. Knocking his partner down, Rikishi pinned Chuck and got the three, making him one half of the new Tag Team Champions. The other half, meanwhile, took his belt as he headed to the back with the beaten tandem.

Undertaker was looking to trade the Hulkster's weight belt in for the Undisputed title that night, but first he'd use it to beat Hollywood Hulk Hogan as he entered the ring for their championship match. Hogan grabbed the belt and returned the favor before the referee finally discarded it and officially started the contest. The icon controlled early with a backdrop and clothesline that sent the Dead Man to the outside floor, then later crotched 'Taker and his "old school" top-rope assault with a superplex from the top. Kicking out of a two-count, the Red Devil focused his attack on Hogan's left knee. Hogan powered out of a submission hold with his good wheel, then hit 'Taker with a double sledgehammer and the big boot. The Hulkster went for the win with the legdrop, but the Phenom blocked it and countered into a half crab.

Reaching the ropes eventually broke the hold, though Big Evil soon almost broke Hogan with a massive Chokeslam to the mat. Suddenly, the power of the *Hulkamaniacs* started surging within Hogan, who kicked out at two and Hulked up! The Hulkster made with the right hands and big boot, then hit the legdrop for the surefire victory… until Undertaker kicked out at two! Shocked, Hogan went for a backdrop, but the American Badass scored a DDT, then grabbed a steel chair while *SmackDown!* owner Vince McMahon started his way down ringside. Hogan kicked the chair in 'Taker's face and nailed another legdrop, but Vince's distraction of the referee prompted him to drag the billionaire into the ring and share the wealth. Hitting a legdrop on McMahon, though satisfying, proved costly, as Undertaker laid Hogan out with a chair shot while the official attended to Vince. The Dead Man then Chokeslammed Hogan in the middle of the ring, and got the three-count to become the new Undisputed Champion! And to celebrate, Undertaker took the steel chair and rammed it into Hogan's throat, then used it to beat on the fallen ex-champion. Hollywood Hulk Hogan had been judged, and sentenced. ■

Stratus recaptures the Women's title from Jazz.

title claim lasted the longest of the lot, until Bubba—blinded by Jazz with a fire extinguisher—powerbombed Trish through a table, thinking it was the *Women's* Champ!

[**"I'm hardcore! I'm hardcore!"**]

Steven Richards took advantage of the situation, pinning the lovely Diva to regain the Hardcore belt.

Fortunately, the debacle between Trish and Bubba Ray sparked a strong alliance, and the two paired up on May 13 for an Intergender match that put Jazz and Richards's respective championships up for grabs. Despite more outside interference from Justin Credible and Crash, Bubba fended off Richards while Trish guaranteed Stratusfaction on Jazz to win the Women's title in front of her hometown Toronto crowd! To add to the celebration, Bubba gave the ex-Women's Champ a taste of his wood by putting her through a table!

Montreal's Molson Centre fans certainly enjoyed the new "Stratus status" at the May 16 *SmackDown!*, especially since Tajiri prevented Torrie Wilson's participation in

LOU THESZ

In Memoriam 1916-2002

Lou Thesz was wrestling personified, a Superstar long before the term was ever associated with the business. From the moment he defeated Everett Marshall for his first National Wrestling Association title on December 29, 1937, to the end of his sixth and final NWA Championship at the hands of Gene Kiniski on January 7, 1966, Thesz's accomplishments and contributions to wrestling could fill dozens of squared circles. Defeating Wild Bill Longson on July 20, 1948 began a nearly eight-year reign where Thesz unified the National Wrestling Association title with Championships from other promotions, most notably, the National Wrestling Alliance (NWA) title.

Honored for his achievements with a Lifetime Achievement Award from World Wrestling Entertainment during *In Your House: Badd Blood* 1997, Thesz passed away of complications from open-heart surgery on April 28, 2002. He continues to be honored, however, and missed whenever a WWE Superstar launches himself onto an opponent with a Lou Thesz Press. ∎

a swimsuit competition against Stacy Keibler. The crowd even forgave Torrie's "replacement" for wearing red hot lingerie in place of the bikini she'd forgotten! Stacy also saw red...first from anger that Trish stole her heat, then from embarrassment after the Women's Champ dumped her to the outside floor on her derriere!

Stacy whined her way backstage to Mr. McMahon, who'd console his personal assistant with a title shot against Trish at *Judgment Day*...provided she accepted the contribution services of Reverend D-Von and his new, truly biggest follower, Deacon Batista. The Reverend defeated Triple H in Bridgeport a week ago (with some outside contributions from Y2J, Batista and a steel collection box), and donated one in the "loss" column to Maven earlier in the evening. If Trish had new friend Bubba Ray in her corner at the PPV, Vince wanted Bubba's half brother there to provide protection and offer up a "Saving Grace!"

The virtuous Molly Holly didn't seem to need any kind of protection, though the relationship she started developing with William Regal only reaffirms that *anything* can happen in the WWE! Despite his European title bid falling short at *Insurrextion,* Regal

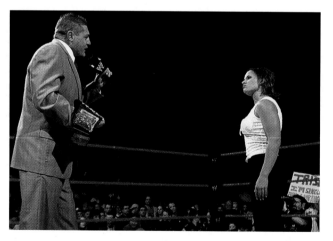

Regal finds virtue in Molly Holly.

would exploit the severe ankle sprain Spike Dudley suffered at the England PPV to declare himself "the greatest European Champion of all time" two nights later on *Raw.* At the May 13 broadcast in Toronto, he'd disclose his gentleman's intentions to Spike's one-time fiancée Molly, who successfully defended her virginal senses against the thong-wearing Terri for the second time in as many weeks. Expressing how nice it was "to find a lady who can make a name for herself in a way other than hiking up her skirt or showing her bosom," Regal requested the honor of escorting her up the ramp, and Molly accepted.

Molly and Regal's new relationship was indeed *Raw,* but there were plenty of kisses to heat things up on *SmackDown!* Stacy Keibler and Mr. McMahon were all kissy-face backstage during the broadcasts, but her advances toward Vince's "can't-miss" prospect Randy Orton, son of wrestling legend Cowboy Bob Orton, was almost a kiss of death for the third-generation Superstar. During the April 25 *SmackDown!,* Stacy falsely accused Orton of hitting on her, so Vince punished the youngster with a tryout match against Hardcore Holly. But the youngster

Orton's *SmackDown!* debut is painful for Hardcore Holly.

Maven eats an elbow from Billy Gunn.

shocked everyone in the Peoria Centre, especially Holly, when he executed a drop-toehold and rollup for the victory!

Upset over the "upset," Holly demanded a rematch on the May 2 *SmackDown!* and, once again frustrated when he couldn't pin Orton, got himself disqualified after low-blowing the rookie and nailing him with a Hardcore Alabama Slam onto the steel stage. Trading in trunks for pinstripes, Holly guest-officiated Orton's match with Lance Storm on May 9, and made sure the youngster tapped out when Storm cinched on a half Boston crab. A save by Big Valbowski set the sides for a tag match in Montreal the following week, where Orton would pull off another upset, this time rolling up Storm for the three-count.

At the May 9 *SmackDown!*, Torrie Wilson gave boyfriend and WWE Cruiserweight Champion Tajiri a well-deserved kiss-*off* during his nontitle bout with The Hurricane. Tired of his demeaning attitude, Torrie got up on the announcer's table and ditched her humbling geisha outfit, revealing herself in a neon blue bra and panties! Driven to distraction outside the ring, Tajiri

lost his match via countout, then lost his girl as the Diva walked out of the HarborYard Arena feeling truly liberated. As for Hurricane, breezing past Tajiri earned him a spot in the Triple-Threat match for the Cruiserweight Championship on May 16. There, the hero would rise above both Tajiri and Billy Kidman at the Molson Centre, where his Chokeslam on the Buzzsaw allowed him to kiss Cruiserweight immortality.

The *Tough Enough* tandem of Al Snow and Maven continued to peck at Billy and Chuck's WWE Tag Team title—starting with their shorts after pantsing the thong-wearing duo on April 25—while Rikishi's Stinkface would bare down on the champs' stylist/manager Rico Costantino in Pittsburgh's Mellon Arena. Despite regaining some dignity with a Six-Man Tag Team win at the May 9 *SmackDown!* in Bridgeport, the threesome lost it in Montreal the following week, when the Phat Man weighed in with a sit-down splash on Rico and embarrassed Billy and Chuck for good measure. Ashamed that they'd allow themselves to be manhandled, *SmackDown!* owner Mr. McMahon told Billy and Chuck they'd have to put their Tag Team belts up at *Judgment*

Day against Rikishi and a partner of Vince's choosing. Little did they or Rico know at the time that Rikishi might have all three men kissing his ass at the PPV, figuratively *and* literally!

With betting men like Test and Christian continuing to pay dearly for their lip service toward Faarooq and Mark Henry, Reverend D-Von decided it wise for the two Superstars to cleanse themselves and donate their vile winnings to the "United D-Von Building Fund" during the May 2 *SmackDown!* Henry's charitable advice to D-Von was "to testify your ass out" of the Mellon Arena locker room before the World's Strongest Man did "something sinful" with the collection plate. D-Von contributed to the tag duo's loss to Test and Christian later that night, distracting Henry from the ring while Christian planted Faarooq with an inverted DDT. Test would collect additional payback in his match with Henry on May 9, hitting the big man low and flooring him with a big boot.

Surprisingly, no one was placing any bets on what transpired between Kurt Angle and Edge up to *Judgment Day.* During the April 25 *SmackDown!*, Angle was about to lift off a canvas and introduce the "morbidly obese" Peoria Centre crowd to his new T-shirt. Kurt assured that wearing the shirt (available only in XXL or larger so he could fit all of his accomplishments on the back) "will give you a feeling you've never had before—you'll feel like *winners.*" Not realizing Edge had earlier switched the shirt for a different one backstage, he became understandably teed off after unveiling a shirt that said "You Suck." Kurt teamed with Albert later that night to defeat Edge and Rikishi, but his attempts to fit Edge into a body cast backfired when the Superstar kicked a tailor-made chair shot back in Angle's direction.

> "Take the money you normally spend on beer and porno and put it to *good* use."

As Lance Storm modeled Kurt's new T-shirt at the May 2 *SmackDown!*, Angle told his hometown Pittsburgh fans, "Take the money you normally spend on beer and porno and put it to *good* use." Edge then

Edge has secretly replaced Angle's new shirt.

Lita's quest for WWE Women's Championship gold was sidelined on April 6, when she sustained a broken neck while rehearsing her own stunts for her role in the series finale of the Fox television series *Dark Angel*. The injury wouldn't be accurately diagnosed for another three weeks, when Stone Cold Steve Austin recommended the former Women's Champion contact Dr. Lloyd Youngblood, a San Antonio, Texas-based surgeon who operated on the Rattlesnake's neck injury in 1999. Upon visiting Youngblood, the Diva underwent successful neck surgery on April 30, when the surgeon used a bone from her hip to fuse her C5 and C6 vertebrae.

Although the injury resulted in her missing a year in the ring, Lita is expected to make a one hundred percent full recovery. She's scheduled back in the squared circle mid 2003, though she continues her WWE duties with numerous promotions, events and charities, and is currently cohosting with Jonathan Coachman on MTV's *Sunday Night Heat*. ■

came out to inform the Mellon Arena crowd of "a better T-shirt" and presented Big Valbowski sporting Kurt's "You Suck" T-shirt, complete with Angle's entrance music!

It was the last straw for Angle, who issued a challenge: the two Superstars would meet once again at *Judgment Day*, and if Edge lost, he'd have his head shaved! Edge agreed to the bet, provided Kurt would do the same if *he* lost. When Kurt hesitantly acquiesced, Edge told him to be prepared—at *Judgment Day*, the gold medalist would be "red, white and *bald*."

> "Be prepared—
> at *Judgment Day* [you'll]
> be red, white and *bald*."

The Hair vs. Hair match was scheduled for the PPV, but the head games would start on the May 9 *SmackDown!* in Bridgeport. Angle used the Trons to show the HarborYard audience what his "weisenheimer" opponent would look like after *Judgment Day*. The sight of an eggheaded Edge made Kurt grin, though his leer turned to a sneer when the next screen shot was of a hairless gold medalist!

Angle called Edge out, though it was Hollywood Hulk Hogan who answered. Pointing out that "Superstar" Billy Graham, Stone Cold Steve Austin and the Hulkster "represent some of the greatest champions the industry has ever seen," Hogan warned Kurt, "If Edge doesn't get you at *Judgment Day*, Mother Nature will!", and rubbed the top of his head! Angle talked trash at the Undisputed Champion, even after the icon's big boot knocked him to the outside floor, until Edge finally silenced him with a spear at the top of the stage.

It was obvious from his interaction with Hogan in the locker room that Edge was thrilled about teaming with his boyhood idol against Angle and Chris Jericho. He might have thought otherwise had he known a sledgehammer-wielding Triple H, brutalized earlier in the evening by Jericho and McMahon, would return to ringside and lay everyone out with his equalizer. Edge confronted Hunter about the incident on May 16 *SmackDown!*, and told him that even though he was ready to shave Kurt Angle bald at Sunday's PPV, "I've a feeling in my stomach...*I want to play The Game.*"

The two Superstars started trading punches when they were suddenly jumped by Jericho and Angle, with Kurt cutting off a lock of Edge's hair. Agreeing to put their differences aside, Triple H and Edge faced their attackers later that evening in a Tag match that quickly grew out of hand. Y2J and The Game's

Jericho just misses Hunter with the Lionsault.

tussle knocked out the ref before spilling out into the Molson Centre crowd, while Kurt tossed a steel chair that connected with Edge's head, then hit a second Angle Slam for the victory. Holding up the lock of hair he'd cut from Edge earlier, the gold medalist was ready for his "mane" event at *Judgment Day*!

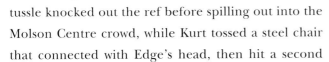

EDGE

HEIGHT: **6'4"**
WEIGHT: **240 lbs.**
FINISHING MOVE: **Edgecution**
CAREER HIGHLIGHTS: **Tag Team Champion (9); Intercontinental Champion (4); WCW U.S. Champion**
2002 HIGHLIGHTS: **Defeating Booker T in hometown Toronto at *WrestleMania X8*; shaving Kurt Angle bald after winning Hair vs. Hair match at *Judgment Day*; winning his eighth Tag Team Championship with Hollywood Hulk Hogan at July 4 *SmackDown!*; winning the WWE Tag Team Championship with Rey Mysterio at November 7 *SmackDown!***

6

JUNE

The Next Big "King"

William Shakespeare's *King Richard III* said it best, "The king's name is a tower of strength." Strength means respect, which a king demands of all his subjects. *Earning* respect in the WWE is precisely why its Superstars endure the grueling tournament that is *King of the Ring*.

KOR's ten-year history actually began on March 27, 1988, when Randy "Macho Man" Savage beat the odds—and four opponents—in Atlantic City's Trump Plaza to win the WWE Championship at *WrestleMania IV*. The tournament remained a fixture throughout WWE house shows for years before earning its own PPV slot in 1993, when Bret "Hitman" Hart went through Razor Ramon, Mr. Perfect and Bam Bam Bigelow to become the crown's inaugural wearer. Stone Cold Steve Austin emerged a King of near-biblical proportions in 1996 in response to comments from finalist Jake "The Snake" Roberts—"You talk about your psalms, talk about John 3:16...*Austin 3:16* says I just *whipped your ass!*" Coveting the crown a year later was Triple H, the only Superstar to date who's won the *Royal Rumble* and WWE, Intercontinental, Tag Team and European Championships. And after an unparalleled rookie campaign that included winning

the *KOR 2000*, Kurt Angle became the first Superstar to reach the finals in consecutive years, only to fall to new King Edge in 2001.

Using a bracketing style akin to the NCAA or World Cup tournaments, the *King of the Ring 2002* offered a field of sixteen Superstars between *Raw* and *Smack-Down!*, with the winner of each match advancing until only four finalists remained to meet at the Pay-Per-View. This year's final four, however, would be offered extra incentive for winning it all: an automatic title shot at *SummerSlam* for the WWE Undisputed Championship, the crowning achievement in professional wrestling.

KOR tournament rounds often play a greater role for its participants beyond advancing to the finals. For Goldust and X-Pac, a first-round victory determined membership within the New World Order, which was "all shook up" on May 20

Booker T shows the European Champion the American plan—whooping his butt.

Raw by an Elvis-garbed Goldust's involvement in *two* nWo losses to the Hardy Boyz, as well as by the return of Kevin Nash. Big Sexy's "win or go home" brand of leadership would soon offer Booker T's "freaky-deeky Oreo cookie" associate a chance to add color to the Black and White, provided he could beat X-Pac in their June 3 *KOR* qualifier. The golden opportunity almost turned into *Raw* reality as Goldust used X-Pac's own Bronco Buster to ride roughshod in Dallas' American Airlines Arena, until a low blow and X-Factor suddenly left the Golden One with shattered dreams, eliminating him from both the tournament and nWo consideration.

Prior to the next June 3 qualifying match, WWE European Champion William Regal told interviewer Jonathan Coachman no one was better suited to royalty than he, though he didn't think nWo opponent Booker T could even *spell* "king." Interrupting, the Bookerman replied, "My boy, G.W. [George Washington], couldn't spell 'king,' either, 'cause he was to busy choppin' down cherry trees and kickin' *your* king's ass in the Revolutionary War—*suckkaaaaa!*" Booker soon crowned Regal with his own European belt to win the match, then raised the roof with a revolution the fans *wanted* to see—the Spin-a-Roonie!

Big Valbowski looked good while advancing past his first-round contest at the June 6 *SmackDown!*, countering Christian's Unprettier with a swing-out powerbomb. Sadly, a brutal May 30 Cage match with Kurt Angle had left *King of the Ring 2001* Edge with a severe shoulder injury, and the unattractive notion of surgery forced him to forfeit his qualifying match. The announcement disappointed not only the Edgeheads inside Oklahoma City's Cox Convention Center, but opponent Chris Jericho as well—the "King of the World" wanted to kick Edge's ass and prove he was also King of the Ring. Instead, Y2J settled for tearing off Edge's sling and smashing the injured arm first into the ring post, then across the steel steps with a chair, until Valbowski dashed down for the save.

Rob Van Dam's June 10 preliminary against Eddie Guerrero promised plenty of heat, Latino and otherwise, following their spectacular Ladder match for the Intercontinental Championship in Edmonton's SkyReach Centre on May 27. High-flying maneuvers, moonsaults, Frog Splashes, and ladder and chairs as weapons made that main-event bout one of *Raw*'s best in 2002, with Mr. Monday Night ultimately climbing the top rung to recapture the Intercontinental belt. Neither competitor had lost a step during their *KOR* qualifying match in Atlanta's Philips Arena, though RVD's educated feet gave way to a heads-up roll-through of Guerrero's Hurracanrana for the one-two-three.

Perhaps most interesting about the June 10 qualifier was what occurred on *Raw* the week *before:* Van Dam, set to partner with Bubba Ray Dudley against Guerrero and Brock Lesnar, was interrupted by Paul Heyman during a prematch interview with the Coach. Heyman looked to provide inclement weather for "the Summer of RVD" with a face-to-face introduction to The Next Big Thing, then later grounded an RVD aerial assault that set up Lesnar and Guerrero finishers for the win. Neither Van Dam nor Lesnar realized it at the time, but the encounter was a sign of things to come at *King of the Ring,* and a prelude to one of the summer's hottest feuds in the WWE.

That said, Lesnar and Dudley didn't need any heat to fire up their own *Raw* feud that started back on May 20, after Bubba defended Trish Stratus from the lecherous advances of agent Paul Heyman and The Next Big Thing. Lesnar, in return, sabotaged Dudley's shot at

William Regal's European title later in the show, and registered a "W" with his facebuster finisher, the "F-5" (the designated classification for the most powerful of tornadoes), in Edmonton the following week. Dudley proved especially Bubba-Tough during their *Raw* qualifying match on June 10, but Heyman's interference powered the F-5 to again blow through Dudleyville (not to mention the Philips Arena), and move Lesnar forward in the tourney.

Test feels the power of The Hurricane.

Still riding high from his May 30 upset over Triple H (via an assist from Undertaker), Test weathered a somewhat scattered Hurricane in their June 13 *SmackDown!* qualifying match. A stretch of ominous notes had baffled the Cruiserweight Champion before his mystery stalker revealed herself on June 6 as *Tough Enough* Women's Champion Nidia, a tempestuous "Hurribitch" with whom the hero had a whirlwind

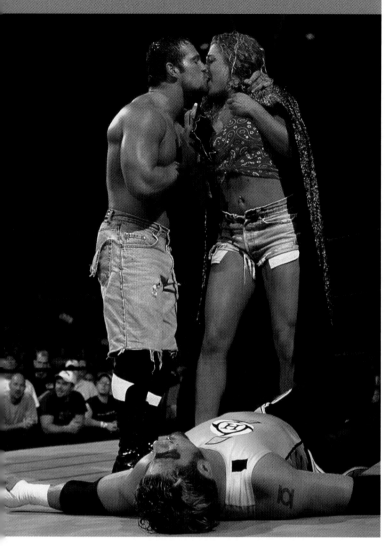

Sweethearts Noble and Nidia celebrate over the fallen hero.

Enough 2 trainer had suffered a rough June 6 loss to Kurt Angle, who felt Holly "screwed" him out of winning that night's Twenty-Man Battle Royal to establish the Undisputed Champion's opponent at the PPV. Meanwhile, a week after helping Christian defeat Torrie Wilson's new beau Maven in a May 30 *SmackDown!* bout that resulted in a broken fibula for the *Tough Enough* Men's Champion, the resentful Japanese Buzzsaw played doctor and administered painful physical therapy upon finding his ex-girlfriend elevating the rookie's leg (among other things) in a hospital bed. Holly was no helpless greenhorn, though—despite a kick to the head and being roped into Tajiri's gut-wrenching Tarantula maneuver, he'd rebound with an Alabama Slam that drove him into the next round.

The Black and White seemed complete after Kevin Nash announced the New World Order's latest recruit at the June 3 *Raw:* the king of WWE "Attitude," Shawn Michaels! Sadly, Shawn revealed a bitter disposition the following week in Atlanta's Philips Arena, reaffirming his June 1 *WWE Confidential* comments that "The Heartbreak Kid" was dead. Michaels explained how he'd literally broken his back for the WWE, only for the fans to steer the company's "promotional machine" from

> **"It was *you,* the fans, who *dumped* me for Stone Cold Steve Austin like a cheap nickel-and-dime prostitute runs to a millionaire!"**

romance. Following a "Test Drive" to the canvas that advanced the big man to the quarterfinals, Nidia and new boyfriend Jamie Noble berated the fallen champion in front of Greenville's BI-LO Center audience, taking the cape and mask that concealed his "secret" identity as Gregory Helms. But moments after Noble's June 20 *SmackDown!* win over Billy Kidman earned him a Cruiserweight Championship match at *King of the Ring,* the eye of The Hurricane plunged Sacramento's Arco Arena into darkness before chokeslamming his antagonist to the mat and recovering his stolen property!

Final *KOR* entrants Hardcore Holly and Tajiri were suffering from their own distractions of late. The *Tough*

HBK over to "3:16" at *WrestleMania XIV.* "As Vince McMahon always said, 'It's *you,* the fans, who determine where we go as an organization.' So it was *you,* the fans, who *dumped* me for Stone Cold Steve Austin like a cheap nickel-and-dime prostitute runs to a millionaire!" Michaels called Nash, Booker T, X-Pac and Big Show out to the ring to address a similar problem that existed within the nWo...then superkicked the Book with some Sweet Chin Music! Accusing the floored Booker of upstaging the Black and White like Austin had done to him, Michaels swore, "*Nobody* will ever steal the spotlight of the nWo again!"

Shawn Michaels's return is a Black and White issue.

Booker was gone from the nWo, but his Book End on X-Pac at the June 17 quarterfinal would not be forgotten by the group, especially since it enabled Rob Van Dam to hit the Five-Star Frog Splash and proceed to the *KOR* semifinals. Unfortunately, neither backstage preparation from a medievally garbed "Duke of Gold," nor the backstage tension Paul Heyman created by

warning the nWo away from ringside, would prevent Brock Lesnar from closing the Book on his opponent's *King*-ly quest. Nor would it stop the Black and White from celebrating Booker's loss with Big Showstoppers for him and Goldust!

The June 20 *SmackDown!* rounded off the *KOR* "final four" at Sacramento's Arco Arena, where Chris Jericho proved "larger than life" in his quarterfinal, countering a powerbomb into the Walls of Jericho that left Big Valbowski no choice but to tap out. Neither Hardcore Holly nor Test had "any quit" in their match, in which Hardcore lived up to his moniker by kicking out of a crushing pumphandle slam. But a simple yet effective big boot to the face gave the final *KOR* spot to Holly's opponent, who told Marc Loyd afterward that after beating Brock Lesnar at the June 24 PPV, "Test is going to be 'The *New* Big Thing'!"

Rob Van Dam. Brock Lesnar. Chris Jericho. Test. Only one would rise as the King of the Ring and challenge the Undisputed Champion at *SummerSlam*.

But *SummerSlam* was months away, and there's no such animal as "status quo" in World Wrestling Entertainment. Undertaker proved that at *Judgment Day*, rising past *Hulkamania* and becoming Undisputed Champion, a kingly station he felt made it his right to open the May 20 *Raw*. The Red Devil exercised that right by beating the hell out of Rob Van Dam with the ringside steps, then inform-

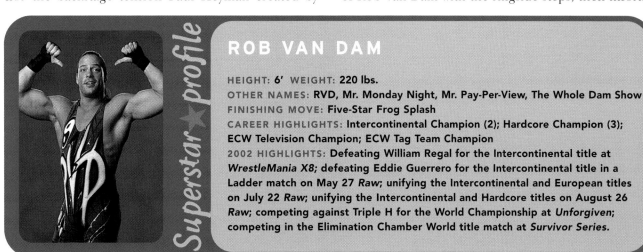

Superstar ★ profile

ROB VAN DAM

HEIGHT: 6′ WEIGHT: 220 lbs.
OTHER NAMES: RVD, Mr. Monday Night, Mr. Pay-Per-View, The Whole Dam Show
FINISHING MOVE: Five-Star Frog Splash
CAREER HIGHLIGHTS: Intercontinental Champion (2); Hardcore Champion (3); ECW Television Champion; ECW Tag Team Champion
2002 HIGHLIGHTS: Defeating William Regal for the Intercontinental title at *WrestleMania X8*; defeating Eddie Guerrero for the Intercontinental title in a Ladder match on May 27 *Raw*; unifying the Intercontinental and European titles on July 22 *Raw*; unifying the Intercontinental and Hardcore titles on August 26 *Raw*; competing against Triple H for the World Championship at *Unforgiven*; competing in the Elimination Chamber World title match at *Survivor Series*.

Undertaker breaks out the soup bones for Randy Orton.

ing the Pyramid crowd in Nashville, Tennessee, it was time to reacquaint everyone "with the number one rule in this company: You *will* respect Undertaker."

A crimsoned Van Dam defied the American Badass (and gravity) with a Five-Star Frog Splash, prompting 'Taker's first—and almost only—title defense later that evening. Mr. Monday Night's spinning heel kick and Rolling Thunder scored the three-count while Undertaker's foot on the rope went unseen by the referee. But when *Raw* owner Ric Flair—himself an expert on blown officiating calls—came down to rectify the error and restart the match, Big Evil capitalized on the confusion, flooring RVD with a Last Ride for the win.

Though no one was worthy enough "to step into my yard and look Big Evil in the eye," the champion demonstrated why the WWE is "the land of opportunity" on May 30 *Smack-Down!*, offering rookie Randy Orton a title shot in Calgary's Pengrowth Saddledome. Undertaker began the match with an eerily cordial handshake, then ended it with a bone-rattling Chokeslam after Orton caught him off-guard with several near-pinfalls. The Phenom was shocked even further afterward by a ringside assault from Triple H, who sent both the champ and his title over the ropes with a message: "You want to talk about giving somebody an opportunity? How about giving *me* the opportunity? Because I guarantee you this: you give me the chance, you won't be leaving with [the Undisputed Championship belt]!" 'Taker would deliver several shots to The Game, all from a steel chair, later in the broadcast, after costing Hunter his match against Test. The attack would also injure Hunter's right elbow badly enough for him to require surgery one month later.

None of this helped the suddenly delicate constitution of Tommy Dreamer, who entertained crowds with nauseating feats like eating his own freshly cut hair and drinking out of a public urinal. Following the May

27 *Raw* beating he received after drinking a cup of Big Evil's chewing tobacco spit (and admitting it tasted pretty good), Dreamer had no stomach for a nontitle contest with the champion a week later, and vomited repeatedly into a bucket on his way to the ring. Cinching a Dragon Sleeper hold that made the former ECW star tap out for the first time in his career, 'Taker further humiliated the fallen Dreamer by pouring the puke pail all over him. But even the Dead Man would turn ghastly pale after Jeff Hardy raced down and *drop kicked* him into the vomit!

Regardless of this spectacular drop, it was Jeff Hardy who went down for the count.

Not appreciating Jeff's idea of "living for the moment," Undertaker called him out and asked, "Are you ready to *die* in that same moment?" at the June 10 *Raw*. Team Xtreme soon answered his challenge with a ladder, from which Jeff vaulted off the top step into a tremendous legdrop on the champion! The Dead Man's hand would eventually pound respect into a handcuffed Jeff on June 17 *Raw,* while brother Matt was restrained by Raven (who lost to Jeff earlier in the show), and forced to watch every moment. As Big Evil later put it to Terri Runnels backstage, "*That's* what happens when people try to make a name for themselves at *my* expense."

While Undertaker secured his reign atop an undisputed throne, business king Vince McMahon wanted Hollywood Hulk Hogan and his "name value" to continue servicing the WWE, despite his dropping the championship to the Phenom at *Judgment Day*. But when the icon announced his retirement at the May 23 *SmackDown!* in Tupelo's BancorpSouth Center ("the very *rectum* of Mississippi," as Vince described), McMahon threatened to sue for breach of contract. "The only way you're going to leave *my* company," he wanted, "is when your body is decomposing in a pine box!" Vince added that as the creative force behind "Hulk Hogan" and "*Hulkamania,*" "I intend to milk *Hulkamania* for every cent I can until the day you *die.*"

Understandably upset, Hogan punched out Vince, flogging him with his weight belt before warding off an assault from Undertaker. At the May 30 *SmackDown!*, he reiterated to Marc Loyd and the Saddledome fans his plans to retire, but revealed there was now some-thing else that meant as much to him as winning the WWE Championship: "a one-on-one confrontation against Vince McMahon, with me *kicking his ass* right in the middle of that ring! And when I do, I'm gonna reach in and tear his black heart out, brother!" Just then, Vince suddenly disrupted the interview, seemingly to offer Hogan the opportunity… and providing just enough distraction for Kurt Angle to whack the Hulkster over the head with a pipe!

> **"I'm gonna reach in and tear out his black heart, brother!"**

The icon recovered later that night to get a piece of Angle (who in less than two weeks after losing his locks at *Judgment Day,* was sporting miraculously regrown

---

In Memoriam
1962-2002

DAVEY BOY SMITH

The wrestling world was shocked and saddened to hear Davey Boy Smith, The British Bulldog, had died on May 18, 2002. Smith, a longtime member of the WWE roster, suffered a heart attack in his sleep and passed away while vacationing at the resort community of Invermere, British Columbia. He was thirty-nine.

A native of Manchester, England, Smith's accomplishments in the WWE were vast, including two reigns as a Tag Team Champion—the first with British Bulldogs partner Dynamite Kid at *WrestleMania 2* on April 7, 1986, the next with brother-in-law Owen Hart on September 22, 1996. His greatest singles claim to fame came at *SummerSlam* in 1992, when he defeated brother-in-law Bret Hart for the Intercontinental title in front of eighty thousand fans at Wembley Stadium. Smith also earned the distinction of becoming the WWE's first-ever European Champion back in February 26, 1997, defeating co-Tag Team Champion Owen at the tournament final held in Berlin, Germany. He'd win the title again after defeating D'Lo Brown on October 26, 1999 *SmackDown!*, only weeks after winning his first Hardcore Championship and choosing to relinquish it voluntarily. A second, and brief, Hardcore reign followed at *Insurrextion* in London on May 6, 2000, shortly before Smith left the WWE. Regardless of whether or not he wore a title, the British Bulldog was, and always will be, remembered fondly by his legion of fans as a champion. ■

"natural hair" that he secured with wrestling head-gear) during his brutal Cage match with Edge. With the ref knocked senseless as Kurt Angle Slammed Edge off the top rope and climbed out of the cage, Hogan ran down and pummeled the gold medalist back inside, where Edge launched into a top-rope spear for the victory. Hogan then added to the celebration by almost "wigging out" Angle!

Vince McMahon was likely pulling out some of his own hair at the June 6 *SmackDown!* in Oklahoma City. his Twenty-Man Battle Royal to determine the No. 1 Contender for the Undisputed title at *King of the Ring* came down to hated finalists Hollywood Hulk Hogan and imminent ex-son-in-law Triple H when both of them went over the top rope simultaneously. Rather than let the "hokey Okies" decide who won, McMahon ordered the two Superstars to compete again that evening. In a rematch from *Backlash,* Triple H would emerge the victor, kicking out of Hogan's legdrop and planting the Pedigree for the three-count. But as the two embraced in a gesture of sportsmanship, they were ambushed by Undertaker and Kurt Angle, who hovered over the fallen figures as *SmackDown!* went off the air.

With the *KOR* Championship match set, all that remained was the signing of the contract, which kicked off—and almost *pre-empted*—the June 13 *Smack-Down!* Once the dotted lines were signed within the red-carpeted ring, McMahon sicced security guards on Triple H while Undertaker attacked. Grabbing hold of a sledgehammer that cleared the ring of 'Taker and the

"See you in hell, Dead Man!"

Long time rivals, can't wait for *King of the Ring.*

hired hands, The Game held *SmackDown!* hostage for almost fifteen minutes, demanding Vince return the Red Devil to ringside or there would be no show. The sledgehammer pulverized the announce monitors and announcer's table, and was about to destroy a fifty thousand-dollar television camera when McMahon finally consented to Hunter's demands...but with a Tag Team match that also included Kurt Angle and Hulk Hogan. Satisfied, Triple H looked directly into the camera with a message for 'Taker—"*See you in hell, Dead Man!*"—then smashed the expensive equipment beyond repair!

During the Tag match, Hunter would be forced to ally himself with the sledge-hammer again when Hogan—

Triple H hammers his point home.

Undertaker Chokeslams Hogan into the canvas.

Undertaker. Not even Vince McMahon could mend the duo's sudden rift to prevent their main-event battle that night, though Triple H's surprise distraction would allow Angle to recuperate from a Big Evil Chokeslam and schoolboy 'Taker for the victory. With Hogan also charging ringside, a free-for-all broke out, and as the last *SmackDown!* before the PPV ended, it was Triple H standing tall as that evening's King of the Ring!

At times it seemed the *SmackDown!* ring was no more dangerous a realm than Vince McMahon's office, which had been a hub for Diva discord of late. Locking lips with Test in Tupelo's BankCorp South May 23 "meant nothing" to Stacy Keibler, but hearing how sensuous new paralegal Dawn Marie kissed up to the boss in Calgary the following week made it only a matter of time before the two women locked horns. Meanwhile, *Tough Enough 2* Champion Linda Miles cinched up with Ivory on WWE June 8 *Velocity*, after the trainer tongue-lashed her and Co-Champion Jackie Gayda for "bothering" Mr. McMahon in his office during *SmackDown!* two nights earlier. Jackie disrupted a potential upset by dislodging Linda from the top rope and leaving her open to an Ivory facebuster, but partnering with Women's Champ Trish Stratus guaranteed Linda satisfaction—and Stratusfaction—against the double team at the June 13 *SmackDown!*

Whether it was defeating a "disgusting and distasteful" thong-wearing Rikishi on May 23, hearing Lance Storm's confession of being Western Canadian ("A sin worse than blasphemy or adultery," said Storm) the following week, or a simple desire to worship his own king, Reverend D-Von continued mounting the sermons on *SmackDown!* He was especially impassioned at the June 13 show, warning masturbators in the BI-LO Center they would surely burn in hell. "Please," he implored, "leave that thing alone!"

Out came Faarooq, who confessed that just because D-Von no longer "partakes. Guess what? I do." Then he got sinful with a Dominator on the Reverend for the quick pinfall victory!

who earlier questioned the gold medalist's "sack" with a one-on-one challenge at *King of the Ring*—was double-teamed backstage by Angle and Undertaker minutes before. Big Evil would painfully learn to respect The Game while Hogan ventured ringside for Angle, who'd find his wrestling tights pulled down to his knees, his wig on the Hulkster's head and his face connecting with a Pedigree and a legdrop!

Angle capped off what was truly more than a bad hair month at the June 20 *SmackDown!*—a promise to make Hogan tap out at *King of the Ring* looked unlikely, since he was too busy hauling his ass out of the ring before the Hulkster could kick it. That didn't stop him from *looking* like an ass during Triple H's victory against former "Mr. Ass" Billy Gunn, when a chair shot intended for The Game instead found his double-team partner,

By this point, Lance Storm believed his countrymen were the victims of too many transgressions—while teaming with Chris Jericho for a June 13 match against Billy Kidman and Big Valbowski, the referee failed to notice Storm lifting his shoulder off the mat before awarding the three-count to Kidman. And when a ring official missed Christian's foot on the rope in a June 20 *SmackDown!* bout with Rikishi, Storm opined the miscue "wasn't an innocent act of incompetence," but "a pattern of inherent prejudice toward Canadian athletes." Accusing the WWF and all Americans of "screwing us every chance they get," Storm screamed, "*America sucks!*" before he and Christian ran out of the Arco Arena.

Billy and Chuck weren't Canadian, though they did look tarnished after losing the Tag Team gold at

Chris Jericho Lionsaults Billy Kidman.

Judgment Day to their stylist Rico Constantino and his unwilling partner Rikishi. Rico fashioned several opportunities to drop the title back to his friends, including a May 30 rematch where the Phat Man's savate kick dropped him on top of Chuck for the pin. But the stylist capitalized on a June 6 Elimination match which required both tag partners to be defeated, first by tapping out instantly to an "agonizing" armbar from Chuck, then tossing Rikishi's foot from the rope, resulting in a three-count. With Billy and Chuck WWF tag kings once again, Rico's troubles seemed behind him...except for *Rikishi's* behind, which came down on him with a king-sized sit-down splash!

As Vince McMahon struggled to maintain his *SmackDown!* regime, things were no better over in Ric Flair's *Raw* fiefdom, especially with Stone Cold Steve Austin remaining a constant thorn in Slick Ric's side. At the May 20 *Raw*, Flair decided to pluck that thorn, informing the Bionic Redneck he was pulling the property of *Raw*—"my property"—from ring matches, and taking away "what makes you tick—the thrill of competition that winds you up every day. As of tonight, you're benched."

Naturally, the Rattlesnake didn't take the news well, downing Flair and Enforcer Arn Anderson with Stunners, then some Steveweisers for himself. Wife Debra tried consoling Stone Cold by taking him to a local Tennessee karaoke bar, but the evening hit another sour note after then-Intercontinental Champ Eddie Guerrero broke a beer bottle over Austin's skull!

Flair and Guerrero expected a pissed-off SOB in Edmonton for the May 27 *Raw*, but were apparently shocked by the hometown return of the Canadian Crippler, Chris Benoit. "It sure as hell feels good to be back," declared the No. 3 *SmackDown!* pick, returning from a major neck injury sustained at the *KOR 2001* Triple-Threat Championship match with Y2J and Austin. Guerreo disrupted the happy moment while

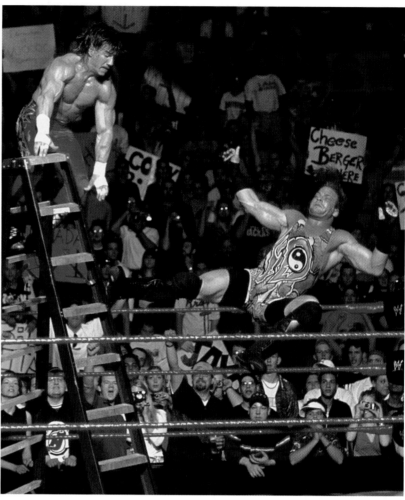

Flair, fearing Benoit might start a fight "like a typical Canadian," banned him from the ring. The ban wouldn't prevent Benoit from sitting ringside and watching Guerreo drop the IC title to RVD in their Ladder match, nor would it stop him from charging the ring when the arriving Stone Cold opened cans of whoop-ass on Latino Heat, Flair and Arn Anderson. Unfortunately for Austin, it was all a trap, as the Rabid Wolverine turned on the Rattlesnake, setting him up for Guerrero's Five-Star Frog Splash!

The conspiracy further unfolded on June 3 *Raw*, with Benoit promising Austin "a very long and painful payback" for his neck injury, and Flair reminding the Dallas crowd their home state hero was benched. Suddenly, on flashed the TitanTron, showing Stone Cold holding a beat-up Arn Anderson. "[Being benched] *sucks*," said Austin, who'd issue a challenge— if he were to beat Flair in a match that night, he was back competing full-time. The Nature Boy agreed to "an old-time *wrestling* match"—*no* punches or illegal

maneuvers—and if *he* won, Austin would remain on the bench "for the rest of your life." After questioning Flair as to "*What?*" a "Nature Boy" is, Stone Cold answered nature's call to an all-day beer-drinking session…and *urinated* on Arn Anderson! He then countered Slick Ric's catch phrase, "To be The Man, you got to *beat* The Man," with his own bottom-line philosophy: "It's better to be pissed *off* than pissed *on!*"

Flair quickly ordered multiple stipulations to the match contract before letting Austin sign it, the most important being that if Stone Cold lost via pinfall or DQ, he'd become the *Raw* owner's personal assistant. Unfortunately, Flair didn't read the contract *language*, which Debra pointed out had clearly specified that *the loser* of the match would become *the winner's* assistant.

WHAT? HAPPENED

Both the fans and the personnel of World Wrestling Entertainment were shocked when Stone Cold Steve Austin decided to no-show at June 10 *Raw*, resulting in his dismissal from the organization. The Texas Rattlesnake had made it no secret in recent months prior to his departure that he'd become unhappy with his role in the WWE; days before his match against Scott Hall at *Wrestle-Mania X8*, Austin expressed in an interview with WWE.com that he wasn't "real excited" with the direction the company had been taking. The August issue of *Raw* magazine reported that he and wife Debra didn't attend the post-*Wrestle-Mania* party that evening, and while everyone headed to Montreal for March 18 *Raw*, the couple decided they were heading home to Texas, despite the fact that Austin's presence at the show was supposed to contribute heavily to the WWE brand extension.

Stone Cold wouldn't show up on *Raw* again until April 1, when the "free agent" signed with the *Raw* brand. By then it was believed the problems had abated, until Austin again made derisive remarks regarding the WWE story lines during the May 31 *Byte This!* on WWE.com. The problems reached their breaking point twenty-four hours before the June 10 *Raw* in Atlanta, when Stone Cold was informed he'd face Brock Lesnar in a *King of the Ring* qualifier and Eddie Guerrero would be the guest referee. This would add fire to the current Austin-Latino Heat conflict. The following day, after arriving at the Philips Arena, Jim Ross learned that Stone Cold had booked a flight back to San Antonio. It was soon decided that since Austin had no intention of returning to *Raw* and settling his differences in person, WWE had no choice but to issue a press release that declared, "Stone Cold Steve Austin is no longer an active member of WWE's talent roster."

WWE owner Vince McMahon and Senior VP of Talent Relations Jim Ross explained the circumstances regarding the situation on *WWE Confidential* on June 15. According to McMahon, what it all boiled down to was that, "...Austin, for whatever reason, was hell-bent on not showing. He got on a plane and went home. He took his ball and went home."

Sadly, the year of the "What?"—still heard extensively throughout arenas everywhere—had become the year of the "Why?" ∎

SHAWN MICHAELS

Superstar ★ profile

HEIGHT: **6'1"** WEIGHT: **225 lbs.**
OTHER NAMES: **HBK, The Showstopper**
FINISHING MOVE: **Sweet Chin Music**
CAREER HIGHLIGHTS: **WWE Champion (3); Intercontinental Champion (3); European Champion; Tag Team Champion (3); World Champion; *Royal Rumble* 1995 and 1996 winner.**
2002 HIGHLIGHTS: **Returning to the WWE spotlight on June 3 *Raw*; defeating Triple H at *SummerSlam*; winning the World Heavyweight title in the Elimination Chamber match at *Survivor Series*; returning to the WWE on June 3 *Raw*; defeating Triple H at *SummerSlam*; winning the Elimination Chamber match to become World Champion; losing World title to Triple H at *Armageddon*.**

Austin fights to break Flair's Figure-Four Leglock.

The error motivated Austin to honor his end of the deal, and despite Benoit's ringside distractions and a Guerrero Frog Splash, the Bionic Redneck offset Flair's Figure-Four and hit the Stunner for the win. Stone Cold was off the bench and quickly on his new personal assistant's case, landing another Stunner before downing some Steveweisers in front of the sold-out crowd!

The idea of Stone Cold Steve Austin lording over Ric Flair was indeed *Raw* with possibilities. But those possibilities ended June 10, when Flair informed the Philips Arena that after showing up to take the Rattlesnake's orders like a man, "Stone Cold Steve Austin decided *not* to show up." That prompted Vince McMahon to head ringside and call Flair "the sorriest excuse of an owner I've ever seen in my life," emphasizing his recent failures had driven *Raw* "right down the *toilet.* You may be a sixteen-time World Champion," he added, "but as an owner...*you suck!*"

Vince then threw down the gauntlet—a No Holds Barred match between him and Flair, with the winner becoming one hundred percent owner of World Wrestling Entertainment! Arn Anderson and just about everyone in Atlanta predicted "an early retirement" for McMahon, but Paul Heyman's advice to "forget about Stone Cold, because you need to start thinking about The Next Big Thing" would prove prophetic in the match result. With his Figure-Four, a bloodied Flair had just about wrested control of the WWE from McMahon...until Brock Lesnar raced into the ring and finished off the Nature Boy with the F-5! Rolling onto Flair for the one-two-three, Vince McMahon was the sole king of the WWE!

> "You may be a sixteen-time World Champion, but as an owner...*you suck!*"

Raw was clearly in a state of transition as the show broadcast from Oakland's Coliseum June 17, but Ric Flair wasn't ready to go home like Austin had. Finding inspiration from Hogan's comeback, Flair signed a contract to wrestle and "prove to myself that I have *at least* one more good run left in me." Plans to start that run with Brock Lesnar veered course, however, when Eddie Guerrero and Chris Benoit approached ringside. Guerrero wanted Stone Cold at the PPV, and called the former sixteen-time World Champion "a worthless

Nationwide Arena
Columbus, OH

UNDISPUTED CHAMPIONSHIP MATCH

Undertaker defeated *Triple H* via pinfall
to retain the Undisputed title

KING OF THE RING TOURNAMENT FINAL

Brock Lesnar defeated *Rob Van Dam*
via pinfall to become the *King of the Ring 2002*

Kurt Angle defeated *Hollywood Hulk Hogan*
via submission

WOMEN'S CHAMPIONSHIP MATCH

Molly Holly defeated *Trish Stratus* via pinfall
to become the Women's Champion

Ric Flair defeated *Eddie Guerrero* via pinfall

CRUISERWEIGHT CHAMPIONSHIP MATCH

Jamie Noble defeated *The Hurricane* via pinfall
to become the Cruiserweight Champion

KING OF THE RING TOURNAMENT SEMIFINAL

Brock Lesnar defeated *Test* via pinfall

KING OF THE RING TOURNAMENT SEMIFINAL

Rob Van Dam defeated *Chris Jericho* via pinfall

For four Superstars, *King of the Ring* 2002 truly represented "The Ride of Your Life," as indicated by the Neurotica theme song that kicked off the tenth annual tournament in Columbus, Ohio's Nationwide Arena on June 23. For one man, however, being declared King meant his ride would end not after the tournament, but at *SummerSlam*, where he would try to lay claim to another man's Undisputed kingdom.

Two of the WWE's very best delivered a thrilling semifinal to open the PPV extravaganza—Intercontinental Champion Rob Van Dam and Chris Jericho were evenly matched from the start, even dropkicking each other simultaneously. Mr. Pay-Per-View made Y2J pay for a missed body press to the outside with a somersault plancha over the ropes. Grounding the aerial assault temporarily with a double-arm suplex and the Breakdown, Y2J rebounded from a split-legged moonsault by rolling into the Walls of Jericho. RVD countered into a near-pin, though nearly lost the match after a missed Five-Star Frog Splash made him easy pickings for the Lionsault. Frustrated by several near-falls, Jericho tried superplexing RVD from up top, but another kick crotched him down to the mat, where the Five-Star found its mark and advanced Van Dam to the finals.

In a postmatch interview inside the ring, Jerry "the King" Lawler asked whom Van Dam preferred meeting in the final. His response, "Whatever." Whether it was Test, Brock Lesnar or Godzilla, "Nothing's gonna keep the *King of the Ring* from being *Rob! Van! Dam!*" Unfortunately, all of his thumb-pointing couldn't prepare Van Dam for a near-hysterical Y2J to blindside him, then lock him in the Walls of Jericho while screaming, "*I'm* the King of the World!" An army of WWE officials came down and made Jericho relinquish the hold, but from the way a clearly hurt RVD left the ringside area, it may have been too late.

Enjoying the show from backstage, agent Paul Heyman laughed at Van Dam's comments. "Godzilla was fake," he said, "but *you*, Brock Lesnar…are *real.*" And it was time for The Next Big Thing to prove it in his semifinal with Test, whose own smashmouth style made their match resemble a Japanese monster movie showdown. Neither man tried outfinessing the other, relying heavily on power moves—Test opened strong with a succession of clotheslines and punches, while the former NCAA Champion emphatically answered back with several counteroffensive slams. Twice Test looked to have victory in his grasp, first with a massive pump-handle slam, then a big boot that had Brock tasting serious shoe leather. Both times Lesnar barely kicked out, worrying Heyman enough to get up on the apron and distract Test before he moved in for the kill. The ploy worked, as Test went after Heyman, allowing Brock to recover and put his opponent up in the F-5. Like all the victims before him, Test didn't get up, and The Next Big Thing was in the finals.

With the tournament to be decided between RVD and Lesnar, Jonathan Coachman went to the *Raw* locker room for thoughts on who might win. Bubba Ray Dudley wished it was himself going to the final, but he was content with finding another way to make an impact. And although he wanted to see Van Dam's hand raised, "I don't think he's making it past The Next Big Thing tonight." Outside the *SmackDown!* locker room with Marc Loyd, Lance Storm was disgusted; what should have been an all-Canadian final between Y2J and Test was now "just all-*American*." Christian chimed in, accusing WWE of being "prejudiced" against Canadian athletes, and that America was the most prejudiced country in the world. Lance reminded Christian not to get sucked into "the pro-American hateful abyss. We need to rise above it, and as Canadians, we need to carry the flag of civility, tolerance and peace."

Jamie Noble and girlfriend Nidia looked like they parked their trailer right outside the arena as they headed ringside for his Cruiserweight Championship match against heroic titleholder The Hurricane. But beneath Noble's lack of class was an accomplished technical ring etiquette, displaying impressive takedowns and combos to wear the hero down. But the champion stood strong, matching Noble move for move and deflecting a top-rope suplex to the outside floor with a superhuman swinging neckbreaker! The match was over as Hurricane covered Noble, but Nidia, having been the hero's one weakness throughout the contest, distracted the referee on the ring apron. Hurricane sent a charging Noble crashing into his girl, then planted him with the Chokeslam. Kicking out, the redneck proved resilient and resourceful—falling against the ropes to bring Hurricane crashing down from the top buckle, he caught the dazed hero with a powerbomb, while Nidia knocked Hurricane's foot off the rope to ensure the three-count. The *extremely* demonstrative couple celebrated inside the ring, as Jamie Noble was the new Cruiserweight Champion.

Eddie Guerrero said hi to pretty much his *entire* family—brothers, kids, nephews and Timmy, the little foster boy they picked up last weekend—before promising Terri that Ric Flair's "one last run" would be to the retirement home, and his only memory would be of Latino Heat putting him there. Guerrero planned to insult the former *Raw* owner even more by beating the dirtiest player with his own game, focusing on the legs and latching on the signature

Figure-Four Leglock. Flair broke the hold, then capitalized on a missed Frog Splash with his own finisher as Chris Benoit made his way to ringside. Finding sanctuary in the ropes, Guerrero soon caught the Nature Boy with a tornado DDT from the corner, but Flair broke up the count, only to get dragged to the outside floor, where Benoit put him in the Crippler Crossface. Guerrero failed to distract the referee, who caught the Rabid Wolverine and argued with him on the outside floor, not realizing Bubba Ray Dudley had raced into the ring and Bubba-bombed Latino Heat! Bubba exited the ring as Flair crawled in and got the one-two-three!

After what Molly Holly had put her through the past few weeks, Women's Champion Trish Stratus was more than up for kicking her pronounced posterior. Molly kept Trish on the defensive in the early goings with a painful armbar hold, though the champion Diva countered with an impressive victory roll for the two-count. After regaining control, the challenger climbed the top rope for a high-risk maneuver, but Trish surprised Molly with an impressive Hurracanrana that sent her crashing down to the canvas. Nailing Trish with a suplex, Molly went up top again, but missed with a Molly-Go-Round that Jim Ross described "could have broken a two-by-four." Yet Molly's butt strength would weigh heavily in the match outcome moments later—reversing a rollup by Trish, the virtuous Diva hooked the tights to pick up the three-count, and steal the WWE Women's Championship.

Kurt Angle—and his hairpiece—were offended that Marc Loyd would call his upcoming match with Hollywood Hulk Hogan "a battle of the real American heroes." Insisting Hogan was one only because Vince McMahon once *told* him he was, Kurt intended to prove he was "legit" by making Hogan tap "faster than Mr. Bojangles on speed." Hogan's early dominance in the contest (his first *King of the Ring* since the inaugural PPV in 1993) suggested he wouldn't be doing so on this night, but a low blow soon put Angle in control, and he'd spend the next several minutes wearing the Hulkster down with a number of holds and a belly-to-back suplex. The gold medalist thought he'd won the match when he connected with the Angle Slam, only to be shocked when Hogan kicked out, then dismayed when he started Hulking up. Hogan delivered the hard rights and the big boot, but opted not to go for the legdrop. Instead, he removed Angle's headpiece, revealing Angle was balder than an American eagle!

Embarrassed, Kurt headed backstage when Hogan made a surprising unveteranlike error—he mocked his opponent while he was down, wearing the headpiece on his head for laughs. Incensed, Angle charged the ring with a chair, only to catch himself with it when Hogan ducked and it bounced off the ropes. The Hulkster went

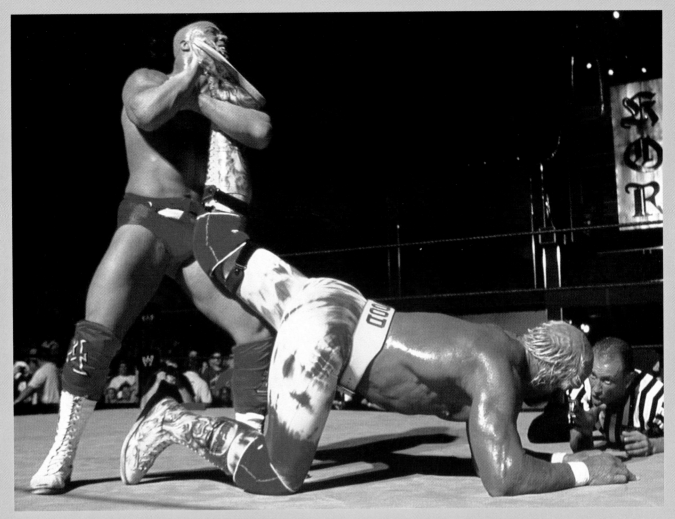

Angle forces an icon to tap out.

for the legdrop, but Angle deflected it and slapped on the ankle lock. Hogan tried ferociously to break the hold, but Angle wouldn't let go. He tried reaching the ropes, but the Olympian kept pulling him back to the center of the ring. In agony and out of alternatives, Hollywood Hulk Hogan did something he'd never done throughout his illustrious career: he tapped out.

As disturbing a visual as that was, Goldust quickly topped it backstage minutes later, as Booker T came face-to-face with "The Rock." He didn't seem too fond of Goldust's impression of the Great One, nor was the real deal who suddenly stood behind the Bizarre One. Rock was at *King of the Ring* for one reason only: to watch the Undisputed Championship match tonight, a match that was bigger than the People's Elbow, the Spin-a-Roonie and whatever it was a "sick freak" like Goldust does.

Where agility faced agility and power fought power in the tournament semifinals, the *King of the Ring* final itself became a strict contrast in styles. Rob Van Dam tried working Brock Lesnar over with a series of forearms and kicks, until the behemoth's powerslam stopped him

in mid-monkey flip. Lesnar dominated the match with numerous high-impact power moves, but Van Dam's educated feet soon exploited a rookie mistake in the corner and scored a near-pinfall with the Rolling Thunder. As Mr. Pay-Per-View went up top and hit the Five-Star Frog Splash, Heyman got up on the ring apron and whiplashed RVD off the top rope, almost costing his client the match when Van Dam fell on top of Lesnar for a near-fall! Van Dam took Heyman out of the equation with a baseball slide, then climbed the ropes again for a lateral press, but Lesnar was waiting for him; catching him in midair, he downed Van Dam with the F-5 for the victory. The Next Big Thing was the King of the Ring, and he had an appointment with the Undisputed Champion at *SummerSlam*.

Determined to make that date with Lesnar, Triple H made his way through the backstage area for his Undisputed Championship match with Undertaker when he ran across the nWo's Shawn Michaels and Kevin Nash. After a seemingly tense moment, the three hugged, with Michaels, Nash and the rest of the Black and White clan wishing Hunter good luck, and they'd be there if he needed them. But The Game was resolute in taking it to the Dead Man on his own as the bell sounded. The champion took control early with the soup bones to Hunter's head, then delivered a hard guillotine legdrop off the apron. Triple H mounted his own offense with a suplex on the outside floor, followed minutes later by whipping 'Taker into the turnbuckle area he'd exposed, dazing the Phenom long enough to deliver a neckbreaker.

From there the pace of the contest quickened, with both men trying to finish each other off. Triple H, favoring his heavily taped right arm (which Undertaker injured on *SmackDown!* a few weeks before), went for the Pedigree, but Undertaker countered with a slingshot to the corner that squashed referee Earl Hebner. Big Evil then followed in with a hard clothesline, but again Hebner took the full impact as Hunter dodged it. All three men were down as The Game and the American Badass collided, but business picked up when The Rock's music suddenly hit! Down came the Brahma Bull, but it wasn't to interfere; he just wanted to chase away guest commentator Paul Heyman, who bragged during the match to J.R. and the King how Brock Lesnar punked out the People's Champ backstage and sent him heading for the People's Highway. Unfortunately, as the ring combatants spilled out toward the announcer's table, Undertaker chose to involve Rock with a kick to the face! Big Evil then grabbed a steel chair to finish off Triple H, but the Great One unleashed a number of rights, then delivered his own chair shot… which unfortunately missed the Dead Man and caught The Game between the eyes, busting him wide open.

Dispensing the Brahma Bull, the Red Devil rolled a barely conscious Triple H inside and delivered the Last Ride. Another referee came in to make the count, only to get thrown out of the ring by an irate Undertaker when The Game kicked out at two. Without warning, The Rock surprised Big Evil with the Rock Bottom, then left the ring as Triple H slowly made his way over to make the cover. With Hebner still recovering, Hunter could only get a two-count, then needed to get the referee's attention again after landing the Pedigree. The distraction proved costly, allowing Undertaker to roll up Triple H and hook the tights as Hebner counted to three. The Undisputed Champion stood tall in the ring, until his trash-talking toward Rock in the back prompted the People's Champ to race down and shut him up with a spinebuster and People's Elbow! Suddenly, The Game repaid Rock for the earlier chair shot with a Pedigree, only to go down again moments later as Undertaker Chokeslammed him to the canvas. The ring was a sight of chaos as *King of the Ring* came to an end, meaning the kingdom still belonged undisputedly to the Dead Man walking inside it. ■

piece of crap" who caused his departure. Benoit chided his friend…then accused Flair of taking away *his* chance for revenge on Austin. A Figure-Four from Guerrero culminated a double-team effort on the Nature Boy, whose run would now begin with Latino Heat at *King of the Ring*.

At that point, WWE Women's Champion Trish Stratus was still enjoying her run as queen among Divas, though Molly was closing in on her throne in the weeks leading up to *KOR*. After losing a May 27 Intergender match to Trish and former fiancé Spike Dudley, Molly's new gentleman friend William Regal showed his brass, supplying a pair of knux to polish off the Women's Champ. But when she tried the same stunt after Trish's "Stratusfying" Lingerie match victory over Terri a week later, Molly was clobbered by the Women's Championship belt, then had the Diva's ring bottoms dropped on her face.

"You've got a *huge* ass!"

During a June 10 backstage interview Trish told her pure and virtuous rival to face facts: "You've got a *huge* ass!" Those comments prompted Molly to put her *tuchus* on the line and challenge the Women's Champ to a match that would either earn her a title shot at *King of the Ring*, or the future embarrassment of wrestling in a thong! Thankfully, Molly put the "junk in her trunk" to good use with a Molly-Go-Round, somersaulting from the top rope and lading full force on Trish for the win. After celebrating her victory by choking Trish with the same bottoms she'd discarded the week before, Molly left her even worse for wear during June 17's Mixed Tag match, bouncing the champion's head off the announcer's table while D'Lo Brown went Sky High on Crash Holly for the

TOP **Molly Holly bridges Trish for a near fall.**

LEFT **Christopher Nowinski gets frisked by event staff.**

pinfall. With *King of the Ring* looming, it appeared Trish's derriere suddenly belonged to Molly.

It was around this same time that the ever-refined European Champion Regal started associating himself with a higher class. *Tough Enough* runner-up Christopher Nowinski had finally attained his dream of entering the squared circle...though he did so as a ticket holder among *Raw's* sold-out audience in Atlanta on June 10, slipping Regal a pair of brass knux that laid out new Hardcore Champion Bradshaw. Seven days later, Spike Dudley tested the Harvard grad's *Tough Enough* schooling, but a clear size advantage and full nelson bomb graded the varsity-lettered heel with his first "W." Nowinski and Regal then enrolled in an after-school beating on Spike, but quickly dropped out when Bradshaw's run-in threatened to educate them to the moves that made him an All-American offensive tackle at Abilene University.

Most *Raw* Superstars already knew Bradshaw to be a headmaster in the School of Hardcore Knocks, possessing a smash mouth style that earned him the Championship title held previously by Steven Richards (minus an incredulous three-second reign by Terri Runnels, who pinned Richards when their May 27 backstage interview ensued into a melee among Jacqueline, Shawn Stasiak and Boss Man). Richards dropped the title to the tough Texan in Dallas on June 3, but not because of the bullrope, cowbell, saddle or buffalo horns used in the slobberknocker bout. Rather, it was a Clothesline from Hell delivered, ironically, on an interfering Spike Dudley.

Bradshaw takes the Hardcore title from Steven Richards.

kingdom? Addressing that question in Oakland during the June 17 edition of *Raw*, the WWE chairman said it was true, "and I don't like it any more than you fans do." He hoped Stone Cold would return to the WWE one day, though the company would continue on. As part of that process, Vince added a stipulation that the winner of the *King of the Ring* tournament would get a shot at the WWE Undisputed Championship at *SummerSlam*. Then directing his attention to Austin watching at home, McMahon hoisted a beer from ringside, said, "Thank you, Stone Cold. Thank you for the memories," took a sip and left the can in the middle of the ring as he walked out.

Vince McMahon was king of the WWE again...but what of Stone Cold Steve Austin's apparent departure from the *Raw*

PAGE TURNS TO RETIREMENT

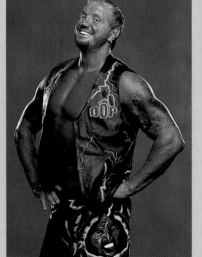

On June 11, almost one year after joining World Wrestling Entertainment, Page Falkinburg—Diamond Dallas Page—decided to call it a career. After learning recent neck problems would require extensive corrective surgery and rehabilitation, the ever-positive DDP saw it as a good thing—and a good time—to end his in-ring career shortly after being at *WrestleMania X8* and defending the WWE European title in front of sixty-eight thousand fans. Not bad for a guy who started as a manager twelve years ago, moved on to being a color commentator and then a "jobber" helping promote other wrestlers. But it was Page's work ethic that earned him the notice of World Championship Wrestling fans over the past seven years (the company was sold to the WWE in 2001). In his time with WCW, the master of the Diamond Cutter became TV Champion, a two-time U.S. Champion, a coholder of five Tag Team titles and a two-time World Champion.

The greatest battle Page ever won, however, was not in the ring. His determination and support from wife Kimberly helped him overcome the dyslexia that plagued him throughout most of his life. In addition to learning how to read, Page showed he knew how to write as well, penning his first book *Positively Page—The Diamond Dallas Page Journey* in 2000. Page and Kimberly remain extremely active with helping children fight illiteracy, having founded the charity foundation Bang It Out for Books. And that's not a good thing. That's a *great* thing. ∎

Despite the gesture, McMahon fully expected the Bionic Redneck to show up that evening and apologize for his actions, so he ordered his lookouts to make sure Austin found his way to the ring the moment he entered the Coliseum. In fact, McMahon was so convinced Austin had arrived by the end of *Raw* that he went down to ringside and called him out, with a beer ready for the one-time King of the Ring.

A king did walk down the *Raw* runway...but McMahon nearly went into shock when he saw it was a *Scorpion King*—"the Livin' Fool, Brahma Bull, Jabroni-Beatin', Pie-Eatin', Walkin' Fast, Whuppin' Ass, People's Champ, *The Rock!*"

Vince McMahon is stunned by The Rock's return.

The Great One asked why Vince looked so surprised, then quickly cut him off—*it didn't matter* what he thought! He gave McMahon fifteen seconds to clear the ring, then chucked the beer can in his direction. Rock admitted he hadn't planned on returning until July, but after Austin's departure, he'd be damned if he didn't come back to the people. "Every single time I walk into a WWE locker room, every time I step into a *SmackDown!* locker room, I see the eyes of guys who are here because they *want* to be here," he said. "And if there's anybody in the back who *doesn't* want to be with this company... then do like the slogan says and *'Get the "F" Out'!*"

With the crowd on its feet, The Rock said he hadn't returned just to move on, but to move *up*, starting with *King of the Ring*. "Austin can take his ball and go home," he added, "but as far as The Rock is concerned, this *is* home. *If ya smell what The Rock is cookin'!*"

When *King of the Ring* started in 1993, the Pay-Per-View became a crowning achievement for those Superstars not wearing a major WWE title at that point in their career, the most notable being the tournament's first winner, Bret "Hitman" Hart. In later years, the tournament evolved into a showcase that promoted the Superstars on the verge of breaking out. The 2002 tournament winner actually earning an automatic Undisputed title bid at *SummerSlam*. Below is a quick reference list of past Kings, and the opponents they defeated in their respective tournaments.

1993: BRET "HITMAN" HART—defeated Razor Ramon, Mr. Perfect and Bam Bam Bigelow.

1994: OWEN HART—defeated Tatanka, 1-2-3 Kid and Razor Ramon.

1995: MABEL—defeated Undertaker and Savio Vega.

1996: STONE COLD STEVE AUSTIN—defeated "Wildman" Marc Mero and Jake "the Snake" Roberts. (It was during Austin's post-match interview after defeating Jake that "3:16" was born—"Austin 3:16 says I just whipped your ass!")

1997: HUNTER HEARST-HELMSLEY (TRIPLE H)—defeated Ahmed Johnson and Mankind.

1998: KEN SHAMROCK—defeated Jeff Jarrett and The Rock.

1999: BILLY GUNN—defeated Ken Shamrock, Kane and X-Pac.

2000: KURT ANGLE—defeated Chris Jericho, Crash Holly and Rikishi.

2001: EDGE—defeated Rhyno and Kurt Angle.

2002: BROCK LESNAR—defeated Rob Van Dam. ■

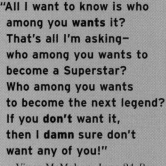

"All I want to know is who among you **wants** it? That's all I'm asking— who among you wants to become a Superstar? Who among you wants to become the next legend? If you **don't** want it, then I **damn** sure don't want any of you!"

—Vince McMahon, June 24 *Raw*

Ruthless "Vengeance"

Ruthless aggression. **That's what made Vincent Kennedy McMahon "an unqualified success." It was ruthless aggression that enabled him to "kick the asses" of every wrestling promoter in North America, the U.S. courts and eventually his company's greatest rival, World Championship Wrestling. And it was ruthless aggression that resonated from the WWE owner on June 24 Raw, in a message loud and clear to not only his Superstars surrounding the ring at Cleveland's Gund Arena, but to all of World Wrestling Entertainment.**

"**I** *want to know here tonight…as you stand here on my ring…which one of you has that quality?*"

Shawn Michaels, along with Kevin Nash, X-Pac and Big Show, apologized for their tardiness at McMahon's *Raw* assembly that evening, but he assured his boss that when it came to the personification of ruthless aggression, "You've got no bigger and no better Superstars than the nWo." Booker T, with Goldust uncomfortably close by his side (and describing themselves as "so tight…hell, we're practically *married*"),

stepped up and suggested otherwise, daring his former "4-Lifers" to come get some. McMahon sanctioned a Tag match that evening that sent The Book into a

Vince McMahon puts the WWE Superstars on notice.

Spin-a-Roonie, and a poor Aussie-accented Golden "Crocodile Hunter" on an expedition into the "vile, nasty" nWo locker room. Inside, he'd discover a sleeping "Showpapotamus" on the couch, "smelling like a kangaroo crotch sack," then lure "the X-Pac" ("a bandana-wearing grease rat," he described. "Be very careful—they tend to *suck*.") into a backstage chase, and head-on into a trashcan lid wielded by the Bookerman!

Stern backstage encouragement from Nash and Michaels powered their nWo buddies to a winning performance that night, with Big Show converting the celluloid freak's Golden Globes kick into a Showstopping-Chokeslam. But "Darthdust's" spirited words in New Hampshire the following week provided *Raw* force to a lightsaber-swinging "Obi-Book Kenobi," who declared, "It don't matter if you're a stormtrooper or the nWo—your ass is about to get waxed by the five-time Master Jedi Champion!" Booker first got medieval on X-Pac backstage, evening the sides after Big Show and Kevin Nash put a hurting on the Bizarre One minutes before a Tag match.

> "It don't matter if you're a stormtrooper or the nWo—your ass is about to get waxed by the five-time Master Jedi Champion!"

Now a one-on-one, the contest spilled over to the outside floor, until a Booker kick made the behemoth drop the ringside steps on himself, giving him a countout victory.

After the match, Show received nWo disapproval in the form of Nash's fist, which Michaels downplayed as "tough love" from a dysfunctional family that was suffering because they were missing an injured member. The Superstar Michaels meant, however, *wasn't* X-Pac. "In the very near future," he announced, "you will see...none other than the *newest* member of the New World Order...*Triple H.*"

Shawn wasn't concerned about *SmackDown!* exclusivity with The Game (who underwent elbow surgery after *King of the Ring*)—at July 8 *Raw,* he reminded Philadelphia's First Union Center how he, Nash, Scott Hall, X-Pac and Hunter were The Kliq that ran together in the WWE five years ago. Then again, Michaels *was* annoyed that his friend had yet to respond to his backstage offer at *King of the Ring*, where he told Hunter the Black and White would be there for him. Not one to be ignored, Shawn expected Triple H's answer by the July 21 Pay-Per-View *Vengeance,* warning, "You will either make the best decision of your life...or the *last.*"

That ultimatum became moot after that evening's Ten-Man Tag Team main event, which paired the nWo with Eddie Guerrero and Chris Benoit against Booker T, Goldust, Bubba Ray and Spike Dudley, and Intercontinental Champion Rob Van Dam. Nash, returning to ring action for the first time in over three months, tagged in and leveled The Book with a boot to the face... only to collapse on the floor and clutch at his knee in agony. While the referee saw to the fallen nWo leader, Michaels intervened with the Sweet Chin Music on Booker, giving Big Show the three-count. But Nash's torn quadriceps—ironically, the same injury Triple H suffered in 2001—did irreparable damage to the New World Order, as Vince McMahon announced at the July 15 *Raw* that the nWo was officially no more.

News of the Black and White's demise made Booker's day, despite a truly awful "Coach-a-Roonie" that had him wondering if interviewer Jonathan Coachman was black *or* white. Several chair shots and a Chokeslam through the announcer's table would leave Booker black and *blue* that evening, though victorious a second time over a disqualified Big Show. Frustrated, the giant demanded a No-Countout, No-DQ contest at *Vengeance* to finish the Book, and their ongoing feud.

"**W**ho among you has that one single ingredient?"

Vince McMahon knew of one wrestler who "unquestionably" met his criteria, though he wasn't standing among his *Raw* brethren in Cleveland on June 24. "Brock Lesnar didn't give a damn how he won *King of the Ring,*" he explained, "nor *should* he. He won because of ruthless aggression."

The billionaire's remarks bothered Intercontinental Champ Rob Van Dam nearly as much as his controversial loss to Lesnar in the *KOR* final less than twenty-four hours before. Brock was a man of few words, though earning an Undisputed title shot at *SummerSlam* allowed agent Paul Heyman to coat-tail on Mr. McMahon's comments

Big Show tables his feud with Booker T.

> "Tonight, I'm going to show you the *meaning* of 'ruthless aggression.'"

at The Next Big King's *Raw* coronation. "*No man,*" he insisted, "has the need, has the obsession, has the compulsion to be the champion more than The Next Big Thing, Brock Lesnar!" Van Dam responded with an attack Jim Ross described as "*urinating*" all over the coronation, knocking Lesnar to the outside floor!

"Brock Lesnar *cannot* wait until *SummerSlam* to become a champion," pleaded an irate Heyman inside the office of WWE owner Vince McMahon. "Brock Lesnar should be a champion *now.*" McMahon approved an IC title match that night between RVD and Heyman's client. Lesnar interrupted Jonathan Coachman's interview with Van Dam to tell him, "Tonight, I'm going to show you the *meaning* of 'ruthless aggression.'" School was in session during the contest, but it was RVD's educated feet doing the teaching—a split-legged moonsault threatened a three-count over Lesnar until

RVD "urinates" over Lesnar's coronation.

RVD's educated feet connect with The Next Big Thing.

Heyman's interference drew his client a disqualification, and himself a Five-Star Frog Splash. It also bought the King of the Ring time to regroup and powerbomb Mr. Monday Night through the *Raw* announce table!

There was no rematch in Manchester's Verizon Wireless Arena on July 1—Ric Flair, still seeking retribution after Lesnar cost him *Raw* ownership on June 10, answered Brock's open challenge to all ring veterans backstage, but not even the Nature Boy's ring expertise could withstand the fury of the F-5. Meanwhile, Van Dam matched win for win by reversing European Champion William Regal's double-arm suplex and going sky with the Five-Star, then called out Brock to settle their differences in the ring. Heyman restrained his client, however, advising that they meet on "a grander scale" in an Intercontinental Championship match at *Vengeance*.

At the First Union Center a week later, Heyman mocked the "Philadelphia animals" that supported his now-defunct ECW brand and provided the means to sign "...the man that will dominate this industry for the next ten to twenty years." But the agent wasn't expecting Tommy Dreamer to head ringside and innovate some violence on Lesnar with a Singapore cane, nor was he prepared for Van Dam's spinning heel kick, or for Mr. Monday Night to catapult across the ring and nail him with a steel chair-enforced Van Terminator! Payback came during the evening's Ten-Man main event. Provoked into chasing Shawn Michaels towards the TitanTron, RVD instead ran into an F-5 that leveled the Intercontinental Champ on the steel stage!

With the prospect of inflicting further damage to both Van Dam and Ric Flair at the July 15 *Raw*, Heyman sucked up to Lesnar's tag partner and likely *SummerSlam* opponent, Undertaker. Lesnar's agent insisted his client was "thrilled" about teaming up with the Undisputed Champion. 'Taker, however, urged

Heyman and his client to hope that he'd lose the belt in his Triple-Threat match at *Vengeance,* or they *would* meet at the next PPV. "I've made a career out of taking the 'next big thing' and making them famous," he explained, "and I make them famous by making them *disappear."*

The evening's Tag encounter proved even more explosive than anticipated, with all four participants hitting their signature moves throughout the match. Leaving Flair a twisted mess with his finisher, Lesnar caught a Five-Star Frog Splash that looked to seal the win for Van Dam—who realized too late that Undertaker was still the legal man in the ring. The American Badass powered down the Last Ride for the hard-fought victory, but it was Lesnar who celebrated with a devastating F-5 on his own partner! Leaving the belt on top of the fallen Phenom, Brock exited the ring, confident that he'd walk away with Van Dam's Intercontinental Title at *Vengeance,* and cap off an undisputed "Summer of The Next Big Thing" at *SummerSlam!*

Undertaker gets swept up in the F-5.

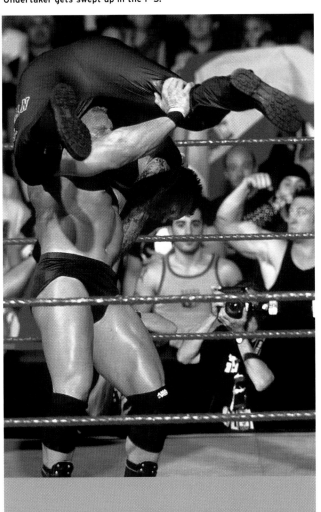

As Undertaker had reminded Brock Lesnar and Paul Heyman backstage before their July 15 Tag match, there was still a matter of him making it to *SummerSlam* as the Undisputed WWE Champion. First Big Evil would have to overcome the obstacles that lay ahead at *Vengeance*—the self-dubbed "poster boy" for ruthless aggression, and the Brahma Bull whose interference almost cost Undertaker his title at *King of the Ring.*

Not even the Chicago Allstate Arena fans' chorus of "You suck!" could dampen Kurt Angle's spirits at the June 27 *SmackDown!* He was coming off a great week that included a surprise nontitle win over Undertaker, and making the immortal Hollywood Hulk Hogan tap out at *King of the Ring.* Kurt felt so good that he even shed the hairpiece he'd worn since *Judgment Day,* though he was soon scratching his head. John Cena, a six-foot-one inch, two hundred-forty pound prospect, called up that day from Ohio Valley Wrestling, answered Angle's open challenge to locker-room up-and-comers. An incredulous Kurt asked, "What is the one quality *you* possess that makes you think you can walk out here, come in the ring and face the very *best* in the business?" Cena responded, *"Ruthless aggression!"* He then hammered away at the medalist, collecting *ten* two-counts before a desperation rollup gave Angle the victory. Despite the loss, the approval of the crowd and wrestlers backstage, including a *rare* handshake from Undertaker, suggested a Superstar was born that night.

Kurt would attribute Cena's performance to having the flu, but the only "bug" he'd been suffering of late was one of *jealousy*—he was sick of being overlooked by the Undisputed Champion, who at that point was advising the Chicago fans to set their VCRs July 11, when The Rock made his return to *SmackDown!* "But now for the *bad* news," he added. "I'm gonna beat The Rock down, and *make him pay* for ever stickin' his nose in my business." Angle came out and challenged Undertaker to a title shot on *SmackDown!* next week. The Dead Man offered to kick his ass for him right there, then had to refrain from laughing when Kurt

UNDERTAKER

HEIGHT: 6'10" WEIGHT: 328 lbs.
OTHER NAMES: American Badass, Big Evil, Red Devil, Phenom, Dead Man
FINISHING MOVES: Last Ride powerbomb; Chokeslam; "Takin' Care of Business"
(Dragon Sleeper); Tombstone Piledriver
CAREER HIGHLIGHTS: Undisputed Champion (4); Tag Team Champion (6);
WCW Tag Team Champion; Hardcore Champion
2002 HIGHLIGHTS: Beating Ric Flair in a No-Disqualification match at
***WrestleMania X8;* defeating Hollywood Hulk Hogan for the Undisputed**
Championship at *Judgment Day;* defending the Undisputed Championship in a
Triple-Threat match at *Vengeance;* facing WWE Champion Brock Lesnar first at
Unforgiven,* then in a "Hell in the Cell" Match at *No Mercy.

explained he'd just had a "tune-up match" with rookie John Cena that night. But he was serious when he added, "Any *time,* any *where,* any *how*...it's *on,* man." Still feeling disrespected, Angle asked to touch the title, then threw it in 'Taker's face and gave him a taste of the ankle lock before leaving the ring.

Jeff Hardy resorts to a chair to break 'Taker's hold.

A *SmackDown!* contest was scheduled with Angle in three days, and Vince McMahon gave the Dead Man good news just before his July 1 *Raw* Ladder match against Jeff Hardy. "At *Vengenace,* whether you're champion or not, you've got The Rock." 'Taker couldn't

believe his ears, "*Whether* I'm champion or *not?*" Realizing he'd stepped in something, Vince could only reassure the Dead Man he'd face The Rock at *Vengeance,* "no matter what." But "what" almost happened in Boston's Fleet-Center on July 4—as 'Taker prepared Angle for the Last Ride, Kurt countered by wrapping his legs around the Phenom's neck. Fading fast from the triangle choke, Undertaker lowered Kurt to the canvas, pinning him...

Angle and 'Taker draw to *Vengeance.*

only to start tapping just as the referee counted three. After several minutes of heated debate, ring officials finally declared the match a draw, with Undertaker retaining the belt. The controversial decision incited Vince McMahon. In a taped segment on July 8 *Raw,* he announced, "At *Vengeance,* it will be Undertaker versus Kurt Angle...versus The Rock in a Triple-Threat match for the Undisputed Championship."

Atlantic City's Boardwalk Hall erupted in anticipation on July 11 as finally The Rock had come back to *SmackDown!*...and he invited *Halloween: Resurrection* star and "...the undisputed champion of hip-hop" Busta Rhymes to the ring for a pie-eatin', ass-whoopin' rendition of "Under the Boardwalk!" The Great One then got down to business, and the Dead Man at *Vengeance*. "You think you got a problem with the Brahma Bull?" he asked. "You have no idea—and The Rock means *no idea!*—what problems you're gonna have after The Rock takes your title! You got something to say to The Rock? Well, The Rock has one thing to say, very simple, Undertaker: *Just bring it!*"

Instead, out came Kurt Angle, who suggested Rocky's absence might have messed up his sense of reality. "The reality is, Undertaker *isn't* the one you're going to have to worry about at *Vengeance;* it's *me.*" Perhaps Rock would have been concerned…if he recognized who was talking to him. The bald guy sort of looked like Kurt Angle, wore the "Calvin Klein Donkey-Nuts"

> **"The Rock has one thing to say, very simple, Undertaker: *Just bring it!*"**

cologne Kurt wore, and that "A" on his ring attire *might* have stood for "Angle," or the crowd's "asshole" chant, or even "anus." But then it hit the People's Champ, who playfully sang, *"Somebody got a haircut…"* Rock then admitted he was genuinely impressed with the talent that showed up on *SmackDown!* "We've got The Rock, Busta Rhymes and *Dr. Evil himself!*" Seeing as his nemesis knew how to sing, Kurt offered to make Rock *tap* at next week's show. But the Brahma Bull didn't want to wait, and made Angle submit to his own ankle lock, then Undertaker attacked, Chokeslamming both Rock and Angle to the canvas, talking trash at the downed People's Champ before exiting the ring.

Backstage minutes later, Rock wondered if the Coach shrunk and turned white when Marc Loyd started asking him questions. Pushing Loyd aside, Rock said he'd been gambling earlier in A.C. on a slot machine called *Vengeance*, and three Brahma Bulls came up. Since he was feeling lucky, he figured Angle and 'Taker should just have their scheduled Tag match that evening, because the clock was ticking on the Dead Man's reign as Undisputed Champion—ten days and counting! Fortune would also favor John Cena, who'd pin Y2J in the Tag contest after a hard right from Undertaker broke up a Lionsault. But both Angle and Big Evil's luck hit "Rock Bottom" as the Great One attacked and laid the smack down!

In a taped interview for the July 18 *SmackDown!*, Big Evil gave Michael Cole and his *Vengeance* opponents the bottom line, "The Rock and Kurt Angle are going to find out why Undertaker is the American Badass, and why that ring is *my yard*. I'm coming to take the yard. If you're caught in it, you're going to *pay.*" The yard in this case was Wilkes-Barre, PA's First Union Arena at Casey Plaza, where 'Taker joined Cole and Tazz on commentary for a one-on-one between Rock

Rock's not quite sure who this bald guy is.

Ruthless aggression abounded with a *Vengeance* at the Joe Louis Arena on July 21—in the *Raw* and *SmackDown!* locker rooms, between the brands' General Managers as they vied for Triple H, even at the announce table, where minutes before the Pay-Per-View started, *SmackDown!* commentators Michael Cole and Tazz demanded that *Raw* announcers Jim Ross and Jerry "the King" Lawler split the show in two. The matches hadn't even started, and it was already one hell of a night.

The wood broke out big-time in the PPV's first contest, a Tag Team Tables match between Bubba Ray and Spike Dudley against Chris Benoit and Eddie Guerrero. Requiring both tag partners to be put through tables sounded like a match born in Dudleyville, but it was the Canadian Crippler and Latino Heat dictating the pace early. Spike moved one table as Bubba caught a dual-powered superplex off the top rope, while Bubba deflected Spike from tasting wood set up in the corner. Despite suffering the Crippler Crossface, Spike soon finished Latino Heat with the Dudley Dog through a table at ringside, only to get slammed through one by the Rabid Wolverine moments later. Benoit next set Bubba up for a German suplex through a table, but the reversal and Bubba Bomb ultimately polished off the Crippler, giving the Dudleyz the hardwood win.

Backstage, new *Raw* GM Eric Bischoff told Jonathan Coachman how proud he was to see *his* Superstars show such ruthless aggression in the Tables match, though he was concerned to see his most ruthless prospect, Triple H, heading into the *SmackDown!* General Manager's office. Having given Bischoff the chance to make his sales pitch after *SmackDown!* a few days ago, Hunter explained he now wanted to hear Stephanie's, and went inside.

Cruiserweight Champion Jamie Noble just about pitched a fit during his Title match against former title holder Billy Kidman. Instead, he settled for throwing trashy girlfriend Nidia into Kidman when the battle spilled to the outside floor, buying himself time to injure Kidman's arm with a modified armbar. Kidman fought through the pain and nailed the back of the redneck champ's head with an Enziguri, then landed a top rope powerbomb for a two-count. Enough of Noble's wits remained, however, to roll away from a Shooting-Star Press, then floor Kidman with a massive underhook powerbomb to retain his Cruiserweight Championship, and ensure at least one more night of he and Nidia living in the lap of trailer park luxury.

When it came to winning the Undisputed Championship, Kurt Angle wasn't listening to any "ifs" from Marc Loyd

Joe Louis Arena
Detroit, MI

TRIPLE-THREAT UNDISPUTED CHAMPIONSHIP MATCH

The Rock defeated *Undertaker* and *Kurt Angle*; Rock pinned Angle to win the Undisputed Championship

CRUISERWEIGHT CHAMPIONSHIP MATCH

Jamie Noble (w/Nidia) defeated *Billy Kidman* via pinfall to retain the Cruiserweight title

EUROPEAN CHAMPIONSHIP MATCH

Jeff Hardy defeated *William Regal* via pinfall to retain the European title

John Cena defeated *Chris Jericho* via pinfall

INTERCONTINENTAL CHAMPIONSHIP MATCH

Rob Van Dam defeated *Brock Lesnar (w/Paul Heyman)* via disqualification to retain the Intercontinental title

NO-COUNTOUT, NO-DISQUALIFICATION MATCH

Booker T defeated *Big Show* via pinfall

TAG TEAM CHAMPIONSHIP MATCH

Lance Storm & Christian defeated *Hollywood Hulk Hogan & Edge* via pinfall to win the Tag Team titles

TAG TEAM TABLES MATCH

Bubba Ray & Spike Dudley defeated *Eddie Guerrero & Chris Benoit* by sending both men through tables backstage; he was dealing only with *"whens."* Suddenly, Paul Heyman approached Kurt and introduced him to his *SummerSlam* opponent, Brock Lesnar. The gold medalist wasn't intimidated, and couldn't wait to face the next big Intercontinental Champion. But he had news for him, "This isn't the Summer of Brock. It's all-year Angle. Got it?" As Lesnar smiled and moved on with Heyman, Angle muttered, "I *hate* pompous people."

That being the case, Angle could be grateful not to see William Regal in his rematch with Jeff Hardy, who made the ever-arrogant Brit cry at July 15 *Raw* by defeating him for the European title. Mr. Xtreme's aerial antics kept Regal reeling at first, until his Swanton Bomb was harshly greeted by the ring veteran's knees. Crippling the Hardy air attack with a series of forearms and a half nelson back suplex, Regal was suddenly stunned to tears again when Jeff surprised him with a schoolboy rollup for the one-two-three! Jeff received backstage congratulations from Ric Flair and Hollywood Hulk Hogan, who joked that maybe he'd climb the top rope someday and deliver a *"Hulkamaniac* Swanton Bomb!" Both legends agreed the idea was no more preposterous than Vince McMahon's new general managers. Flair worried that the WWE's young turks would get caught in the crossfire of a ruthless power struggle, while Hogan opined Stephanie and Bischoff would become either "the *single* best thing" for the industry, or the *worst.*

Chris Jericho intended to make sure newcomer John Cena wouldn't have to worry about such things, since he planned on annihilating the rookie with a chair before their match officially started. But as Cena grabbed the chair and brandished it against Y2J's back, the King of the World painfully discovered that being green didn't make the kid yellow. Jericho's experience responded to the strong start with the Breakdown, but Cena's ruthless aggression dealt the cocky Canadian a top-rope super-plex for the two-count. A Y2J dropkick decimated Cena's oncoming corner splash, but his decision to go for the Walls of Jericho when his Bulldog and Lionsault promised a likely win resulted in a "larger than life" upset—Cena countered the submission move into a rollup for the three-count!

Whatever Triple H and Stephanie McMahon were negotiating inside the *SmackDown!* office, it kept Coach and a very anxious Eric Bischoff glued to the outside door. The *Raw* GM's distress only grew when Stephanie's lawyer arrived and entered the room with legal documents. At ringside, there was no apprehensiveness in Brock Lesnar—The Next Big Thing took the Intercontinental title from the referee's hands and slung it over his shoulder, as if he'd already beaten Intercontinental Champion Rob Van Dam. Despite their vast contrast in ring styles, both Superstars entered the match with the same game

plan—to keep the other man grounded. For Lesnar, that meant preventing the champ from using the top rope, while for Mr. Pay-Per-View, keeping the six-foot-four-inch behemoth off his feet was essential. RVD met success with a drop toehold that tripped his opponent face-first into the corner, but a crossbody attempt to the outside proved disastrous when Lesnar caught and rammed him into the ring post. Van Dam tried again with a moonsault, yet again Brock's strength countered with a jarring power-slam to the outside floor.

"The Whole Dam Show's" aerial persistence finally produced results when a top-rope kick to Lesnar's chest and the Rolling Thunder earned a two-count. Brock got up and stalled a Five-Star Frog Splash by going into the F-5, which Van Dam reversed into a midair DDT. RVD then hit the Five-Star and covered Lesnar, but Paul Heyman broke up the count by pulling the referee to the outside floor, drawing a disqualification for his client. Brock and RVD continued fighting after the bell, with Van Dam gaining the advantage and looking to celebrate his win with a Van Terminator. Unfortunately, Heyman held Van Dam's leg long enough for Lesnar to deliver first a fisherman's suplex, then the F-5 onto the steel chair! If the crowd hadn't heard the match was awarded to RVD, they wouldn't know it by the way The Next Big Thing stood over him in the ring.

The mind games continued backstage as Stephanie McMahon exited her office with a disgruntled look on her face. Eric Bischoff beamed at the thought that Triple H didn't sign, until she revealed he *did.* Irate, Bischoff started yelling at The Game as he came out of the office, only to look like an ass as Hunter told him to back off. He only signed his *divorce* papers; he hadn't decided between *Raw* or *SmackDown!* yet. Embarrassed, Bischoff swore to the Coach, "He's mine. Just watch...he's *mine."*

Most people already counted out Booker T the moment Bischoff granted Big Show a No-Countout, No-Disqualification Match for *Vengeance.* The Book's chances looked even slimmer on the outside floor, when Show's fist drove a chairshot back into his opponent's face. But the No-DQ aspect worked more *for* the Bookerman than *against* him—he choked the giant with a camera cable, nailed him with a TV monitor and spring-boarded off the main commentator's table with a scissors kick that cut Big Show down through the Spanish announce counter. Back in the ring, Show prepped Booker for the Chokeslam, but a low blow set the big man up for a new move—a 360-degree top-rope legdrop called the Houston Hangover! With literally his biggest victory since joining the WWE, Booker T capped off his night with a well-deserved Spin-a-Roonie!

There was much uncertainty over the past few weeks as to who would emerge the Undisputed Champion at

Vengeance's Triple-Threat match; not even Dawn Marie and Torrie Wilson could agree who'd win while they appeared at the World in Times Square. One answer that *was* forthcoming, however, was Triple H's decision. Both Eric Bischoff and Stephanie McMahon made their cases to him at ringside one last time, taking shots at each other along the way. Admitting he felt stuck between "an arrogant prick" and "a cold-hearted bitch," the free agent was ready to return to *SmackDown!* when Shawn Michaels intervened. Weeks before, the former Showstopper promised to reunite Triple H with his nWo buddies at *Vengeance*, but since Vince McMahon disbanded the faction last week, there were now only two things for Hunter to consider: "friendship and fun," the idea being that there could be no greater fun than two best friends making Bischoff's life "a living hell." Such an offer sounded too good for Hunter to pass up, and with that, The Game was back on *Raw*.

Bischoff gloated over Stephanie in the ring, explaining the difference between them: "I have testicles…and you *don't*." Stephanie left the ring, but not before giving Bischoff a slap so hard his testicles could feel it. She later assured Marc Loyd backstage that she was also in the process of hurting him where he lived; she was in direct contact with every *Raw* Superstar already, and when the time was right, from under Bischoff's nose, "I'm going to rip the heart right out of *Raw*."

Triple H's decision elicited mixed reaction backstage. Rikishi was disappointed since Hunter was a leader for the younger Superstars in the *SmackDown!* camp; Booker T was down with The Game going *Raw*, but if he got in his business, the *next* game they'd play would involve getting his ass kicked by the five-time WCW Champion! (And Goldust added they had "the bigger joysticks" to do it!) And Lance Storm and Christian… well, they didn't care. They were busy spouting off their Un-American rhetoric in the ring before their Tag Team match against Champions Edge and Hollywood Hulk Hogan, a "real American fraud" who, like America, was "past his prime and living in past glory." The Canadian combo doubled up Edge in the early going, but the red, white and blue waved proudly when the red- and yellow-clad Hogan tagged in and unloaded the big boot on Storm. A reverse DDT by Christian only helped Hogan Hulk up, and bought himself the big boot and legdrop. Storm broke up a certain three-count, then met the Hulkster with a superkick after Christian knocked him to the outside floor.

Edge picked up where his partner left off, cleaning house on the challengers until Storm avoided a spear that caught the official. While the ref recovered, Test charged the ring and smashed Edge with a big boot, allowing Storm to make a cover. Amazingly, Edge kicked out, while Rikishi stormed down and ensured Test could no longer interfere. Edge laid Storm out with the spear, but while Hogan and Christian's battle occupied the referee, Chris Jericho raced in and nailed Edge with one of the Tag belts! Storm covered him for the one-two-three, and the Tag Team Championship headed for the Great White North.

"Red, White and Blue Machine" Kurt Angle wouldn't have time to talk with Eric Bischoff backstage, or to think about his offer to join *Raw*; he had a Triple-Threat Undisputed Title match to win. But when the contest started, The Rock and Undisputed Champion Undertaker ignored the gold medalist while they jawed at each other, looked at Angle, then ignored him again! Kurt got their attention by shoving them, though it came with their right hands. Having fought one another so often in the past, it was no surprise that each Superstar knew the others' signature maneuvers; nevertheless, it was still exciting to watch them *execute* their opponents' moves—The Rock caught the Phenom with a Chokeslam, then slapped the ankle lock on Angle. Kurt countered the move and delivered the Rock Bottom on the Great One, only to be scooped up in the Angle Slam…by Undertaker!

The Brahma Bull soon caught 'Taker with a People's Elbow, but Angle slammed him onto the announcer's table outside, then raced in to cover the Dead Man. The champion kicked out, then went "old school" on the medalist, walking the top rope and coming down with a shot that busted Angle open. The referee took a bump while Rock and Deadman, Inc. countered finishers again, allowing Angle some payback with a chair shot on 'Taker and an Angle Slam on the People's Champ. Unable to get the three-count on either Superstar, Kurt got caught in a sharpshooter, though the move left the Great One susceptible to a Last Ride from Undertaker, whose pinfall victory was thwarted when Angle latched on the ankle lock. 'Taker escaped and got the Olympian up for the Last Ride, until Angle countered with the triangle choke he used to make Undertaker tap on July 4 *SmackDown!*.

Big Evil was just about done when The Rock broke the hold and tried to Rock Bottom Angle. Kurt again went for the ankle lock, which Rocky converted into a near-fall rollup. Minutes later, Angle caught Undertaker in what definitively looked like the match-winning Angle Slam, but his stupid in-ring celebration for executing the move enabled the People's Champ to regain his wits and deliver the final Rock Bottom of the night. Getting the three-count, The Rock had become an unprecedented seven-time champion, and enjoyed his first Undisputed reign! ■

The Great One clotheslines Kurt Angle.

It was strange that Vince McMahon would pose his question while looking straight at Bradshaw on June 24, since ruthless aggression was practically a prerequisite for being Hardcore Champion. Even stranger was Harvard grad and *Tough Enough* finalist Christopher Nowinski. He'd rattled Bradshaw's cage since his June 10 *Raw* debut, which included getting a cheap rollup for himself and William Regal over the Texan and Spike Dudley two weeks later. Nowinski showed no interest in the Hardcore title, he challenged Bradshaw to a straight, *non*-title wrestling match on July 1. Nowinski explained it so Terri and everyone else could understand; the idea of looking over his shoulder for oncoming trashcans and two-by-fours on a 24/7 basis didn't appeal to

and Angle. As the battle spilled outside the ring, Angle ducked a Rock clothesline that caught Undertaker, who paid the Great One in kind before he could land a People's Elbow on his gold medal opponent. Rocky won the match via a DQ, but received a pounding from the Phenom, who in turn caught a steel chair from Angle. Kurt then slapped his ankle lock on Rock and, though the match had already ended, made him tap out. With *Vengeance* on his mind and ruthless aggression on his side, the psychological win made Kurt Angle more than ready to add the Undisputed Championship around his waist.

him. "I prefer to compete in a more civilized manner, " he said, "where the most dangerous weapon is *not* a table or a chair. It's *intelligence.* "

> ## "I prefer to compete in a more civilized manner, where the most dangerous weapon is *not* a table or chair. It's *intelligence.*"

Whatever his reasoning, Nowinski was smart enough to exploit his opponent's inability to kick his Hardcore habits, using a cowbell behind the unsuspecting official's back to kayo Bradshaw for the upset. But the victory apparently backfired on Nowinski, since it earned him a Hardcore Title match at July 15 *Raw*. The scholar offered to let himself be pinned, then almost caught Bradshaw off-guard with a quick small package rollup.

" **W**ho has enough ruthless aggression to reach *for the stars as you never have before?*"

Trish catches Victoria with a kick to the mid-section.

Breaking the count, the big Texan chased Nowinski to the back, only to be blindsided by another WWE newcomer—Johnny "The Bull" Stamboli, a former WCW Hardcore and Tag Team Champion trained in the WCW's Power Plant facility. With the 24/7 Hardcore rule in effect, Stamboli pinned Bradshaw, and just two weeks after making his *Heat* debut became the WWE Hardcore Champion...for a few minutes, anyway. Bradshaw would soon recapture the belt with a surprise Clothesline from Hell that nearly decapitated the hot-blooded Italian.

Cena, Nowinski and Johnny The Bull were part of a growing movement in World Wrestling Entertainment, one that seemed to go hand-in-hand with Vince McMahon's "ruthless aggression" credo. Christened the "Generation Next"

in *Raw* magazine's September 2002 issue, these young stars weren't waiting for their big break; they were *making* their opportunities.

Indications of the movement had already been seen; Brock Lesnar was a prime example. Randy Orton and David "Deacon" Batista had already established themselves on *SmackDown!*, and made very strong showings against each other in three separate Tag encounters. Orton partnered with Faarooq (June 27), the Big Valbowski (July 4) and Mark Henry (July 11), while Reverend D-Von provided guidance for Batista, who'd pick up the win in all three contests with powerful spinebusters, twice on Orton and once on the World's Strongest Man.

There were more new faces coming up to play, including six-foot-six-inch, two hundred-sixty-pound Sean O'Haire, a two-time WCW Tag Team Champion whose modified Death Valley Driver generated solid *Heat* with victories over Justin Credible on June 30, then Shawn Stasiak on July 14; Shannon Moore, formerly of WCW's "3-Count" boy band (of which "Sugar" Shane Helms, aka The Hurricane was also a member), who dropped his July 13 *Velocity* debut against Tajiri, but delivered a top-rope corkscrew moonsault that was no laughing matter for Hugh Morrus the following week. OVW alum Victoria looked impressive in her first match as a WWE Diva on the July 7 *Heat*, despite finding Trish Stratus too hot to handle. Clearly, the door had been left wide open, and there was plenty of new talent walking through it.

"Larger than life" Superstars like Chris Jericho didn't seem to care about the company's sudden infusion of new blood; he was more interested in using a chair to put the legendary Hollywood Hulk Hogan out to pasture on the ringside steps during the June 27 *SmackDown!* Jericho was surprised to hear his own theme music and to see Edge make his dramatic return. He paid Y2J back by saving the icon Edge had worshipped since childhood. Only three weeks had passed since looming shoulder surgery, at Jericho's hands, had forced Edge to forfeit his *King of the Ring* quarterfinal to Y2J. A medical reevaluation and physical therapy, however, determined the operation unnecessary, and Edge made sure Jericho felt every bit of his healed shoulder with a spear to the midsection!

At the July 4 broadcast in Boston, Jericho accepted Vince McMahon's offer of a chance to meet Edge at *Vengeance;* then John Cena entered the WWE owner's office. Vince commended Cena for the ruthless aggression he'd shown against Kurt Angle last week, and McMahon got another look at it when Jericho

berated the "disrespectful" rookie for interrupting his meeting. Cena slapped Chris' face, provoking a confrontation that evening which saw the hometown native baffle the first-ever Undisputed Champion with numerous counterholds and near-pinfalls. A "Flash Back" sleeper hold slam, combined with added leverage from the second ring rope, gave Y2J the one-two-three. But it was Cena who looked like "King of the World," delivering a sidewalk slam that sent his adversary reeling to the outside floor.

Y2J gets a taste of ruthless aggression from John Cena.

Y2J received more bad news the following week—his *Vengeance* match was put on hold. Edge and Hogan won the Tag Team Championship from Billy and Chuck on Independence Day, and McMahon thought they should defend their title at the Pay-Per-View. But shock quickly replaced disappointment after an Undertaker fist broke up Jericho's Lionsault, allowing tag partner John Cena to score the quick pinfall. Shock then turned into frustration at the July 18 *SmackDown!;* unable to finish the greenhorn cleanly in singles competition, Jericho resorted to a low blow, drawing the disqualification. Chris snapped and whaled away at the youngster's back with a steel chair

UNDRESSED TO THRILL

Less than one week after crowning the *King of the Ring 2002*, World Wrestling Entertainment uncovered its "Queen of the Scene"—the scene being the World in New York City's Times Square, site of the first-ever *WWE Divas Undressed* competition that aired on TNN June 29. Eight WWE Divas—Terri, Dawn Marie, Torrie Wilson, Stacy Keibler, Trish Stratus and *Tough Enough* Champions Nidia, Jackie Gayda and Linda Miles—put their bodies on the line as they competed for the coveted "Golden Thong" award. Jonathan Coachman hosted the event, while Michael Cole ensured ecstatic co-commentator Jerry "the King" Lawler didn't whip out his "magistrator." The panel of judges consisted of Edge, Paul Heyman, Jazz, Al Snow and Maven, while the packed house of WWE fans were the clear winners of the night.

The competition consisted of three categories: Lingerie, Bra and Panties, and Fantasy Free-For-All. The "free-for-all" portion unfortunately came in the first round for Trish, who strutted her under-wares to the Stratusfied crowd until the ever-bitter Jazz (still sidelined after ACL surgery) laced into her with a crutch. Trish, a strong favorite going into the contest, was unable to continue, further emphasizing it was any Diva's thong to win.

Walking down the World ramp for each round in their attire of desire, the sexy contenders bared well under all of the shapely curves the evening offered, not to mention the bumps. Virginal Molly Holly, the Women's Champion, literally winged it in "angelic" garb on stage to protest the degrading contest, until security dragged her from the stage kicking and screaming. One could hardly blame them for *not* running towards elderly Mae Young when she came out on the runway during the Bra and Panties portion; if anything, they ran in the *opposite* direction! A King-cam backstage in the Divas' dressing room threatened to reveal all several times, yet cruel Fate not only denied Lawler of his royal treats, but also chose to sic Mae on him!

Crowd reaction seemed to lean towards Jackie in the Lingerie portion, while all eyes steered towards Dawn Marie and Stacy during the Bra and Panties segment. But it was Torrie Wilson putting the Free-For-All competition to bed in her nightie, complete with one tasty lollipop! Not even an all-day sucker like Rico, who'd been running the show backstage, could dampen the moment...despite taking the stage wearing feathered headgear and a bra and panties himself! (Even *Mae* was more preferable!)

When all was said and *undone*, Torrie Wilson was declared the winner of the first-ever Golden Thong award. Of course, with the Divas being as competitive *outside* the ring as they are inside, jealousy got the better of some of them, resulting in a more violent "Free-For-All"! Needless to say, the experience means Torrie will face only stiffer competition when she defends her golden G-strap at *Divas Undressed* in 2003! ∎

until ring officials pulled him away. Amazingly, the assault didn't stop Cena from showing up on the *Sunday Night Heat* that preceded *Vengeance,* or from challenging Y2J to one more match at the PPV. "Jericho'll find out that I'm not only the rookie with ruthless aggression," he promised, "but I'm also the rookie who's gonna *kick his ass!*"

> ["I'm not only the rookie with ruthless aggression, but I'm also the rookie who's gonna *kick his ass!*"]

New Tag Team Champions—Hollywood Hulk Hogan & Edge.

From the instant the icon entered Boston's FleetCenter to his classic "Real American" theme song, to the moment Edge covered Chuck following twin big boots and legdrops, winning the Tag Team Championship on the Fourth of July *SmackDown!* was an indescribable moment for young stud Edge and the immortal Hogan. It was the first time the forty-eight-year-old Hogan officially wore Tag Team gold. While it was the eighth go-round for Edge, perhaps it was his sweetest, since he was sharing it with the legend he grew up watching in Toronto. The tandem successfully defended their titles in a rematch

Superstar ★ profile

CHRIS BENOIT

HEIGHT: 5'10"
WEIGHT: 235 lbs.
OTHER NAMES: Canadian Crippler; Rabid Wolverine
FINISHING MOVE: Crippler Crossface
CAREER HIGHLIGHTS: Intercontinental Champion (4); Tag Team Champion
2002 HIGHLIGHTS: Returning to the ring for the first time in a year at May 27 *Raw;* defeating Rob Van Dam to win the Intercontinental Championship at July 29 *Raw;* winning the Tag Team Title tournament at *No Mercy;* smacking Tag Team partner Kurt Angle over the head with a beer bottle at the *SmackDown!* Halloween party October 31; competing in a Triple-Threat Tag Team Championship match at *Survivor Series.*

the following week, from the site of *WrestleManias IV* and *V*, though they'd collide with a new force that made its feelings about Atlantic City, and the rest of the United States, all too clear.

"On behalf of the citizens of the world," and mostly his Canadian homeland, Lance Storm kept his promise to beat an American on June 27 *SmackDown!* with a superkick to the face of the World's Strongest Man, Mark Henry. Fellow Canadian Test wasn't so fortunate in his match, and felt the referee's decision to disqualify him reeked as bad as Rikishi's Stinkface, since it was the Phat Man who shoved him into the official. Joined by Christian, the three "Un-Americans" (originally called "Anti-Americans") invaded ringside as *SmackDown!* kicked off in Boston on July 4. They interrupted Lilian Garcia's rendition of "America the Beautiful" to inform "ignorant" American youths everywhere that Independence Day *wasn't* "...the day Will Smith saved the world from a bunch of aliens," and to shout out a birthday message for "the most hypocritical nation in the world: *America sucks!*"

Taking exception to the Un-Americans' tirade, Rikishi came down and jumpstarted a match against Storm, who'd score the pinfall after Christian preoccupied the referee while Test nailed the Phat Man with a big boot. Rikishi overcame a similar ploy against Test on July 11, landing a Samoan drop for the win, but leaving himself open to attack from Christian and Storm. Racing down to help Rikishi were new Tag Champs Hogan and Edge, who cleaned house as the Boardwalk Hall fans' "USA!" chants reached a frenzied pitch. The save drew all six participants into a *SmackDown!* contest the following week, where ironically,

The "Un-Americans"—Christian, Lance Storm and Test—demand to be heard.

fellow Canadian Edge scored the win with an Edgecutioner on Storm. With the victory, Hogan and Edge demonstrated they were ready not only to defend their belts against Christian and Storm at *Vengeance*, but that, win or lose, they would stand united against the Un-Americans.

"**W**ho has enough ruthless aggression to excel beyond your wildest dreams?"

If Vince McMahon didn't think the WWE Divas could get ugly, then he was sorely mistaken. Torrie Wilson, Stacy Keibler and Dawn Marie may not be known for their in-ring prowess, but while parading their scantily clad wares on June 27 *SmackDown!* to preview that week's *WWE Divas Undressed* competition at New York City's the World, the three got into a shoving match that showed they were quite capable of ruthless aggression. Torrie walked away with the Golden Thong award at the event where less was more, then sparked some intense fireworks at July 4 *SmackDown!* when she not only liberated Stacy of her clothing in a Bra and Panties match, but stripped down to her own star-spangled lingerie!

The Phat Man overpowers Test.

On *Raw* three nights earlier, *Tough Enough 2* Co-Champion Jackie Gayda showed Mr. McMahon personally that she was *Undressed* to impress at the upcoming competition, before teaming up with the virginal new Women's Champ Molly Holly against fellow *TE2* Champion Linda Miles and former Champion Diva Trish Stratus. Before the match, Molly glared at Trish while declaring herself honored, "…to bring *dignity* back to the WWE Women's title by *earning* it, not by being a sleazy tramp who *sleeps* her way to the top." Naturally offended, Trish admitted to Molly she'd felt bad about making butt jokes, "But now, it'll be my pleasure *to kick your fat ass!*" Linda took care of Jackie while Trish kept up her end of the team, Bulldogging Molly off the ropes for some personal Stratusfaction!

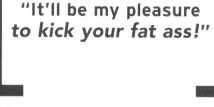

"It'll be my pleasure to kick your fat ass!"

Ironically, high-and-mighty Molly would also show some *Raw* thigh on July 1, though not by her own volition. She was beating up smartmouth Jackie, who'd been blaming the Women's Champ backstage for losing last week's Tag match, when Trish stormed the ring and pulled down Molly's tights, revealing what the King cried out as "granny panties!" Embarrassed, Molly was quick to remind her adversaries that she was *no* pantywaist—interrupting Torrie Wilson during her beachside bikini photo shoot in Atlantic City on July 11, she insisted she was Women's Champion because of her physical and mental skills, "not because I can prance around in my underwear." She proved her point on *SmackDown!* that night by cinching Torrie in a combination submission/pin, then emphasized it at *Raw* four days later, scoring a back suplex and putting her posterior weight on the ropes for some payback on Trish.

For some Superstars, unleashing ruthless aggression was their ticket to thriving in the WWE. For seasoned journeymen like Tommy Dreamer and Raven, however, it was necessary for their survival in the company. Dreamer had become known in the organization as the crazy guy who ate strange things or drank from the toilet. Raven was a bitter birdbrain who walked out on his *Sunday Night Heat* color commentary position alongside Jonathan Coachman on May 26, protesting what he considered to be inadequate star treatment. Seeing the pair as wrestlers who failed to realize their potential, Vince McMahon ordered them to compete June 24, with the loser to be cut from *Raw.*

Recalling the experience to Terri on July 7 *Heat*, Raven said the experience made him feel "…like a

Raven puts the boots to Matt Hardy.

UNDER NEW MANAGEMENT

Vince McMahon's nominations of Stephanie McMahon and Eric Bischoff as the new General Managers for *SmackDown!* and *Raw* were, to say the least, shocking. Not only had he hired a daughter who eight months before tried taking over World Wrestling Entertainment, but he now employed the one man who spent years and millions of dollars in an open attempt to destroy his company! Both GMs offered the ruthless aggression Vince sought to have land the two brands, and both wasted no time going to war with each other. As fans continue to debate over which WWE brand is better, a tale of the tape might offer more insight. ■

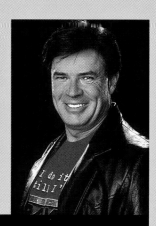

STEPHANIE McMAHON		ERIC BISCHOFF
General Manager of *SmackDown!*	**OCCUPATION**	General Manager of *Raw*
Establishing herself as the WWE's dominant female	**OBJECTIVES**	Puts "E" in the WWE
Make *Smackdown!* the No. 1 brand		Making *Raw* the No. 1 brand
Former owner of Extreme Championship Wrestling	**CAREER HIGHLIGHTS**	Former President of World Championship Wrestling
Former Women's Champion		Created *WCW Monday Nitro* (which beat *Raw* in the ratings for eighty-four consecutive weeks)
Former wife of Triple H		Creative genius behind the New World Order
Signed Undertaker, Chris Benoit, Eddie Guerrero, Matt Hardy, Crash Holly, Big Show and Brock Lesnar to exclusive *Smackdown!* contracts	**2002 HIGHLIGHTS AS WWE GM**	Signed Triple H, Chris Jericho, Lance Storm, Test, Christian, Billy, Chuck, Rico, D-Von, Stacy Keibler, Maven, Randy Orton, Al Snow, Big Valbowski, Hurricane, Batista, Scott Steiner, Ivory and Sean Morley to exclusive *Raw* contracts
An advocate of exclusive Cruiserweight Division		Reinstated the World Heavyweight Championship
Reinstated the WWE Heavyweight and Tag Team titles		Unified European, Hardcore, Intercontinental Titles with World Heavyweight Championship
		Created the Elimination Chamber
		Introduced 3 Minute Warning
Smart, manipulative	**PROS**	Smart, manipulative
Thinks on her feet		Thinks on his feet
Gives as good as she gets		Martial arts black belt
A McMahon through and through		Major ass-kisser
Emotions get the better of her	**CONS**	As often as he can (also drove WCW into the ground; too many deals under the table)
Lacks heavy-duty business experience, based on failed ECW Alliance		
Has slowly earned *Smackdown!* Superstars' respect	**WHAT OTHERS THINK OF THEM**	Sleeps with one eye open

Billy Kidman drives Jamie Noble to the mat.

pawn in some megalomaniacal billionaire's chess game." Perhaps, but it produced results. Planting Raven with a Death Valley Driver, the victorious Dreamer reawakened from the match as the Innovator of Violence, a nickname he'd introduce to Brock Lesnar on *Raw* the following night, then remind fellow ECW alum Steven Richards in a bloody Singapore Cane match win on July 15. Meanwhile, only minutes after his *Raw* presence was to be felt nevermore, the departing Raven was given a painful parking lot sendoff

from Matt Hardy, paying him back for his role in the Undertaker-staged assault from a week before. But Raven's grappling game *Heat*ed up—he notched a victory against Matt on June 30, put Dreamer to sleep with the DDT-styled Raven Effect in their July 7 rematch and gave Hardcore Champ Bradshaw a run for his money in a losing cause on the July 15 *Heat*.

New Cruiserweight Champion Jamie Noble and girlfriend Nidia were enjoying the "new money" lifestyle—not to mention a *full*-sized bed for their new trailer—that came with his title. Hooking Chavo Guerrero and Hurricane in his "Trailer Hitch"—a submission move similar to a reverse figure-four—for consecutive *Velocity* wins on June 30 and July 7, the rural Superstar was convinced that so long as he held the belt, he and Nidia would never be poor again. But his hold started loosening after a Billy Kidman powerbomb gave the high-flyer and Hurricane a July 11 *SmackDown!* Tag win over him and Tajiri (who two weeks before fell to a Shooting-Star Press in the same Tag matchup). It was announced at the July 18 *SmackDown!* he'd face Kidman in a Cruiserweight Championship match at *Vengeance;* Noble's fear of losing his "meal ticket" prompted him to sneak-attack the No. 1 contender only moments after he'd beaten Tajiri with another Shooting-Star Press. Nidia added to the low-class assault in her usual gutter-trash fashion, slapping the face of the already-helpless Cruiserweight.

Contributing to Eddie Guerrero's loss to Ric Flair at *King of the Ring* set the stage for an intense rivalry between Bubba Ray Dudley and Latino Heat, but it was Vince McMahon's lecture on ruthless aggression that helped set the tables for *Vengeance.* Ordered to compete on June 24 *Raw,* Guerrero countered the Bubba Bomb and hooked the tights for a cheap rollup win, though paid for it afterwards with a powerbomb through some wood. Chris Benoit ran down and ambushed Bubba Ray with the Crippler Crossface, prompting Spike to join his half-brother in Tag Team payback on July 1. The Bubba Bomb cooled off Latino Heat for the win, but Benoit—wrestling in his first match in a year—German-suplexed Spike through a ringside table, then Crossfaced Bubba into position for a Guerrero Frog Splash.

Picking a fight with the first "sucka" to mouth off at July 8 *Raw,* a frustrated Guerrero became further outraged when Booker T rolled him up for the three-count. Benoit joined Eddie in a double-team effort, but soon cleared the ring after being outnumbered by Goldust and some chair-swinging Dudleyz. The Book

and Goldust later returned the favor, preventing a Guerrero/Benoit beatdown after Bubba tapped out to the Crossface in his match against the Rabid Wolverine. With nothing settled at the evening's ensuing Ten-Man Tag match, or at the Six-Man Elimination match on July 15 that featured Jeff Hardy and William Regal, it was decided that Benoit and Guerrero would face the Dudleyz at *Vengeance,* in a Tag Team Table match to determine whose wood would splinter first.

"**W**ho has enough ruthless aggression to make the necessary sacrifices of mind, body and soul in order to be a success in this company?"

Vince McMahon knew just how to push Jeff Hardy's buttons on June 24—he knew "Mr. Xtreme" wanted respect in the WWE. And since he'd been buzzing around Undertaker in recent weeks, there was no one more qualified at making people famous "the old-fashioned way" than the Undisputed Champion. Vince gave Jeff a non title match on *Raw* that evening…*without* Team Xtreme brother Matt in his corner. The brothers seemed all right with that stipulation backstage, as Jeff verbalized what both understood (though it eventually became evident that Matt realized it in a different way)—with no Tag titles on *Raw,* "We've got to go our own way and become stars ourselves. I'm going to be a star again, or I'm going to die trying."

> ## "I'm going to be a star again, or I'm going to die trying."

'Taker didn't have an easy time against Jeff—the fast, agile Hardy kept the six-foot-ten-inch. three hundred-twenty-eight-pound Phenom off-balance with high-risk maneuvers like a plancha to the outside floor. The size difference and more than a decade of destruction ultimately caught up to the young daredevil as he was taken for a Last Ride. But as Undertaker rode his bike up the *Raw* ramp, he stopped when he heard a battered Jeff get on the mic. "You've beat my ass time and time again," he yelled, "but we're not done. I want a match for the WWE Undisputed title...*my* match to beat you...a *Ladder match!*" Being a glutton for punishing others, Big Evil accepted.

Respect in the form of the Undisputed title would dangle high over the ring in Manchester throughout the entire *Raw* broadcast on July 1, while backstage an Xtreme underdog's confidence soared. Jeff explained to Terri that he'd been in several of the greatest ladder-oriented contests in WWE history, while Undertaker had been in *none.* "There's a saying here in New Hampshire, 'Live Free or Die,'" he added. "I'm living for the moment. I'm *not* dying tonight."

Mr. Xtreme taunted death from the moment he approached ringside and sat on Big Evil's hog. Inside the ring, two ladders quickly became potent offensive weapons—a battering ram for 'Taker, a diving board for Jeff to propel over the top rope and onto the Phenom outside the ring—in a match that put both Superstars on a level playing field. In fact, only 'Taker's last-ditch Chokeslam from the top step would end Mr. Xtreme's climb for the gold. Undertaker

[
"You haven't broke me, 'Taker...I'm still standing!"
]

started riding off with the Undisputed title, then returned to the ring and gave Jeff a Last Ride for good measure. But as he started leaving again, Jeff lifted himself up with the ropes, grabbed hold of the mic and said, "You haven't broke me, 'Taker...I'm still standing!" The Undisputed Champion grabbed Hardy, ready to deliver the killing blow...then raised

The new General Manager of *Raw* —Eric Bischoff?!

his exhausted opponent's hand. Even Undertaker, a man who demanded total respect, couldn't help but admire such grit and determination, and on that night, the Red Devil gave Jeff Hardy his due.

His name was entered in the loss column, but the Ladder match had firmly cemented Jeff's career as a singles competitor, and a main player in the *Raw* roster. And WWE gold *would* surround his waist in "Extreme Country" Philadelphia a week later—a reverse Bulldog and Swanton Bomb left William Regal a sobbing mess backstage, while the fans hailed Jeff as the new European Champion.

Of all the surprises that unfolded in the month since his "Ruthless Aggression" address, it was Vince McMahon himself providing the greatest ones at the July 15 *Raw*. From New Jersey's Continental Airlines Arena, Vince announced not only the disbanding of the nWo, but the hiring of two General Managers—one for *Raw*, and one for *SmackDown!* Both with complete authority and responsibility over their respective brands. "It's time to shake up *Raw*, *SmackDown!* and the entire World Wrestling Entertainment brand," he proclaimed, "and by God, the shake-up begins *tonight.*"

Michaels's return. The sudden departure of Stone Cold Steve Austin. The dispersion of the nWo. In a year when World Wrestling Entertainment had already seen more than its share of surprises, it took Vince McMahon only one night to deliver one of the biggest blows in sports entertainment history. The first was hiring the former head of World Championship Wrestling who tried putting him out of business, and nearly succeeded. The second? That these once sworn enemies were now standing on stage and *hugging* each other.

Bischoff sauntered down the ring and introduced himself, smiling as he asked the crowd, "When Vince was out here a couple weeks ago, talking about ruthless aggression, just who the hell do you think he was talking about?!" He then recalled his days raiding

> "It takes a real son of a bitch to be successful in this business. So, from one son of a bitch to another, allow me to introduce you to the new General Manager of *Raw...Eric Bischoff*!"

Speculation regarding the *Raw* GM's identity ran rampant throughout the audience and the Superstars backstage—candidates ranged from Mick Foley to Paul Heyman, from Vince's brother Rod to his son Shane, who'd confront his father backstage for the first time since selling his WCW stock to Ric Flair in November 2001. Shane knew who Vince had hired, and warned he was "a parasite, and he's going to screw this company over, royally." But the billionaire remained steadfast with his decision as he walked on stage and made his big announcement.

"It takes a real son of a bitch to be successful in this business," Vince said. "So, from one son of a bitch to another, allow me to introduce you to the new General Manager of *Raw...Eric Bischoff!*"

The return of Hollywood Hulk Hogan and the New World Order. Rock versus Hogan. The Draft. Hogan winning the Undisputed title at *Backlash*. Shawn

the WWE locker room and convincing Superstars like Hogan, Randy Savage, Hall and Nash, Roddy Piper, Bret Hart and others to sign with WCW. "What I really did," he clarified, "was take this little family business, this 'McMahon monopoly,' and gave it one swift kick in the crotch. And it was *sweet.*"

Signing Alundra Blayze and having her throw the WWE Women's Championship belt in the trash on *WCW Monday Nitro*. Going live with *Nitro* two minutes early every week and revealing the results of *Raw*'s then-taped main events so fans didn't have to tune in. Creating a "cutting-edge" faction like the nWo. Bischoff credited his ruthlessly aggressive moves as the reason why *WCW Monday Nitro* beat *Raw* for eighty-four consecutive weeks, and how it forced McMahon to change the way he did television. Ironically, such moves were the impetus behind Vince's decision to make Bischoff his new *Raw* GM.

"I was surprised," Bischoff admitted. "*Damn* surprised. But then I thought about it, and it made sense. If there's *one* person who can take this struggling franchise and turn it into a national media powerhouse…well, that would be Eric Bischoff!"

Bischoff declared his first official act would take place at *Vengeance*, where he'd sign to *Raw* the one Superstar he never could get to jump ship and join WCW—Triple H. He also assured the *Raw* wrestlers backstage that they'd generally like working for him, since he was a winner. "Let's face it," he said, "the WWE *needs* me, and the fans *deserve* me. I promise that I'm here to put the 'E' in 'WWE.' "

> ## "Let's face it, the WWE *needs* me, and the fans *deserve* me."

Backstage in the locker room, many Superstars agreed—there was something in Bischoff's words, but it *wasn't* "entertainment." Former WCW employees like Booker T couldn't believe their eyes, while Ric Flair, whose memories of Bischoff were hardly good, eyed his new boss warily. Only Big Show looked happy about the news—with Nash down and the nWo out, the big man saw the arrival of his old WCW boss as a personal saving grace, and he used their history to convince Bischoff to sanction a No-Countout, No-DQ match against Booker T.

Eric spent the rest of the show making his presence known to everyone on *Raw*. He sucked up to Undisputed Champion Undertaker while ignoring Hardcore Champion Bradshaw, who'd lose his title briefly that night to Johnny the Bull. But as Bischoff rubbed elbows with the new Hardcore Champ backstage, Bradshaw charged in with a Clothesline from Hell to recapture his title, then properly reintroduced himself to the new GM.

As for Bischoff's sole interest in signing Triple H at *Vengeance*, he picked up his cell phone as *Raw* closed that evening and left a message—he was a huge fan and couldn't wait to meet him at *SmackDown!* that week. But the message Bischoff left wasn't for Hunter; it was for *The Rock*.

"The Bisch" was pure *Raw* as he walked into Wilkes-Barre's First Union Arena for July 18 *SmackDown!*. Saying hello to the brand Superstars, rubbing elbows…he wasn't wasting any time trying to make *his* show No. 1. When he ran into the one man who knew him better than most, one knew the *Raw* GM was only making small talk with Hollywood Hulk Hogan while he looked for Triple H and The Rock. Shameless as ever, Eric insisted he wanted to say hi to his buddy…then asked where Edge was and if he and Hogan were a package. Hogan asked about negotiating, which Bischoff credited the Hulkster as the guy who taught him to *always* negotiate. As he walked off, Hogan muttered, "Negotiate, my *ass.*"

Before long, Eric came across the Great One and laid his cards on the table—he wanted him on *Raw* next Monday. "What, you think The Rock is gonna go to *Raw* because of *you?!*" he asked, as if he couldn't believe the question. "No-no-no-no-*no*. The Rock *is* going to *Raw* live this Monday night…but it's because of what The Rock does at *Vengeance* this Sunday night! And when he won the Undisputed title, he planned to go on *Raw*, on *SmackDown!*, *The Osbournes*, *The Sopranos*, even on *Frasier* "and kick him right in the nuts!" Bischoff couldn't stop himself from laughing, telling the People's Champ how he wished he'd had him back on *WCW Monday Nitro*. That gave Rock reason to smile—"Yeah, well while you were on *Nitro*, giving all your creative genius and creative input to WCW… The Rock was doing his part about putting your company *out of business.*" And with that, the Brahma Bull left a seething Bischoff in the locker room.

Vince McMahon professed amazement as he walked onto the First Union Arena stage—never had he seen his wrestlers look so concerned about his announcement on *Raw.* To alleviate matters, he informed his *Raw* Superstars that they could freely negotiate with the *SmackDown!* GM, while his *SmackDown!* employees could follow suit with Bischoff. And with that came the announcement of his new General Manager for *SmackDown!*—another ruthless, aggressive individual who had almost put the WWE out of business, but failed. "The only difference is that the *Raw* audience deserves Bischoff as their new GM, but the *SmackDown!* fans may *not* deserve their new GM." And out came Vince's daughter, *Stephanie McMahon.*

Like her new entrance music suggested, *SmackDown!*'s new General Manager appeared "All Grown Up" as she welcomed everyone to *her* show. Gone was the bratty, whining, Billion Dollar Princess exiled from the WWE just under four months ago. Now her tone was all business, and that business concerned the *Raw* "parasite" wandering around backstage.

"I won't allow Eric Bischoff to steal your *SmackDown!* Superstars," Stephanie swore, and her promise included soon-to-be ex-husband, Triple H. "The egg is going to be on your face, Bischoff, when you're left standing there, and Triple H leaves *Vengeance* and comes back home to his fans on *SmackDown!*"

Unfortunately, the yolk looked to be on Stephanie, whose first official act was to throw Bischoff out of the building. She soon caught up with her estranged spouse before he entered a limo inside the backstage parking lot, and asked to talk "strictly business" about staying with *SmackDown!* The Game cut her off—he'd make his decision after listening to all sides at *Vengeance.* Suddenly, he looked Stephanie over, leaned in and asked her, "You gaining weight?" then smirked as he entered the limo. The window then rolled down, attracting Stephanie's attention... only to come face-to-face with Eric Bischoff. "Don't worry, Steph," he said, "I think you look *great!*" Bischoff laughed as the car drove off, yelling to the irate *SmackDown!* GM that he'd see her at *Vengeance.*

The Billion Dollar Princess, Stephanie McMahon is GM of *SmackDown!*

"The egg is going to be on your face, Bischoff!"

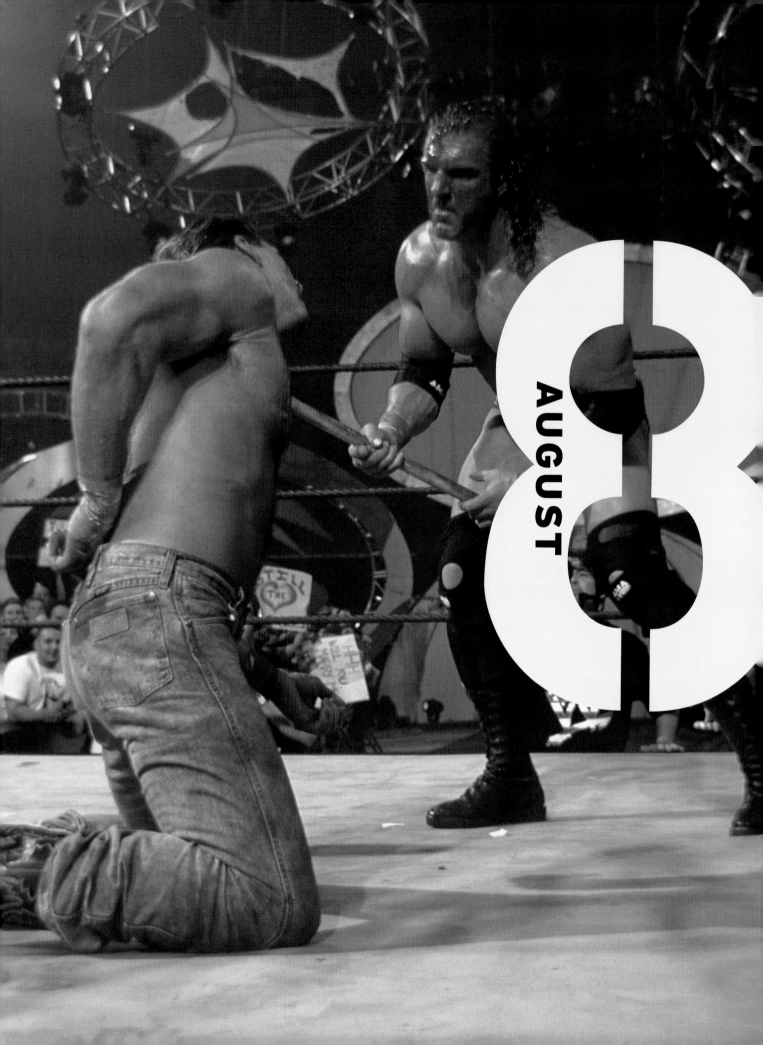

AUGUST 8

"F5: WIND ESTIMATE: **261-318 m.p.h.**
TYPICAL DAMAGE: **Incredible damage. Strong frame houses leveled off foundations and swept away; automobile-sized missiles fly through the air in excess of 100 meters (109 yds); trees debarked; incredible phenomena will occur.**
—*Fujita Tornado Damage Scale*
T. Theodore Fujita, University of Chicago
National Weather Service Storm Prediction Center
National Oceanic and Atmospheric Administration (NOAA)

Summer Slammed

From the fury of *Vengeance* emerged a new Undisputed Champion, one whose recent box-office success with *The Scorpion King* had also made him one of Hollywood's hottest new actors. But the jabronis in Tinseltown would have to wait—the *people* smelled what The Rock was cookin' again.

The Brahma Bull wouldn't have to look far for his opponent at the next Pay-Per-View—*King of the Ring* had already established a No. 1 Contender who stormed through every opponent he faced. It had been a long, hot summer in the Tri-State area, but a tornado—an *F-5*, to be precise—was headed towards Long Island's Nassau County Veterans Memorial Coliseum. And its time of arrival was August 25, 2002—*SummerSlam*.

Weeks before the "Rock vs. Brock" storm hit New York, however, an air of mystery unfolded at the July 29 *Raw* in North Carolina's Greensboro Coliseum Complex: who assaulted Shawn Michaels in the parking lot? Best friend Triple H didn't know, but he'd become hell-bent on finding out.

Granted, The Game had Pedigreed Michaels in Grand Rapids, MI's Van Andel Arena seven nights earlier, and he knew Shawn was waiting for him in the parking lot while he headed ringside. Hunter wasn't looking for a

Raw comes to a screeching halt for the Showstopper.

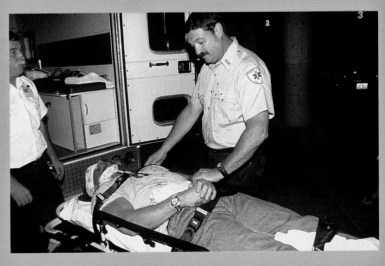

fight, though; he staged a return to D-Generation X greatness so he could give his best friend "a cold, hard slap on the face of reality"—the reality being that Shawn's career as "the Showstopper" was over, ended four years ago by a broken back. "The Game has passed you by," said Hunter, who was offering his best friend a choice, "You can *try* to fight me…or you can say, 'Screw pride.' You can walk down to this ring, you can accept your role, you can accept your disabilities, and you can accept being my manager."

[
"I'm going to exercise my right as an American citizen to beat him from one side of this arena to the other."
]

A response would have to wait. A floor manager directed Hunter towards the parking lot, where he'd find several WWE Superstars surrounding an unconscious Michaels, his face bloodied by the smashed window of a nearby car. As Shawn was placed into an ambulance, an impressed Eric Bischoff pulled the Cerebral Assassin aside, saying, "I guess this means you're not friends anymore. I heard you didn't play well with others, but *man…*!" With a reply to the *Raw* General Manager that would make a deaf man blind, Triple H stormed off.

The investigation would start with the events that transpired July 29. The suspects were many starting with Bischoff's new *Raw* acquisitions, Test and Tag Champions Lance Storm and Christian. Carrying an upended U.S. flag to symbolize "…the upside-down beliefs and values of American society," Storm promised a "distinctly Un-American" impact on the show, "and that impact will strike a blow for freedom and justice." But Michaels interrupted the tirade, and demanded Bischoff bring him Triple H. "I'm going to exercise my right as an American citizen to beat him from one side of this arena to the other." Not

appreciating HBK's interruption, or his comments towards the Un-Americans, Storm guaranteed that Shawn, like every other American, would soon be put in his place.

Storm's threats that evening would also pertain to the American Badass. Undertaker was providing Harvard grad Christopher Nowinski an "old school" beatdown and a second Last Ride in as many weeks when he was laid out by Test's big boot and a Storm and Christian

Sgt. Slaughter can't stomach any more of the Un-Americans.

"conchairto." After waving their upside-down American flag in victory over the unconscious Phenom, the Un-Americans headed backstage, discussing "one more piece of business to take care of." Soon after, Michaels' body was discovered lying in the parking lot.

Joined by his Un-American allies backstage at Maryland's Baltimore Arena for August 5 *Raw*, Storm bragged to Terri, "Just like America, Undertaker has been humbled, emasculated and exposed to the world as a weakened bully that is no longer feared or even respected." Further gibberish regarding presidential acts of "American aggression" that slaughtered innocent civilians overseas boiled the red, white and blue blood of Sgt. Slaughter, who came out and challenged Test to a match. The Un-American accepted, then continued the faction's own terrorist campaign by blindsiding the retired ring great before he could even enter the squared circle. But the threesome wouldn't be so brave when Triple H soon approached them backstage with a sledgehammer and some questions regarding last week's "unfinished business." Christian confessed that they were looking for Shawn Michaels, but someone had beaten them to it. The Game bought their story, but warned if he learned otherwise, "I'm going to make the Un-Americans un-*conscious.*" He then drove his point home by sledgehammering a nearby table.

The Un-Americans didn't realize it at the time, but they'd find common ground with an emerging enemy; Booker T also was a suspect in Shawn Michaels's assault. The five-time WCW World Champion certainly had the motive—following a scissors kick victory over Eddie Guerrero on July 29—The Book bumped into Michaels backstage and pointed out how Triple H's Pedigree assault had reminded him of his own embarrassing dismissal from the New World Order on June 10 at the hands of HBK. Intent on finding The Game, Shawn explained that was a business decision, not personal,

Booker T takes Latino Heat.

and he had bigger things to worry about. As Michaels moved on, Booker told Goldust on the side, "Sounds to me like a personal invite to an ass-whoopin'."

The backstage comments prompted a visit from Triple H on August 5. Booker T and Goldust—accompanied by the leg-humping "Minidust," his answer to being "ripped off" by the latest *Austin Powers* film—were preparing for a Tag match against William Regal and Christopher Nowinski. Book told Hunter, "I don't give

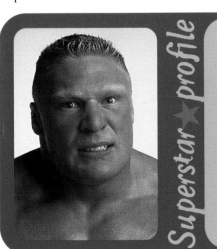

Superstar ★ profile

BROCK LESNAR

HEIGHT: 6'4"
WEIGHT: 295 lbs.
OTHER NAMES: The Next Big Thing; Here Comes the Pain
FINISHING MOVE: F-5
CAREER HIGHLIGHTS: Undisputed Champion; *King of the Ring 2002*
2002 HIGHLIGHTS: Making his WWE debut on March 18 *Raw*; being named the No. 8 *Raw* pick at the Draft March 25; winning the tournament at *King of the Ring*; defeating Hogan at August 8 *SmackDown!*; defeating The Rock to win the Undisputed Championship at *SummerSlam* (he became WWE Champion when the titles split in September).

a damn about what happened to Shawn Michaels; in fact, I'm *happy* about it. But I didn't do it. I'm clean." The Cerebral Assassin took his word for it, then raised his sledgehammer and cautioned, "If I find out you're lying to me, I'm going to introduce you to *my* little friend."

Hunter's next suspect was Big Show. The giant reminded Michaels that he hadn't forgotten his "tough love" superkick from three weeks before. Shawn didn't look so tough without the nWo surrounding him. The *Raw* GM brought out a merciless streak in Show, giving him the thumbs-up after he pummeled Spike Dudley (already beat up after his Tag Team Tables match at *Vengeance*) that night. Show then chokeslammed Bubba Ray on top of his half-brother and through a table. Trish Stratus almost suffered a similar fate on July 29,

following an Intergender Tag victory over the big man and Women's Champion Molly Holly, until Bubba Ray tried adjusting Show's attitude with a massive chair shot. The outraged big man felt slighted when Michaels, busy searching for Triple H, rebuffed his complaints over what transpired in the ring, muttering, "Maybe I ought to *make* you have time for me."

The fact that Big Show was seen lurking around backstage only moments before Michaels's attack was reason enough for Triple H to put him high on the list of suspects. But the big man was in no mood to answer Hunter's questions on August 5—he'd just lost a Table match to Bubba Ray after being suckered by the seductive Trish, then nailed in the midsection by a Baltimore Ravens helmet-wearing Spike Dudley. Between the humiliating

CONTINENTAL CROSSOVER

Eric Bischoff celebrated his first week as *Raw*'s General Manager with a controversial decision to unify the WWE European and Intercontinental Championships on July 22. The belt had changed hands thirty-six times since February 26, 1997, when British Bulldog Davey Boy Smith defeated brother-in-law Owen Hart in Berlin, Germany, in the final round of the inaugural European Championship tournament. During its brief-yet-prestigious five-year history, two men—D'Lo Brown and William Regal—each held the European title four times, while four other Champions— Shawn Michaels, Triple H, Kurt Angle and Chris Jericho—went on to become WWE or World Heavyweight Champions. The title was officially consolidated into the Intercontinental Championship when Jeff Hardy fell to Rob Van Dam in a Ladder Unification match at July 22 *Raw*. ■

EUROPEAN CHAMPIONSHIP HISTORY

WON BY	DATE WON	WON BY	DATE WON
Davey Boy Smith	2/26/97	Eddie Guerrero	4/3/00
Shawn Michaels	9/20/97	Perry Saturn	7/23/00
Triple H	12/11/97	Al Snow	8/31/00
Owen Hart	1/20/98	William Regal	10/16/00
Triple H	3/16/98	Crash Holly	12/2/00
D'Lo Brown	7/14/98	William Regal	12/4/00
X-Pac	9/21/98	Test	1/22/01
D'Lo Brown	10/5/98	Eddie Guerrero	4/1/01
X-Pac	10/18/98	Matt Hardy	4/26/01
Shane McMahon	2/15/99	Hurricane Helms	8/27/01
Mideon	6/21/99	Bradshaw	10/22/01
D'Lo Brown	7/25/99	Christian	11/1/01
Jeff Jarrett	8/22/99	Diamond Dallas Page	1/31/02
Mark Henry	8/23/99	William Regal	3/21/02
D'Lo Brown	9/26/99	Spike Dudley	4/8/02
Davey Boy Smith	10/26/99	William Regal	5/6/02
Val Venis	12/12/99	Jeff Hardy	7/8/02
Kurt Angle	2/10/00	Rob Van Dam	7/22/02
Chris Jericho	4/2/00		

Big Show helps Bubba Ray Dudley meet the mat.

only announcement that matters tonight is as of this moment on… *Raw is Jericho*!"

The "majestic King of the World" welcomed Baltimore's "pathetic, common morons" to "Monday Night *Jericho*" on August 5, since *Raw* was now *his* show. He explained he'd been lured away from the *SmackDown!* brand "…because Eric Bischoff knows the difference between a Superstar like Chris Jericho and a has-been like Ric Flair." That's when Triple H headed ringside and confronted Jericho. The Game didn't give a flying crap why Jericho made the move; he just wanted to know if he'd ambushed his best friend, as a measure of revenge for losing the Undisputed title to Hunter at *WrestleMania*. Jericho denied the alle-

loss and Triple H's accusations, Show confessed he *wished* he'd hurt Michaels, and stormed off.

One other possible culprit surfaced. On the same night Shawn Michaels was ambushed, a campaign between Ric Flair and Undisputed Champion The Rock resulted in a hard-fought match. That ended cleanly with a Rock Bottom on the Nature Boy. Flair had remained in the ring afterwards to make a very important announcement, only to be interrupted by a steel chair between the eyes. His attacker picked up the mic and proclaimed, "The

> "I don't think you've got the balls to do what someone did to Shawn Michaels."

gation, pointing out it was Triple H who Pedigreed his own best friend only two weeks ago. Hunter reminded Jericho he was in the ring when the assault occured, yet chose to believe his denial. "I don't think you've got the balls to do what someone did to Shawn Michaels," he told him, and moved on.

Raw GM Eric Bischoff wouldn't have been a likely candidate to assault Shawn Michaels himself, though the ruthless aggression he displayed since becoming *Raw*'s General Manager indicated he had the stroke to orchestrate such an attack. After all, it was his July 22

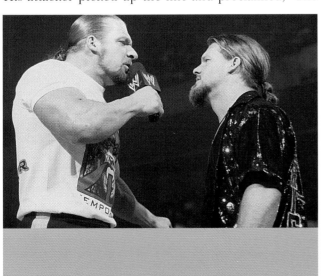

Triple H accuses Jericho of the attack on Michaels.

announcement that Michaels would play "a supporting role" as Triple H's manager that led to The Game Pedigreeing his best friend later that night. Bischoff also didn't appreciate the former Showstopper interrupting his new Un-American family members the following week; it became obvious to Bischoff that loose cannons like Michaels would continue trying to undermine his authority unless he took drastic action.

While The Game used a sledgehammer to weed out the guilty party on August 5, the *Raw* GM decided to help his prize Superstar, setting up a live satellite feed from San Antonio so Hunter could talk with HBK directly. Seeing Michaels on the TitanTron, his face bruised and battered, Hunter expressed guilt over what happened to his best friend, and swore whoever was responsible was "a marked man." But then Michaels revealed the police in Greensboro had given him the security footage from the parking lot's cameras. Running the footage on the TitanTron clarified nothing at first, but then Michaels explained how modern technology was able to enhance the tape's images. Running the enhanced footage, it became sickeningly clear to everyone watching who was standing over Shawn Michaels' body in the parking lot on July 29. "It was *you*, Hunter."

The Cerebral Assassin, his head bowed down, said nothing for a moment. Then, with a smile of pure evil, he looked up at the TitanTron and answered, "You're *damn right* it was me, Shawn."

Triple H wanted to prove a point: that Shawn Michaels, his best friend and cofounder of D-Generation X, a former WWE World Heavyweight, Intercontinental, European and Tag Team Champion, was now "weak and vulnerable." That's why he *needed* to be The Game's manager, "...so I could *protect* you. Shawn. I could have crippled you in that parking lot, but I *didn't.*" Hurt and disappointed over Hunter's comments, the former Showstopper admitted he wasn't in the best of shape, but according to his doctors, "I'll be one hundred percent

["I will finish the job, Shawn! I will *cripple* your ass!"]

by say...*SummerSlam.*" Triple H laughed, asking if that was some kind of challenge, to which Michaels responded, "You're *damn right.*"

No longer laughing, Hunter told Shawn to face facts. "You can't wrestle anymore! 'HBK' is *dead!*" he yelled. "There's a new Game in town. And Shawn... You go through with this, and *I won't stop.* I will finish the job, Shawn! I will *cripple* your ass! And what then? What if, when it's all over, you can't walk anymore? What if, when it's over, you can't pick up your two-year-old son anymore? What if, when this is over, you can't hold your wife anymore? Or even worse, what if you can't satisfy your wife anymore, as *a man?*"

"I know I can't wrestle anymore," Michaels replied. "I know I'm no longer the Showstopper. But I can still *fight.*" And Shawn decided that at *SummerSlam* he would walk down to the ring one last time, "not to wrestle, but to fight. And fight *you*, Hunter. And in front of the entire world, I'm going to show my little boy that sometimes...you've got to fight to be a *man.*" With that, Michaels got out of his chair, pulled off his mic and walked off camera.

While Michaels recuperated at home in San Antonio, Triple H set the record straight with his "disappointed" Seattle KeyArena fans at August 12 *Raw*—"I used Shawn Michaels to get to the top, just like Shawn Michaels used me to *stay* at the top." The fact was, according to Triple H, he was better than Shawn Michaels ever was, even in his prime...though *not* because of the fans that chanted his name over the past eight months. He realized it was trying to accommodate those cheers "...that made me sick, that made me soft, that made me weak to the point where I got beat by an old piece of crap like Hulk Hogan." But that was over now—Hunter's sole objective for *SummerSlam* wasn't to fight

METAL'S BRASS BOY

Becoming a bona fide rock star wasn't happenstance for the King of the World. Then again, maybe it was, since it was this past July when Chris Jericho, a.k.a. the arrogant, egotiscal Moongoose McQueen (sound familiar?), and his band Fozzy released *Happenstance*. An Atlanta-based band that includes guitarist and cofounder Rich Ward and several members of the metal band Stuck Mojo, Fozzy's sophomore effort for Megaforce Records offered four new songs, including the title track and "To Kill a Stranger," plus several covers (among them Judas Priest's "Freewheel Burning" and Black Sabbath's "The Mob Rules"), and established the group as no mere flash-in-the-heavy-metal-pan.

Music critics lauded the follow-up to 2001's self-titled debut, while the usually *louder* than life Jericho's—Moongoose's—lead vocals rocked the 25,000 metalheads attending Germany's "Bang Your Head Festival" in July, then headlined "Global Meltdown," the WWE's *Global Warning* after party in Melbourne, Australia's Festival Hall August 10. Fozzy next caught serious airwaves on the August 19 *Raw* in Norfolk, then MTV and WNEW's *The Eddie Trunk Show* in New York in November, before taking over the World for a concert that month. So the next time the ass-clowns sitting in the nosebleeds of Section 108 want to jeer Chris Jericho and all of his ring accomplishments, do Moongoose McQueen and Fozzy a favor and *shut the hell up!* ■

> "You want to show your son what it means to be a man? Then when this is all said and done, Shawn, you take your son, and put him on your lap while you're sitting in your wheelchair, and you point out to him what a *real* man looks like. You point him out to *me* on TV."

or defeat Shawn Michaels, but to *maim* him. Having ended careers in the ring before (Mick Foley), Michaels would be no different. "You want to show your son what it means to be a man?" Triple H asked. "Then when this is all said and done, Shawn, you take your son, and put him on your lap while you're sitting in your wheelchair, and you point out to him what a *real* man looks like. You point him out to *me* on TV."

The Game's comments were cut short by The Rock, making his way down the ramp to address *Summer-Slam* challenger Brock Lesnar, whose attempted mind games by sitting in the first row were about to earn him "a front-row ticket to a Brahma Bull ass-whoopin'!" But Hunter sidetracked his longtime rival, provoking him to a fight in the ring until Brock's interference allowed him to Pedigree the Undisputed Champion. As a result, Rock and Triple H would become part of the evening's Eight-Man Tag match, though neither would factor into the decision. But Eric Bischoff, knowing how big a Triple H-Rock match would be for *Raw*'s ratings, decided they would go one-on-one in Virginia's Norfolk Scope Arena on August 19.

As the main event neared that evening, the Cerebral Assassin entered the ring with two pieces of business to discuss. He wanted to inform Brock Lesnar that he'd done him a favor by having Bischoff alter the nontitle bout with Rock to a No-Disqualification match. Hunter promised to leave enough of the Great One to make it to *SummerSlam*…provided that when Lesnar showed up on *Raw* with his shiny new Undisputed Championship belt, "know that *I'm* going to be waiting for you." But first Triple H needed Shawn Michaels to sign and return some paperwork, or there could be no

match at *SummerSlam*. "This paper says that when—not 'if,' but *when*—I cripple Shawn Michaels, *when* I leave him a bloody pile in this ring, *when* I leave Shawn Michaels in a wheelchair for the rest of his life, that I cannot be held legally responsible," he explained. "These papers, when signed, state that I can have my way with Shawn Michaels at *SummerSlam*, and there is not a damn thing that anybody can do about it."

The Game's comments prompted Eric Bischoff to "show his ass" and protect his own *Raw* interests, should Michaels sustain any permanent damage. "As far as WWE is concerned," he told Triple H backstage, "officially, your match will never happen." But Hunter had the faxed document with Michaels's signature and smiled. "Oh, but it *will* happen, Eric," he said, adding that it would be "the most brutal match that anyone has ever seen. The last image that anyone has of Shawn Michaels is going to be of a bloody, crippled mess in that ring. And regardless of whether you sanction it or not, it will be an image that lives in their minds, in *your* mind and in *my* mind, forever."

The No-DQ matchup between The Rock and Triple H would quickly shape up to be another classic, though Brock Lesnar's ringside presence and Rock injuring his ribs on the outside barricade gave The Game a clear advantage. The Great One fought past the pain valiantly until Hunter rammed him with the steel steps. Stalking Rock with a sledgehammer he'd grabbed from under the ring, he prepared to show Michaels what awaited him at *SummerSlam*. But Hunter wasn't prepared for Shawn to actually show up and start pounding on him. If the Showstopper's injuries had cost him a step or two, then someone forgot to tell him; moments after delivering Sweet Chin Music that sent an attacking Brock Lesnar out of the ring, he'd soar over the top rope, landing on top of the Cerebral Assassin and several security guards on the outside floor. Rock had run into the crowd in pursuit of Lesnar, so the match ended in a no-decision. But Shawn Michaels achieved a small victory that night—if Triple H was expecting the Heartbreak Kid to be easy prey at *SummerSlam,* he was going to be sorely heart-*broken.*

While the three Un-Americans beared up to Triple H's cross-examination, none of them were getting off scot-free for their other crimes on *Raw.* Lance Storm and Christian almost dropped their Tag Team titles to the Hardy Boyz on August 5 after Matt's Twist of Fate and Jeff's Swanton Bomb laid out Storm. Christian disrupted the referee's count by pulling Jeff out of the ring and clobbering him with one of the tag belts. The action drew a disqualification, meaning they retained the title. However, Test's attack drew the chain-wielding fury of Undertaker, who chased the cowardly Canucks backstage as they escaped in a nearby car, 'Taker then continued after them on a commandeered police motorcycle!

Booker and Goldust had better luck in tag action that night—the Golden One avenged a brass-knuckled loss to Regal at the August 4 *Sunday Night Heat* when his inverted atomic drop on the Brit left him open to

Booker's scissors kick. The victory prompted them to add some "Goldmembers" to their waists, so Goldust made a *Raw* proposition to GM Eric Bischoff the following week—should The Book beat Lance Storm one-on-one that night, they would get a Tag Team title shot at *SummerSlam.* Bischoff liked the idea…though *not* Minidust's personal attempt to "seal the deal" by attaching himself to the GM's leg! During the contest, Christian's ringside interference tripped Booker up as he went for his finisher, but Goldust returned the favor with a right hand to Storm's face, setting him up for the scissors kick and the three-count. Test raced in to gang up on Booker and Goldust, but again met resistance when the Dead Man arrived to help fend off the Un-American sneak attack.

The Un-Americans chose to stand their ground in the arena that night. Bischoff announced they would all face off in an Eight-Man Tag match that also featured The Rock and Triple H. Backstage with Terri, Storm and Christian were sickened about having to defend their belts against jive-talking freaks who only further proved America was "the United States of *Embarrassment.*" An extremely confident Test, meanwhile, was thrilled that Bischoff sanctioned a match with Undertaker at *SummerSlam,* where he promised to enter and *bury* the so-called American Badass in his own yard. Amazingly, Test proved he could do it during the Eight-Man main event; 'Taker chokeslammed Storm, then propped Christian up for the Last Ride, but the Un-American's

REY MYSTERIO

Superstar ★ profile

HEIGHT: **5'3"**
WEIGHT: **165 lbs.**
FINISHING MOVES: **West Coast Pop; 619**
CAREER HIGHLIGHTS: **WWE Tag Team Champion; WCW Cruiserweight Champion (5); WCW Tag Team Champion (3); WCW Cruiserweight Tag Team Champion**
2002 HIGHLIGHTS: **Making his WWE debut at July 25 *SmackDown!;* defeating Kurt Angle and Chris Benoit to win the WWE Tag Team titles with Edge on November 7 *SmackDown!***

World Wrestling Entertainment continued its international odysseys on August 8-10 with a twenty-plus hour flight to Melbourne, Australia, where the Superstars unleashed the *Global Warning Tour*. The event marked the WWE's first live event in the land down under since 1986, so both the company and Aussie fans were determined to make the most of it. In a vein similar to the annual *Fan Axxess* weekend that precedes *WrestleMania*, the WWE hosted fan *Frenzy* at the Crown Showroom August 8 and 9, consisting of eight sold-out two-hour sessions and a plethora of interactive exhibits for over eight thousand fans, including calling matches through fantasy play-by-play; autograph sessions and in-ring Q & A's with WWE Superstars; trivia competitions; waging interactive war with others via XBOX's *WWE Raw* video game; and the WWE Hall of Fame exhibit. WWE *Global Warning Tour* after hours hubs were also stationed for the three nights, hosting WWE-themed nights and offering ticket giveaways to the *Global Warning Tour* event.

Rico greets fans at *Fan Axxess* down under.

In addition to entertaining their international fans inside the squared circle, the Superstars took time to help those less fortunate at the Charity Gala August 9. The black-tie dinner at the Plaza Ballroom gathered Melbourne's elite to pool their resources and aid for Challenge, a nonprofit support network for children and families living with cancer and other life-threatening blood disorders. The evening included dinner, music and an auction of donated items and collectibles, including three items which Triple H purchased—three life-sized portraits of The Rock, Hulk Hogan and The Game himself.

After enjoying a special pre-show hospitality function with an exclusive number of supporters, the Superstars kicked off an historic *Global Warning Tour* event in Colonial Stadium August 10. The crowd of 56,734 shattered the stadium's attendance record, set previously by rock legends the Rolling Stones; in return, they got nothing *but* satisfaction from the WWE. Rikishi started the evening off with a kickass win over Rico in a *"Kiss* My Ass" match, then made sure the reluctant stylist "Stinkfaced" up to his end of the bargain. Mark Henry next power-slammed the way to victory for himself and Randy Orton against Reverend D-Von and Batista, while Nidia's trashy ring-side distractions allowed redneck Romeo, Jamie Noble, to retain his Cruiserweight title over The Hurricane.

Pretty boys Billy and Chuck didn't look so good to the Aussie crowd, nor were they tough enough to beat the tandem of Chavo Guerrero and Hardcore Holly that night. Un-American Test's disparaging remarks about Australia fueled Kurt Angle to an Angle Slam for the Red, White and Blue win, while Lance Storm and Christian kept the Tag Team gold for Canada, with Storm using one of the belts to shut down Billy Kidman and fellow high-flyer Rey Mysterio. A fast, high-impact contest between Chris Jericho and Edge ended with a simple small package on the King of the World, while Torrie Wilson stripped Stacy Keibler of her arrogant attitude—and her clothes—in a Bra and Panties match. The main event proved just as exciting, as The Rock retained his Undisputed title in a Triple-Threat match with Brock Lesnar and Triple H, who joined the Brahma Bull after the match to lay the smack down, plus dual People's Elbows, on agent Paul Heyman.

Despite losing his match to Edge, Y2J continued the special evening over at Festival Hall, an establishment long considered a home of rock and wrestling, where his band Fozzy powered "Global Meltdown—the *Global Warning* After Party." Sadly, though, the party eventually came to an end, as the Superstars packed up and headed back to the States the next day. But the weekend will be remembered by both wrestlers and fans for a long time...at least until August 2003, when the WWE plans not only to issue another *Global Warning* to Melbourne, but to extend it to Sydney and Brisbane! ■

Angle admires a native Australian for its natural hair.

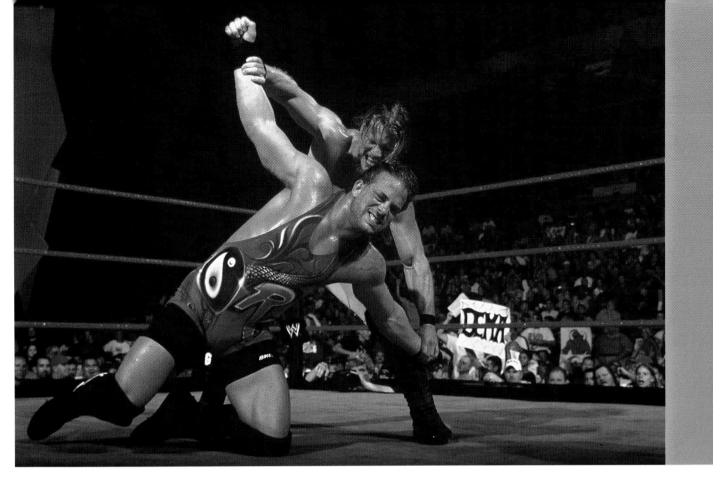

Chris Jericho works the shoulders of Rob Van Dam.

big boot annihilated the Phenom, and provided the win for his team.

Undertaker opened the August 19 *Raw* with a very public proclamation, "Just like my country…*I don't take no shit.*" The Norfolk Complex crowd's "USA!" chants grew as the Dead Man declared he wasn't afraid to pledge allegiance to his flag, or to pledge that at *SummerSlam* he'd show Test, the Un-Americans or anyone disrespecting his country "…what happens when you screw with America. I'm *not* the All-American Boy…but I *am* the American Badass."

Riding down to ringside on his own motorcycle with the upside-down Old Glory, Test got in the Dead Man's grille, telling him, "For the longest time, I thought it was just *America* that sucked. But standing here, in front of you, I realize…*you* do, too." 'Taker responded with a series of soup bone-sized rights and lefts, until Storm and Christian raced down to help their fellow Un-American. But the Phenom wasn't alone, either, as Booker T and Goldust made the save and cleaned

house. The Book got on the mic and told the retreating faction that even though it was six days early, *Summer-Slam* would start *tonight*, in a Six-Man Tag match.

The ensuing matchup heated up quick, with all six participants slugging it out on the *Raw* ramp. Goldust would soon kick the match into high gear with a "Golden Globes" to Christian in the corner, though Test quickly followed up with a big boot to the Bizarre One. Undertaker took his personal vendetta with the big Canadian to the outside floor, while Christian caught Booker with a reverse DDT. Goldust went for the Curtain Call, but a distraction from Storm allowed Christian to nail him with one of the tag belts, and power his team to another Un-American victory.

Chris Jericho hadn't appreciated the ringside interruption from "Cerebral *Ass*" Triple H on August 5, especially to implicate him in something that was later revealed that the *accuser* was the culprit. As The Game headed backstage, Y2J went back to berating Baltimore's "losers" and explaining the difference between him and Ric Flair…only to be interrupted again by Rob Van Dam. RVD came out to welcome Chris to *Raw,* but he had to ask, "Between your comment and those clothes…what have you been *smoking*?" With the crowd's support and the thumbs pointed towards him, Van Dam issued a challenge to meet in the ring tonight and added, "There can be only *one* true 'Mr. Monday Night,' and that's *me—Rob! Van! Dam!*"

> "Between your comment and those clothes...what have you been *smoking*?"

The discussion quickly evolved from a "Y2J-RVD" shouting match to an exchange of blows, with Jericho catching Van Dam with the spinning heel kick and exiting the ring fast. The two met again later that night in an evenly matched contest, until RVD shoved Jericho off the ropes, nailing the referee in the process. Capitalizing on the downed official, Jericho brought in a chair and delivered several shots to his opponent's midsection and spine. Then, without warning, Y2J also tasted steel, as the Nature Boy raced in and laid him out, allowing Van Dam to recover and hit the Five-Star Frog Splash for the victory.

Y2J offered some payback on August 12 *Raw,* tagging with Big Show and making Flair's partner Bubba Ray Dudley submit to the Walls of Jericho. But Flair once again got the drop on Jericho, literally catching him with his pants down and chopping him to the canvas before Big Show chased him away. Humiliated and outraged, Y2J told Jonathan Coachman backstage that he'd show the Nature Boy and everyone else "…what a multi-dimensional, multi-talented Superstar does." Not only would he and his band Fozzy perform live on August 19 *Raw,* but at *SummerSlam,* he'd prove Flair was "a washed-up has-been," while Chris Jericho was "the *true* King of the World."

The night of the big concert, Jericho approached the *Raw* stage and interrupted Triple H, who was in the ring talking about Shawn Michaels. Y2J just wanted to let The Game know he agreed with him—beyond sharing sheer hatred for one another, they were both facing has-beens at *SummerSlam.* But then Chris retracted his comparison, realizing he was facing an *easier* opponent in "ass-clown" Ric Flair, "a man with only one-tenth of my talent, one-tenth of my charisma and one-tenth of my legendary status in this business." Without warning, the dirtiest player in the game dumped a trashcan over Y2J's head, then pushed him down the ramp and told him, "The only thing you do better than me, pal, is *talk trash!*"

Backstage, an extremely pumped Flair explained to Terri that Jericho had started something he just wasn't big enough to get away with, until his "larger than life" adversary surprised him with a trashcan of his own, and busting the Nature Boy wide open. Fozzy's concert performance would go on as scheduled that evening, opening with "To Kill a Stranger" from their new album *Happenstance.* But it was a crimson-faced Flair who'd play the last number on Jericho, as he chased the "Ayatollah of Rock and Rollah" off the stage with a guitar, then destroyed the stereo equipment! And the former sixteen-time World Heavyweight Champion was planning an encore performance at *SummerSlam.*

As evidenced by the *Raw* arrivals of Chris Jericho and the Un-Americans, many of the battles heating up for *SummerSlam* were the product of a territorial war waged between Eric Bischoff and *SmackDown!*'s GM Stephanie McMahon. Embarking in a high-stakes game of one-upmanships, both General Managers wanted their respective show to reign supreme, and both were willing to do *anything* to make sure it happened.

From the onset, "The Bisch" sought to establish *Raw* as *his* show, using elements from his days of running WCW; repositioning commentators Jim Ross and Jerry "the King" Lawler beside the *Raw* stage. The real changes began on July 22, when Bischoff announced he would unify Jeff Hardy's European Championship with Rob Van Dam's Intercontinental title in a Ladder match. Admittedly, the *Raw* GM deserved to be pleased with himself; he'd sanctioned a contest where both Mr. Xtreme and Mr. Monday Night delivered high-impact offense from two ladders, including a Hardy Swanton Bomb and a sunset flip-turned-powerbomb from RVD. A top-rung Five-Star Frog Splash ultimately proved the finisher for Jeff, as Van Dam climbed the top rung and claimed a now-unified title.

RVD barely had the belt around his waist before Bischoff set up a No. 1 Contender's match that night. Reminiscing over the classic "Best-of-Seven" series Chris Benoit and Booker T had back in WCW, Eric decided the Rabid Wolverine and The Book would compete once more, with the winner facing Van Dam the following week. Booker's bruised ribs from

Steven Richards sticks it to Tommy Dreamer.

Vengeance, coupled with having his head rammed into an exposed turnbuckle, enabled Benoit to lock on the Crippler Crossface for the submission win, though he wouldn't have those advantages against RVD seven days later. In a showcase of ring expertise, the two battled tooth and nail—Benoit dodged the full impact of a Five-Star while Van Dam escaped the Crossface on two occasions. Unfortunately, Benoit rolled through after the second time and pinned RVD, placing his feet on the ropes for added leverage to win the Intercontinental title.

Another title the *Raw* GM decided to concern himself with was the Hardcore Championship, which always had a healthy turnaround thanks to its 24/7 rule. Only one week after dropping the European title in a Unification Ladder match against RVD, Jeff Hardy Swanton Bombed Bradshaw from the top of a ladder to capture the Hardcore Title on July 29 *Raw*. The reign was extremely short-lived, however, as Johnny "The Bull" Stamboli (who Bradshaw pummeled on *Heat* a night earlier) surprised Jeff with a spinebuster and pinned him to win the belt. Bradshaw recovered and primed himself to retake the championship with a Clothesline from Hell on The Bull, until a charging Tommy Dreamer nailed the big Texan with a kendo stick, then pinned Johnny for the three-count and the title.

Bradshaw didn't wait to meet the new Hardcore Champion in the ring for their *Raw* title bout on August 5—he started the fight backstage, putting Dreamer's head through some glass as the two fought their way towards ringside, then delivering a powerful fallaway slam off the second rope. But Dreamer would battle back, ultimately driving Bradshaw down with a DDT on the steel steps and scoring the pinfall. He next defended successfully against Steven Richards on August 12 *Raw*, despite a stipulation that permitted Dreamer and Richards only one weapon apiece. Oddly enough, Dreamer brought a Singapore cane down to ringside, but he'd pick up the pinfall with the steel chair that accompanied Richards.

Dreamer's most extreme challenge came August 19, when he and eight other former Hardcore Champions—

Edge spears Chris Jericho.

including *Terri Runnels*—met in the squared circle. From the *Raw* stage, Bischoff announced that the 24/7 Hardcore rule was "no more, over, finished, done, bye-bye," and whoever held the title at the end of six minutes would be declared the Hardcore Champion. Understandably, Terri didn't stick around as the bell rang, while Bradshaw quickly rang Dreamer's bell with a Clothesline from Hell to win the title. The belt changed hands once again after Crash Holly nailed Bradshaw with a bullrope, then fended off Spike's Dudley Dog by throwing him outside the ring. Bubba Ray Dudley powerbombed Crash through a table, only to become preoccupied with Bradshaw while Dreamer took advantage and scored the pinfall. Dreamer would barely manage to hang on after Bubba's superplex, but by the end of six minutes he would walk out the Hardcore Champion.

Undoubtedly, Dreamer was relieved; he no longer

had to keep looking back to see who might attack him and where. Then again, maybe he did—without warning, the Big Red Machine's music and pyro erupted! For the past several weeks, the *Raw* and *SmackDown!* TitanTrons spontaneously aired clips of Kane, who'd been off the WWE's active roster since being injured on April 8. Each promo would run ominous messages, all of which led to one clear conclusion: "The Fire Still Burns." The only hot debate that remained was whether it would burn on *Raw* or *SmackDown!*

While Bischoff was moving and shaking on *Raw*, Stephanie McMahon was making some surprise leverage moves of her own for her first *SmackDown!* At the close of July 22 *Raw*, she exited a limousine in the Van Andel parking lot and threatened to kick Bischoff in the testicles he bragged about at *Vengeance*. It appeared Eric gained the upper hand when Brock Lesnar and Paul Heyman suddenly arrived...until Stephanie opened the limo door for her new employees to enter. "Tell me, since I don't have any," Stephanie said, back inside the vehicle, "how does it feel to get kicked in your testicles?" As the limo took off, she yelled out that if Eric wanted to see The Next Big Thing, he'd have to watch *SmackDown!* Bischoff, meanwhile, screamed over and over that he would knock her out.

From Indianapolis' Conseco Fieldhouse, Stephanie ushered in an exciting new era for *Smack-Down!* with her first show on July 25—the newly signed Brock Lesnar would interfere in several matches that night, plus deliver an F-5 to Hollywood Hulk Hogan that cost him and The Rock a Tag Title match against new Champions Christian and Lance Storm. Stephanie also made good on the Edge-Chris Jericho match postponed from *Vengeance* by putting them in a steel cage, where a bloodied Edge hit an "Electric Chair" that sent Y2J crashing down from the top rope, then climbed up and over to get the victory. And last but not least, high-flying masked luchador Rey Mysterio leaped out from under the *SmackDown!* stage and made an amazing WWE debut, highlighted by the "619" (a swinging kick between the first and second ring ropes that also stands for the San Diego area code) and a springboard hurracanrana to roll up Chavo Guerrero Jr. for the pin.

Unfortunately, the threat of Eric Bischoff's presence loomed large, as did the possibility of *SmackDown!* Superstars defecting over to *Raw*. After receiving flowers with a note saying "*SmackDown!*'s loss is *Raw*'s gain," Stephanie spent most of the evening chasing down leads that suggested Edge, Jericho and Kurt Angle were among those planning to jump ship. Both Edge and Y2J insisted they were happy being on *SmackDown!*, though when Stephanie learned Kurt was on the phone with someone named Eric, and that Bischoff was in the parking lot, she thought for sure

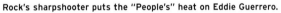

["Tell me, since I don't have any, how does it feel to get kicked in your testicles?"]

she'd lost the gold medalist to the *Raw* GM, who yelled from the sunroof of a departing limo, "*Smack-Down!*'s loss is *Raw*'s gain!" Stephanie's disappointment turned to relief when Kurt walked up behind her, telling her he'd been talking to his *brother* Eric and that he had no contact with Bischoff. She wouldn't discover until the following Monday's *Raw* that Y2J and the Un-Americans were her deserters.

"Steph, Steph...when are you ever going to learn?" Bischoff mocked at ringside on July 29 *Raw*. "When Eric Bischoff knocks you out, you *don't* get up." But it was Stephanie delivering the next one-two punch at August 1 *SmackDown!*. After finding Bischoff in her office backstage at North Carolina's Charlotte Coliseum, security escorted him from the room and McMahon informed Eric that The Rock and Edge were in the main event. Figuring Bischoff would buy his way to a front-row seat for the contest that night,

Rock's sharpshooter puts the "People's" heat on Eddie Guerrero.

Stephanie headed ringside and clarified her earlier statement—it wasn't Edge *versus* The Rock, "but the team of Edge *and* The Rock, facing my newly acquired *Raw* talent—Latino Heat, Eddie Guerrero, and new Intercontinental Champion Chris Benoit!" An irate Bischoff climbed over the railing to get to Stephanie, only to be stopped by security and escorted from the building.

Losing the Intercontinental belt to *SmackDown!* was an especially bitter pill for the *Raw* GM to swallow, but he had an ace up his sleeve, one who'd worked closely within Stephanie's camp over the past few weeks. It was difficult for Stacy Keibler to get in Stephanie's good graces; that she'd provided specific "services" for her father until recently certainly didn't help, nor did Bischoff slipping into Stephanie's office unnoticed one week before. When Dawn Marie arrived with time-sensitive documents that Stephanie had requested during the August 8 broadcast in Virginia's Richmond Coliseum, it wasn't too surprising that Stacy played the Diva and accepted them, then told Stephanie the

papers were never delivered (something about Dawn meeting Mr. McMahon at the Marriott). It also wasn't a shock that after giving the documents to Bischoff, Stacy would be introduced on *Raw* four nights later as his latest acquisition...though it *was* a crowning moment for Jerry "the King" Lawler as she dropped her pants and performed a table dance on the *Raw* announce table!

Signing up a Diva delight like Stacy Keibler was yet one more example of Eric Bischoff's credo since taking over *Raw:* to put the "E" in World Wrestling *Entertainment*, or to make sure *Raw* had the talent and the Superstars to do so. But God help those who *didn't* entertain Bischoff after *three minutes.*

Shawn Stasiak and D'Lo Brown became the first victims on July 22, after appealing to appear regularly on *Raw*. Bischoff gave them three minutes to impress him and win a spot by fighting each other, but warned "it's not going to be pretty" if he were forced to entertain

Rosey and Jamal issue a "three minute warning."

the fans. Despite strong ring efforts from both men, "The Bisch" never really gave them a chance. When their three minutes were up, he provided the entertainment in the form of two enormous Samoan bruisers, who annihilated both Stasiak and D'Lo. Jamal and Rosey made an even larger impression on July 29, after the Fabulous Moolah and Mae Young pestered Bischoff to let Moolah talk about her new autobiography in the ring. Eric caved, telling them he had a three-minute hole to fill, though he wouldn't even wait that long before supplying the ladies with "the last chapter." Moolah received a butt splash in the corner, while Mae was left motionless by Jamal's thunderous top-rope splash. Laughing as the two women were stretchered out, Bischoff asked the audience to give Jamal and Rosey a big hand, "because *that's* entertainment!"

The General Manager acknowledged that it wasn't the nicest thing to do, but he wanted to make a point. "Things *happen* on Eric Bischoff's *Raw,*" he explained. "The people on this show all know that Eric Bischoff is in charge. All I have to do is snap my fingers, and things just happen."

Ring announcers Howard Finkel and Lilian Garcia were the next to share some entertaining moments on August 5—the *Raw* GM decided that since both wanted the main announcer's spot so bad, they should compete for it. He had them provide tag lines following the trailer debut of the Vin Diesel film *xXx,* but when the competition turned ugly with Finkel and Lilian trading barbs, Eric decided things had gone on "just a little too long. Let's say, about *three minutes* too long." As Jamal and Rosey entered the ring, Howard suddenly put the "Fink" in "Finkel," saving his own hide by sacrificing Lilian to a devastating Samoan drop and top-rope splash.

It was moments like those why Bischoff declared himself "the Undisputed King of Sports Entertainment," and why he thought, "*Raw* will *always* outperform *SmackDown!,* because I, Eric Bischoff, give the people

what they want." That included having Minidust perform in the ring on August 12, but after only a few cartwheels and a "Min-a-Roonie," Eric decided he'd stopped being entertaining about three minutes ago. With that, Jamal and Rosey came out and put a sizable hurt on Goldust's diminutive friend, all the while providing Bischoff with a big laugh.

One thing Eric hadn't found very amusing, however, was Chris Benoit taking the Intercontinental Championship to *SmackDown!* Fortunately, the sensitive documents Stacy provided him included Rob Van Dam's contract, which contained a rematch clause for the title. With the papers in Bischoff's possession, Benoit would *have* to defend the belt against Van Dam at *SummerSlam.* But as the GM stressed to RVD the importance of bringing the title back at August 19 *Raw,* Big Show expressed a big problem with being overlooked for

> "All I have to do is snap my fingers, and things just happen."

the title shot. Eric turned down the giant's request for a one-on-one with RVD that night, though Mr. Monday Night thought a "good match" would loosen him up for *SummerSlam.* Unfortunately, the good match—and Big Show's temper—got out of hand, with Show throwing the steel steps into the ring. Afraid *Raw*'s best chance of recapturing the IC belt was about to be sent to the hospital, Bischoff intervened, yelling, "*Dammit, three minutes!*" Out raced Rosey and Jamal, who used the steps to hold Show down long enough to keep him down with the top-rope splash.

Stephanie was furious backstage at Seattle's KeyArena on August 15—Stacy Keibler had potentially ruined all of the work that went into bringing the Intercontinental Championship over to *SmackDown!,* since Chris Benoit had to defend the belt against Rob Van Dam at *SummerSlam.* Her only comfort that night was that she'd secured another *Raw* member three days earlier, after RVD put his

Sensitive Billy runs into the fist of Hardcore Holly.

No. 1 Contender's spot up against Jeff Hardy. Much like their previous encounter, the Superstars put their bodies on the line with their high-risk acrobatics, one of which accidentally knocked the referee down. Suddenly, Matt Hardy raced in, but instead of helping his brother out, he nailed Jeff with the Twist of Fate, allowing Van Dam to climb the ropes and deliver the Five-Star Frog Splash for the victory.

There were signs Matt was going through tough times of late—he refused to accept dropping a *Sunday Night Heat* match to Steven Richards on July 28,

regardless of the fact that Richards had used the ropes to pin him. A top-rope Twist of Fate gave Matt the win over Richards in an August 4 *Heat* rematch, but with Jeff enjoying more success in individual competition—and more title opportunities, judging from Eric Bischoff's coin toss to see who'd face RVD—it became evident that Matt's problem wasn't with Richards, but with jealousy over his brother.

With Team Xtreme no more, Matt headed for August 15 *SmackDown!*, making his presence felt moments after Hardcore Holly and The Hurricane rescued partner Shannon Moore, who'd just dropped the Six-Man Tag match to a "One and Only" slam and was being triple-teamed by Billy, Chuck and Rico. Backstage, Hurricane, Moore and an unimpressed Holly stayed their tongues while Matt spouted off. "How awesome was *that*?" he said. "What a reaction when my music hit, I ran everybody out of Dodge, made the save for you guys…it was *perfect*. And I want you to know that for you guys, I'll always be there, no thanks ever needed. And I don't think there's a question in anyone's mind that *SmackDown!* is ready for Matt Hardy…*Version 1.*"

> **"…for you guys, I'll always be there, no thanks ever needed."**

Perhaps, but Hurricane and Moore noticed a week later that "Version 1's" timing needed work—they'd already beaten and cleared the ring of Tajiri and Cruiserweight Champ Jamie Noble when Matt raced down and soaked up the Crown Coliseum crowd's cheers, then had his pals hoist him up on their shoulders. Taken back by Hurricane's "hometown boy" observation regarding the North Carolina fans' reaction, Matt insisted *all* crowds loved him. To prove his point, he returned to the ring and posed to his entrance music for the audience, until Chavo Guerrero came out and challenged him to a match. Matt eventually gained the advantage, but as he went for the Twist of Fate, Kane's pyro suddenly exploded. Startled, Matt looked towards the *SmackDown!* TitanTron, while Chavo capitalized on the distraction and schoolboyed Version 1 for the one-two-three. Outraged, Matt argued with the referee that *everyone* knows a match automatically ends when an explosion goes off in a building, and that his decision was "the biggest travesty since Earl Hebner screwed Bret Hart in Canada!"

While Matt Hardy closed his eyes to the reality surrounding him, other budding *SmackDown!* Superstars decided to open theirs. Batista had continued to practice delivering the pain Reverend D-Von preached upon his *SmackDown!* ring opponents, laying out Big Valbowksi and ringside partner Hardcore Holly after Valbowski's win over D-Von on July 25, then spinebusting Rikishi following the Reverend's losing effort a week later. But when Batista attacked after Mark Henry's power-slam victory over D-Von on August 8, the Phat Man charged the ring and challenged him to an impromptu match. Batista would dominate the contest, yet suffered his first loss after a missed cheap shot from D-Von dazed the powerhouse long enough for Rikishi to nail him with a superkick.

From the look in his eye and the way he threw the Reverend through a backstage door the following week, it was obvious that Batista had no intention of turning the other cheek. The clincher came during their August 22 Tag match against Rikishi and John Cena, when D-Von got on Batista's case about catching *both* cheeks of a Stinkface, despite the fact that his partner had just run in and helped him. Fed up, Batista gave D-Von a spinebuster, leaving the Reverend out and on his own to suffer a top-rope rump-shakin' loss from the Phat Man.

Edge, Rey Mysterio and John Cena were three Superstars Stephanie McMahon clearly saw as being the future of *SmackDown!*, and all three made a strong case for themselves under the brand's new leadership on July 25, working together to fend off off an Un-American attack against Edge after his steel cage victory over Jericho. Rey followed up his high-flying debut victory with an equally impressive win over Tajiri on August 1, while Cena also continued his winning streak, countering a Test powerbomb with a rollup pin on July 25, then a top-rope clothesline over Rico the following week. But the "future" of *SmackDown!* soon discovered that some of

Angle goes head-to-headlock on Cena.

raced down and made the save on the rookie, while Angle, having been disqualified for Benoit and Guerrero's interference, was hardly grateful for their "help." It had been the latest mishap for Kurt in recent weeks—he'd dropped a decision to Mark Henry on July 25 after Brock Lesnar charged down and F-5'd the World's Strongest Man, poorly explaining later that he was only trying to bail Kurt out of trouble. Informing Angle his days as *SmackDown!*'s "Number One Man" were over, The Next Big Thing screwed him over again on August 1, disrupting a match with Hollywood Hulk Hogan to determine who would face Lesnar on August 8 *SmackDown!*. After Kurt fell into the referee, Brock raced down and nailed Hogan in the head, but the official recovered just as Angle used a steel chair on the icon, and the match was awarded to the Hulkster.

its present members had problems with their growing stature in the WWE, and looked to slow their progress down to further themselves in the company.

The feud started while Cena dropkicked Kurt Angle into the steel steps during their August 8 matchup, only to get blindsided by new Intercontinental Champ Chris Benoit and Eddie Guerrero. Mysterio and Edge

Having had his share of memorable one-on-ones against Benoit in the past, Kurt's hostile history with the Canadian Crippler momentarily resurfaced following his loss to Cena. But Guerrero got between them, and convinced them to focus their energies elsewhere.

The World's Strongest Man taps out to the ankle lock.

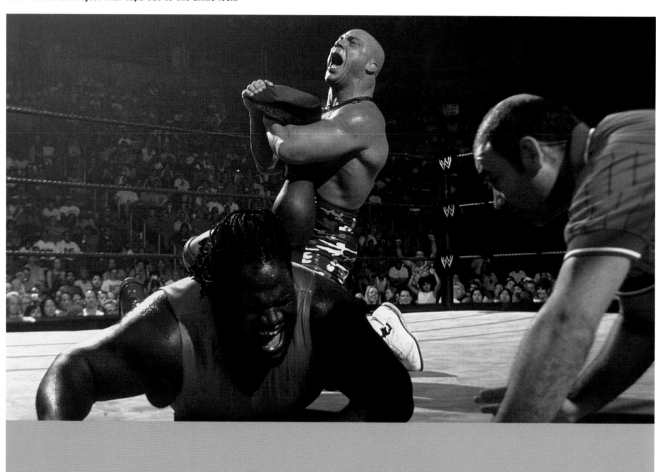

> **"Make sure Dorothy, the Tin Man and all the Munchkins know that your butt is mine at *SummerSlam*!"**

"They say Mysterio, Cena and Edge are the future," he said. "Well, I say *we* are. And I say how about *us* against *them*?" Everyone was for the Six-Man Tag match that ensued that evening, though once again Angle would find himself in the loss column, this time after Mysterio hit the gold medalist with the 619 and springboard hurracanrana to pick up the win.

"What the heck is going *on* around here?" Angle asked Marc Loyd backstage, feeling the referee had screwed him over. He'd been pinned by "a freakin' twelve-year-old" who wasn't even the legal man in the ring. "He's probably an illegal citizen," Kurt added, "and if he had *any* integrity whatsoever, he'd come forward and forfeit the match. But integrity isn't a part of his *extremely* limited vocabulary, is it?" When he continued insisting a week later that Mysterio's win didn't count, the masked luchador confronted him. "How about we hit it off at *SummerSlam*, so I can *make* it count?" he asked, inciting a laugh from Angle until he realized Rey was serious. "If there's one thing I can't stand, it's a little man with an attitude," Kurt said. "You're on. Make sure Dorothy, the Tin Man and all the Munchkins know that your butt is mine at *SummerSlam*!"

Angle's comments led to an argument that had Mark Henry inviting him to "follow the yellow brick road" towards ringside. Kurt picked up the win via submission after slapping the ankle lock on Henry, but he'd leave the ring seeing red when a Mysterio 619 busted Kurt open. Angle didn't even wait for Rey and Edge's Tag Team match against Eddie and Chavo Guerrero to end later that night. He pulled Mysterio out of the ring and put him in the ankle lock. Edge saved his tag partner from serious injury, avoiding an Angle Slam and catching him with a spear.

Mysterio told Michael Cole on August 22 *SmackDown!* he proved he could "hang" with the likes of Kurt Angle when he pinned him. Kurt interrupted the interview, and suggested to Rey that his mask was on too tight. He then advised him to "sit back, relax and grab a high chair or a booster chair or whatever it is you need to see a monitor" while he treated him to "a dose of reality." Angle promised to give tonight to Billy Kidman what Rey had coming to him at *SummerSlam*—"a beating that's going to make you want to run for the border." But Kidman proved much tougher than Kurt anticipated, especially after Mysterio's usual "pop-out" stage entrance got Kurt thinking he might get jumped during the match. And that's precisely what happened, shortly after the referee caught a clothesline intended for Kidman. Chasing Mysterio away from ringside, Angle didn't realize until it was too late that the ref had recovered and counted him out, giving Kidman the win. Angle snapped, taking his frustrations out on Kidman with an Angle Slam over the top rope, all the while he thought about how he would break Rey Mysterio at *SummerSlam*.

Like Mysterio, Eddie Guerrero also was looking for respect. He first demanded it from the new Undisputed Champion on July 22 *Raw*, complaining how he had to discipline his two young daughters when he discovered they had a poster of The Rock hanging in their bedroom. When the Great One joked that he couldn't figure out if he was talking to Cheech or Chong, Guerrero decided to teach him some respect in a nontitle contest. But it was The Rock doing the teaching later that evening, catching Eddie with a People's Elbow for the victory. After being further dissed in a loss to Booker T the following week, Guerrero decided he'd make his future elsewhere, and jumped ship with new Intercontinental Champion Chris Benoit over to *SmackDown!*

Perhaps that's why Edge's attitude seemed to light a fire under Latino Heat—he wasn't ready to move aside

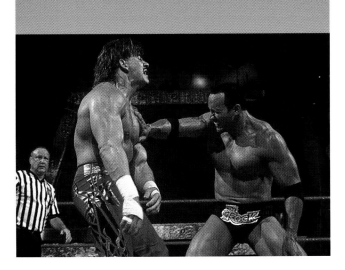
The Brahma Bull knife-edges Eddie Guerrero.

for anyone claiming to be the future of *SmackDown!* Eddie decided he and nephew Chavo would take Edge and Mysterio down a peg in tag action on August 15. But his plan fell by the wayside when Kurt Angle attacked Mysterio and drew a disqualification, while Guerrero found himself speared into the ring barrier on the outside floor. Scheduled to meet Edge one-on-one at *SummerSlam,* Eddie enlisted Benoit's aid and got an early jump on his adversary at the August 22 *SmackDown!,* attacking him backstage only minutes after they'd ambushed The Rock at ringside. Upset that their vendettas endangered the upcoming Pay-Per-View's main event, *SmackDown!* GM Stephanie McMahon decided Guerrero and Benoit would meet Edge and The Rock later that night, in a Tag match that ended with Edge planting Guerrero with another spear. If Latino Heat was ever going to get respect, he'd have to earn it from Edge at the PPV.

The WWE Women's Division looked good as always, though Bischoff and Stephanie's company war threatened to make life in the ring more complicated—and dangerous. Intergender tag team rules had previously specified that the Divas and male Superstars weren't allowed to compete against one another in the ring, but Bischoff changed the rules so that whoever was in the ring was fair game. The stipulation made its mark right away on July 22 *Raw,* in a match that paired Bubba Ray Dudley and Trish Stratus against William Regal and Women's Champion Molly Holly. Bubba infuriated Molly by turning a test of strength into a dance step, but Regal wouldn't dance around with Trish—while Bubba went for a table outside the ring, Regal caught her with a back suplex and the STF for the submission. Trish called for a rematch on July 29, and despite an alleged pulled muscle leading to Regal's spot being more than filled by Big Show, got the victory after Bubba hoisted Molly up on his shoulders, setting her up for a top-rope clothesline.

Christopher Nowinski, meanwhile, might have welcomed the change in Intergender tag rules, hinting that he'd like to wrestle the Women's Champion in a manner that didn't include the ring. Nowinski and William Regal were backstage on August 5 *Raw* when Molly introduced them to Victoria, a newcomer who'd grab a huge upset win that evening after faking an injury to sucker-kick Trish in the face, then hold onto the ring ropes to pin her. Pulling the new Diva to one side, Nowinski asked her to confirm rumors of Molly being a virgin. When she did, he muttered to Regal, "Not for long." The following week, he'd bust Spike Dudley's chops about not being able to "seal the deal" with his former fiancée, then childishly joke with a stagehand, "Before long, Molly Holly's going to be *my* vale-*dic*-torian." Had she heard his comments, Molly might not have been so quick to team with him against Spike and Trish that night, even if he did counter Spike's Dudley Dog into a double underhook and slam for the three-count.

Based on what he did to Lilian Garcia with Jamal and Rosey on August 5, it wasn't hard to figure out how much *Raw* respect Howard Finkel had for women. The following week "The Fink" was "truly sorry…sorry you didn't get what was coming to you *sooner*!" He'd swallowed his pride watching her work in the ring, though he was quick to add, "That's a hell of a lot better than what *you* had to swallow to get your job here!" Finkel soon learned just how funny his comments towards Lilian were, however, when Trish Stratus entered the ring for a match and slapped him across the face!

> ## "That's a hell of a lot better than what *you* had to swallow to get your job here!"

Trish Stratus shoves Stacy and "The Fink" into the mud.

Raw GM Eric Bischoff told Trish and Stacy Keibler on August 19, *"No one* really cares about women's wrestling." He just wanted to give the fans "what they really want"—a Bra and Panties Mud Wrestling match! Stacy got down-n-dirty, pushing her scantily clad opponent off the *Raw* stage and into the nearby mud pool, but it was Trish coming up with the clean win, rolling Stacy up just outside the pool for the three-count. As Howard Finkel came to Stacy's aid, Trish decided on more payback for Lilian, and pushed him into the mud. Stacy seemed to share Trish's sentiment regarding the Fink's recent actions, and decided to lay into the ring announcer with a few shots of her own.

Over on *SmackDown!*, Cruiserweight Champion Jamie Noble may have had a Diva in his corner, but he was hardly a gentleman. For one thing, he was all too happy to share his girlfriend Nidia with other men, including unwilling *SmackDown!* announcer Michael Cole on August 1, since "he makes the wrestlers look good" and Noble wanted his public image elevated in the broadcasts. But the redneck wasn't so friendly when it came to Nidia's ring competition. During mixed tag action on August 8, Nidia would receive a well-deserved spanking from Torrie Wilson over partner Billy Kidman's knee, but Noble's distraction allowed his woman to roll Torrie up for the "schoolgirl" victory. The Cruiserweight Champion contributed to the outcome again when the Divas met in singles competition a week later, clotheslining Torrie in the ring and providing his girl with an easy three-count.

When it came to Nidia, *everything* was easy. She allowed a visit to the women's locker room by "Number One *SmackDown!* Announcer" Funaki on August 22, while she was getting dressed for that evening's Women's Championship match with Molly Holly. Molly was also in the locker room, and she didn't applaud Nidia's "loose" attitude of letting Funaki come by and admire her breasts. The argument prompted Nidia to declare she'd remove her top if she won the belt that night, exposing herself to the Fayetteville crowd as the new Women's Champion. Funaki would be ultimately disappointed, however, as the pure and wholesome Molly overcame Jamie Noble's ringside interference and took Nidia down with the Molly-Go-Round for the one-two-three.

Molly Holly shows Nidia how easy it is to lose.

The Next Big Thing didn't even bother with a cane, instead opting to finish the Superstar off with a hard-core F-5. But he would return to the ring after Rock defeated Eddie Guerrero, only to take the Undisputed title from the referee's hands and look it over before dropping it at the champion's feet. Lesnar and agent Paul Heyman had plans elsewhere, plans which included accompanying General Manager Stephanie McMahon over to *SmackDown!*

The Conseco Fieldhouse crowd expected the highly anticipated "Rock vs. Brock" buildup to *SummerSlam* to catch fire at the July 25 *SmackDown!* Again, Lesnar decided to make his impact elsewhere first, drawing a disqualification for Kurt Angle during his bout with Mark Henry. He later disrupted The Rock and Hollywood Hulk Hogan's bid for the Tag Team Championship, breaking up Hogan's leg drop and cover on Un-American Christian, then flooring the icon with an F-5 and signaling to Rock as he left ringside that the Undisputed Championship would be his.

The People's Undisputed Champion had his usual backstage fun on July 29 *Raw*, first intimidating Jonathan Coachman about that story he heard regarding him, his microphone and his special cow Bessie, then throwing Coach out of the room when he confessed,

> **"The Rock will bring the whoopin'. You bring that *candy ass!*"**

"It was just *one* night." He'd also practice his Nature Boy strut shortly before that evening's match with Ric Flair. But there was no playing around when it came to addressing The Next Big Thing's mind games. "The Rock doesn't play games, but The Rock will make one exception for you," he said. "It's called 'Just Bring It,' and it's real simple—The Rock will bring the whoopin'. You bring that *candy ass!*"

F or a rookie on a quest to become the youngest Undisputed Champion in WWE history, twenty-four-year-old Brock Lesnar didn't seem overly concerned about his upcoming title match with the Great One at *SummerSlam*. In fact, Lesnar ignored The Rock on his way down the *Raw* ramp on July 22, choosing to focus his attention on Tommy Dreamer and their Singapore Cane match. Unlike Dreamer's extreme attack a few weeks back,

Nassau County Veterans Memorial Coliseum Uniondale, NY

UNDISPUTED CHAMPIONSHIP MATCH

Brock Lesnar defeated *The Rock* via pinfall to become the new Undisputed Champion

UNSANCTIONED STREETFIGHT MATCH

Shawn Michaels defeated *Triple H* via pinfall

Undertaker defeated *Test* via pinfall

INTERCONTINENTAL MATCH

Rob Van Dam defeated *Chris Benoit* via pinfall to become the new WWE Intercontinental Champion

TAG TEAM CHAMPIONSHIP MATCH

Lance Storm & Christian defeated *Booker T & Goldust*; Christian pinned Booker T to retain the Tag Team titles

Edge defeated *Eddie Guerrero* via pinfall

Ric Flair defeated *Chris Jericho* via submission

Kurt Angle defeated *Rey Mysterio* via submission

AUGUST 25, 2002

For the past fourteen years, no matter what the weather, *SummerSlam* has determined what kind of a season it was for the WWE and its Superstars. The Summer of 2002 proved no different inside Long Island's Nassau Coliseum—a Canadian storm front threatened to rain down its cloud of anti-American hatred. A ring legend sought to prove he could still take the heat inside the squared circle. A Showstopper forced to retire before his time entered the ring once more to find relief from the personal tempest caused by his best friend. And the monthlong heat wave behind the "Rock vs. Brock" debate would finally come to an end.

At five-feet-three-inches, Rey Mysterio made a huge impact in just his first month on *SmackDown!*, and he looked to come up even bigger at his first Pay-Per-View with a victory over Kurt Angle, who sized the high-flyer up as a snot-nosed punk interfering in his business. Rey opened the match strong by surprising Angle from behind, then kept him off-guard until Kurt deflected a head scissors takedown. The gold medalist tried wearing down the cruiserweight with a half-crab maneuver and an Angle Slam, but Rey countered both moves before pulling the top rope down, sending Kurt flying to the outside. The referee stopped the lochador from following his opponent to the outside, until Mysterio leaped over his head and landed on Angle! Back in the ring, Kurt slapped on the ankle lock, but Rey got the hold broken before regaining the momentum with a 619 between the ropes. The two soon battled off the top rope, where Angle countered a Mysterio hurracanrana and rolled the maneuver into the ankle lock, forcing Rey to tap out.

Confident that *Raw* General Manager Eric Bischoff couldn't top her *SmackDown!* stars' ring performance, GM Stephanie McMahon felt pretty good as she entered her office...until she found "The Bisch" already sitting inside. Since both brands were represented at *SummerSlam*, the two agreed to share the one office, though their war of words would continue into the night as they watched to see whose WWE brand offered the better product.

Chris Jericho might have seen Ric Flair as a washed-up has-been, though he'd quickly find the Nature Boy able to match him toe-to-toe and blow-for-blow. A Y2J clothesline took the fight to the floor, where he slammed Flair into the ringside barrier before climbing up top and crashing down on the back of his head. Back in the ring,

Slick Ric eventually mounted a comeback, pulling Jericho off the ropes and following in with his customary knife-edge chops. Avoiding the Lionsault, Flair put Y2J in a half-crab, until the larger than life Superstar countered with Flair's signature Figure-Four Leglock. Flair grabbed the ropes at the same time he started tapping out, forcing the referee into a tough decision to break the hold. Moments later, the dirtiest "has-been" in the game took full advantage of the questionable call, landing a low blow that softened Jericho up for the Figure-Four submission.

In the locker room, Paul Heyman was pumping up his client. It was time for Brock Lesnar to take The Rock out and murder his title reign, like he'd killed *Hulkamania*. It was time to show everyone that The Next Big Thing had arrived. Meanwhile, Eddie Guerrero entered his contest looking to halt Edge, the so-called "future of *SmackDown!*" And after dodging a second spear that sent his opponent sailing outside, he saw a golden opportunity. Edge had hurt his left shoulder in the fall, so Guerrero poured on the Latino Heat, smashing it into the steel steps and wrenching the arm like he wanted to take it home for a souvenir. Edge fought back with a suplex to the outside floor, then crashed down on Guerrero from the top rope. Eddie's dropkick averted another spear attempt, though his frog splash was met with Edge's knees to his mid-section. Neither an Edgecution nor a successful frog splash could finish the other man off, but as Guerrero went up top again, Edge yanked him down and caught him with the spear, giving the young Superstar the hard-fought pinfall win.

Backstage, Un-Americans Lance Storm and Christian told Jonathan Coachman they couldn't wait to expose Booker T and Goldust as "American shams," even if they *had* to carry their upside-down American flag in front of the "lazy, unresponsive and spoiled" Long Island fans that typified U.S. audiences. The Book and the Bizarre One defended Old Glory with an opening barrage on the Tag Team Champions, who double-teamed Goldust in the wrong side of town when the referee missed the tag to Booker. The crowd's "USA!" chants rallied Goldust to duck a Storm and Christian "*conchairto*" and deliver a double clothesline to make the tag. Booker cleaned house, following a missile dropkick and near-fall on Christian with the face-down flapjack to the canvas. A Storm superkick missed its target and floored the refer-ee, while Booker's scissors kick to both Un-Americans powered him to the Spin-a-Roonie. A superkick to Christian earned more than a three-count, but before the downed ref recovered, Test invaded the ring and hammered Booker with the big boot, giving the Un-Americans the one-two-three to retain the belts.

A brief visit to the World saw Cruiserweight Champion Jamie Noble bolster girlfriend Nidia to "devour" a crowd member on the couch. Watching the action from their office backstage, Bischoff thought Nidia's attitude would make her a fine *Raw* acquisition, then badgered Stephanie that like the trashy Diva, Rob Van Dam was about to come out on top against *SmackDown!*'s Chris Benoit, and bring the Intercontinental title back to *Raw*. Mr. Pay-Per-View opened the interpromotional matchup with the educated feet to Benoit's midsection, while the Rabid Wolverine regrouped and forced his opponent to the mat. RVD crumpled to the canvas after the IC Champ delivered a jarring suplex, then further hurt himself when Benoit's knees disrupted his split-legged moonsault. Benoit missed a flying headbutt from the top rope, but regained the advantage with the Crippler Crossface when Van Dam failed to hit the Five-Star Frog Splash.

RVD made it to the ropes to break the hold, only to be sent flying to the outside and into the barrier. Van Dam soon recovered with a foot sweep, but the Crippler avoided the Rolling Thunder and latched the Crossface again. Again Van Dam escaped, then countered the relentless Benoit's third bid at the submission hold with his own Crossface attempt. Kicking out of the Rolling Thunder and several near-falls, Benoit went for the win with a top-rope suplex, but RVD converted it in midair with a body slam, then landed the Five-Star Frog Splash to become the new Intercontinental Champion. Backstage, Bischoff celebrated the *Raw* victory by trying to rub it in the *SmackDown!* GM's face. Stephanie simply turned towards Bischoff, laughed in his face and exited the room, looking like she knew something that would more than offset the loss.

Undertaker may not have considered himself a role model, but he was an American Badass poised to defend his country's honor against the Un-American Test. After scoring a hip-toss, the Dead Man started going "old school" on the big Canadian's arm when Test shoved the referee into the ropes, crotching 'Taker in the process. Amazingly, Test continued dominating the Phenom, slamming him into the steel steps and working over his shoulder and arm. Then he made the mistake of trying to match punches with Big Evil's soup bones, which caught him with a DDT and a successful old school shot to the arm. The two countered several high-impact moves until Undertaker scored a Chokeslam, but as he set Test up for the Last Ride, Lance Storm and Christian charged the ring. 'Taker answered the Un-American attack with Chokeslams for both men, but then ate Test's big boot to the face. Unable to secure the pin, Test brought a chair inside, but 'Taker smacked it into his face, then drove home a victory for Old Glory with a Tombstone to the canvas. Grabbing an American flag from the crowd, Undertaker climbed the ropes and held it high, celebrating more than just a tremendous win with the Nassau Coliseum fans.

That even Eric Bischoff wouldn't sanction Triple H's match against Shawn Michaels was testament that it would be an ugly, bloody affair…for the Heartbreak Kid, who hadn't wrestled in four years. Coupled with the fact that he'd suffered a broken back, no one—not the fans, not Bischoff and certainly not The Game—could anticipate the one-time Showstopper tossing Hunter over the ropes, then following him to the outside with a reverse plancha! Withstanding a shot into the ring barrier, Michaels went Hardcore on Hunter with a trashcan to the skull, then landed a double axe-handle smash from the top rope. The Cerebral Assassin avoided the Sweet Chin Music and went to work on HBK's sweet spot, punishing him with a series of backbreakers and elbows before smashing a steel chair across Shawn's lower back. Michaels kicked out of a pin attempt, then tried for one of his own, so Hunter busted him open with a DDT down onto the chair. Again Michaels kicked out, frustrating The Game to the point of whipping Shawn with his own leather belt, then producing a sledgehammer from under the ring.

Fighting back before the sledgehammer could come into play, Michaels soon worked his way out of an abdominal stretch and went upstairs. But The Game pushed referee Earl Hebner into the ropes, dislodging Shawn and leaving him hanging upside-down. Triple H followed in for another shot with the chair, then used it to hit an agonizing backbreaker. Refusing to be pinned, Michaels countered a Pedigree with a groin shot, then planted Sweet Chin Music to send the chair back into Hunter's face, making him a bloody mess. Looking like the Showstopper in his prime, Michaels caught Triple H with the flying forearm and back body drop, then hammered him with the chair before sending him to the arena floor. Outside, he Bulldogged his former friend onto the ring steps before finding an item that helped catapult HBK into WWE Superstardom: a ladder. Shawn used it to batter The Game around, but he still couldn't get the three-count, even after a superplex off the ropes. Triple H threw the steel stairs into the ring, only for a drop toe-hold to bring him crashing down onto them.

Taking the fight back outside, Michaels set Hunter up on a table, and from the top rope delivered a tremendous splash that sent both men through the table! Both the action and the ladder went back inside as HBK, like he had in his *SummerSlam* Ladder match with Razor Ramon in 1995, climbed the top rung and came crashing down with the flying elbow drop. The fans were on their feet as Michaels geared up for the Sweet Chin Music, until Triple H blocked it and went for the Pedigree. Suddenly, Shawn countered the finisher with a rollup, and got the one-two-three! The Nassau Coliseum erupted as the victorious Heartbreak Kid started celebrating in the ring,

but then the party came to a screeching end; without mercy, Triple H smashed the sledgehammer into Shawn Michaels' back, laying him out instantly, then continued to pummel him with the lethal instrument. Ring officials and paramedics rushed to the scene of the carnage, as one man's personal triumph against all odds had suddenly turned into tragedy, while the loser of the match headed backstage, smiling over having accomplished what he promised to do.

Before the Undisputed Championship match got underway, ring announcer Howard Finkel declared that *SummerSlam* was the first Pay-Per-View he'd announced inside the Nassau Coliseum since *WrestleMania 2* in 1986. "It's a little something called 'commitment'," he stated, adding that major league baseball might be going on strike (it didn't), "but you WWE fans will *always* have The Fink." Suddenly, Trish Stratus made her way to the ring, but Howard wasn't impressed. After everything Trish had done to him over the past few weeks as payback for sacrificing announcer Lilian Garcia to Rosey and Jamal on August 5 *Raw*, she had no right to keep harassing him, even in "an arena of Long Island skanks." But Trish only came out to apologize and tell him what a sexy voice he had, and that she had a surprise for him. The two hugged, as the notion of her puppies and his wiener coming together in a dog-eat-dog world pleased Fink to no end. Then she introduced the *real* surprise behind him: Lilian, who slapped Howard silly, then nailed him with the low blow before exiting the ring with Trish.

At the age of twenty-six, The Rock became the second-youngest World Champion in WWE history (the first being the late Yokozuna). Fast-forward four years to *SummerSlam,* where he'd enter Nassau Coliseum wearing his unprecedented seventh Heavyweight title. Waiting in the ring for him was twenty-four-year-old Brock Lesnar, The Next Big Thing, whose sights were set on making his first-ever major championship an Undisputed one. After weeks of training and preparation, the time for talk was over, as the Brahma Bull charged towards the ring and took the fight to the challenger. Brock answered with a powerful backbreaker and several shoulders into the ribcage before sending Rock to the outside, where agent Paul Heyman contributed a few cheap shots of his own. Lesnar clotheslined the Brahma Bull over the barrier, then continued the fight back inside the ring with a German suplex. The People's Champ started fighting back until Heyman tripped him, allowing Lesnar to regain the advantage.

Brock's ring inexperience showed as he went in prematurely for a spear, but caught only ring post. The Brahma Bull connected with several clotheslines before downing The Next Big Thing, then knocked Heyman off the apron with a right hand and finished slapping on the sharpshooter. Refusing to tap out, Lesnar actually started winning some of the Nassau Coliseum fans over. Heyman came to his client's aid again, tossing a chair in the ring and distracting the referee on the apron, until Rocky invited him inside the hard way. The diversion allowed Lesnar to ram the chair into the Great One's already-tender ribs, then put the squeeze on the Undisputed Champion with a bone-crunching bearhug. Brock instantly resumed his grip after suplexing Rock down to the canvas, but just as it looked like the People's Champ was down and out, he picked himself up off the mat and punched his way out.

A low blow from Rock earned mixed reactions from a suddenly split crowd, while Lesnar forced his shoulders into the midsection again. Brock's inexperience sent him into the ring post again, while the Great One made him pay with a trip over the top rope. Rock cleared the Spanish announce table of its monitors, then whipped Brock into the post after catching Heyman trying to

sneak up on him. The agent bought himself a one-way ticket through the announce table, courtesy a Rock Bottom, while Lesnar caught one moments later in the center of the ring. But Brock once again won some fans over—and shocked the hell out of The Rock—after kicking out of the pin and nailing a Rock Bottom on the Brahma Bull! Rocky barely kicked out at two, and it soon appeared the rookie's inexperience had finally cost him—Rock converted a whip to the ropes with the spine-buster, then set the big man up for the People's Elbow. But before the champion could deliver the blow, Brock sprang up and clotheslined him! The Next Big Thing went for the F-5, but Rock battled out of it with the right hands, then set him up for another Rock Bottom. Suddenly, Brock countered the finisher and connected with the F-5, then pinned Rock for the one-two-three! Only five months since starting his career at World Wrestling Entertainment, Brock Lesnar had shocked the world and become the youngest-ever Undisputed Champion! ■

With a hook of the leg it's Brock over Rock!

Lesnar clearly wasn't making friends wherever he went—at the August 1 *SmackDown!*, Kurt Angle and Hollywood Hulk Hogan agreed to a contest just for the opportunity of facing him next week. But Brock used their dislike for him to his advantage—after blowing through his match with an F-5 on World's Strongest Man Mark Henry, he went backstage to tell Hogan he hoped to square off against him, then expressed similar sentiments to Angle minutes later. Ultimately, the young powerhouse's interference in the ensuing bout would cost both men—the match decision for Kurt, and for Hogan a second F-5 in as many weeks.

The evening's main event proved even more chaotic, especially with Stephanie putting the screws to Eric Bischoff by debuting new *SmackDown!* members Chris Benoit and Eddie Guerrero. Nevertheless, tag partners Edge and The Rock looked to have the match in hand until Lesnar walked down and distracted the Undisputed Champion, allowing Benoit to slap on the Crippler Crossface. Rocky had no choice but to tap out, but as Brock laughed his way back up the ramp, out came Hogan, brandishing a steel chair and laying the rookie out at the top of the stage!

Youth and size were on Lesnar's side, but no *Hulkamaniac* worth his salt considered Hogan the underdog before their August 8 match. Paul Heyman certainly didn't, and he begged his client not to visit Hogan's locker room and antagonize the icon who made a career of rising from the ashes of defeat, and was as adept as anyone in or out of the ring when it came to mind games. "You're so young, full of life," Hogan told Brock backstage. "You've got the world in the palm of your hand. No injuries...man, you've got it made. But if *I* was you, I'd lay it *all* on the line. Put it all up for grabs and prove the point you're trying to prove. If *I* was you, I would put my shot at the WWE title at *SummerSlam* on the line tonight. *If* I was you. Then again, you're *not* Hulk Hogan, are you?"

The rookie took Hogan's bait; the winner of their match would face The Rock at *SummerSlam* in seventeen days' time. Heyman just about hit the wall, convinced Brock had been played and suckered right out of title contention. Even worse, before Heyman could appeal to Stephanie McMahon about the situation, she applauded him and Brock on their "stroke of genius"—whether it ended up "Rock vs. Brock" or "Rock vs. Hogan, Part II," the *SummerSlam* main event was "a win/win situation for *SmackDown!*" Meanwhile, the Hulkster admitted to Marc Loyd backstage that conventional wisdom might say he didn't have a chance against the seemingly unstoppable Lesnar. "But conventional wisdom doesn't take into account that there's 15,000 *Hulkamaniacs* that'll rise to their feet and scream their lungs out for me," he added. "It's *Hulkamania*, not Brock Lesnar, that's unstoppable." That being the case, Hogan had just one question to ask: "What'cha gonna do, Brock Lesnar, when *Hulkamania*, and 15,000 *Hulkamaniacs*, run wild on you?"

> **"It's *Hulkamania*, not Brock Lesnar, that's unstoppable. What'cha gonna do, Brock Lesnar, when *Hulkamania*, and 15,000 *Hulkamaniacs*, run wild on you?"**

As had happened so many times throughout his illustrious career, Hogan would reach deep within himself and battle his way back, ultimately taking his opponent down with the big boot and the legdrop. This time, however, Brock Lesnar would do what so few have been able to—he'd kick out of the pin. As the Hulkster went for another leg drop, Heyman caught him by the ring apron, slowing him long enough for Brock to recover and take Hogan down with the F-5. Lesnar decided to add to the tremendous punishment, putting the icon in a bearhug. Checking to see if Hogan was still conscious, the referee watched Hogan's hand drop once, twice...then a third and final time. The official called

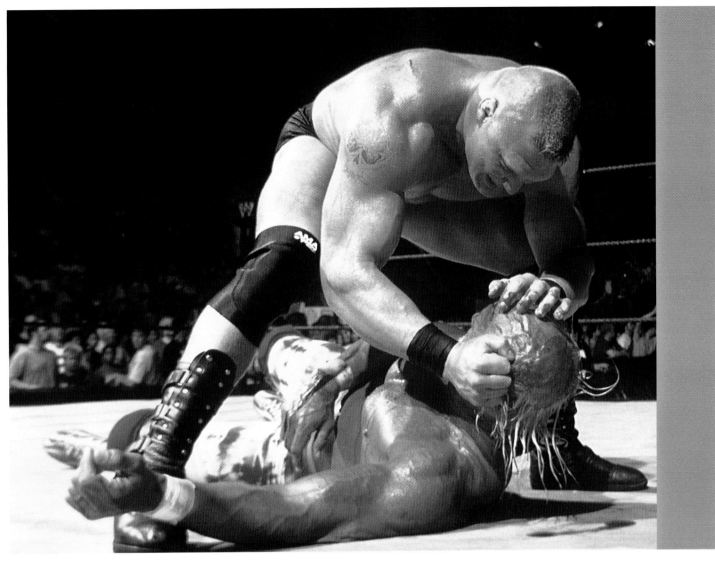

Out of control, Lesnar revels in his victory over Hogan.

for the bell, and Brock Lesnar had earned his greatest victory to date—a win over the Immortal Hulk Hogan.

But it wasn't enough—blood was already coming from Hogan's mouth when Lesnar decided to inflict more damage. The Next Big Thing whaled on his prey with a steel chair as fans called out for The Rock. Even Paul Heyman begged his client to stop, fearing he might kill Hogan. But Lesnar was too far into it, and he continued until the icon could no longer get up. Smearing Hogan's blood across his chest, Lesnar lifted his beaten opponent's head, then told him to stay down. At that very moment, it appeared as if *Hulkamania* had been destroyed.

Focusing his attention towards The Rock once more, Lesnar purchased a ringside seat for August 12 *Raw*, wearing a bright red *Hulkamania* T-shirt as a visual reminder of the savage beating he'd given Hogan. His stay was brief, but effective—his mere presence instigated a fight between the Brahma Bull and arch-rival Triple H, and left Rock open to a Pedigree before Eric Bischoff had him evicted from the building. The incident also allowed Paul Heyman to reiterate at the August 15 *SmackDown!* that the Hulkster wasn't his client's "ultimate trophy on the mantle," but "a damned stepping stone." "Better than a letter, better than a phone call, better than an email," he explained, "Brock Lesnar *used* and *exploited* Hulk Hogan to send a message to The Rock. And that message reads loud and clear, like a neon sign: the blood of *Hulkamania* is on Brock Lesnar's hands, and the People's Blood will be on Brock Lesnar's hands at *SummerSlam*!"

It was Rikishi's ass on Heyman's face later that evening, when the Phat Man—sickened by what they'd done to Hogan—stepped up and challenged Lesnar to a contest. Ultimately, despite giving Brock "a piece of the Kish," not even the three hundred-fifty-pounder could withstand the power of the F-5. Lesnar's outside ring presence had contributed to Rocky tapping out to the Crippler Crossface two weeks before, but the Undisputed Champion insisted backstage, "There ain't no way—and The Rock means *no way!*—that The Rock is gonna tap *twice*." As for Lesnar's message, the Great One had one for him as well, as he motioned with his hand and gave it to him in German, Chinese and "American Way, USA—*Just bring it, bitch!*"

> "There ain't no way—and The Rock means *no* way—that The Rock is gonna tap *twice*."

The Rock remained true to his word about not tapping out that night, even when Lesnar's arrival led to a staredown that allowed Benoit to blindside Rock and lock on the Crippler Crossface again. From the outside floor Lesnar urged him to quit, but the Great One refused; reaching the ropes to break the hold, he recovered quickly enough to surprise the Rabid Wolverine with the Rock Bottom, giving him the one-two-three. Locking eyes with Brock once more, the victorious Rock also seemed to succeed in registering a new look from his *SummerSlam* challenger—one of uncertainty.

Knowing he'd reached Brock, the People's Champ refused to buy into any more of Lesnar and Heyman's ploys as he prepared for his *Raw* No-Disqualification match against Triple H on August 19. He laughed off a package of photos featuring a battered, bloodied Hulk Hogan from his *SmackDown!* bout with Lesnar, then scoffed at Jonathan Coachman over rumors that Brock was in the building. The Great One was only interested in facts. "The fact is that The Rock stands before everyone as the Undisputed Champion," he said. "Fact: The Rock, for one month, has been *begging* Brock Lesnar to just bring it, and he has brought *nothing*. Until Brock actually brings it to The Rock, he'll *never* be known as The Next Big Thing, but always The Next Big *Bitch!* Fact: The Rock is going to say this one last time: *Just. Bring. It.*"

Triple H was certainly intent on bringing it to his arch-rival that evening, as The Game did a number on his ribs before all hell broke loose with Lesnar and Shawn Michaels showing up at ringside. Lesnar ran off as Rock challenged him to come to the ring, then chased after him in the crowd. But neither Brock nor Heyman were running at August 22 *SmackDown!*, as the agent declared that Rock and Brock would finally collide that night, just three days before *SummerSlam*. Lesnar taunted the Undisputed Champion to come out and face him, and he was glad to oblige. "Tonight will be a night like no other," Rock said on the *SmackDown!* stage. "No 'Just bring its.' No 'Stick it up your candy asses.' No 'If you smell what The Rock is cookin'.' And quite frankly, Brock Lesnar, seeing that you flat-out refuse to bring it to The Rock, The Rock will just have to bring it to *you*."

Unfortunately, as Rock started heading down the runway, Benoit and Eddie Guererro blindsided him, further banging up his bruised ribs and making The Next Big Thing laugh as he was assisted backstage by officials. Benoit and Guerrero's subsequent attack on Edge minutes later would lead to that evening's Tag Team headliner, where the Great One Rock Bottomed Benoit and Edge speared Latino Heat for the win.

Lesnar would once again approach ringside, this time accepting the Great One's invitation to bring it into the squared circle. But he wouldn't stay long—after getting in a few shots around the ribs, Lesnar was sent flying over the ropes by a tremendous right hand. Rock invited him back in, though Heyman held his client back. But nothing could break the icy stares coming from both athletes as *SmackDown!* came to a close.

[**"Seeing that you flat-out refuse to bring it to The Rock, The Rock will just have to bring it to *you*."**]

The Rock wonders if Brock Lesnar will ever "Just bring it."

9

"Hell of a thing, killin' a man.
Take away all he's got, and all he's ever gonna have."
"Yeah, well...I guess he had it comin'."
"We all got it comin', kid."
—William Munny to the Schofield Kid, *Unforgiven*

"You desire to be in this business, you sacrifice.
You sacrifice the time with your kids.
You miss them growing up, but you have a goal in mind.
You know that one day, all the sacrifices that you make,
it's going to make it easier for your children.
You just hope you're there to enjoy it."
—Undertaker

Sins "Unforgiven"

Paul Heyman told everyone his client was The Next Big Thing. No one listened. Heyman proclaimed his man would be crowned King of the Ring, yet his words fell on deaf ears. He warned one and all that the former NCAA Champion would destroy *Hulkamania*, then defeat The Rock for the Undisputed title at *SummerSlam*. Again, Heyman was ignored. "Well, listen to *this*," said a smiling Brock Lesnar, who addressed the crowd on the "sacred ground" of Madison Square Garden at August 26 *Raw*. "I'm just twenty-five years old...and I'm the youngest WWE Undisputed Champion in history! I'm the youngest *ever*! And nobody—*nobody*!—can beat me!"

Less than twenty-four hours had passed since Lesnar claimed his very first, and most important, title in all of sports entertainment. Having arguably achieved the single greatest rookie season in WWE history, Brock looked invincible, and had every right to feel that way. Though when Shawn Michaels's music suddenly filled the venue, the MSG fans erupted, thinking HBK was going to take issue with Lesnar's comment.

Sadly, the cheers quickly turned to jeers, as Triple H came out on stage and posed like the former Showstopper before yelling for the music to be cut. "That is the last time you will ever hear that Shawn Michaels crap!" he yelled, and he might have been right; Michaels won their vicious, unsanctioned *SummerSlam* contest, only to feel the head of a sledgehammer smashed into his surgically repaired back. Not expecting Shawn to walk again, much less enter another ring, Hunter made his way down the ramp and reminded Brock that when he appeared on *Raw* with his shiny new championship, he would be there waiting. Getting in the champion's face, he asked, "Are you man enough to play The Game?"

Before any response could be given, Undertaker's music hit, and the Phenom walked down to the ring.

Undertaker has seen Lesnar's type before.

bout, charging ringside after Undertaker's corner assault on Triple H momentarily put the referee out of commission. Lesnar smacked his championship belt across 'Taker's skull, allowing The Game to pin him for the three-count and become the No. 1 Contender.

Alerted that *SmackDown!* General Manager Stephanie McMahon was in a limo out back, Bischoff got in her face and ordered her to leave, though he couldn't stop himself from gloating about his historic evening; between the new champion's debut and the No. 1 Contender, the past twenty-four hours favored everything *Raw*. But as The Next Big Thing and his agent approached, Stephanie asked Bischoff, "Triple H is the No. 1 Contender...for *what*?" Brock and Heyman entered the limo while she silenced Bischoff's protests that both brands feature the Undisputed Champion. "No, Eric...it's the *champion's prerogative* which show he wrestles on," she said, "and *I* happen to pay Brock Lesnar a whole lot of money to be exclusive to *SmackDown!* Tonight, history *has* been made, because this is the *last* night *Raw* will ever see an Undisputed Champion." With that, the limo drove off, adding some dust to the crow Bischoff had just eaten.

Looking straight at Lesnar, 'Taker explained that he got first crack at the young blood, "Because as the No. 1 Contender, I need to know...are you really The Next Big Thing, or The Next Big *Bitch?*" Triple H nailed the

[

"I need to know...are you really The Next Big Thing, or The Next Big *Bitch*?"

]

Dead Man from behind, allowing him and Brock to double-team him into the corner. But Undertaker quickly bounced back, clotheslining the champion and pummeling the Cerebral Assassin to clear the ring. Hunter was ready to step back in and fight, then rethought his decision and backed off.

Raw General Manager Eric Bischoff, already over-joyed about having Brock Lesnar back on his show as the Undisputed Champion, announced that Undertaker would take on Triple H to establish the No. 1 Contender. Before the match, Terri asked Heyman and Brock backstage who they preferred to face, to which Lesnar snarled, "It *really* doesn't matter." But the champion seemingly made his preference known during the

A very proud Stephanie McMahon welcomed everyone to Uncasville, Connecticut's Mohegan Sun Arena for the August 29 *SmackDown!* "Home of the Undisputed Champion, Brock Lesnar!" Pointing out that The Next Big Thing's exclusivity to *SmackDown!* nullified *Raw's* No. 1 Contender, she announced "a single elimination style series of matches, with the winner of the last match being named the No. 1 Contender to face Brock Lesnar for the Undisputed title." The *SmackDown!* GM didn't waste any time starting the tournament, which began with a rematch from *SummerSlam* between Edge and Eddie Guerrero. Reeling from a missile dropkick and spear, Latino Heat avoided the Edgecution by heading to the outside floor. He threw in a chair that Edge intercepted, but as the referee sent it back outside, Guerrero produced another chair that a charging Edge speared into head-first. Latino Heat climbed up top and delivered an unnecessary Frog Splash to advance to the next round.

Guerrero's next opponent would be Rikishi, who told Marc Loyd backstage that he looked to advance all the way and "….take care of unfinished business with The Next Big Thing" who F-5'd him a few weeks back. Eddie interrupted the interview, suggesting Rikishi's diaper was cutting off the circulation to his head. "Oh, wait…that's your *ass!*" he laughed, then got serious and warned the Phat Man to pull his head *out* of it; he was facing Latino Heat, *not* Brock Lesnar. Soon after the bell rang, Rikishi narrowly missed a Stinkface on Guerrero, though he'd settle with a corner splash and thrust kick for the three-count. But his victory was tainted by a sneak attack from Chris Benoit, who put the big man in the Crippler Crossface until Edge made the save.

Annoyed with the Rabid Wolverine's interference, Stephanie McMahon entered Benoit into the No. 1 Contender's competition. The Canadian Crippler was up for it, and since he'd already done a number on Rikishi's arm, it wasn't long before he exploited the injured appendage and Crossfaced the Phat Man for the submission victory. Following the match, Marc Loyd pointed out to Kurt Angle backstage that he hadn't been named in the tournament yet. The arrogant

Edge takes it to Eddie Guerrero.

Angle told Loyd, "Didn't you ever hear of 'Save the best for last'?" He was just informed he'd face Benoit for the No. 1 Contender spot, and once he went through him, it was on to Brock Lesnar, who was going to learn that he might be the champion, but he wasn't the best.

Lesnar F-5's Mattitude out of Version 1.

Unfortunately for Matt Hardy, he was about to discover just how good The Next Big Thing was. Harassing Stephanie to put him in the tournament, Matt stepped over the line after disconnecting the *SmackDown!* GM's phone conversation with a *Raw* Superstar in attendance who talked about jumping ship. Since Matt wanted to face Brock so badly, the infuriated Stephanie put him in a non-title match that night. Thrilled he'd been granted "the first step," Matt's chances of taking his final ones increased outside Lesnar's locker room, where he informed Paul Heyman and "Number One *SmackDown!* Announcer" Funaki, "It's not the era of Brock. It's the era of Matt Hardy," and that "WWE Attitude" would now be referred to as "WWE *Mattitude!*" Version 1 earned a painful Mattitude adjustment in the match, which ended quickly with Brock countering a Twist of Fate into the F-5 for the win. And to make sure Matt remembered whose time

it was, Lesnar re-entered the ring and drove home the point with a pair of powerbombs.

As for the *Raw* Superstar Stephanie spoke with earlier, Dawn Marie entered the office with a signed contract, prompting the excited *SmackDown!* GM to change the final No. 1 Contender's match between Kurt Angle and Chris Benoit into a Triple-Threat match. Before Benoit and Angle locked up in the ring, Stephanie came out on stage and introduced her newest acquisition, *Undertaker!* The Mohegan Sun crowd went wild as the Dead Man rode his bike down the ramp and entered the ring, where his opponents quickly went to work on him. Several times the pair double-teamed the Phenom, at one point locking on the Crippler Crossface and ankle lock simultaneously, only to refuse each other the killing blow. After dropping 'Taker with the Angle Slam, Kurt charged towards Benoit, who sent the gold medalist over the top rope. But then Undertaker caught the Crippler and sent him on the Last Ride, getting the one-two-three and moving one step closer to the very thing he came to *SmackDown!* for: the WWE Undisputed title.

With her No. 1 Contender in place, Stephanie McMahon sanctioned a title match between Undertaker and Brock Lesnar for *Unforgiven*. But Eric Bischoff, with briefcase in hand, opened September 2 *Raw* in Milwaukee's Bradley Center with a bombshell that would affect both brands, their Superstars and their fans. "Brock Lesnar likes to refer to himself as the Undisputed Heavyweight Champion of the World," he stated, "but ever since my competitor persuaded him to become exclusive *SmackDown!* property, I would say that that title is very, *very* disputed." Bischoff bottom-lined that the *Raw* fans deserved their own champion, exclusive to their brand, and his candidate for the role "...proved and convinced Undertaker...that it's much better to jump to *SmackDown!* and be a big fish in a little pond, than to swim with the sharks on *Raw.*" With that, Bischoff invited Triple H to the ring, opened his briefcase and unveiled the World Heavyweight title. "You may recognize this World Championship," he said, "because you were the last man to officially wear it. It's been worn by some of the greatest champions in the history of this industry, and now it will be again. Ladies and gentlemen...*your new World Champion, Triple H!*"

Triple H dons the World title.

Holding the now-exclusive *Raw* belt high, Triple H offered a less-than-gracious acceptance speech; most others might say they don't deserve it, "But then, I'm not a lot of guys, am I?" he smirked. "*Nobody* should be the World's Heavyweight champion more than The Game." A booming "*Woooo!*" suddenly interrupted Hunter, and the crowd rose to its feet as Ric Flair made his way ringside. The Nature Boy agreed with Bischoff's decision to reactivate the World title— "*Raw* deserves its own champion"—and that Triple H was the man to wear it. "The problem I have is that you wore it *once;* I wore it *sixteen* times. And nobody gift-wrapped it, brought it out in a gold Haliburton and *gave* it to me. I *won* it, right here, by busting my ass in the middle of this ring."

Flair's suggestion that Triple H *earn* the right to walk out of the Bradley Center with the belt rubbed Bischoff and the fans the right way. But rather than pull a *Smack-Down!* and hold some "bogus" tournament, the *Raw* GM declared that for the first time in history, World Champion Triple H would face the Nature Boy that night. Both men supposedly considered the match an honor and a privilege, until Triple H disrespected Flair, blowing off his handshake and sucker-punching him.

Other *Raw* Superstars would have a problem with The Game being handed the World title. Backstage, Bubba Ray Dudley threatened to smack the smug look off Triple H, who presumed he was just jealous. "This ain't the look of jealousy," Bubba said. "It's the look of *hunger.*" Becoming World Champion was a hunger everyone in the *Raw* locker room had, and since Lesnar walked away with their opportunity last week, "That belt that Bischoff just gave to you...is *our salvation.*" Chris Jericho, meanwhile, had a match with Intercontinental Champion Rob Van Dam that night, yet he couldn't believe "...a fifty-three-year-old, over-the-hill *has-been*" like Ric Flair was awarded the first shot at the new title. Though Flair reminded Y2J of his figure-four victory over him at *SummerSlam,* Jericho still wanted the Nature Boy to beat Triple H. "One of these days," he explained, "you and me are going to have a rematch.

Superstar ★ profile

MATT HARDY

HEIGHT: 6'2"
WEIGHT: 225 lbs.
FINISHING MOVES: Twist of Fate; Version 1
CAREER HIGHLIGHTS: European Champion; Hardcore Champion; Tag Team Champion (5); WCW Tag Team Champion
2002 HIGHLIGHTS: Severing ties with brother Jeff on *Raw* and striking out on his own at *SmackDown!*; developing a whole new "Mattitude"; beating Undertaker twice on *SmackDown!*

And if you're the World Champion...when we have that rematch and I beat the living hell out of you, then that title goes back where it belongs."

Prior to the match, *Raw* commentators Jim Ross and Jerry "the King" Lawler interviewed via satellite one Superstar whose focus was more on the man than on the title he now wore. "HBK" Shawn Michaels was wheelchair-bound after Triple H smashed a sledge-hammer between his shoulder blades, but he expected to walk again once he went through all the rehab and physical therapy. As for the man who put him in the chair, Michaels had only one message: "Triple H... don't hunt what you can't kill. And what goes around," he said, suddenly brandishing a sledgehammer, "is *definitely* gonna come around."

> **"Don't hunt what you can't kill. And what goes around is *definitely* gonna come around."**

If Triple H heard any of Shawn's warning, he didn't acknowledge it when he locked up with the Nature Boy that evening. As it was, he'd have his hands full with Flair, who fought the World Champion tooth and nail, eventually cinching him in the Figure-Four. The Game reached the ropes to break the signature hold,

then sent the referee to the outside after shoving Flair in his path. A low blow set Flair up for the Pedigree, and Triple H retained his new title. Hunter exited the ring laughing as Chris Jericho attacked and put Flair in the Walls of Jericho, but the beatdown was cut short when Rob Van Dam raced in and made the save. The Game ran back to handle Van Dam, but RVD's educated feet quickly dealt with both him and Jericho, clearing both men from the ring.

Incensed over what happened, Triple H demanded Bischoff give him a match against Van Dam that night. Jericho overheard the discussion and got in Hunter's face, since he was already scheduled to face RVD. Eric tried abating the tensions by making it a Tag Team contest, pairing the Cerebral Assassin with Y2J against Van Dam and Flair. The two Superstars didn't like each other, but they were able to work together and double-team Van Dam from the onset, until Flair came down and evened the sides. The Nature Boy's Figure-Four would get the better of Jericho on the arena floor, while Triple H tried capitalizing on a distracted referee by using his World Championship belt on Van Dam. Instead, a kick from Mr. Monday Night sent the belt into The Game's face, buying him enough time to climb up top and connect with the Five-Star Frog Splash for the one-two-three! The Game's first night as World Champion would end on a bad note, with Van Dam holding the belt along with his own Intercontinental title.

Since Eric Bischoff reinstated the World Championship for *Raw*, Brock Lesnar's belt would now exist as the WWE Heavyweight title, starting with the September 5 *SmackDown!* in Green Bay, Wisconsin's Resch Center. It was there Stephanie McMahon arranged for Lesnar and Undertaker to have a face-to-face meeting to promote their upcoming *Unforgiven* matchup, though Paul Heyman implored The Next Big Thing to first concentrate on his non-title match against Randy Orton, who trained with Brock while going through the system together. Whether or not the behemoth was overly focused on Undertaker would soon become moot; Lesnar rolled through a top-rope crossbody and rose to his feet with Orton in tow, then F-5'd the third-generation Superstar for the victory.

Shortly afterwards, in a darkened room backstage, Stephanie held court between the Dead Man and the WWE Champion, with Heyman in his corner. Brock didn't have a lot to say to Undertaker. He just pointed out his vast amateur background—four-time All-American, two-time Big Ten Champion, and the 2000 NCAA Heavyweight Champion—before reviewing his brief but unprecedented career in the WWE. "Not even a year in the business," he said, "and I come to *King of the Ring* and win it, no problem. And then I crucify Hulk Hogan. I took Hulk Hogan's blood, wipe it with my hands and wipe it across my chest. Why? Because I loved every minute of it, that's why. And then came *SummerSlam*: The Rock, the 'Great One.' Yeah, and that's when I brought the Undisputed Championship home. I am the WWE Champion. And tonight, I went out and brutalized Randy Orton; didn't even break a sweat. You see, I'm twenty-five years old—*twenty-five*—and I'm the youngest WWE Champion in history. How old are *you*?"

Undertaker had seen Lesnar's look more times than he could count—the look that said no one could beat him. He admitted Brock was very impressive from where he sat, but noted that in his youth lay inexperience.

Stephanie McMahon arranges a sit down.

"Son, you ain't been tested yet," he said. "You brag about wiping Hulk Hogan's blood all over you. Have you ever had to wipe *your own* blood out of your eyes? Have you ever fell down and felt ribs sticking out where they were broken, and wonder when your next breath was going to come? Or figure out how you were going to win a match? No, of course not, and do you know why? Because there ain't no one beat you up yet. That's gonna change real soon, because *I'm* gonna take you to a place you ain't ever been. I'm gonna beat you up. I'm gonna *bust* you up. And then, if you survive that, then you *might* have something to brag about. Life makes no exceptions, and neither do I. To me, it's all about the fights, Brock, and you ain't had those fights yet. At *Unforgiven*...your ass is *mine*, boy."

Mock-congratulating the Phenom on his "brilliant" speech, Paul Heyman got personal about Undertaker's distracting "family situation." 'Taker and Stephanie both warned Heyman the conversation had nothing to do with family, but the agent begged to differ. "It's *all* about family," he said, pointing to Lesnar's WWE title. "To my client, *that's* family. But *you* not only have to train for Brock Lesnar, you have to tend to your pregnant wife Sara at home." Despite another Undertaker warning, Heyman continued to press, informing him that if Brock caused any "irreparable harm" that rendered 'Taker unable to provide for his family, "I want you to know, the giving man that I am, that I will *definitely* take care of your lovely wife, Sara. But I *refuse* to take care of your unborn child!" The table cleared as the outraged Dead Man shoved Heyman down and went eye-to-eye with The Next Big Thing. Worrying about what might ensue, Heyman convinced Brock to walk away, though it was clear that neither man had any intention of backing down when it came time to meet at *Unforgiven*.

["I will show you the *real* meaning of 'extreme'!"]

It had come to Eric Bischoff's attention that several *Raw* Superstars were unhappy with the way—"No matter how much he may have deserved it," Bishoff noted—Triple H was given the World Title, so he offered them a chance to "put up or shut up" at September 9 *Raw*. From the Hilton Coliseum of Ames' Iowa State University, Bischoff announced Jeff Hardy, Rob Van Dam, Chris Jericho and Big Show would participate in a Fatal Four-Way Elimination match, from which the winner would get a shot at the World Championship at *Unforgiven*.

The matchup sounded to everyone's liking, especially to a daredevil like Jeff, who often thrived in specialty matches. Besides which, the contest provided an opportunity for some personal payback against Y2J, who was disqualified in their August 26 *Raw* match for refusing to break the Walls of Jericho after Jeff reached the ropes. Unfortunately, Mr. Xtreme confessed to Jonathan Coachman that he wasn't feeling a hundred percent, following a Rosey and Jamal beatdown Bischoff ordered on *Raw* a week ago, after getting some bad information that Jeff was jumping ship to *SmackDown!* Jeff cut his interview short when he saw the *Raw* GM, who blew off the mishap and told Jeff no thanks was necessary for including him in the Elimination match.

"*Thank* you?!" he yelled. "I'm in the match tonight because I *deserve* to be in the match, not because of *you*!" Jeff warned Bischoff that if he ever pulled another stunt like last week, "I will show you the *real* meaning of 'extreme'!"

Rob Van Dam was on a roll since winning the Intercontinental Championship back at *SummerSlam*. He followed up his classic confrontation against Chris Benoit with an even more amazing victory on August 26 *Raw*, one which unified his belt with Tommy Dreamer's Hardcore title. The two friends had taken it to the extreme with a ladder, on which RVD delivered a spinning legdrop onto a chair while Dreamer was caught between rungs. As for pinning

Triple H in last week's Tag match, Van Dam saw it as "just another day in the life of Mr. Monday Night." But Ric Flair illustrated that if he could walk away the victor in the Fatal Four-Way, "I know, without a shadow of a doubt, that you *will* be the next World Champion."

Arrogant as ever, Chris Jericho chomped away at an apple while informing Terri he expected a fruitful result in the Fatal Four-Way. "Ass-clown" Triple H may have been given the World Championship and ruined his Intercontinental title shot against Van Dam last week, but he had a plan to help him become No. 1 Contender, and ultimately help bring the World title back to where it belonged, "…around *my* gorgeous waist."

Jericho's plan included fellow competitor Big Show, who expressed giant problems with the *Raw* General Manager on September 2—not only had Bischoff sicced Rosey and Jamal on him two weeks prior, but giving Triple H the reinstated championship was beyond his comprehension. "Why don't you hand *me* the World title?" he snarled. "I'm seven-foot-two and five hundred pounds. *Nobody* can do what I can do in that ring." Eric dared him to *earn* a No. 1 Contender spot, which Show guaranteed during the evening's match with Tommy Dreamer. But the big man would have to settle for a DQ win after Dreamer fell back on his defunct Hardcore ways and hammered him repeatedly with a chair. Given another chance with the Elimination match, Big Show couldn't believe Jericho's proposal to work together against RVD and Jeff Hardy, nor did he appreciate Johnny Stamboli's locker room advice to listen to Y2J. Grabbing "The Bull" by the throat, Show advised him to keep his mouth shut; he was going to come up big, and get that top Contender spot on his own.

Triple H didn't care who won the Fatal Four-Way, and he denied Coach's allusion

regarding any trepidation towards Rob Van Dam after last week. He also casually dismissed Bubba Ray Dudley's accusation that Triple H was avoiding him by arranging a non-title match that evening against Bubba's half-brother Spike. But Hunter wouldn't have an easy time discarding the runt of the Dudley litter, who was coming off a rollup win against Raven at the September 8 *Sunday Night Heat.* Spike low-blowed his way out of a second Pedigree, then almost pulled off a major upset with the Dudley Dog. Barely escaping the near-fall, the Cerebral Assassin pulled out the victory after countering a second Bulldog finisher into a sleeper hold, then inflicted further punishment on the unconscious Spike until Bubba raced in for the save.

Though he claimed not to care about the Fatal Four-Way result, Hunter became as engrossed watching it as the *Raw* fans in the Hilton Coliseum. Big Show allied himself briefly with Y2J until he gave the big man a chair shot, looking for the hat trick after using it on RVD and Jeff Hardy. The referee, just getting back to his feet after Van Dam landed on top of him, saw the giant with the chair and disqualified him,

Jeff Hardy lands the Swanton Bomb on Big Show.

prompting a furious Big Show to leave behind three Chokeslams for the remaining competitors. Jeff and RVD double-teamed Jericho before turning against each other, during which Mr. Xtreme gained the upper hand and went for the Swanton Bomb. Y2J pushed Jeff off the top rope, however, then hit the Lionsault to eliminate him.

Jericho and Van Dam turned things up a notch by risking several high-impact moves, though Triple H's presence on stage distracted RVD long enough for Jericho to roll him up for a two-count. RVD's lightning-quick agility regained the advantage after slingshotting Jericho into the turnbuckle he exposed, then finished him with a Five-Star Frog Splash for the one-two-three. Van Dam then locked eyes with The Game, who looked visibly upset that his World title might be in jeopardy against "The Whole Dam Show."

Whether it was confidence, inexperience or just plain foolhardiness was debatable; the fact was, Brock Lesnar just didn't sweat facing Undertaker. And he certainly wasn't concerned with Hardcore Holly, long considered one of the toughest men within the WWE, when they grappled to kick off *SmackDown!* in Minneapolis' Target Center on September 12. Coming off a rollup victory to shut Matt Hardy's mouth seven days ago, Holly wasn't afraid of taking it to Brock Lesnar, though Lesnar was *no* Matt Hardy. The Next Big Thing's strength ultimately dominated the match; not long after dropping Hardcore on his head with a powerbomb, Lesnar finished him off with the F-5 for the win.

Not surprisingly, Undertaker wasn't afraid of Lesnar, either. He'd faced too many "invincible" opponents over the past twelve years to start running scared now. What *was* unexpected, however, was seeing the Phenom arrive at the Target Center with his very pregnant wife Sara, especially after Paul Heyman's comments last week. Not that he needed to justify his reasons to Marc Loyd outside his dressing room, but the Dead Man explained she wanted to see some friends and

General Manager Eric Bischoff's decision to unify the WWE Hardcore title with the Intercontinental title brought an end to nearly four years of turbulent title reigns. It was appropriate that WWE owner Vince McMahon awarded the newly formed title to Mankind at *Raw* November 2, 1998, since Mick Foley's entire career exemplified the very nature of the championship. There were two main rules for a Hardcore match, the first being there were no rules. A Superstar could use anything they can get their hands on to help them win the match, which over the years saw very imaginative weapons come into play.

The second rule for the Hardcore title came into existence during *Raw* on March 13, 2000, when Crash Holly said he'd defend his Hardcore title 24 hours a day, 7 days a week. And so the 24/7 Hardcore rule was born, meaning that with a little luck and a referee to count a pinfall, Hardcore immortality could happen any time, anywhere…and often did. As a result of the stipulation, fans would often witness several title changes during a single match, the most being *ten* in a Hardcore Battle Royal at *WrestleMania XV*. Before Rob Van Dam defeated Tommy Dreamer to unify the titles on August 26 *Raw*, it's estimated that the Hardcore Championship changed hands over *two hundred-thirty* times in its forty-six-month history. The following is a partial list of those who won the belt on either *Raw, SmackDown!* or a Pay-Per-View event. ■

WWE HARDCORE TITLE HISTORY

WON BY	DATE WON	WON BY	DATE WON	WON BY	DATE WON
Mankind	11/02/98	Gerald Brisco	5/18/00	Al Snow	3/11/02
Big Boss Man	11/30/98	Crash Holly	6/12/00	Maven	3/14/02
Jesse James	12/15/98	Gerald Brisco	6/19/00	Spike Dudley	3/17/02
Hardcore Holly	2/14/99	Pat Patterson	6/19/00	The Hurricane	3/17/02
Billy Gunn	3/15/99	Crash Holly	6/25/00	Mighty Molly	3/17/02
Hardcore Holly	3/28/99	Steve Blackman	6/29/00	Christian	3/17/02
Al Snow	4/25/99	Shane McMahon	8/21/00	Maven	3/17/02
Big Boss Man	7/25/99	Crash Holly	9/24/00	Raven	3/28/02
Al Snow	8/22/99	Perry Saturn	9/24/00	Bubba Ray Dudley	4/1/01
Big Boss Man	8/24/99	Steve Blackman	9/24/00	Raven	4/15/02
British Bulldog	9/7/99	Raven	12/25/00	Tommy Dreamer	4/15/02
Al Snow*	9/7/99	Al Snow	1/22/01	Steven Richards	4/15/02
Big Boss Man	10/12/99	Raven	1/22/01	Bubba Ray Dudley	4/15/02
Test	1/17/00	Hardcore Holly	2/8/01	Steven Richards	4/29/02
Crash Holly	2/24/00	Raven	2/8/01	Booker T	5/4/02
Pete Gas	3/13/00	Billy Gunn	2/25/01	Crash Holly	5/4/02
Crash Holly	3/13/00	Raven	2/25/01	Booker T	5/4/02
Tazz	4/2/00	The Big Show	2/25/01	Steven Richards	5/4/02
Viscera	4/2/00	Raven	3/19/01	Bubba Ray Dudley	5/6/02
Funaki	4/2/00	Kane	4/1/01	Raven	5/6/02
Rodney	4/2/00	Rhyno	4/19/01	Justin Credible	5/6/02
Thrasher	4/2/00	The Big Show	5/21/01	Crash Holly	5/6/02
Pete Gas	4/2/00	Chris Jericho	5/28/01	Trish Stratus	5/6/02
Tazz	4/2/00	Rhyno	5/28/01	Steven Richards	5/6/02
Crash Holly	4/2/00	Test	6/14/01	Terri	5/27/02
Hardcore Holly	4/2/00	Rhyno	6/25/01	Steven Richards	5/27/02
Crash Holly	4/3/00	Mike Awesome	6/25/01	Bradshaw	6/3/02
Perry Saturn	4/13/00	Jeff Hardy	7/12/01	Johnny The Bull	7/15/02
Tazz	4/13/00	Rob Van Dam	7/22/01	Bradshaw	7/15/02
Crash Holly	4/13/00	Jeff Hardy	8/13/01	Jeff Hardy	7/29/02
Matt Hardy	4/24/00	Rob Van Dam	8/19/01	Johnny The Bull	7/29/02
Crash Holly	4/27/00	Kurt Angle	9/10/01	Tommy Dreamer	7/29/02
British Bulldog	5/6/00	Rob Van Dam	9/10/01	Bradshaw	8/19/02
Crash Holly	5/11/00	Undertaker	12/9/01	Crash Holly	8/19/02
Bobcat (a Godfather Ho)	5/15/00	Maven	2/7/02	Tommy Dreamer	8/19/02
Crash Holly	5/15/00	Goldust	2/28/02	Rob Van Dam	8/26/02

*After winning the Hardcore Title, the British Bulldog presented it to Al Snow.

Big Evil takes Matt Hardy for the Last Ride.

McMahon to make a match that evening. Though Matt was in no position to "demand" anything, the *Smack-Down!* GM acquiesced, "Since you're so full of your 'Mattitude,' I'd *love* to see what you do to Undertaker." Matt guaranteed victory, while everyone else thought he'd assured himself a trip to the hospital…until Brock Lesnar and Paul Heyman accompanied him to the ring. Referee Mike Chioda was on his game, however, and tossed first Heyman, then Lesnar, the moment they started interfering in the match.

Undertaker controlled the bout from that point, but as he closed in for the kill, the *SmackDown!* TitanTron suddenly came to life, and showed Heyman terrorizing Sara in the dressing room. "Sara, how are you going to take care of your infant child when Brock is through with your husband, with your invalid Undertaker?" Heyman asked as he walked towards her. Matt picked up a cheap countout win as 'Taker left the ring and raced backstage, but the Phenom didn't give a damn. Storming into the dressing room, he wrapped his hands around the sleazy agent, only to get his brains scrambled by a massive chair shot from The Next Big Thing! Brock next hovered over Sara, smiling as he put his hand around her pregnant belly and said, "Life's a bitch." The WWE Champion and his agent exited the room, while the badly shaken Sara tended to her unconscious husband.

family living in the area. Matt Hardy suddenly interrupted to congratulate the Phenom; he thought having "a little Undertaker running around the house" was "awesome," then ranted on about one day having "a little Matt Hardy, Version *2,*" complete with all of his Mattributes. Hopefully, that wouldn't include a penchant for overstepping his bounds; Matt tried barging the dressing room to congratulate the mother-to-be, only to earn himself a hard shove into the wall.

Thinking Undertaker was in sore need of a "Mattitude adjustment," Version 1 demanded Stephanie

Eric Bischoff wanted to make the September 16 *Raw* especially interesting for Denver's Pepsi Center and his *Unforgiven* main eventers. With only six days till the Pay-Per-View, he arranged for Rob Van Dam and Triple H to defend their Intercontinental and World Championships against opponents of his choice. The Game was fine with having a match, though the fans' "RVD" chants, plus hearing "The Same Damn Crap," that he'd lose to "The Whole Dam Show" at *Unforgiven*, were getting under his skin. "I've got the body, the ability, the talent and the brains," he argued, "and Rob Van Dam doesn't stand a chance in the ring with me." The "One of a Kind"

Superstar's music interrupted Hunter, and though he entered the ring calm and confident, he'd express concern for his opponent. "Dude…you are *seriously* stressed out, *big* time," he noted, advising him to shake the anger he radiated. If he was angry because he'd seen Van Dam's "cool moves" in the ring, RVD justified that's what he was all about, "That's why all these fans love *me*…I'm amazing."

Triple H confirmed he *was* angry, but it was "a gift" that made him a World Champion who sold out arenas and headlined PPVs. Van Dam cut him off to acknowledge his accomplishments, "You've proven time and time again that, brother, *you* can spit some water!" An over-the-top impression of The Game's ring entrance had the Pespi Arena audience in stitches, and even Hunter confessed he could see why the crowd loved RVD. "They love you because you're just like them…a *gross underachiever,*" he said. "For all your athleticism, for all your cool moves, for all your great talent and ability, you're not going to amount to a damn thing in this business. Fact is, RVD, you are *not* championship material, and you will *never* be the World's Champion."

Rob suddenly understood where Triple H's anger came from; he was upset because Van Dam's fans didn't chant "H-H-H!" But he had bad news for The Game—it *wasn't* going to happen. "The fans are a little too busy and *way* too excited chanting the name of their favorite Superstar, and the *next* World Champion: *Rob! Van! Dam!*" The Cerebral Assassin attempted a kick to the midsection, but Van Dam caught his foot and spin-kicked him to the mat. Triple H was left lying in the ring, while the "RVD" chants he so hated grew louder than ever.

Hunter was down yet far from out, though he wouldn't say the same for Ric Flair. An embarrassed Nature Boy stewed backstage after dropping a match to Eric Bischoff's latest *Raw* acquirement, a man Triple H described as incapable of even holding

[**"I've got the body, the ability, the talent and the brains."**]

Flair's jock. Belittling the former sixteen-time World Heavyweight Champion he once idolized, Hunter said he'd lost his instincts and guts, and urged the "pathetic" Flair to "do everybody a favor" and retire. "*'Pathetic'*?!" yelled Slick Ric. "'Pathetic' is walking around with the most coveted trophy in this sport—the World Championship—without *earning* it! *That's* pathetic! And as far as Ric Flair goes, you don't know what I'm all about, and never will! You also don't know what I'm capable of, either!" Smirking as Flair left the room, Triple H muttered, "Oh, I think I *do* know, Ric."

Chris Jericho, meanwhile, assured Eric Bischoff he'd "redeem" last week's loss to Rob Van Dam by taking his Intercontinental title. Though he'd come close a few times in the contest, RVD's educated feet took control, setting Y2J up for the Five-Star Frog Splash.

RVD insists he's earned the title shot.

Brock Lesnar makes easy work of John Cena.

But as he climbed up top, he noticed Triple H at ringside, and changed his trajectory to splash him on the outside floor. Back inside, Jericho tried whipping RVD into Hunter, though a reversal sent Y2J crashing into The Game, forcing him into the ring. Van Dam floored Triple H with another kick, though this time Jericho would be around to apply the Walls of Jericho and force RVD to tap out. The new Intercontinental Champ exited the ring, while the Cerebral Assassin delivered a Pedigree that laid Van Dam out.

Backstage, a rapturous Jericho broke out the bubbly and celebrated with the *Raw* GM backstage. But Y2J made one more request of Bischoff, knowing Ric Flair was "on the lowest rung of the ladder...he's losing it," he wanted the Nature Boy in an Intercontinental title match at *Unforgiven,* to redeem the loss he suffered at *SummerSlam.* Totally into the idea, Eric gladly granted Chris the match, and a "larger than life" Y2J screamed, *"I am! The King! Of! The! World! Woooo!"*

Triple H still didn't know who his opponent was as he prepared to defend his World title, but Rob Van Dam wouldn't wait to find out before he got his licks in. Officials eventually pulled RVD away from ringside, but not before he busted the champion open with his own belt. While Hunter pulled himself together, his opponent made his way to the ring. Jeff Hardy saw a golden opportunity in keeping Xtreme pressure on the crimsoned Game, clotheslining him from atop the security barrier on the outside while landing the Twist of Fate and a Swanton Bomb on the inside. A foot on the rope saved Triple H from a three-count, while a late rally enabled him to catch Jeff in the sleeper hold for the win. But The Game wouldn't come out of the match feeling like a winner, as RVD returned to the ring and finished what he started, capping off an offensive flurry with a devastating Five-Star from the top rope. As Triple H slipped out of

"I am! The King! Of! The! World! Woooo!"

consciousness, his last vision was of his *Unforgiven* challenger holding the World title as if he were born to carry it.

Paul Heyman was extremely worried for his client's safety as *SmackDown!* rolled into Colorado Springs' World Arena on September 19. Convinced Undertaker would seek retribution for last week's assault, the agent informed Stephanie McMahon that he'd hired a team of off-duty police officers to protect Brock Lesnar. The *SmackDown!* General Manager also had some information to impart—the Phenom's wife had gone into false labor that morning and was taken to the hospital. Thinking the American Badass wouldn't be at *SmackDown!,* Heyman reacted like a huge weight had been removed, until Stephanie replaced it with an even heavier one— Sara was released from the hospital that afternoon, and Undertaker was trying desperately to make it to the arena. "If I were you," she cautioned, "I'd keep that security *real* close."

The agent heeded Stephanie's words, keeping security tight around him and Lesnar throughout the broadcast, and pleading with Brock to make his match against John Cena a short one. Cena's reputation for ruthless aggression continued to make him a Superstar on the rise, regardless of a losing effort to Reverend D-Von at August 29 *SmackDown!,* or a winning endeavor against Chavo Guerrero on September 7 *Velocity.* Unfortunately, not even his ruthless aggression would stop Brock from honoring Heyman's request, easily reversing a crucifix attempt into an F-5-powered victory. Throughout it all, the agent still remained nervous, to the point where he psyched both himself and Lesnar out of leaving the arena, for fear the Dead Man might attack them in the parking lot.

Like Brock, Matt Hardy wasn't afraid of Undertaker, though one could understand why The Next Big

Thing felt no reason to worry. Version 1 was simply too self-absorbed to know any better. He'd use last week's countout victory over the Phenom to bolster himself among *SmackDown!* friends like The Hurricane, and offered the hero a chance to realize his potential by facing him in the ring. But when The Hurricane began storming ahead in the match, Matt opted for the low-blow, then caught his "friend" with the Twist of Fate for the win.

Before long, another storm brewed inside the World Arena—Undertaker had finally arrived and made a beeline for the ring. "Tonight's got nothing to do with business. This is strictly *personal*," he announced to the crowd. "Brock Lesnar…I'm gonna teach you a lesson, so get your ass out here, or I *will* come back there and find you! Last week, as you put your hand on my wife and unborn child, you said that life

is a bitch. Well, I'm here to tell you, punk…*payback's a bitch!*"

To his credit, The Next Big Thing accommodated the American Badass, despite Paul Heyman's vocal protests all the way down the ramp. Brock entered the ring and got right into it with Undertaker, shoulder-blocking him into the corner. Deadman, Inc., quickly traded places and broke out the soup bones for

> ## "Tonight's got nothing to do with business. This is strictly *personal!*"

Lesnar, then sent him to the outside floor. Suddenly, Matt Hardy raced in and attacked, though he wouldn't take up much of the Phenom's time. 'Taker swatted Matt away like a fly, then chased after Lesnar and Heyman, who made their way backstage. He caught up to them just moments too late—the security guards kept Big Evil at bay while they carted Lesnar away in handcuffs. Heyman told Undertaker that putting Brock in protective custody wasn't for his own good, but "for *your* benefit." The Dead Man would just have to exercise patience for another three days, when nothing would restrain him or The Next Big Thing at *Unforgiven.*

Lesnar rises to Undertaker's challenge.

A boiling pot of anti-American sentiment continued to stew after *SummerSlam,* as did Lance Storm, Christian and Test's heated rivalry with Booker T and Goldust. Despite a scissors kick giving The Book a singles victory over Christian on August 26, the Un-Americans cooked up a *Raw* scheme to torch the U.S. flag in the middle of Madison Square Garden. But as Test prepared to ignite Old Glory in the ring, Kane's pyro suddenly exploded! Unfortunately, as had been the case in recent weeks, no Big Red Machine came out. Booker and Goldust raced down to stop the desecration, but the Un-Americans

The Big Red Machine Chokeslams Test.

Booker didn't tackle any Un-Americans on *Raw* the following week, though his scissors kick clipped William Regal for a proud Labor Day victory. Backstage, Storm and Christian found it funny that an American like Coach would speak to them of pride regarding their Handicap match against Kane that night. "Americans wouldn't know pride if it slapped Lady Liberty across her fat face," said Christian, and that included the "big, red burnt-up freak" who ruined last week's flag-burning ceremony. The Tag Team Champions planned to take great pride in ruining him, though it looked like they'd fall short of the mark when Storm's superkick nailed his partner instead of Kane, who Chokeslammed Storm for the victory. Test ran down and surprised the Big Red Machine with a big boot, but another attempt to burn the flag in public this time lit a fire under Bradshaw, who charged in and helped Kane clear the ring once again.

The momentum was clearly with Kane and Bradshaw as they looked to capture the Tag Team belts from Christian and Storm at September 9 *Raw*, but the big Texan wanted the Iowa crowd to know they weren't just interested in winning for themselves. "We don't know a better place than right here in the heartland of

fought them off as Test once again put the igniter towards the flag. Suddenly, another pyro explosion occurred, and Kane made his long-awaited return to the ring! The crowd erupted into a "USA!" mantra as the seven-foot monster Chokeslammed the three Un-Americans to hell and cleared the ring. Booker T celebrated by giving the MSG crowd *"exactly* what they paid to see"—the Spin-a-Roonie, which the Big Red Machine followed up with another move the people *wanted* to see—the *Kane*-a-Roonie!

America," he explained, "and we *damn* sure don't know a better time than *right now* to bring those titles home!" Their chances looked good when Kane chokeslammed Storm, whose missed missile dropkick floored the referee moments before. Test raced in and caught the Big Red Machine with a second big boot in as many weeks, though Bradshaw made him pay for it with Clothesline from Hell. Sadly, he wasn't expecting William Regal or his "power of the punch," which allowed Christian to pin the Texan for the three-count.

Bubba and Trish enjoy an Intergender Tag win.

The disappointed fans booed as the Un-Americans not only retained the Tag Team title, but apparently added a brass-knuckled ally to their ranks. Even Christopher Nowinski seemed bothered that his mentor had joined forces with the faction, though Regal pointed out to him that he'd been Un-American "…ever since I came to this ghastly country." The Brit further demonstrated his animosity by pairing with Test against Booker T and Goldust later that evening, though it soon looked like World War III as Kane, Bradshaw, Storm and Christian charged the ring and pounded away at one another. Although no winner was declared in the match, the retreating Un-Americans and the crowd's booming "USA!" chants gave a strong indication of who they thought won.

It was learned later that week that Bradshaw paid a steep price in defending his country's honor; he'd torn his left biceps (an injury similar to the one Kane suffered in April) during the Tag Title match and would be out of action for six months. Fortunately, another proud American would stand in his place. Bubba Ray Dudley dominated both singles and tag competition of late—the Bubba-bomb powered first him and Spike over Regal and Nowinski on August 26, then gave himself and Trish Stratus an Intergender Tag Tables win over Nowinski and Women's Champ Molly Holly on September 2. Steven Richards blindsided Bubba while he confronted new World Champion Triple H on September 9, though he'd pay for it in the ring that night with a jarring Bubbabomb from the second rope. A week later, Bubba gave Christian a powerbomb that would have made him and his half-brother Tag Team Champions, but the referee was busy tending to Spike, whom Storm and Christian threw to the outside floor and through a table. Christian capitalized on the distraction and rolled Bubba up for the three-count, but by then the loss meant nothing to him. The assault on poor Spike, however, guaranteed the Un-Americans had made themselves a Bubba-Tough enemy.

The Un-Americans sought to assert themselves further at the last *Raw* before *Unforgiven*, though both Test and William Regal would come up short in their matches against Booker T and Kane, respectively. Booker took and passed his former tag partner with a surprise rollup win, while Kane won his contest via disqualification when Test, Storm and Christian attacked him in the ring. Booker, Goldust and Bubba Ray stormed the ring in and sent the Un-Americans running up the ramp again, which prompted The Book to hold some truths to be self-evident. "You suckers ain't got no heart… ain't got no guts…and most definitely ain't got no Spaldings!" That said, Booker laid down the challenge:

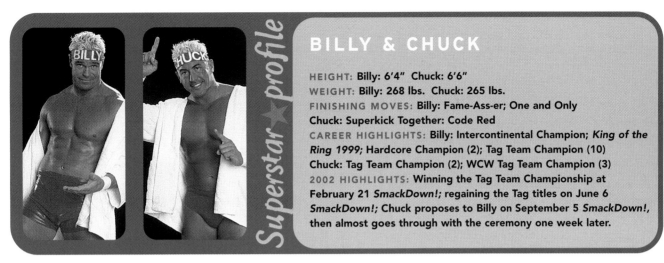

Superstar ★ profile

BILLY & CHUCK

HEIGHT: Billy: 6'4" Chuck: 6'6"
WEIGHT: Billy: 268 lbs. Chuck: 265 lbs.
FINISHING MOVES: Billy: Fame-Ass-er; One and Only
Chuck: Superkick Together: Code Red
CAREER HIGHLIGHTS: Billy: Intercontinental Champion; *King of the Ring 1999*; Hardcore Champion (2); Tag Team Champion (10)
Chuck: Tag Team Champion (2); WCW Tag Team Champion (3)
2002 HIGHLIGHTS: Winning the Tag Team Championship at February 21 *SmackDown!*; regaining the Tag titles on June 6 *SmackDown!*; Chuck proposes to Billy on September 5 *SmackDown!*, then almost goes through with the ceremony one week later.

an Eight-Man Tag match at *Unforgiven*. The Un-Americans talked it over and accepted, though Booker didn't have to ask anyone on his team; he knew that Bubba, Goldust and Kane "…can most definitely dig that, *suckkaaa!*"

The elimination series Stephanie McMahon held on August 29 *SmackDown!* not only determined a No. 1 Contender for Brock Lesnar, but kick-started several existing grudges in the process. And after the following week's Six-Man Tag match between Undertaker, Edge and Rikishi against Kurt Angle, Chris Benoit and Eddie Guerrero, those conflicts would escalate towards the aptly named *Unforgiven*.

While preparing in the locker room for the Six-Man main event, Latino Heat told Kurt Angle that he wanted revenge after being "robbed" in the tournament by Rikishi and his big ass. Kurt, on the other hand, blamed his loss in the Triple-Threat final round on Eddie's "gap-toothed pal" Benoit. "There's no way I'd ever let these Olympic shoulders get pinned on the mat by some redneck biker," he said, mocking that the Rabid Wolverine was more like a "Rabid Puppy-Dog" or "Rabid Chihuahua." Entering the room in time to hear the disparaging remarks, Benoit got in Angle's face and dared him to prove he was the better man, but Guerrero told them to save it for the match— "Tonight, the war is out there!"

For two guys who couldn't stand each other, Benoit and Angle worked well together throughout the match,

even if it was usually through Guerrero. But the teamwork dissolved when a Stinkface on Angle gave Benoit a good laugh, which in turn outraged Kurt and prompted a harsh exchange of words. Not even Eddie could stop them from hammering each other to the outside floor, leaving poor Latino Heat alone in the ring with Edge, Rikishi and Undertaker. The outnumbered Guerrero tried buddying up to them, though Edge made sure his face became particularly familiar with Rikishi's ass before sending him over to Undertaker for a Last Ride that gave their team the win.

Deadman, Inc. snuffs out the fires of Latino Heat.

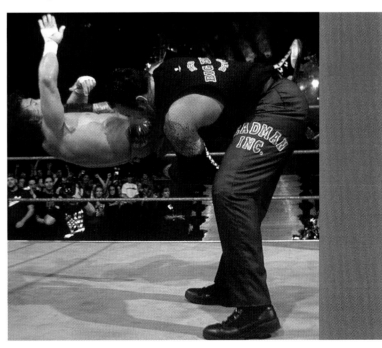

If people thought what happened to Guerrero was funny, then the events that unfolded at September 12 *SmackDown!* were a laugh riot. Humiliated by last week's contest, Latino Heat recruited cousin Chavo for a Tag match against Edge and John Cena. Los Guerreros pulled away with a hard-fought victory after Eddie's frog splash immediately followed Chavo's brainbuster to Cena. Latino Heat next had Chavo drop his tights and position himself a la Rikishi so he could push a dazed Edge into a Latino Stinkface. Edge caught Eddie with a low blow at the last second, however, then shoved his face into the posterior of his unknowing nephew, who laughed the whole time. Eddie looked sick as he headed backstage and threatened to kick his nephew's ass, while all Chavo could do was apologize and try to make his uncle feel better by telling him, "I wiped, *I wiped!*"

Kurt Angle thought it was funny to be in *Mini*-sota for a *SummerSlam* rematch with Rey Mysterio that night, though he hadn't found anything humorous about Chris Benoit laughing at him last week. Kurt promised "*two* holy unions" in the Target Center if he caught the Crippler cackling at him again—Billy and Chuck's wedding, "and your face and my fist!" Unfortunately, the gold medalist made a laughing stock of himself when he tried to issue a warning to Mysterio. "You're a boy in a man's world, and I'm a man who *loves* to play with boys! No, wait…What I meant to say is, you're a boy and I'm a man, and tonight I'm going to *love* to manhandle you…Hold on a second, *shut up!* Rey Mysterio, you remember this, pal: you're a boy and I'm a man. When you and I get together tonight, I'm gonna get on top of you and…No, no, *no!*" The luchador mercifully

Chavo Guerrero administers a painful armlock to Kidman.

came out and ended Angle's tantrum, only to come up just short of the mark when Kurt jumped up to the top rope and Angle Slammed him for the win.

Benoit was all business as he headed out for his match against the usually good-natured Rikishi. The

"You're a boy in a man's world, and I'm a man who *loves* to play with boys! No, wait…What I meant to say is, you're a boy and I'm a man, and tonight I'm going to *love* to manhandle you… Hold on a second, *shut up!*…No, no, *no!*"

Phat Man's strength helped him escape another Crossface, but the Rabid Wolverine's relentless attack put him in control as he went up top for a flying head-butt. Suddenly, Angle appeared and pushed Benoit off the ropes, giving the Crippler a DQ win. The gold medalist didn't care, however; he just wanted to have a good laugh at Benoit's expense, and did so by holding his arms in the corner while Rikishi delivered a long, hard Stinkface. Minutes later, Benoit headed into Stephanie McMahon's office and demanded a match with Angle at *Unforgiven*. He didn't have to work hard at convincing the *SmackDown!* GM, who knew from the two Superstars' past encounters that it would be an automatic classic. Getting the nod, a pleased Benoit promised, "When Kurt Angle sees my smile, he *will* feel my pain!"

Eddie Guerrero told Chavo he had two goals going into their Tag match against Edge and Rikishi on September 19: that Edge's "pretty little face" would get messed up, and that "he's never going to lack respect for Latino Heat again!" A failed double team on Rikishi, however, soon had Chavo's kisser falling victim to a Stinkface, though the young Guerrero got his revenge by kayoing the Phat Man with a TV camera while the official was distracted. Chavo pinned Rikishi for the three-count, while Eddie caught Edge between the eyes with a steel chair that busted him open. Talking trash in the face of the bloodied, unconscious Superstar, Latino Heat fulfilled one half of his goals, though he'd have to wait until *Unforgiven* to finish the job.

Earlier in the evening, Kurt Angle interrupted Stephanie McMahon, Billy and Chuck, and proved that in addition to being a master at ankle locks, he had a gift for putting his foot in his mouth. He likened the tandem's commitment ceremony last week to "a bad episode of *Three's Company*," telling them he didn't rely on "pathetic" publicity stunts during the 1996 Olympics. "I certainly didn't try to make out with Carl Lewis, I can assure you of that!" he added. "I won an Olympic gold medal with a broken freakin' neck!" Chuck asked what Kurt thought it meant when

the crowd chanted "You suck!" but Angle wasn't biting at the implication that he was gay. "I don't have a problem with gays," he insisted. "In fact, gay people *love* me! *Everybody* loves me! I'm freakin' adorable!" But neither Billy nor Chuck might think so if one of them accepted his challenge to a match that night, "We'll *see* which one of us sucks!"

> "I don't have a problem with gays. In fact, gay people *love* me! *Everybody* loves me! I'm freakin' adorable!"

Stephanie agreed to the challenge, provided Kurt found a Tag partner; she wanted Billy and Chuck ready for their upcoming Interpromotional match at *Unforgiven*. That was fine with Angle, who invited "Will and Grace" to pick his partner for him. Billy and Chuck's eyes lit up at the invitation, and so did Angle's when they selected his partner to be Chris Benoit, the man he'd face at *Unforgiven*. The tongue-tied medalist thought teaming up with Benoit would be a hard one to swallow, then corrected himself and said he didn't care who he teamed up with, since he'd be the one climbing up on top of Billy or Chuck for the three-count. The crowd went into hysterics as Kurt just gave up and said he'd see Billy and Chuck in the ring.

Amazingly, Benoit and Angle again established themselves as a formidable tag pair, matching the more experienced Billy and Chuck move for move. Victory was assured when Kurt converted Chuck's superkick into the ankle lock, but Benoit, refusing to let his partner hog the glory, sent Angle to the outside floor and latched Chuck into the Crossface. Billy recovered to make the save, while Chuck followed up with a super-kick on the Wolverine to get the "W." The outraged medalist re-entered the ring and Angle Slammed the Crippler, then put him in the ankle lock until Benoit countered with the Crossface. WWE officials were

Terri and Stacy engage in *Raw* pillowtalk.

eventually able to pull the two ring technicians apart, but there was no way they could prevent their egos from clashing at *Unforgiven.*

Whoever said "all's fair in love and war" had obviously never stepped inside the squared circle, or been a part of *Raw* or *SmackDown!* Eric Bischoff and Stephanie McMahon's ongoing battle to become the top WWE brand had run pretty much neck and neck from a competitive standpoint, but new twists would develop along the road to *Unforgiven,* a road that became paved with three-minute warnings, same-sex weddings and "Hot Lesbian Action."

Bischoff was exceptionally proficient at reaching new highs in lows, particularly when it came to "making history" on *Raw* and giving people their three minutes of fame. WWE Hall of Famer Jimmy "Superfly" Snuka had become Jamal and Rosey's latest *Raw* victim on August 26, after Eric set the ring legend up with a video tribute and a WWE Lifetime Achievement Award at Madison Square Garden. "The Bisch" also

sanctioned the first-ever Tuxedo/Evening Gown match, a classic confrontation which saw Trish Stratus and Stacy Keibler help Lilian Garcia strip Howard Finkel down to his briefs, which in turn removed him from the *Raw* announcer's job.

Stephanie, meanwhile, enjoyed squashing Bischoff's night, plus the rest of his week, by making newly Undisputed Champion Brock Lesnar and Undertaker exclusive to *SmackDown!* Bischoff countered on September 2 by officially disputing the championship and reinstating the World title as an exclusive to *Raw.* As a bonus, he decided to pit Stacy Keibler's "assets" against Terri's "pillows" in "Eric Bischoff's First-Ever In History Lingerie Pillow Fight match." Jerry Lawler was probably up all night after guest-officiating a contest that included a "King"-sized bed in the center of the ring, though he was perfectly positioned as scantily clad Terri hooked Stacy's legs up high for the exciting victory. Unfortunately, Stacy ruined the dream matchup by literally clocking poor Terri with a

Staples Center
Los Angeles, CA

UNFORGIVEN®

WWE CHAMPIONSHIP MATCH
Brock Lesnar (w/ Paul Heyman) and *Undertaker* fought to a draw; Lesnar retains the WWE title

Chris Benoit defeated *Kurt Angle* via pinfall

WOMEN'S CHAMPIONSHIP MATCH
Trish Stratus defeated *Molly Holly* via pinfall to become the new Women's Champion

WORLD CHAMPIONSHIP MATCH
Triple H defeated *Rob Van Dam* via pinfall

INTERPROMOTIONAL MATCH
Rosey & Jamal (w/ Rico) defeated *Billy & Chuck* via pinfall

Eddie Guerrero defeated *Edge* via pinfall

INTERCONTINENTAL CHAMPIONSHIP MATCH
Chris Jericho defeated *Ric Flair* via submission to retain the Intercontinental Title

EIGHT-MAN TAG TEAM MATCH
Kane, Booker T, Goldust & Bubba Ray Dudley defeated *Un-Americans (Test, William Regal, Lance Storm & Christian)*; Kane pinned Storm

SEPTEMBER 22, 2002

With matches putting national, sexual, personal and interpromotional pride on the line, the events that unfolded inside Los Angeles' Staples Center resulted in acts *Unforgiven*, nor easily forgotten. Political fireworks flew as Kane, Goldust, Booker T and Bubba Ray Dudley kicked off an explosive Eight-Man Tag Team match against Un-Americans, Lance Storm, Christian, Test and William Regal. Tempers ran high early, and it wasn't long before all eight men slugged it out in the ring. Test caught the Big Red Machine with the pump-handle slam, but fell to a scissors kick that sent Booker T into a Spin-a-Roonie. Regal took Bubba Ray to the outside floor after a Bubbabomb primed Christian for the Bizarre One's Golden Globes. Test dropped Goldust with the big boot, but fell to a top-rope clothesline from Kane, who also converted a Storm superkick into a Chokeslam from Hell, getting the one-two-three for the USA!

Ric Flair wanted to beat new Intercontinental Champion Chris Jericho not just for the belt, but to refute Triple H's recent claims that he no longer had what it took in the ring. As usual, Jericho underestimated the Nature Boy, who took whatever Y2J could dish out, then dominated after launching him to the outside floor. Back inside, Jericho tried keeping himself upright after Flair avoided the Lionsault, only for his knee to give out on him. Flair backed off and turned away from the agonized Jericho as the referee called for a trainer to check on his knee. But the King of the World beat the dirtiest player at his own game, showing his knee was fine as he sprung up and attacked Flair while his back was turned, then locked on the Walls of Jericho to make the Nature Boy tap out.

Eddie Guerrero demanded respect from Edge, who entered the ring only three days after receiving a mild concussion at the hands of a Latino Heat chair shot. Guerrero would use that to his advantage throughout their *SummerSlam* rematch, starting with a tornado DDT from the second rope. Edge eventually mounted a comeback, converting Guerrero's Hurracanrana into a sit-out powerbomb, then later spearing him into a turnbuckle Eddie exposed moments before. But as Edge climbed the ropes to deliver a superplex, Guerrero rammed his head into the exposed turnbuckle, then sunset-flipped from the top of the ring post into a powerbomb. Grabbing a handful of tights with the rollup insured a pinfall victory for Latino Heat.

Booker T and Bubba show the Un-Americans no forgiveness.

Earlier in the evening, Stephanie McMahon assured Billy and Chuck backstage that winning their Interpromotional match against Rosey and Jamal would be more in the best interests of *SmackDown!* than her not having to "French-kiss a lesbian." Preferring to see Stephanie engaged in "Hot Lesbian Action" over kissing her ass, Eric Bischoff employed a different motivational technique, telling Rosey and Jamal they were representing not only *Raw* in their first official match, but their GM. And heading to the ring with them would be Rico, the man who knew Billy and Chuck "inside and out." The massive Samoans worked over Chuck, usually as a double team, before he finally tagged in Billy, who went to town on them and knocked Rico off the ring apron. Jamal went up top, but Chuck sent him quickly crashing down to the mat, allowing Billy to hit the Fame-Ass-er. Rico entered the ring, only to get clocked with a hard right and sent back out the hard way, but the diversion was enough for Jamal to nail Billy with a devastating Samoan drop for the victory.

Visiting the locker room shortly before his World title match, champion Triple H told challenger Rob Van Dam he didn't have the passion to take the belt from him, then pointed to Flair, a man who *used* to have that craving. Holding the Nature Boy back, RVD said he'd rather hang with a so-called "loser" like Flair than an alleged winner like Hunter, who left the room laughing. But it was Mr. Pay-Per-

View having a laugh early in the contest, using his agility to keep the Cerebral Assassin off-balance with several side head-lock takeovers, then mocking Triple H's usual water-spit entrance. A failed somersault plancha attempt to the outside put Triple H in control, who soon started aping RVD on the top rope until Van Dam kicked him down.

Fighting out of a sleeper hold, The Whole Dam Show elevated the pace, scoring several near-falls with spinning heel kicks and the Rolling Thunder. But as he avoided Triple H coming off the ropes, the referee took a hard shoulder that knocked him to the outside floor. The incident proved costly for Van Dam, whose spinning heel kick and Five-Star Frog Splash guaranteed two certain pinfalls. Triple H finally grounded RVD with a low blow, then pulled a sledgehammer out from under the ring. Van Dam kicked it back in Hunter's face, and while both men struggled to get up, Ric Flair stormed the ring and grabbed the sledgehammer. Flair stalked Hunter with the weapon, only to suddenly smash it into Van Dam's midsection! The Cerebral Assassin connected with the Pedigree on a defenseless RVD, while Flair helped the ref recover and make the three-count. A pleasantly surprised Triple H and the Nature Boy embraced inside the ring, while a betrayed Van Dam lay on the canvas in pain.

Backstage watching the match, D'Lo Brown told Billy Kidman he had a feeling that Flair was up to something, though he wasn't expecting to see Eric Braeden—the actor who plays the conniving Victor Newman on *Young and the Restless*—enter the room. Being a huge *Y&R* fan, D'Lo had to ask the daytime TV star, with all those hot, fine women on the popular soap, does he ever get any "off-screen action"? As a married man for many years, Braeden couldn't really comment on such things, though Dawn Marie spoke volumes for the actor when she showed up and said he's with her.

The Women's title match was the latest, and perhaps greatest chapter in the intense rivalry between champion Molly Holly and Trish Stratus. Molly established herself as the more vicious aggressor, both technically on the mat and on the arena floor, where she slammed Trish's face into the ring steps. But Trish's heart and determination kept her in the contest, countering the virtuous champion's straightjacket maneuver into a near-fall. Converting Trish's attempted Hurracanrana into the Tree of Woe and a vicious handspring, Molly went for the kill as she whipped her opponent into the ropes. But Trish caught Molly completely off-guard, twisting herself into a bodyscissors position and nailing the Stratusfaction to capture the Women's title for a third time. Emotional over her hard-earned victory, the new champion expressed to the Coach at ringside how she loved entering the ring every night to experience moments like this one.

Any time Chris Benoit and Kurt Angle hook up in the ring is a guaranteed five-star matchup, and their *Unforgiven* contest was no different. Angle and Benoit punished each other before engaging in what looked like a yard sale on suplexes—Kurt tried following a series of German suplexes with the Angle Slam, but Benoit responded with a German leverage flip that sent the gold medalist flying face-first into the canvas. As Benoit headed up top, Angle met him and delivered a fierce belly-to-belly off the ropes. Both Superstars soon tried earning their reputations as masters of submission, with Angle twice reversing Benoit's Crippler Crossface into the ankle lock, and vice versa. Kurt soon surprised the Rabid Wolverine by putting him in his own Crossface, which Benoit converted into a pinfall, using the ropes for leverage to get the three-count.

Paul Heyman confirmed Marc Loyd's observation that Brock Lesnar's approaching WWE Championship match against Undertaker had become personal. Trying to take away what The Next Big Thing had worked all his life for made it personal, which meant Brock "was going to be personal back." Lesnar added that he felt no remorse about terrorizing Undertaker's wife, nor would he feel any for what he was going to do to the Dead Man. "When you have no remorse, you have no problem being unforgiven."

An ecstatic Eric Bischoff let the victorious Jamal, Rosey and Rico take some ladies out for a *Raw* Hollywood night on him (they could even mention *his* name if they wanted anything), while he headed ringside with his girls—"Peaches" and "Cream"—before the WWE Championship match. Addressing the keyed-up crowd, Bischoff announced that L.A. wouldn't stand for Los Angeles, but for *Hot* "Lesbian Action!" then welcomed Stephanie out for a little three-way action. The lesbians took off their tops and rubbed up against Stephanie, but "The Bisch" stopped them before the first kiss fell. He wanted this to be the most humiliating experience in Stephanie's life, so he brought out Hildegard, "the ugliest, fattest, most physically repulsive lesbo I could find…and she's done prison time!"

Bischoff howled as the enormous Hildegard started getting it on with Stephanie, though quickly became stupefied when it seemed the *SmackDown!* GM was *enjoying* it! Suddenly, Hildegard laid out Bischoff with a superkick, then removed her disguise to reveal Rikishi! Stephanie hoisted up the rear of his trunks, while the Phat Man backed that ass up and gave Bischoff what seemed like an eternal Stinkface!

Fun time came to a screeching halt as Brock Lesnar went face-to-face with Undertaker, with the WWE title at stake. The champion's inexperience showed as the American Badass threw him out of the ring several times, then took him "old school" by walking the ropes and coming down hard on The Next Big Thing. Heyman tried distracting the referee, only to catch a big boot from Big Evil, though it enabled Lesnar to regroup and mount an offense. Lesnar focused on 'Taker's midsection, injuring his ribs after a series of shoulder blocks and ramming him into the steel post. As the fight spilled to the outside, Big Evil hurled Brock into the ring barrier, but another Heyman diversion allowed Lesnar to bust 'Taker open with the WWE title. Undertaker's soup bones eventually regained the advantage, though the referee went down in the corner just before the Phenom hit Lesnar with the Chokeslam.

Matt Hardy stormed the ring to help The Next Big Thing, but there was no helping him out of a Last Ride to the canvas. Heyman supplied Lesnar with a chair when he countered a Tombstone and sent 'Taker crashing into the referee, but Brock wouldn't get to use it. Undertaker floored him with the big boot, then bashed the chair over the champion's head, making him bleed for the first time in his WWE career. Fighting past the pain, Brock back-body-dropped his way out of a Last Ride and set 'Taker up for the F-5. But the Dead Man countered his finisher as well, and the match broke down into an all-out slobberknocker in the corner. While trying to regain control of the match, the referee took his third bump of the night, giving him no choice but to call for the bell. Officials swarmed the ring to separate the combatants, though Lesnar left only after Undertaker Chokeslammed him to the mat. The Dead Man didn't win the WWE Championship, but he would get the better of The Next Big Thing, sending him backstage the hard way—right through the *Unforgiven* stage sign! ∎

timepiece-loaded pillow, then tarred and feathered her Diva opponent in the ring before leaving.

The experience wouldn't be quite so pleasurable for Bischoff, who received word that a *Raw* member was going to *SmackDown!* to join a family member. The news prompted Eric to stop a match between Jeff Hardy and Crash Holly that evening. He knew Jeff had wanted to settle scores with his estranged brother Matt, "but hey, a little *notice* would have been nice," he

World's Strongest Man takes Tajiri's best shot in stride.

said. "It didn't have to be a month's notice; hell, it didn't have to be a week's notice. It could have been *three minutes'* notice!" Rosey and Jamal entered the ring and put a hurting on Jeff, while Bischoff promised anyone else wanting to leave *Raw* for *SmackDown!* would get the same. From a safe distance on stage, Crash Holly suddenly made an announcement: "Mr. Bischoff, I just thought you should know that Jeff isn't the one leaving for *SmackDown! I* am!" Crash then headed up the ramp to join his cousin Hardcore Holly and the competition.

Stephanie and Bischoff's rivalry headed to the sidelines there was something in the air at September 5 *SmackDown!*, and it *wasn't* just the ever-agile Rey Mysterio, who victory-rolled Billy for the three-count. Rico, who'd fallen to Mysterio's springboard Hurracanrana on *SmackDown!* one week before, didn't want Billy to get too upset about the loss, since his partner, Chuck, was about to make it the greatest moment of his life. The excited stylist instructed Chuck "to dig deep into those tights and pull out the love!" Thankfully, Chuck produced a small box containing a ring, while Rico guided him to go down on one knee and pop the question.

"Billy," Chuck said nervously, "I know we've been partners in the ring for a long time, and I was just wondering...I want you to be my partner for life." Billy, who seemed as surprised as the Resch Center crowd, thought a moment before giving his answer—a resounding "Yes!" Chuck topped off the "storybook moment" by placing the ring on Billy's finger, then embraced while a tearful Rico joined in the celebration.

Even though Billy and Chuck made their share of enemies since pairing up, many of the *SmackDown!* Superstars applauded them on the joyous occasion, including World's Strongest Man Mark Henry, who congratulated the happy couple en route to his match

[**"I know we've been partners in the ring for a long time, and I was just wondering...I want you to be my partner for life."**]

> "This is *exactly* what makes this country so great! In what other country will you find a beer-drinkin' Texas cowboy, a big red freak, a gold freak and the five-time, five-time, five-time, five-time, *five-time* WCW Champion kickin' some Un-American ass, and *still* have time to check out some Hot Lesbian Action?! Only in America, man!"

(and subsequent running powerslam victory) against Tajiri. Even *SmackDown!* commentator Tazz, who dropped the Tag Team Championship to them back in February, was happy for the partners, even after Michael Cole explained that Billy's acceptance of Chuck's proposal made them *more* than "a tag team for life."

Reverend D-Von, however, thought it was sinful and immoral, telling Stephanie in her office, "If I'm not mistaken, it says Adam and Eve, not Adam and *Steve*!" Stephanie informed D-Von she'd just approved Billy and Chuck's request to hold a commitment ceremony at next week's *SmackDown!*, so he should get over his petty concerns and remember that it's also immoral to impersonate a man of the cloth. D-Von wouldn't speak of the matter again, especially after suffering another fall from Stephanie's grace two weeks later, when she learned that evening's match loss to Batista prompted the "Reverend" to fire his former Deacon, making the six-foot-five powerhouse a free agent.

To no one's surprise, Eric Bischoff also detracted the commitment ceremony on September 9 *Raw,* calling it "a publicity stunt." Granted, it ignited a media circus—the *New York Times, Variety, New York Post, ESPN*…everyone was talking about the event. Bischoff said Stephanie McMahon could have her same-sex controversy, because he planned to go one better, and he didn't mean the Fatal Four-Way match he'd just announced. "For the first time in the history of this show…hell, for the first time in the history of this damn *company*…I've got some beautiful women who are going to take part in some 'HLA'…*'Hot Lesbian Action'!*"

The Hilton Coliseum fans wholeheartedly approved the decision, which earned interesting reactions from

Raw Superstars like a water-spouting Spike Dudley, who had a hard time swallowing his meeting with the lesbians Bischoff selected. Christopher Nowinski was ready for some "HLA" until William Regal slapped some sense into him. "You're the smartest man here, and all you can think about is looking at some scrubber lesbians, or rogering Molly Holly? You're a bloody Harvard graduate—start *acting* like one!" While answering Coach's questions regarding his upcoming Tag match against Un-Americans William Regal and Test, Booker T was interrupted by his Kane-masked partner Goldust, the Big Red Machine himself, and Bradshaw, who asked if anyone was up for "some girl-on-girl." To everyone's surprise, Kane raised his hand, while Booker told Coach, "This is *exactly* what makes this country so great! In what other country will you find a beer-drinkin' Texas cowboy, a big red freak, a gold freak and the five-time, five-time, five-time, five-time, *five-time* WCW Champion kickin' some Un-American ass, and *still* have time to check out some Hot Lesbian Action?! Only in America, man!"

Bischoff came out to some cheers for a change as he stated his personal commitment to offer "the finest in culture, class and sophistication. So, ladies and gentlemen, please welcome the lesbians!" Tanya and Jenny entered the ring while the *Raw* GM started up the crowd with an "HLA" chant, then provided scintillating play-by-play for the girls to strip to their underwear, do plenty of touching, smacking and holding, and top it off with "…a nice, slow, warm, wet kiss." The girls really started heating up the *Raw* ring when Bischoff suddenly stopped them. "There's this old television adage that sex and violence always sell," he said, "and

Rico attends to every detail of Billy and Chuck's commitment ceremony.

we've certainly had plenty of sex out here, haven't we? You two have been great, but I think this show has gone on just about long enough. I think it's gone on about *three minutes* too long." Out came Rosey and Jamal, and down went Tanya and Jenny, so to speak. Rosey placed the fallen lesbians on top of each other, while Jamal flattened them with a top-rope splash. And Bischoff laughed himself silly throughout it all.

The big day had arrived for Billy and Chuck on September 12 *SmackDown!*, but poor Rico was a mess; he'd argued with the caterers about having *two* grooms on the wedding cake, the singers were stuck in traffic and Stephanie McMahon had politely refused to be a witness at the commitment ceremony. Stephanie asked him to understand—"I have really, *really* bad luck at weddings of *any* type," she said, but the stressed-out stylist soon guilted her into it. Later that night, Rico trekked out to a *SmackDown!* ring beautifully arranged with ivy around the

> ["I have really, *really* bad luck at weddings of *any* type."]

ropes and a dais for the couple to stand under, then welcomed everyone to an historic event where "two pioneers will boldly go where no men have ever gone before." With Stephanie and an elderly minister in place, he next presented Billy and Chuck, both wearing traditional tuxedos and name-embroidered red cummerbunds as they walked the aisle to the lively wedding march, "It's Raining Men."

Some might have wondered if they were attending a funeral, considering the speed with which the minister spoke, but things livened up when Chuck began the vows. "Billy, when I first met you, the only thing I knew was that you were a great tag team competitor, and… well, your name was 'Mr. Ass.' But, Bill, now it's *more* than 'Mr. Ass.' Bill, I know you've worn the Tag Team gold on numerous occasions, but now you've captured something even greater…something unbelievable. Billy, you've captured my heart."

Then it was Billy's turn, as he smiled at his intended and said, "Chuck…*Damn* that was corny, even for *you!* 'Captured your heart'? But seriously, that's what makes you so special. And that's why I'm happy to ask you to be my tag team partner, permanently." Billy slipped a ring onto Chuck's finger while Rico, tears welling up, presented the partners' most…*touching* moments together on the *SmackDown!* TitanTron, in a video montage entitled "Our Love Story." The minister slowly proceeded onward, asking if there was anyone present who thought Billy and Chuck should not commit themselves to each other. Fans' chants of "Just say no!" were drowned out when The Godfather's entrance music suddenly blared!

The escort-servicing Superstar headed ringside with his "Ho Train," revealing that they pulled into Minneapolis because he needed to speak some truth. First, he asked Billy what happened to him—his fine ladies used to like him so much that "I had to ask you to stay away, 'cause the *cookies* were givin' up too much free *nookies!*" Then there was "Chuckie P.," who Godfather remembered as a legendary, albeit not particular, skirt-chaser who liked "…the *heftier* ladies of the stable, if you know what I mean." That being the case, Godfather had just one question: "*What in the hizzell is goin' on in here?!*"

Stephanie looked puzzled while a suddenly nervous Rico shooed away Godfather and his "good-time girls," then told the minister to jump ahead to the end of the ceremony. Billy and Chuck were also sweating as they hesitantly pledged themselves to one another,

then stopped the ceremony before the minister could finish. Chuck told Rico things weren't supposed to go this far, while Billy revealed the ceremony was just supposed to be a publicity stunt. "We aren't gay!" he said. "I mean, we got nothing against gay people. As a matter of fact, if I *was* gay, I probably wouldn't marry Chuck. But that guy ain't pronouncing us *nothing!*" The minister did have something else to pronounce.

[**"The bond that Chuck and Billy have is sacred, and that will never change. It doesn't matter if it lasts fifty years, sixteen months or three minutes."**]

"Commitment is a very special thing," he said. "The bond that Chuck and Billy have is sacred, and that will never change. It doesn't matter if it lasts fifty years… sixteen months…or three minutes.…

"*Wait* a minute," the minister added, his voice suddenly changing. "Did I just hear myself say…'*three minutes*'?" Stephanie, Billy and Chuck, and Target Center attendees were too shocked to move as the elderly figure straightened up and peeled off a mask, revealing himself as *Eric Bischoff!* Bischoff grabbed Stephanie while Rosey and Jamal stormed the ring and joined Rico in a hellacious beatdown of the tag tandem. The *Raw* GM then shoved Stephanie towards Jamal, who crushed her with a Samoan drop! A top-rope splash seemed destined until a horde of *SmackDown!* Superstars made the save, chasing the *Raw* attackers and Rico out of the Target Center. But the damage was done, and the *Raw–SmackDown!* war had just shifted in Bischoff's favor.

Raw's General Manager wanted to comfort his fans on September 16 and clarify that last week's *SmackDown!* appearance was "a one-time shot…because even I, Eric Bischoff, can provide the most riveting moment in the history of *SmackDown!* only so often." In addition to his triumphant return to *Raw,* he brought a new friend who helped make the wedding farce possible—Rico. Rewarding his newest recruit with a match against Ric Flair, one which saw the stylist pick up a lucky upset win (and prompted Triple H's verbal barrage against the Nature Boy), Bischoff also announced that both Rob Van Dam and Triple H would put their respective championships up that night. "And hey, if it changes the title picture at *Unforgiven*, I'll deal with it later," he said. "Because I'll be *damned* if anyone will accuse Eric Bischoff of providing boring, typical, standard television. I'll leave that to Stephanie McMahon and *SmackDown!*"

True, Bischoff's *Raw* was pushing the envelope, though it also generated a large group of female protestors outside the Pepsi Arena that evening. Coach learned that the "IOW," the International Organization of Women, a women's rights group whose spokesperson demanded to speak with Eric Bischoff. Surprisingly, the GM allowed them in the building, though all became clear when he figured he had "a few minutes" to spare. After having a good laugh in telling the audience how he believed women were as smart and powerful as men, Bischoff invited the IOW members to a public forum inside the ring. But as the group spokesperson voiced grievances regarding *Raw*'s exploitation of women in degrading matches, plus having two lesbians perform sexual acts, it dawned on Eric—"I'm surrounded by a hoard of lesbians!" Inciting the crowd to chant "HLA," Bischoff then realized the faction might just be looking for their fifteen minutes of fame. "Well, ladies" he said, turning serious, "I don't have fifteen minutes. As a matter of fact—"

SmackDown! feels the power of 3 Minute Warning

Before Bischoff could finish, one of the women kicked him straight in the groin, leaving him writhing on the floor in pain. The other IOW members cleared out while his attacker removed her wig and glasses, revealing herself as Stephanie McMahon! "What was that you were going to say, Eric?" she yelled. "*Three minutes?*" On cue, Billy and Chuck charged the ring and delivered the Code Red on Bischoff! Jamal and Rosey raced in for the save, only to get laid out by Billy's Fame-Ass-er and Chuck's superkick, respectively. Stephanie then led her *SmackDown!* tandem out through the cheering crowd, having exacted a more than suitable revenge.

A few minutes later, a still-pained Bischoff threw out a challenge to Stephanie for an Interpromotional match at *Unforgiven*—*Raw*'s Jamal and Rosey against *Smack-Down!*'s Billy and Chuck. And with the challenge came a stipulation: "If Chuck and Billy win," he explained, "I'm going to give you what you've been wanting since the day you showed up here: I will kiss your little ass." However, if Jamal and Rosey won, "…since you like to dress up like a lesbian, at *Unforgiven* you get to perform some Hot Lesbian Action right in the center of this ring!"

Stephanie provided her eagerly awaited answer at *SmackDown!* three nights later, telling everyone that as far as the challenge was concerned, Bischoff was on. Billy and Chuck then made their way to the ring to set the record straight. Billy admitted that as much he was looking forward to the Interpromotional match, he wasn't sure which way he'd go afterwards; he could either continue teaming with Chuck, or he could pursue a singles career. Chuck interrupted his partner, "So, what you're saying is…you go *both* ways? There's no shame in that." Relieved, Billy answered, "That's right, Chuck, and I know how excited you are to go down…to Los Angeles this Sunday and beat Rosey and Jamal at *Unforgiven!*"

> ## "I'm going to give you what you've been wanting since the day you showed up here: I will kiss your little ass."

Billy and Chuck proved they were ready for the PPV after scoring an impressive win against Kurt Angle and Chris Benoit that night, while Stephanie and Bischoff poorly concealed their animosity towards one another during a live satellite chat. Stephanie asked Eric how his "Bischoffs" were doing after the *Raw* kick she gave them, while he wondered how the "McMahon Family Dynasty" would react when their "low-brow" little princess would have to perform some Hot Lesbian Action at the upcoming PPV. The *SmackDown!* fans reacted favorably as "The Bisch" got them chanting "HLA!", then as Stephanie accepted the stipulations from "the bastion of good taste." She also warned Eric that when Billy and Chuck won, "It will be me in the middle of the ring, bending over so you can pucker up, purse those pouty lips and…" Bischoff cut her off—"And *what*, Steph? Smooch some McMahon tush?"

"That's right," she said, though admitted that if his team were to win for some bizarre reason, and she had to perform some HLA, "Who knows, Eric? I might just *like* it."

10

OCTOBER

> "'Hell in the Cell'...just saying it I have a nightmare. That's a match that after twenty years in this business may have taken my career away forever. I don't like to think about it. I hate the fact that they have these matches. There's no winner; only a survivor. And if you survive, your life will never be the same, anyway. It's brutal, it's vicious, and it may have ended what I love to do, and that's to be a referee in this industry. This match...I just pray for the guys that are in it tonight. There's nothing else you can do. And I hope for myself that my shoulder heals. It may, it may not... but don't ever put me in that cell again. Ever."
>
> —Referee Tim White, relating his Hell in the Cell experience at *Judgment Day*

Tyrants Without Mercy

Inside the squared circle, there's no room for mercy. It's a lesson which the Brothers of Destruction, Kane and Undertaker, have taught, and learned, throughout their years in the WWE. This time, however, the cruelty of their enemies would pervade outside the ring and into their personal lives. Even more, *Raw* and *SmackDown!*'s General Managers continued to raise the bar in their ongoing brand war, sanctioning matches and stipulations that showed *No Mercy* for their Superstars as the October 20 Pay-Per-View approached.

The chaos began with Booker T and Goldust, who from a locker room backstage Anaheim, California's Arrowhead Pond offered their *Raw* colleagues a special television presentation on September 23: "*Stank Wars: Rikishi's Ass Strikes Back.*" The Phat Man's *Unforgiven* Stinkface on *Raw* General Manager Eric Bischoff was an image the Bizarre One joked as "...unbearable since Chris Jericho's last Fozzy concert." New *Raw* acquisition Rico, however, found the footage and everyone's laughter "despicable," and tattled on the others to Bischoff, who took his foul mood out on the crowd that booed him as he entered the ring. "Let me just get this straight," he said. "A couple of weeks ago, I infiltrate *SmackDown!* I make sure I leave Stephanie

McMahon *laying*, and her entire locker room comes out to save her? And last night [at *Unforgiven*], I get beaten to a *pulp*. I get *humiliated*, and not *one* of my *Raw* Superstars shows up to stop it?! And now I hear that they're *laughing* at me?"

Bischoff had other news for his wrestlers: WWE owner Vince McMahon had officially put a freeze on all *SmackDown!* and *Raw* contracts, meaning Superstars could no longer jump between shows unless there was an official trade. Though Eric was able to cut a few deals before the deadline, the fact was, "If you're on *Raw*, you belong to *me*. No options, no choices. You are here to *stay*." With that, he called out Booker T, who tried stifling a laugh as the *Raw* GM

Booker T jokes over the *Raw* GM's *Unforgiven* performance.

confronted him about the backstage show-and-tell and asked if he thought what Rikishi did was funny. "You damn *skippy*, hippy!" he roared, then asked his boss, "After last night, does 'HLA' still stand for 'Hot Lesbian Action,' or *'Huge, Lumpy Ass'*?!"

That was the final straw for Bischoff, who explained he didn't have all night to teach Booker respect; he only had about *three minutes,* which cued enforcers Rosey and Jamal to storm the ring. Booker fought off the mammoth Samoans, then spinebustered Rico as he jumped into the fray. But the overwhelming numbers and a Samoan drop soon forced him to the mat, with a superkick from Jamal halting an attempted save by Goldust moments later. Upon congratulating the trio backstage, "The Bisch" decided to drive home his point by putting Booker in a match against Rico, and Goldust against Intercontinental Champion Chris Jericho, who disputed the earlier comments regarding Fozzy ("We are *huge* rock stars!") and begged to get his hands on the Bizarre One. Eric granted his wish, putting the Intercontinental title up in the process, much to the dismay of the King of the World.

Y2J almost earned himself a Golden Globes kick in the corner during his match that evening, but the referee's intervention allowed the Intercontinental Champion

to recover with a missile dropkick off the ropes and latch on the Walls of Jericho, forcing Goldust to submit. Booker's luck wasn't much better—despite the scissors kick to Rico for the one-two-three, he was quickly triple-teamed when Rosey and Jamal attacked again. Jamal splashed the Book, then Goldust as he tried aiding his partner. Laughing at both Superstars' expense as they were helped backstage by WWE officials, Bischoff sarcastically asked the tandem what they thought of facing Rosey and Jamal in a *Raw* Tag match in Booker's hometown of Houston next week. The Book's response silenced his boss: "I think you are what you eat. Eric, I think you're an *asshole!*"

Since returning to *Raw* action in late August, Kane was tearing up the competition, and having fun doing it. After powering his team to victory over the faction at *Unforgiven,* the Big Red Machine and a mystery partner of his choice entered a *Raw* Tag Team title match on September 23 against champions Lance Storm and Christian. The Arrowhead

Goldust is trapped in the Walls of Jericho.

Pond crowd were blown away when the mystery partner was revealed as The Hurricane, who'd decided to make the leap over from *SmackDown!* Not even outside interference from Test and William Regal could prevent the winds of change that night, as the "All-AmeriKanes" delivered dual Chokeslams to Storm and Christian, with Kane covering Storm to win the Tag titles.

Catching up with the new champions backstage, Terri asked Hurricane why Kane chose him as his partner. The one hundred ninety-pound superhero thought it

The Hurricane Chokeslams Storm.

Hurricane suggested it was time to party at the Hurricave, but Kane had one more thing to add: he leaned into Terri, planted a passionate kiss on the lips and yelled, *"Yeeaahhh!* Now I'm ready to go celebrate!"

Ric Flair addressed the nation after Union Underground's live performance of the *Raw* theme "Across the Nation," and explained his *Unforgiven* actions that sabotaged Rob Van Dam's World title bid only twenty-four hours before. The Nature Boy claimed that World Champion Triple H was right to call him "pathetic," and doubt his passion, guts and instinct; "I cared more about what *you* thought I was doing than I cared about myself," he revealed. Rather than waste time mentoring unappreciative younger Superstars, Flair decided he'd focus on the World Champion who idolized him since childhood, and

> **"I'm gonna teach him how to high-style and profile...how to be a Rolex-wearin', limousine-ridin', jet-flyin' son of a gun!"**

was obvious—"We both wear masks, we both use the Chokeslam and we both have the most impressive physiques in the WWE!" Kane had a different reason: "He's a *freak*, just like me. Just like all those Kanenites out there. And you know what, Terri? Freaks are *cool!*"

take The Game to another level. "I'm gonna teach him how to high-style and profile...how to be a Rolex-wearin', limousine-ridin', jet-flyin' son of a gun!" he said. "But most of all, I'm gonna teach Triple H how to be the World Champion as long as he *wants* to be."

Superstar ★ profile

KANE

HEIGHT: **7'**
WEIGHT: **326 lbs.**
OTHER NAMES: **The Big Red Machine; Big Freak'n Machine**
FINISHING MOVE: **Chokeslam**
CAREER HIGHLIGHTS: **WWE Champion; Intercontinental Champion (2); Tag Team Champion (7); WCW Tag Team Champion; Hardcore Champion**
2002 HIGHLIGHTS: **Lifting Big Show and throwing him over the top rope at the *Royal Rumble*; winning the World Tag Team Championship with The Hurricane on September 23 *Raw*; winning the Intercontinental Championship on September 30 *Raw*; facing World Champion Triple H in a "Champion vs. Champion Winner Take All Match" at *No Mercy*.**

And the payoff would be to end his own career the way he started it, "…on top, living as high as I possibly can, every day of my life."

An infuriated Rob Van Dam, his ribs taped from the previous evening's Sledgehammer attack, planned a shortened life span for Flair as he headed down the *Raw* ramp, but he wasn't prepared for Triple H to jump him from behind. The Cerebral Assassin and Flair stomped away on RVD, with Hunter yelling that he couldn't win, until Bubba Ray Dudley stormed down and scared the attackers off with a chair. Minutes later, a fed-up Bubba conveyed to Jonathan Coachman backstage that this *wasn't* the Triple H or Ric Flair show. "This is *Raw*!" he yelled. "This is the *fans'* show! And I'll be *damned* if I have to sit through one more Triple H or Ric Flair speech ever again!"

Eric Bischoff intervened—*Raw* was *his* show, meaning *he* called the shots. As for Hunter and Flair, Bubba and RVD had them in Tag action later that night, though Bischoff cautioned Van Dam to watch his bruised ribs. But the injury did nothing to slow down Mr. Monday Night's educated feet inside the ring, or from going up top for a Five-Star Frog Splash as Bubba set Flair up on a table. Unfortunately, Triple H sent RVD flying from the top rope to the outside floor, then snapped Bubba's neck off the ropes, enabling Flair to hook the tights and grab a cheap rollup win. But the evening wasn't a total loss—before Hunter could inflict further punishment on RVD with a sledgehammer, Bubba's low blow and powerbomb allowed his partner to climb up top again, and this time connect with a legdrop that sent The Game crashing through the wood.

In a fashion similar to the way he promoted *WCW Monday Nitro*, Eric Bischoff stood in the ring of Houston's Compaq Center on September 30 and promised viewers thinking about watching *Monday Night Football* that they'd find "the *real* action" on *Raw*. There would be three title matches that night, including World Champion Triple H against Bubba Ray Dudley, and Intercontinental Champ Chris Jericho taking on Kane. In addition, Bischoff announced "something unprecedented" for *No Mercy:* "The Intercontinental Champion facing the World Champion, winner take all!"

Realizing some might consider such a contest a little unorthodox or radical, the *Raw* GM pointed out, "That's what Eric Bischoff is all about." Which brought him to his next subject: the special guest in the ring who was still recovering from a broken neck suffered last April, but appeared to have a mouth that worked all-too-well during a recent interview with WWE.com. Asked whether *Raw* or *SmackDown!* was the better show, Lita answered *SmackDown!* was "definitely better, by far. And I don't think it's the talent on the show." Replied Bischoff, who called the Diva "basically worthless" after her accident, "Why, Lita…you

A wrong answer gets Lita a 3 Minute Warning.

little *bitch.*" Lita tried explaining that she meant the *Raw* Superstars might respect Bischoff more if he respected them, but he didn't give a damn about her opinion. Instead, he'd just give her a chance "to do a little make-good"; about *three minutes'* worth.

Down came Rosey, Jamal and Rico, who backed the Diva into a corner. Jeff Hardy's attempt to stop them earned him a superkick, though the Houston fans rose to their feet as fellow Texans Booker T and Goldust made the save and cleared the trio from the ring. They also drew Bischoff's ire; they obviously hadn't learned their lesson after last week's ass-kicking, and since they had a match against Rosey and Jamal later, the GM ordered, "We do it *now*. Start the damn match!" The impromptu contest almost worked against the less experienced Samoan tandem—Rosey gave Booker just cause to do a Spin-a-Roonie after he splashed his own partner while trying to disrupt a cover. But Rico's superkick to Goldust on the outside left no one to rescue Booker from a Rosey powerslam and Jamal top-rope splash for the victory.

As the trio celebrated backstage, Coach approached them and asked what their ultimate goal was. Rico thought his was apparent; he came to *Raw* to lead "the most dominant team the WWE has ever seen" to Tag Team gold. "And if anybody tries to stop us," added Jamal, "we *will* let them feel the *'3 Minute Warning!'* "

> **"If anybody tries to stop us, we *will* let them feel the '3 Minute Warning!'"**

Last week's complaints that Kane and The Hurricane "robbed" them of their Tag belts was a warning sign that things weren't going well for Un-Americans, Lance Storm and Christian. Seven days later, they'd shifted the blame towards each other—Christian faulted Storm for letting himself get pinned, while Storm

wished his backup wasn't someone "…who screams like a little girl when he gets Chokeslammed by *The Hurricane.*" William Regal and Test broke up the argument, telling Storm to get it together for his match against Randy Orton and start re-establishing the Un-Americans as a dominant force. But Orton, who made a successful transition from *SmackDown!* to *Raw* last week with an impressive top-rope crossbody win over Steven Richards, would shock the Canadian ring technician, countering a rollup with one that gave him the victory.

Donning announcer Jim Ross's black 200x Resistol hat and walking down the runway, Christian asked Storm who should feel more stupid, "*You* for dropping the ball again, or *me* for dressing like a local!" But his on-the-spot challenge to beat the "all-American pretty boy" Orton worked against him. A unique-looking neck-breaker caught him unawares for a three-count, elevating the third-generation Superstar's blue-chip status and earning Ross's gratitude upon

Christian, a truly Un-American cowboy.

returning his hat to him. Backstage, Regal told the bickering Storm and Christian to observe the "tag team harmony" between him and Test against Tommy Dreamer and RVD. But harmony quickly grew into discord after Van Dam's superkick set Test up for a Dreamer schoolboy and the one-two-three. Christian and Storm headed ringside while Test and Regal got into a shoving contest, and before long all four Un-Americans pounded away at each other. RVD and Dreamer broke up the argument by clearing the ring, but the damage was done; Storm and Regal stayed behind as Test and Christian returned backstage. The Un-Americans were no more.

No joy in Dudleyville, Triple H retains the World title.

On an evening already crowded with tension, Bubba Ray Dudley brought a table into the ring, propped it into a corner and spray-painted the letters "HHH" on it. The table was *reserved*, and whether it was during his World title match with Triple H, or another night down the road, Bubba guaranteed The Game's ass would go through the wood. The moment was about more than him or some tables. "Tonight is about every single one of those guys in the locker room who have been *forced* to play The Game," he declared. "It's about every single one of you fans who never had the benefit of having something *handed* to you. It's about going out there and breaking your back, and earning everything you've got. So maybe tonight *is* about me. It's about me beating Triple H and *earning* the right to be called the new World Champion!"

Joined by Ric Flair at ringside, the Cerebral Assassin came out and learned just how hungry his challenger was. Dudley looked Bubba-Tough in the early going until Triple H hurled him to the steel steps on the out-

World Wrestling Entertainment said goodbye to its second most prestigious title, the Intercontinental Championship, when it was absorbed into the World Championship at *No Mercy*. The title celebrated a distinguished twenty-three-year career, originating when a tournament in Brazil declared WWE Hall of Famer Pat Patterson its first champion back in September of 1979. Since then, twelve Intercontinental Champions have worn the gold, though only three—Pedro Morales, Chris Jericho and Kane—defended the belt after a reign as WWE Champion. The crown also became the first WWE male-dominated title to be worn by a woman, when Chyna captured her first of three Intercontinental titles at *Summer-Slam* in August 2000. This was the third title to become unified since Eric Bischoff became *Raw*'s General Manager in July. ■

WWE INTERCONTINENTAL TITLE HISTORY

WON BY	DATE WON	WON BY	DATE WON	WON BY	DATE WON
Pat Patterson	9/11/79	Razor Ramon	5/19/95	Kurt Angle	2/27/00
Ken Patera	4/21/80	Jeff Jarrett	5/21/95	Chris Benoit	4/2/00
Pedro Morales	12/8/80	Shawn Michaels	7/23/95	Chris Jericho	5/4/00
Don Muraco	6/20/81	Dean Douglas[3]	10/22/95	Chris Benoit	5/8/00
Pedro Morales	11/23/81	Razor Ramon	10/22/95	Rikishi	6/22/00
Don Muraco	1/22/83	Goldust	1/21/96	Val Venis	7/6/00
Tito Santana	2/11/84	Ahmed Johnson	6/23/96	Chyna	8/27/00
Greg Valentine	9/24/84	Marc Mero[4]	9/23/96	Eddie Guerrero	9/4/00
Tito Santana	7/6/85	Triple H	10/21/96	Billy Gunn	11/23/00
Randy Savage	2/8/86	Rocky Maivia	2/13/97	Chris Benoit	12/10/00
Ricky Steamboat	3/29/87	Owen Hart	4/28/97	Chris Jericho	1/21/01
Honky Tonk Man	6/2/87	Stone Cold Steve Austin	8/3/97	Triple H	4/5/01
Ultimate Warrior	8/29/88	Owen Hart[5]	10/5/97	Jeff Hardy	4/12/01
Rick Rude	4/2/89	Stone Cold Steve Austin	11/9/97	Triple H	4/16/01
Ultimate Warrior[1]	8/28/89	The Rock[6]	12/8/97	Kane	5/20/01
Mr. Perfect	4/23/90	Triple H	8/30/98	Albert	6/28/01
Texas Tornado	8/27/90	Ken Shamrock[7]	10/12/98	Lance Storm	7/23/01
Mr. Perfect	11/19/90	Val Venis	2/14/99	Edge	8/19/01
Bret Hart	8/26/91	Road Dogg	3/15/99	Christian	9/23/01
The Mountie	1/17/92	Goldust	3/29/99	Edge	10/21/01
Roddy Piper	1/19/92	The Godfather	4/12/99	Test	11/5/01
Bret Hart	4/5/92	Jeff Jarrett	5/25/99	Edge	11/18/01
Davey Boy Smith	8/29/92	Edge	7/24/99	William Regal	1/20/02
Shawn Michaels	10/27/92	Jeff Jarrett	7/25/99	Rob Van Dam	3/17/02
Marty Jannetty	5/17/93	D'Lo Brown	7/27/99	Eddie Guerrero	4/21/02
Shawn Michaels	6/6/93	Jeff Jarrett	8/22/99	Rob Van Dam	5/27/02
Razor Ramon[2]	9/27/93	Chyna	10/17/99	Chris Benoit	7/29/02
Diesel	4/13/94	Chris Jericho	12/12/99	Rob Van Dam	8/25/02
Razor Ramon	8/29/94	Chris Jericho/Chyna	12/30/99	Chris Jericho	9/16/02
Jeff Jarrett	1/22/95	Chris Jericho[8]	1/23/00	Kane	9/30/02

[1] After winning the WWE Championship at *WrestleMania VI*, Ultimate Warrior surrenders the Intercontinental title. Mr. Perfect wins a tournament final to capture the vacated belt.

[2] Shawn Michaels is stripped of the title for not defending it; Razor Ramon is declared champion after winning a Twenty-Man Battle Royal.

[3] Shawn Michaels suffers an injury that forces him to surrender the title to challenger Dean Douglas.

[4] Ahmed Johnson forfeits the championship due to injury; Marc Mero captures the vacated title in a tournament final.

[5] While defeating Owen Hart for the title at *SummerSlam*, Stone Cold Steve Austin suffers an injury that forces him to forfeit the belt. Owen Hart wins the vacated title back in a tournament final.

[6] Refusing to defend the championship, Austin surrenders it to The Rock.

[7] Triple H forfeits the title due to injury; Ken Shamrock wins the vacated belt in a tournament final.

[8] A dual pin results in Chris Jericho and Chyna being declared co-Intercontinental Champions. Jericho wins sole ownership of the title during a Triple-Threat match at *Royal Rumble*.

side, from where the Nature Boy lent a hand, and a series of kicks. Bubba soon rallied his way back in the match, then powerslammed some payback when he caught Flair going up top. Unfortunately, a Bubba Bomb and pinfall were wasted while the referee saw Flair out of the ring, and The Game shortly reversed another attempt into a Pedigree for the three-count.

Backstage, Chris Jericho expected a similar result, thinking Kane's chances of beating him for the Intercontinental Championship were as real as Terri's chest. But Jericho's "glorificent" feeling faded when mild-mannered ace reporter Gregory (Hurricane) Helms interrupted his interview. Looking at Helms like he was completely insane, Jericho had news for him: "Freaks are *not* cool. Freaks are *losers.*" Citing Goldust and Booker T as prime examples while epitomizing himself as a "cool" champion and "*huge* rock star." Y2J wouldn't be intimidated by "...some kind of giant, red freak jackass in a 'crazy, scary' mask." Interestingly, he decided he had nothing more to say and left when Kane appeared in the room. Terri, however, wanted to add something regarding Kane's buss from last week: a hot-and-heavy kiss of her own! Helms looked awestruck as the Big Red Machine smirked. "What can I say? Chicks *dig* the mask."

Booker T, on the other hand, *didn't* dig Jericho's "loser" remark, and confronted him about it backstage. Y2J asked Booker to be honest—losing *was* what he did best, so he really should show the first Undisputed Champion, current Intercontinental Champ and future World Champion more respect. Book pointed out that

Jericho uses the ringpost to make things uncomfortable for Kane.

["Freaks are *not* cool. Freaks are *losers.*"]

the King of the World was on his way to becoming a star in the film "*I Just Got My Ass Whooped By The Five-Time WCW Champion, Right Here In H-Town, Ass Clown!* Now can you dig that..." Jericho cut him off (though Booker later got his "sucka!" in just before Chris headed out to the ring); he had a match to get ready for, and a visit to make to Triple H's locker room. The Game, trying to enjoy a post-victory shower with two ladies, didn't appreciate the intrusion, though Y2J promised that what he had to say would prove *very* interesting.

One could only speculate the Intercontinental Champ was negotiating an arrangement with Triple H for his match against Kane, especially after Ric Flair interfered in a pinfall attempt and took some cheap shots from the arena floor. The referee soon ordered the Nature Boy to leave the ring area, though the diversion was enough for Jericho to gain the advantage. Focusing heavily on the Big Red Machine's left leg, Chris cinched an excruciating figure-four leglock around the ring post. Again, Kane battled his way back until Triple H raced down and intervened several times, including some cheap shots on the outside floor and distracting the official while Jericho nailed the back of Kane's leg with a chair. Refusing to quit, Kane eventually escaped the Walls of Jericho, and as Y2J went for another chair shot, the Big Red Machine's big boot smacked the steel straight back into his face! Kane next delivered a bone-jarring Chokeslam to the canvas, then picked up the pinfall to become the new Intercontinental Champion!

Though the stage was now set for Kane and Triple H to meet in what promised to be an awesome Champion vs. Champion match at *No Mercy,* that wouldn't stop Eric Bischoff from raising his *Raw* stakes in Las Vegas' Thomas and Mack Center on October 7. Joined by several showgirls backstage, "The Bisch" presented the *"Raw* roulette," a wheel that determined every type of match for the evening while symbolizing the best elements of Sin City—"sex, sin, lust, greed, danger, unpredictability…it's all right here."

The first spin of the night kicked off *Raw* in main-event style: Booker T versus the Big Show in a Steel Cage match. Big Show had split a pair of contests against Jeff Hardy recently, dominating with a Chokeslam win on September 23, then coming up short a week later in a ring countout decision during which Bischoff, annoyed by Jeff's run-in to save Lita, had pressured Mr. Xtreme to impress him. Booker nailed Show with several scissors kicks before heading for the top of the cage, but the

giant surprised everyone with his own mobility, climbing the top rope and stopping Booker. Still, not even that impressive feat could protect Show from a low blow that drove him back down to the mat, while Booker climbed up and over the cage for the victory.

A Spin-a-Roonie celebration wasn't to be, however; Chris Jericho blindsided Booker T on the outside floor, ramming his head into the cage and busting him open. Justifying the attack to Terri backstage minutes later, Jericho blamed Booker's accosting and "sucka" remark last week for causing him to lose the Intercontinental Championship and a World Title shot at *No Mercy.* But the blood on Jericho's hands would serve to remind Booker and anyone else just who he was, "The very first-ever Undisputed Champion, the undisputed King of the World, and most important of all, a very dangerous and unbalanced individual. And one thing Chris Jericho is *not* and never *will* be is a sucka. *I* am *not* a *sucka!"*

Triple H wasn't too happy, either; the *Raw* roulette wheel had just spun him into a non-title Blindfold match. The Game guaranteed Bischoff that if this was some effort to keep him away from new Intercontinental Champion Kane, "It's not going to do any good… before this night is over, Kane's life will never be the same." Ric Flair stayed behind as Hunter stormed off;

"The Bisch" plays *"Raw* roulette."

before Bischoff chose Triple H's opponent, the Nature Boy wanted to introduce the vivacious Mandy and Sandy, who'd anxiously await the *Raw* GM inside his hotel suite later that night. It wouldn't be surprising if Flair's "gift" was to also improve his own stock with Bischoff, who came down on Slick Ric last week for not yet producing an ex-*SmackDown!* talent he'd promised to sign.

Whatever Flair's reasoning, it seemed to do the trick for Triple H, who'd meet D'Lo Brown for the Blindfold match. D'Lo recently relinquished his *Sunday Night Heat* commentary position to Lita so he could concentrate on inducting opponents into his "Sky High Hall of Fame." Shawn Stasiak became the finisher's most recent inductee at the September 26 *Heat,* though Raven escaped with a low blow and DDT one week later. Whereas Triple H had a distinct advantage under normal conditions, being forced to wear a hood put him on uneasy equal footing with D'Lo, who eventually connected with the Sky High on the Cerebral Assassin. But Flair once again came to the World Champion's rescue, getting in the ring and

Vegas gives showgirl Regal a *Raw* deal.

in the referee's face while Hunter lifted his hood up long enough to locate and Pedigree D'Lo for an easy three-count.

Both Triple H and D'Lo might have kept the blindfolds on had they known about the next contest. "Lady Luck" continued to be a harsh mistress for William Regal after Bischoff's spin of the wheel called for him and Goldust to wrestle dressed as Las Vegas show-girls! The Bizarre One didn't think the horrified Brit should have a problem with it—"Your country has a queen. Now *you* can be one, too." Goldust looked like a natural as he and several lovely ladies kicked up their heels inside the ring. Regal, however, resembling what J.R. described as a poor man's Dame Edna, was forced out to the ring by security, dressed in uncomfortably high heels and a truly unflattering outfit. In firm control of the match, Goldust was ready to bring down the house—and Regal in particular—with the Golden Globes, until Lance Storm's sudden ringside presence caught his eye and drew him to the outside. The diversion allowed Regal to fish out the brass knuckles from his showgirl outfit, then clobber Goldust for the upset.

As for the *real* WWE Divas, Bischoff informed WWE Women's Champion Trish Stratus and Stacy Keibler that their match had already been decided: a Paddle on a Pole match for the Women's title. Knowing how much of a competitor Trish was, however, the leering *Raw* GM opted to "go for dou-

Flair's run-in with the ref sees to Triple H's win.

ble or nothing" on the wheel, which conveniently stopped at "Bra and Panties match"; the first woman to strip her opponent down to her bare essentials would win the belt *and* get to spank the loser with the paddle. The Divas treated the Thomas and Mack Center audience to plenty of Stratusfaction in the ensuing bout, during which both women's tops came off. Stacy's spin-kick put victory and Trish's pants in her grasp, but the Women's Champ reversed the move and yanked off Stacy's bottoms for the win. Stacy tried spoiling the moment with a cheap kick to the head and grabbing the paddle from up top, but Trish quickly intercepted it and spanked the leggy Diva out of the ring.

The Women's Champion started heading back up the ramp when she ran into the Diva who'd been a constant thorn in her side over the past few weeks. Since joining the WWE in early July, Victoria's malicious streak became increasingly apparent in competition, particularly against Trish, who bested her and Molly Holly during a *Raw* Triple-Threat title match on September 23. One week later, prior to their one-on-one title match, Victoria initiated a vicious backstage assault on the champion, then drew herself a disqualification during the bout with a blatant chairshot that left Trish down and out. Determined not to let herself be bullied around a third time, Trish took it right to the powerful Diva, but Victoria again established herself as the dominant female, executing a devastating moonsault inside the ring, then sending the Women's Champ crashing into the steel steps outside.

Backstage, Coach asked Victoria why she continued instigating the attacks, yet her response was as enigmatic as the woman herself. Claiming Trish would understand what it was all about when she beat her for the Women's title, she added, "I did this to show the whole world who Trish Stratus *really* is. Why don't you ask 'Princess' about her past? About the things *she's* done? The people *she's* hurt? She'll deny it, but I know the truth. Because she hurt *me*, and now it's *her* turn to get hurt."

["[I've] died and gone to puppy heaven."]

It seemed the only person *not* hurting that evening was Eric Bischoff, who relentlessly enjoyed the matches he spun from the wheel. From the TitanTron he'd inform new *Raw* member Al Snow and Test they'd compete in a Hardcore rules-styled "Las Vegas Street Fight." It's a safe bet Snow never showed any of his *Tough Enough 3* students how to handle a bowling ball inside a ring, though he put one to good use in striking Test and picking up the "W". Bischoff next put Jerry "the King" Lawler and Steven Richards in a "It's Legal in Nevada" match, with the winner being given a free ride on The Godfather's extensive "Ho Train." The beauties waiting at ringside were precisely the encouragement Lawler needed to counter Richards's piledriver attempt into a sit-down pinfall victory. It certainly looked good to be the King as the escorts entered the ring and surrounded Lawler, whose expression J.R. likened to having "died and gone to puppy heaven."

Of all the matches Bischoff put together in Las Vegas, it was the main event he set up for Kane and Hurricane that he'd be most proud of: a Tables, Ladders and Chairs match with the renamed *World Tag Team* titles on the line. And Eric knew of no better participants to recruit than Christian, Bubba Ray Dudley and Jeff Hardy, three halves of the tag teams that immortalized the TLC matches at *SummerSlam* in 2000 and 2001's *WrestleMania X-Seven*. Instructed to each find a partner (in effect, making the TLC match a four-team contest), Christian found one in Chris Jericho, who suggested that since they both lost WWE gold to Kane over the past two weeks, they could work together and rob him of the Tag Team belts. Bubba asked Tommy Dreamer to pair with him for the extreme matchup, then made the offer to his half-brother Spike when he learned how much it meant for him to be part of a TLC title match. Jeff Hardy wouldn't have to look very hard for his partner; Rob

Of the many types of matches World Wrestling Entertainment has sanctioned, the most dangerous one has arguably been "Hell in the Cell." The No Disqualification contest takes place within a sixteen-foot-high, twenty-five-foot-wide steel cage enclosed from top to bottom, though its combatants often find a way to continue their battle at the very top of the Cell, until one wrestler is pinned or submits.

Careers have been shortened or outright ended as a result of these bloody trips to "Hell," of which there have been only seven since the inaugural contest at *In Your House: Badd Blood* in October 1997. Remarkably, the unforgiving steel has *not* claimed Undertaker as one of its victims; he's survived *five* of these matches, including the most recent one against WWE Champion Brock Lesnar at *No Mercy*, and shares the most wins with Triple H at two. The following is a brief, brutal history of "Hell in the Cell" and its crimsoned participants.

OCTOBER 6, 1997: Undertaker and Shawn Michaels were the first entrants into Hell in the Cell, sacrificing body and soul in a blood-stained, thirty-minute-plus bout that saw the Showstopper catapulted face-first into the steel cage, and sent crashing through the announce table. But just before Undertaker could finish Michaels with the Tombstone, his estranged brother Kane made his WWE debut and cost the Phenom the match. It was Michaels's only trip to Hell, though many cite his performance in the contest as one of the contributing factors that cut his career short.

JUNE 28, 1998: The *King of the Ring* tournament was out-shined by a Hell in the Cell match between Under-taker and Mankind that's considered by many as one of the greatest matches *ever*. The Dead Man started the match atop the Cell with a broken foot, though it didn't stop him from throwing Mick Foley *off* the Cell and through the Spanish announce table. Foley somehow continued the match, even after 'Taker Chokeslammed him through the top of the cage and onto a thumbtack-covered canvas. The devastating impact, coupled with a chair that landed on his head during the fall, resulted in Foley blacking out, suffering a dislocated jaw, losing several teeth (one of which went through his *nose*) and creating a hole through his lower lip. Undertaker won the match, while Foley's gutsy performance achieved WWE immortality.

MARCH 28, 1999: In his third Hell in the Cell contest, Undertaker faced off against the Big Boss Man at *WrestleMania XV*. Despite being hand-cuffed to the cage and beaten repeatedly with a nightstick, the Phenom's prior experiences in Hell would help him prevail over the Boss Man, who found himself strung up and hung from up top by Undertaker accomplices Edge, Christian and Gangrel.

FEBRUARY 28, 2000: Only Mick Foley's Cactus Jack persona would be crazy enough to challenge WWE Champion Triple H for his title within Hell in the Cell, then leave himself *No Way Out* of having to retire if he lost. In another blood-filled battle during which a bed of thumbtacks and a barbed-wire two-by-four came into play, Cactus and The Game beat each other senseless in and on top of the Cell, until the champion back-body-dropped his opponent through the top of the cage. The resulting impact created a hole through the canvas, and allowed The Game to get the three-count and end Mick Foley's spectacular Hardcore wrestling career.

DECEMBER 10, 2000: The aptly deemed *Armageddon* hosted the first-ever Six-Man Hell in the Cell, during which The Rock, Stone Cold Steve Austin, Triple H, Rikishi and Undertaker vied for the WWE title. Defending Champion Kurt Angle, still in his rookie year, defied the overwhelming odds facing him, pinning a laid-out Brahma Bull after a long, bloody and exhausting affair. The highlight of the match came when the Dead Man Chokeslammed Rikishi from the top of the cage and onto the back of a pickup truck, an amazing feat that laid up the Phat Man for some months afterwards.

JUNE 19, 2002: Neither Chris Jericho nor Triple H were Undisputed Champion by the time they faced *Judgment Day* within Hell in the Cell, but their bitter rivalry would not be silenced any other way. Both Superstars bled from the onset of the hellacious battle, during which referee Tim White suffered a serious shoulder separation that forced officials to open the Cell door and rescue him. The Cerebral Assassin would DDT the "larger than life" Jericho through the Spanish announce table before they took their fight up above. A barbwire-wrapped two-by-four cut both men's flesh to ribbons before Y2J latched the Walls of Jericho on Triple H. But The Game would escape the submission move, then Pedigree Jericho on top of the steel-meshed cage to remain undefeated in one-on-one Hell. ∎

Van Dam emerged from the locker room and said, "Tables, Ladders and Chairs? Dude, *yeah*, I'm in!"

Kane didn't seem concerned about the TLC match putting him at a disadvantage against Triple H come *No Mercy*. "I've been fighting the odds for a long time," he told Terri, "but for the first time in my life...I'm happy." And with an opportunity at the PPV to become the first-ever WWE Superstar to hold the World Tag Team, Intercontinental and World titles simultaneously, Kane, his Kanenites and Triple H knew he could do it. Suddenly, a panicked Coach interrupted the Big Red Machine, to warn him that Triple H and Ric Flair were beating up Hurricane. Kane raced to his partner's aid, though he was too late; the hero was beaten unconscious on the floor, while his attackers fled the scene of the crime.

Kane pulls Bubba Ray Dudley off the ladder for a Chokeslam.

Being forced to defend the World Tag titles *alone*, in one of the WWE's most perilous matches, wouldn't stop Kane from entering the ring with a furious onslaught. The ladders came into play early, with everyone trying to climb up top and grab the Tag belts that were suspended in the air. Kane brought Bubba Ray crashing down off one ladder with a Chokeslam to the canvas. Jeff Hardy followed up a chairshot to Kane with a top-rung leg drop that sent the Big Red Machine through a table. Christian delivered a neckbreaker to Van Dam from one ladder, while Y2J bulldogged Bubba off another. Meanwhile, Jeff floored Kane with the Poetry in Motion, then held a chair for RVD to sail across the ring and deliver a top-rope Van Terminator into the Big Red Machine's face.

After pushing down a ladder to catapult Jericho to the outside floor, Spike's attempted Dudley Dog on Christian soon sent him flying through a table outside the ring. Bubba paid Christian back with a devastating Bubbabomb off two ladders, then back-bodydropped Jeff through a table to the outside. RVD finished off Bubba with a Van Daminator, yet the World Tag titles fell short of his grasp when Jericho caught him with a steel chair. But just as it looked like Y2J was clear to climb the ladder and grab the belts, Kane climbed up the other side and Chokeslammed Jericho from the top rung! Reaching up and grabbing the titles, the Big Red Machine single-handedly won a five-star Tag match that had bodies littering the ring area.

Suddenly, amid one of Kane's greatest moments, Triple H came out to the *Raw* stage and brought his world crashing down around him. "You said this is the happiest you've ever been in your life?" he asked. "Well, let me ask you a question, Kane: How happy is *Katie Vick*?" The Big Red Machine stood in shocked silence as The Game continued, "I know, Kane. I know it all. Ten years ago, you *killed* her. That's right, Kane...*you* are a *murderer*!"

Kane's happier, more open personality was nowhere to be seen by the time *Raw* opened in Montreal's

Bell Centre on October 14. Refusing to even comment on Triple H's accusation, it was clear the Cerebral Assassin had gotten inside his head with only six days to go before their "Winner Take All" match at *No Mercy*. And the result would prove costly that evening, when Kane and Hurricane defended their World Tag titles against Chris Jericho and Christian. Christian prompted Kane to chase him up the ramp, leaving Hurricane alone with Jericho. The hero countered the Walls of Jericho into a rollup, but Y2J reversed it into his own pinfall, adding his feet on the ropes for extra leverage while the ref counted to three. By the time Kane returned to the ring, Jericho and Christian were leaving as the World Tag Champions.

While the champagne poured backstage, Goldust and several WWE officials restrained Booker T, who obviously hadn't forgotten about Jericho's attack last week. But he simmered down after hearing Eric Bischoff congratulate the new Tag Champs, then inform them they'd defend the belts against Booker and Goldust at *No Mercy*. Eric stifled Jericho's protests about having just won the titles, though Booker was down with the challenge. "One way or another," he said, looking at Chris, "this sucka's ass belongs to me!" But the King of the World would have the final say

Kane struggles to keep hold of his World Tag title.

during Booker's Falls Count Anywhere match with the Big Show, which spilled into the ladies' locker room showers. A towel-covered Trish Stratus watched in horror as Jericho gave Big Show an easy pinfall win after smashing the former five-time WCW World Champion with a steel chair, then got in the barely conscious Booker's face and yelled, "Who's the 'sucka' *now*, you ass-clown?!"

Christian's former tag partner, Lance Storm, appeared to land on his feet as well. In addition to picking up a superkick-powered victory over Johnny "The Bull" Stamboli during the October 6 *Sunday Night Heat*, he solidified an alliance with William Regal after helping him secure the win against Goldust in the last week's Las Vegas Showgirls match. Regal joined Jim Ross and Jerry "the King" Lawler on commentary as Storm went head-to-head against Al Snow, though seemingly left in a snit after J.R. aired a shot of him in his showgirl attire on the TitanTron. But Regal made his true intentions known with his cheap shot at Snow from the ring apron, enabling Storm to land a superkick for the win.

Sadly, Snow's night *outside* the ring proved no better. Approaching former student Christopher Nowinski backstage, the *Tough Enough* head trainer told him how proud he was that the first *TE* runner-up never gave up on his dream to join the WWE. But Nowinski's tone soured the moment when he replied, "Yeah, I did it...no thanks to *you*. By the way, nice loss tonight." The arrogant Harvard grad then headed out for his match against Tommy Dreamer, who first got in Nowinski's face when he smashed it with a Singapore cane on September 9 *Raw*, then again two weeks later after teaching him new kinds of pain in a classroom brawl. It seemed Dreamer was about to go up 3-0 when he intercepted Nowinski's Singapore cane attack, until Snow abruptly showed up at ringside and grabbed the cane from Tommy's hands. The intervention left Dreamer off guard and defenseless against a full nelson slam

that gave Nowinski the one-two-three upset. A visibly pissed-off Dreamer glared at Al, who looked ashamed about betraying his friend as he headed back up the *Raw* ramp.

Betrayal was allegedly something Victoria could relate

[**"Who's the 'sucka' *now*, you ass-clown?!"**]

to as she revealed to Coach the details of her history with Trish Stratus. Recalling how the two were fitness models when the WWE first expressed interest in them, "Trish acted like my friend. She told me how great it would be for us to be Divas *together*. But she never let me get my chance." After a long time languishing in the developmental leagues, Victoria eventually made it to the WWE, and now her ruthless aggression earned her an opportunity to win the Women's Championship at *No Mercy*. "It's true... I'll do anything to get what I want," she admitted. "Unlike Trish Stratus, who will do any*one*." At that point, the Champion Diva calmly approached Victoria, then gave her a vicious slap across the face and left.

Trish and Victoria continued their feud in the ring later that night, hammering away at each other before their Tag contest even started. Their respective partners, Jacqueline and Molly Holly, would determine the outcome of the bout, with Jacqueline following up her October 6 *Heat* victory over the virginal Diva with a DDT for the three-count. But it was Victoria who walked tall after the match, pummeling first Jacqueline, then Trish outside the ring until officials separated them. Once again it became clear that the Women's Champion couldn't simply outpower Victoria, which meant she'd have to come up with another game plan if she wanted to defend her title successfully at *No Mercy*.

I f anyone in the WWE best exuded the attitude of "What have you done for me lately?" it was Eric Bischoff. He sounded content while praising Jeff Hardy, Spike Dudley and Rob Van Dam, all of whom

CHRISTIAN

HEIGHT: 5'10"
WEIGHT: 215 lbs.
FINISHING MOVE: The Unprettier
CAREER HIGHLIGHTS: Intercontinental Champion; Tag Team Champion (9); Light Heavyweight Champion; European Champion
2002 HIGHLIGHTS: Wrestling Diamond Dallas Page in his hometown at *WrestleMania X8;* founding the Un-Americans with Lance Storm and Test; winning the World Tag Team Championship with Lance Storm at *Vengeance;* winning the World Tag Team Championship with Chris Jericho on October 14 *Raw.*

were bruised and battered after last week's excruciating TLC match. But he had a funny way of showing his appreciation: he instructed Jeff to prepare for a match against Rico, then told Spike to "take a hike" and say hi to Bubba, who was convalescing from a major concussion suffered in the TLC match. As for RVD, Bischoff promised "the biggest night in your life" at *No Mercy,* a match with the man who thwarted his World title contention at *Unforgiven,* Ric Flair. Van Dam liked the sound of that, though Eric had one more surprise for the Superstar and the *Raw* crowd in Montreal that night: a Canadian Lumberjack match. "That's right," he said. "Twenty guys surrounding the ring, with a leather strap. And just picture this: inside that ring…RVD, one-on-one with Triple H!" With that, "The Bisch" laughed, "And they said I couldn't top TLC!"

As for Triple H's accusations concerning Kane, the compassionless *Raw* GM later assured the crowd that the Big Red Machine would compete in the PPV's "Winner Take All" match, regardless of his frame of mind. And since that historic match was to mark the last time the Intercontinental title would be represented, Eric brought out the WWE's *first* Intercontinental Champion, Montreal's own Pat Patterson. Bischoff swore he had the utmost respect for the retired ring great, yet after airing a video tribute of the Intercontinental Championship on the TitanTron, Eric sicced Rosey and Jamal on Patterson, telling him, "Just like the Intercontinental title, your three minutes are just

about up!" The attacking Samoans' size and strength quickly proved too much for both Patterson and Gerald Brisco, who raced down to help his longtime friend. But Rosey and Jamal unexpectedly found themselves on the receiving end of a beatdown from some of their former victims, including Big Show, D'Lo Brown and Jeff Hardy, whose Swanton Bomb took care of their partner Rico earlier that evening. Clearing the ring of Bischoff's enforcers, the trio sent Rosey and Jamal a message that what goes around often comes around.

It seemed there was no consoling the Big Red Machine after he and Hurricane lost the World Tag titles to Chris Jericho and Christian, though it wasn't because they dropped the belts. Triple H had told the whole world something horrible about Kane's past, and he couldn't hide it any longer. It would take a beauty to tame the beast inside Kane, as Terri suggested her friend tell everyone his side of the story, or he'd be in no frame of mind to beat The Game come *No Mercy.* Heeding her advice, Kane came out to the ring and bared his soul to the fans.

"Katie Vick was a friend of mine," he started, "and Katie Vick is dead. But I *didn't* kill her. It was an accident, and I am *not* a murderer." Recalling how the two were friends back when he started wrestling about ten years ago, Kane explained that they'd been at a party where Katie had had too much to drink. "I decided I should drive her home," he remembered. "I wasn't real familiar with a stick shift, but Katie insisted that we take her car. It was dark…the road was slick because it was raining, and an animal jumped right out in front of us. I swerved to avoid it, but the car spun out of control and went off the road. I broke my arm…but Katie was killed instantly. It *was an accident,* but it's something that I have to live with, and something I've thought about every day since. So, the only thing that I have left to say is what I said to Katie's parents…I'm *sorry.*"

Suddenly, Triple H came out to the *Raw* stage and mocked the Big Red Machine's "touching" story. He also pointed out that Kane omitted a few details, including eyewitnesses at the party reporting that he'd also been drinking, and that there were empty beer cans inside the car and around the accident scene. "More importantly, Kane," he continued, "why don't

you explain to the world how when doctors did the autopsy on Katie Vick's body, they found *your* semen?" The Game got to his point: Kane considered Katie much more than a "friend," though she didn't seem to feel the same way. And while Kane may not have been charged with murder or manslaughter, facts were facts: he killed Katie Vick. But Hunter had one other question: "Did you *force* Katie Vick to have sex with you while she was alive? Or did you just *wait* and do it to her when she was *dead?*"

Kane didn't, or *couldn't,* respond. Instead, he chose to leave the Bell Centre, warning Hurricane that he'd do something regrettable if he stayed. Terri, meanwhile, confronted the Cerebral Assassin, who said the police reports backed up his claims. And while he didn't want to enter the same ring with a murderer, he planned to

Rob Van Dam hits Triple H with the Rolling Thunder.

take care of the Big Red Machine at *No Mercy*. "Kane might be able to take the life of a sweet girl like Katie Vick," he stated, "but he will *never* be able to take my title." As for Hunter's Canadian Lumberjack match later that night, he would overcome the odds like always and beat Rob Van Dam. "The fact is, Terri, I am The Game," he added, "and to quote a friend of mine, whether you like it or you don't like it...*I am. That. Good.*"

Hunter cut down his odds moments before the non-title match, using a forklift to trap half of the lumberjacks inside a room. Having only the lumberjacks he wanted out at ringside gave The Game a distinct advantage over Van Dam, who several times felt the leather straps beating against him on the outside floor. But RVD continued to fight back, and the sides evened up when the trapped lumberjacks eventually made their way to ringside and

Angle and Benoit: WWE's most reluctant tag team.

pounded away at their counterparts. Mr. Monday Night caught Triple H with the Five-Star Frog Splash, but the opportunity was lost as the referee was restoring order on the outside floor. Hunter used the Championship belt on Van Dam to pick up a cheap three-count, but he wouldn't be able to handle the sudden arrival of the Big Red Machine, who obliterated everyone in his path as he made his way to Triple H. Kane hammered away at both The Game and Ric Flair until the Nature Boy's low blow allowed them to escape. Triple H watched fearfully as Kane Choke-slammed one lumberjack after another; instead of breaking the man behind the mask, Hunter realized his personal effrontery had succeeded too well in creating the soulless monster he depicted Kane to be. A monster hell-bent on taking it all from The Game at *No Mercy*.

The intensity felt between the Superstars on *SmackDown!* proved just as fierce as those on *Raw*, particularly after the events of *Unforgiven* just four days before. *SmackDown!* GM Stephanie McMahon created a competition that would see friends turn on each other, and enemies work together towards a common goal. And mercy would be a trait shared only by losers.

The ball started rolling at the September 26 *Smack-Down!* inside California's San Diego Sports Arena, when Kurt Angle entered Stephanie McMahon's office and asked for a rematch with Chris Benoit, who hadn't *really* won their *Unforgiven* match "because he cheated, and cheaters never win." Stephanie expected Kurt to make such a request, but she had something else in mind—a Triple-Threat main event between Angle, Benoit and Rey Mysterio. The masked luchador's presence didn't sit well with the gold medalist—this was Mysterio's hometown "and he was born here, like, *eight* years ago"—however, Angle guaranteed he'd walk away with the one-two-three. Rey countered, "Not if I hit you with the *619*."

To Marc Loyd's surprise, Benoit was almost complimentary about Angle backstage; the fans might chant "You suck!" whenever Kurt heads to the ring, but as a wrestler, "…he's one of the toughest, technically sound SOB's I've ever been in the ring with." Kurt wasn't so gracious as he addressed the crowd prior to the Triple Threat match; he wanted to make sure Rey had the "911" number to go with his 619, and after Benoit's illegal victory at *Unforgiven,* he should feel right at home with the illegal aliens among the San Diego fans! As the match got underway, Angle and Benoit tore into each other, at times almost using Mysterio like a weapon with which to batter each other. But Rey soon capitalized on his adversaries' rivalry, taking his shots while Benoit and Angle traded finishing moves. He broke up Angle's sleeper hold on Benoit with a 619 through the ropes that nailed both men, then disrupted a Crippler Crossface with a springboard dropkick. Benoit sent Angle over the top rope, but as he tried doing the same to Mysterio, Rey literally rebounded with the West Coast Pop for the rollup victory.

While nothing appeared settled between Angle and Benoit that evening, Eddie Guerrero and Edge looked to end their several-month feud with a No-Disqualification match that proved even more spectacular than their previous bouts at *SummerSlam* and *Unforgiven.* Latino Heat established himself as the aggressor as the ladders and chairs came out, sandwiching Edge between two ladders, then vaulting on top of them from the outside apron. As the two battled to the top of a ladder, Guerrero again blew away the sellout crowd by leaping over Edge and executing a hellacious sit-out powerbomb! Somehow refusing to let himself be pinned, Edge soon took the fight back up on the ladder, where it became his turn to amaze with an Edge-cution that drove a bloodied Latino Heat off the top turnbuckle

and down to the canvas for the three-count. If this was to be the end of their private war, then neither Edge nor Eddie Guerrero could have finished it in finer fashion.

Eric Bischoff might have thought his *Raw* brand's "Winner Takes All" match would steal the show at *No Mercy,* but Stephanie McMahon had her own ideas about how to grab the spotlight. Since the Tag titles were entrenched on *Raw,* Stephanie opened the October 3 *SmackDown!* at the CajunDome in Lafayette, LA, with a major announcement: in addition to that evening's main event-caliber offerings of Edge vs. Kurt Angle and Rey Mysterio vs. Chris Benoit, she held up a pair of championship belts and declared a tournament for the newly formed WWE Tag Team titles. "The new champions will be crowned at *No Mercy,*" she added, "and the first round starts right *now!*"

As promised, the first match of the tournament began right away, with Rikishi and Mark Henry taking on Eddie and Chavo Guerrero. The Phat Man had

Eddie Guerrero pummels Edge.

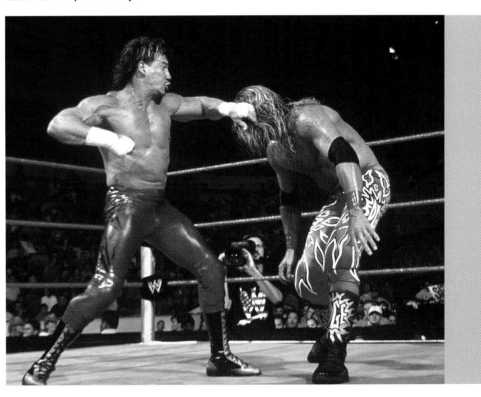

already contributed some "rump-shakin' time" to Chavo just one week before, and the seven-hundred-fifty-pound duo made Los Guerreros a heavy underdog. But when the referee had his back turned, Chavo exploited the moment with a chairshot to Henry's leg. Eddie placed his knee into Henry's back, then pulled back his legs in the "Lasso from El Paso." The World's Strongest Man was forced to submit, allowing Eddie and Chavo to advance to the next round.

The prestige of wearing new Tag Team gold on *SmackDown!* motivated Reverend D-Von and Faarooq to pair up and enter the tournament, a move that survived both their opponents and *SmackDown!* announcers Michael Cole and Tazz, who were expecting Batista to accompany D-Von. Despite each man winning the World Tag titles numerous times (D-Von with Bubba Ray Dudley, Faarooq with Bradshaw), their inexperience as a cohesive unit put them at a disadvantage against Billy and Chuck. D-Von's flying headbutt off the top rope, a move he and Bubba made famous, went horribly wrong when Chuck reversed positions with Faarooq while Billy pushed D-Von off the turnbuckle and into his own partner's groin. But the veteran Faarooq soon bounced back and surprised Billy with a spinebuster, enabling D-Von to get the one-two-three and move them forward in the tournament.

Kurt Angle wasn't concerned with the WWE Tag Team tournament, or his upcoming one-on-one with Edge. He'd rather tell Marc Loyd backstage how Chris Benoit lost the Triple-Threat match to Rey Mysterio last week, and how he would probably lose to him again later that evening. "Why? Because Chris Benoit is a regular person, and regular people make mistakes," he explained. Kurt, on the other hand, was "a freakin' work of art" inside the ring, and he wanted the "You suck!"-chanting fans of Louisiana to realize it. Edge suddenly interrupted the conversation and admitted, "You *don't* suck, Kurt…but you're *not* perfect." Angle said his gold medals told him

differently, though Edge insisted the proof was in the "shiny bald head" he gave Kurt back at *Judgment Day*.

Like their previous battles, Edge and Angle would deliver high-impact offense from the get-go, with neither man able to dominate until a belly-to-belly suplex sent Edge crashing into referee Michael Chioda. With the official unable to make a count, both men wasted finishers on one another before referee Mike Sparks raced in and called the rest of the contest. Angle's top-rope superplex on Edge seemed to end the match as Sparks counted to three, but while he raised Kurt's hand in victory, the recovered Michael Chioda awarded the match to *Edge*, who from his vantage point appeared to have covered Angle. The referees' heated debate turned ugly as Chioda decked Sparks, prompting several officials to run down and restore order, then order the match to continue. Unfortunately for Kurt, Chris Benoit's sudden appearance at ringside would determine the final outcome—he not only prevented Angle from using a steel chair on Edge, but forced the chair to bounce off the ropes and hit Kurt, leaving him wide open for a spear that gave Edge the one-two-three!

Benoit laughed himself all the way back to the *SmackDown!* locker room, where a livid Angle quickly tracked him down and tried to beat the living hell out of him. Several Superstars restrained the men as Stephanie McMahon entered the room and got between them. "The two of you are *going* to get along," she insisted, "because next week, I'm teaming the two of

> **"I'm gonna win this freakin' thing no matter *who* my partner is, even if he is missing a few teeth and a few brain cells."**

you up in the Tag Team tournament! And the two of you *need* to get along when you're in the ring together as partners, or you'll *both* be suspended, without pay, for a year!"

Benoit puts his tag team partner, Kurt Angle, in a Crippler Crossface.

Both Angle and Benoit were shocked by Stephanie's decree. How were they supposed to work together when they couldn't stand each other? But Kurt would quickly dissect a small loophole in Stephanie's statement; she may have ordered them to get along *in the ring as partners,* but that didn't prevent Kurt from messing with the Crippler during other times. That included his match with Mysterio that evening, during which the medalist tied Benoit up on the ropes, allowing Rey to roll him up with a Hurracanrana and get the pinfall victory. The newly formed tag team went right at one another after the match, with Kurt latching on the ankle lock until Benoit reversed it into the Crippler Crossface. Officials ran in to break them apart, no doubt wondering along with everyone else in the CajunDome just how these two egos were ever going to co-exist.

Sharing everyone's concern, Stephanie McMahon reiterated her edict to Benoit and Angle in her office

backstage Phoenix's America West Center on October 10. If they couldn't get along in their tournament match tonight, they'd both be watching *SmackDown!* from their couches at home, without pay, for the next 365 days. Ever the suck-up, Kurt thanked Stephanie for the opportunity to compete in the tournament, "But I'm gonna win this freakin' thing no matter *who* my partner is, even if he is missing a few teeth and a few brain cells." Benoit laughed it off, reminding Angle about losing to him at *Unforgiven.* "You may have been an Olympic Champion," he added, "but you've never been a *Tag Team* Champion. So tonight, you follow *my* lead."

Hanging outside Stephanie's office, Eddie and Chavo Guerrero were in good spirits. Despite catching a dual Stinkface from Rikishi earlier on the show, Chavo's interference enabled his uncle to nail the Phat Man's ankle with a steel chair, then get the submission victory with the Lasso from El Paso. As Benoit exited the room, Latino Heat joked that his buddy looked like he

"Double Trouble," Eddie and Chavo Guerrero Stinkfaced by Rikishi.

just got in trouble with the principal. The Rabid Wolverine wasn't laughing, especially after Chavo mentioned hearing a rumor that Angle planned to take a year off to train for the next Olympics. Eddie added fuel to the fire, warning his *esse* to be careful— "If Kurt's gonna go down, it looks like he wants to take you down *with* him."

With the seeds of doubt planted, Benoit grew even more wary of his partner as they started their first-round match against John Cena, coming off two successive *Velocity* wins over Reverend D-Von (September 28) and Albert (October 6), and Billy Kidman, who rebounded from a September 28 *Velocity* loss to Crash Holly with a win over newcomer Doug Basham the following week. Angle and Benoit seemed more interested in outdoing each other against their opponents until Cena and Kidman rallied back, with Billy hitting the Shooting-Star Press to cover Benoit. Kurt made the save and slapped on the ankle lock, but as Cena tried breaking the hold, Benoit caught the rookie with a shot that sent both him and Angle flying out of the ring. The Crippler latched on the Crossface, forcing Kidman to tap out, yet

neither he nor Angle could celebrate the win without arguing over whose hand should be raised. It also appeared whatever personal bug they had was contagious—Cena blamed Kidman for the loss and challenged him to a match on October 17 *SmackDown!*, during which he'd leverage his feet on the ropes for a cheap backslide victory.

If the tournament win had taken Angle and Benoit's relationship a step forward, Los Guerreros planned to move it several steps back. Chavo tracked the Rabid Wolverine backstage and claimed he and Eddie were jumped by Angle, then lured Benoit into a darkened room and trapped him inside. The sounds of a brief fight erupted from the room, and as everything went quiet, Chavo opened the door and asked his uncle if he got the job done. Eddie came out smiling, holding a folded chair bent nearly in half, and said, "Did *I* get the job done? *Kurt Angle* got the job done, esse!"

> **"Did *I* get the job done? *Kurt Angle* got the job done, esse!"**

The final first-round match of the tournament was to pit Edge and Rey Mysterio against Tajiri and Cruiserweight Champion Jamie Noble. But when Noble left the America West Center following a spat with his girlfriend Nidia, Stephanie made a last minute substitution: WWE Champion Brock Lesnar! The Next Big Thing easily overpowered the tandem at first, but Edge and Mysterio's combined speed and agility eventually sent Lesnar reeling to the arena floor. Edge positioned Tajiri for Mysterio's 619, then speared him for an impressive victory that established them as strong contenders for the WWE Tag titles.

From Toronto's Air Canada Centre, the October 17 *SmackDown!* determined which two teams would compete in the final round of the WWE Tag tournament at *No Mercy.* No longer calling himself Faarooq, Ron Simmons and D-Von gave Edge and Mysterio a run for their money in the first semifinal; Rey hit D-Von with the 619, only to get jolted into the canvas by Simmons's powerbomb. Edge made the save with a spear, then reversed D-Von's Saving Grace DDT into an Edgecution for the win. But as Rey and Edge celebrated in the ring, Eddie and Chavo Guerrero stormed the ring and laid them out, capped off by a Latino Heat Frog Splash on Edge.

Eddie and Chavo thought softening up their opponents four days before *No Mercy* was a sound idea. After all, there was no way Chris Benoit and Kurt Angle could work together and beat them in their semifinal that night, especially after the mind games they played on Benoit last week. But as they entered their locker room backstage, they were surprised to find the Canadian

Angle works Eddie's ankle.

Crippler standing inside, in darkness. Eddie grew increasingly nervous as he reminded his "esse" of their long history together, until Benoit's deafening silence forced them to leave the room. He'd try a similar stare tactic on Angle before their match, but Kurt wasn't intimidated; if he'd wanted to go after Benoit like the Guerreros suggested, "I'd do it to your face." As for training for the Olympics, Kurt asked just how gullible his partner really was. "Look at me! I sure as heck don't need a whole *year* to train for the Olympics!"

Benoit withheld judgment as he and Angle headed out for the tournament semifinal, though Rey Mysterio and Edge would have plenty to say when Chavo and Eddie made their way to the ring. In addition to getting payback against the Guerreros, the duo added some interest with several shots at Kurt and Benoit. As a result, both sides started the match a bit unsteady, though quickly shook off the cobwebs for a fierce, high-impact battle. The turning point came when the referee went down just as Angle positioned Eddie into the ankle lock. Chavo prepared to smash Kurt with a steel chair until Benoit stopped him…and offered his hand in friendship. Chavo gave him the chair, excited that the Rabid Wolverine was about to nail Angle with it. Kurt turned around and thought so as well…until Benoit surprised everyone and knocked Chavo out! Kurt Angle Slammed Eddie as the referee recovered, picking up the three-count to send them to the tournament final! When Angle and Benoit met Edge and Rey Mysterio for the WWE Tag Team Championship at *No Mercy,* they would do so *as* a team.

If Divas like Nidia and Dawn Marie proved anything on *SmackDown!* over the past month, it's that they could be as merciless as any wrestler inside the squared circle. Nidia usually sharpened her claws on anyone who opposed her or her boyfriend, Cruiserweight Champion Jamie Noble, though even Noble would soon find himself on the receiving end of her fury. Dawn, meanwhile, started up a competitive rivalry with Torrie Wilson, but saw a golden opportunity to make their conflict very personal.

Things began innocently enough with a bikini competition between Torrie and Nidia on September 26 *SmackDown!*. Tazz moderated the contest, with Billy and Chuck acting as the guest judges. Unveiling a black bikini, Nidia was hardly the epitome of poise and etiquette—gum fell from her mouth while she danced in the ring (though Tazz was hard-pressed to call it dancing), which she picked up and started chewing again. The fact that Chuck and Billy gave her scores of 6 and 9 respectively had people wondering if they were still shaken up after their *Unforgiven* loss to Jamal and Rosey. When Torrie disrobed, however, it was a totally different story—wearing a skimpy pink number, her sexy, playful dance worked the San Diego crowd and the judges into a frenzy, and earned two perfect 10 scores.

Seeing Nidia upset prompted Jamie Noble, accompanied by Tajiri, to head ringside. Warning Billy and Chuck that nobody screws his girlfriend—"At least, not like that, anyway," he clarified—Noble promised that he and Tajiri would show them "what some *real* competition is all about!" Despite putting up a good fight, it wasn't long before the Cruiserweight Champion was sent flying to the outside floor, while Billy and Chuck scored the win with a Code Red on Tajiri. Outside the ring, Torrie and Nidia also came to blows, though their fight ended moments later as Billy held onto Nidia while Torrie gave her a good spanking. Later that evening, Dawn Marie congratulated Torrie backstage on her "accomplishment"—but instead of winning a bikini contest over "that nothing of a hillbilly," perhaps she'd compete against someone "who has a whole lot more to offer."

Obliging Dawn with a bikini contest the following week, Torrie first entertained a special guest back-

Torrie Wilson savors victory.

stage, her recently divorced father, Al Wilson, who was in Lafayette on business and wanted to see his "little angel." Dawn took it upon herself to say hello to Al, and of course to wish Torrie good luck in their contest. Just before the competition, Dawn approached Al again, now on his own, and asked for his personal opinion of the outfit she wore under her robe. Needless to say, he thought it looked great. As she started to leave, she thanked Mr. Wilson, who insisted, "Call me Al." Unfortunately for Dawn and her white and red-trimmed bikini, Al wasn't the only person in the CajunDome judging the bikini contest; the fans overwhelmingly voted Torrie's tan two-piece and lollipop the winner. Dawn offered to shake the Diva's hand, then surprised Torrie with a slap across the face and threw her out of the ring.

Meanwhile, Jamie Noble returned to his winning ways on *SmackDown!* that night, successfully defending his Cruiserweight title against Crash Holly. No thanks, however, to the ever-graceful Nidia's assistance on the ring apron; she almost cost her redneck boyfriend the match when Crash hurled Noble into her, then rolled him up for a near-fall. The Cruiserweight Champ quickly recovered, then countered a sunset flip and grabbed the ropes to get the three-count.

Still, there was no way Noble would win an argument with his girl at October 10 *SmackDown!*, shortly before he and Tajiri were scheduled to face Rey Mysterio and Edge in the WWE Tag Team tournament. Nidia interrupted Rey's interview with Funaki and made some suggestive remarks to him in Spanish, though his response showed she could become as unbalanced emotionally as she was in a bikini contest. When Noble tried talking with her, she kept walking, totally infuriating the cruiserweight. The ensuing argument led to Nidia throwing Noble's drink on a concerned security guard, who had them escorted out of the building. With Noble out of the tournament match, Stephanie McMahon opted to partner Tajiri with WWE Champion Brock Lesnar, who wouldn't appreciate seeing the Japanese Buzzsaw lose the bout and indicated as such by demolishing his partner with the F-5.

Earlier in the evening, Torrie was almost blown away when she saw Al, who decided to come to Phoenix and surprise his daughter. As excited as she was to see him, Torrie felt somewhat embarrassed, since she was in a lingerie competition with Dawn Marie that night. But as she headed out to the ring, Dawn stopped by and asked for Al's opinion of her latest outfit. Again he seemed impressed, prompting the Diva to give him a kiss on the cheek and tell him how sweet he was. Like the previous week, Torrie was the crowd's overwhelming winner, but it appeared Dawn might also come away with a victory before the evening ended. Torrie was unavailable when she came by her dressing room to congratulate her, though Dawn made sure Al knew how accessible she was. She gave him a copy of the

REIGNING BABE

For the second consecutive year, WWE fans smacked down their Internet votes in October and named Trish Stratus "Babe of the Year." The competition, sponsored by *Maxim*, pitted her against fierce competition from her fellow WWE Divas, but the three-time Women's Champion proved up to the challenge with an online gallery second to none.

After earning the accolade, Trish posted a special thank-you to supporters both on WWE.com and her own website (trishstratus.com). "Being voted 2001 Babe of the Year showed me you were supporting me in all that I did. Becoming 2002 Babe of the Year confirms that you believe in me and all that I do, and it makes me want to go out there every time and deliver one hundred percent Stratusfaction for all of you, the fans, and that is a guarantee!" ■

Torrie watches while Rikishi weights in on Mattitude.

recently published *Divas Undressed* magazine, which happened to have her hotel room key in between the pages featuring her. "It's 604," she whispered in his ear. "I'll be waiting."

Having challenged Jamie Noble to a match at October 17 *SmackDown!*, Nidia promised guest referee Tajiri a lot more than "pillow talk." She'd planned to do to her boyfriend in the ring the same as what she does to him in the bedroom. "I'm gonna come out on top, and I'm gonna have him *begging* for mercy." Noble came out and warned that if she insisted on going through with the match, "You can sure as heck bet it's gonna be like our sex life, baby. It's gonna be *rough*." Nidia retorted, "The rougher, the better," and slapped him across the face.

When it came time to lock up, Nidia's yelling and pushing weren't enough to stop the Cruiserweight Champ from grabbing an easy one-two-three. After the match, Tajiri tried encouraging his argumentative friends to kiss and make up, and they did by deciding to beat *him* up instead! Noble laid the Japanese

> "You can sure as heck bet it's gonna be like our sex life, baby. It's gonna be *rough*."

Buzzsaw out with a Tiger Bomb, then hugged his girl as if nothing ever happened. But Tajiri wouldn't be so quick to forget the incident; in fact, he'd meet Jamie Noble for the Cruiserweight Championship at *No Mercy* in three days. And he wasn't interested whether or not he had the crowd behind him, as his vicious "Kick of Death" to the head of Funaki demonstrated on October 19 *Velocity*. They could save their sympathy for *Noble*.

Torrie wasn't thinking about holding back when she and Rikishi took on Dawn Marie and Matt Hardy in an Intergender Tag match that night, though she didn't know what to think when her father suddenly showed up backstage at the Air Canada Centre. Al said he'd heard she had a match, but Torrie knew better. She saw Dawn Marie give him her room key last week, and cautioned that she was a predator. Al changed the subject and gave his daughter a bouquet of flowers, which Torrie handed over to a makeup woman as she headed out for her match.

Throughout most of the Tag contest, Rikishi and Torrie dominated over Dawn and Version 1, who pretty much killed chivalry by using his partner to shield himself from the Phat Man's Stinkface. He'd make it up to her somewhat by shifting Torrie's small package so that Dawn scored the pinfall, but Rikishi made him pay moments later with a splash into the corner. As he prepared Version 1 for a Stinkface, Torrie stopped him and asked to do it instead. Matt's face lit up as Torrie wedged up her tights; he was ready to take his punishment! But then she changed her mind and let Rikishi do the honors after all!

Sadly, Torrie was crushed in a worse way after the match; discovering that her flowers were actually for Dawn Marie, she tracked her father down in the women's locker room. Hearing voices coming from the shower area, Torrie pulled back the curtain and confirmed her worst fears: Dawn was in the shower with Al (who for some reason chose to keep his clothes *on*)! Devastated, Torrie ran out of the room sobbing, but she'd soon intend to make Dawn cry when they met one-on-one at *No Mercy*.

The WWE Champion and the Dead Man hadn't resolved anything at *Unforgiven*, though that in itself was more of a victory for Undertaker than anyone else could claim. In fact, some wondered if Brock Lesnar might be fearful of meeting the American Badass again, a question "Number One *SmackDown!* Announcer" Funaki dared to ask The Next Big Thing backstage during the September 26 broadcast. Brock offered an answer inside the ring shortly after, beating the hell out of poor Funaki and laying him out with the F-5.

If anyone could beat Undertaker, it was Matt Hardy. Just ask him. Version 1 bragged to Shannon Moore backstage that he had the Dead Man's number the last two times they met in the ring, though he didn't appreciate Moore crediting those outcomes to Brock

Lesnar. Since he had a match with Undertaker coming up next, Matt told Moore to sit tight and see how much Brock would factor into him beating the Phenom again. Lesnar, apparently having heard everything said backstage, wouldn't interfere in the match, and Undertaker took care of Version 1 easily, pulverizing him with the soup bones and dropping him with the Last Ride. But as soon as 'Taker picked up the win, Brock charged the ring and laid him out with the WWE Championship belt, leaving the Phenom sprawled out and a bloodied mess.

Lesnar's agent, Paul Heyman, had some bad news for his client at *SmackDown!* the following week, as per Stephanie McMahon: "You're going to have to give Undertaker a rematch at *No Mercy.*" Not only that, but the *SmackDown!* GM insisted a special stipulation would be added to the contest, though she hadn't yet told Heyman what the stipulation was. Matt Hardy interrupted their conversation, guaranteeing that it *wouldn't* be a Falls Count Anywhere match, like the

> **"[The beatdown Lesnar gave 'Taker last week] will look like nothing—the blood, the guts, *nothing*—compared to what I'm going to do to Undertaker this week."**

one he was about to have with the American Badass. Matt also promised that the beatdown Lesnar gave 'Taker last week "will look like nothing—the blood, the guts, *nothing*—compared to what I'm going to do to Undertaker this week."

If by that Version 1 meant he was going to sustain a longer, more brutal beating at the hands of the Phenom, then it appeared he was on the money. Pummeling Matt in and out of the ring, Undertaker set him up for a Last Ride on top of the *SmackDown!* announce table. Matt countered with a low blow and went for the Twist of Fate, though 'Taker easily blocked it and tossed him on top of the ring barricade. Trying desperately

AllTel Arena
Little Rock, AR

**WWE CHAMPIONSHIP
HELL IN THE CELL MATCH**

Brock Lesnar (w/ Paul Heyman) defeated *Undertaker*
via pinfall to retain the WWE title

WOMEN'S CHAMPIONSHIP MATCH

Trish Stratus defeated *Victoria* via pinfall to
retain the Women's title

WWE TAG TEAM TITLE TOURNAMENT FINAL

Kurt Angle & Chris Benoit defeated
Edge & Rey Mysterio via pinfall to become
the WWE Tag Team Champions

CHAMPION VS. CHAMPION WINNER TAKE ALL MATCH

Triple H defeated *Kane* via pinfall to retain
the World title and unify it with the
Intercontinental Championship

CRUISERWEIGHT CHAMPIONSHIP MATCH

Jamie Noble (w/Nidia) defeated *Tajiri* via pinfall
to retain the Cruiserweight title

Torrie Wilson defeated *Dawn Marie* via pinfall

Rob Van Dam defeated *Ric Flair* via pinfall

WORLD TAG TEAM CHAMPIONSHIP MATCH

Chris Jericho & Christian defeated
Booker T & Goldust via pinfall

OCTOBER 20, 2002

Kane was accused of murder and necrophilia. Undertaker was labeled a womanizer and suffered a broken right hand. But before the night in Little Rock's AllTel Arena ended, the Brothers of Destruction would show their champion opponents *No Mercy* inside the ring.

The Pay-Per-View started with Chris Jericho and Christian defending their newly won World Tag Team Championship belts against Booker T and Christian. The Bizarre One delivered a Golden Globes to Christian, though Y2J soon countered a Curtain Call with the Walls of Jericho, until Booker made the save with a scissors kick to the head. Amazingly, no one was hurt when the middle rope broke around the ring during Jericho's Lionsault attempt, though the turmoil it created, plus the referee's attention towards Booker and Christian's battle on the outside floor, would work in Jericho's favor. Bulldogging Goldust's face into one of the Tag titles, Jericho finished the job with a top-rope moonsault for the three-count.

Backstage, "*SmackDown!*'s Number One Announcer" Funaki had an important question for Al Wilson about daughter Torrie catching him in the shower with the seductive Dawn Marie on *SmackDown!* last week—Why was he taking a shower with his clothes *on*? Al's answer, "I did not have sexual relations with that woman," left the Japanese wrestler/interviewer thinking Al didn't understand English, though the Divas certainly made their feelings towards each other understood in the ring that night. Torrie and Dawn's anger literally steamrolled over the referee at one point, though Torrie eventually got the upper hand, snapping Dawn's neck across the top rope and delivering a swinging neckbreaker for the win.

Rob Van Dam told Jonathan Coachman backstage that he wasn't "a limousine-ridin', jet-flyin', kiss-stealin', wheelin'-and-dealin' son of a gun" like opponent Ric Flair, who screwed him out of the World title at *Unforgiven*. Instead, he Flair-strutted while describing himself as "more of a chair-smashing—*Wooo!*—Frog-Splashing, risk-taking, yinning-and-yanging—Wooo! Wooo! *Wooo!*—Van Daminating dude!" Mr. Pay-Per-View took it right to the former sixteen-time World Champion, whose knife-edge chops and concentrated attack on the left leg enabled him to latch on the Figure-Four Leglock. Reversing the finisher and a second attempt with an inside cradle, RVD regained control of the match after throwing the Nature Boy off the top rope and hitting the Rolling Thunder, then went up top and soared to victory with the Five-Star Frog Splash.

Raw General Manager just about hit the roof when he saw his "property," Big Show, talking with *SmackDown!* GM Stephanie McMahon backstage. Stephanie backed out as the seven-foot two-inch giant, a former WCW and WWE Champion, blamed Bichoff for not putting him in a WWE PPV since *Vengeance*. Bischoff tried cutting the big man down to size—who the hell was he to speak to him like that, or to go talking to Stephanie behind his back? Show grabbed Bischoff and shoved him up into a stack of trays, telling him, "I am one *very* angry giant. *I* should be in the main events, and I suggest you put me there soon...because the next time I get my hands around your neck, I'm going to snap it like a twig."

Tajiri wanted payback in Cruiserweight gold following the *SmackDown!* assault he suffered last week at the hands of former allies, Champion Jamie Noble and Nidia. The rowdy redneck highlighted an early offense with an Electric Chair out of the corner, though the Japanese Buzzsaw readjusted a top-rope moonsault into a running tornado DDT. When it appeared victory might be within Tajiri's grasp, Nidia caught the referee in a liplock while Noble recovered and delivered a Tiger Bomb. Tajiri kicked out, though, as he went for a victory roll, Nidia grabbed her boyfriend's leg to keep him balanced and secure the three-count. Nevertheless, Tajiri picked up some reimbursement after stealing a kiss from Nidia in the middle of the ring, then let the Cruiserweight Champion show him how to kiss her so he could nail him with a kick to the head.

Backstage, Chris Benoit warned Eddie Guerrero that his nephew Chavo was "getting his ass handed to him" by Kurt Angle, but Latino Heat wasn't buying. The cries for help that he heard behind a doorway sounded like those from a little girl, and he knew Kurt would be waiting for him with a chair the moment he opened the door. Suddenly, a battered Chavo came falling out of the room, with Angle coming out behind him. Backstage members would have to restrain Eddie while Angle and Benoit walked away laughing.

Beyond the fact that Kane's Intercontinental Championship was to be unified with Triple H's World title, the "Big Freak'n Machine" sought to unleash hell on The Game after accusations of murdering teenage friend Katie Vick. Withstanding a ferocious opening volley of rights and lefts, Triple H clotheslined Kane to the outside, then kneed him into the steel post. The Cerebral Assassin took firm control back inside the ring, almost obtaining the victory with a sleeper hold. Kane fought his way out with a back suplex, then picked up momentum with a sidewalk slam and top-rope clothesline. Ric Flair suddenly stormed the ring, resulting in the referee getting knocked down while the Big Red Machine chased after him, and supplied

Hunter with the World title, which The Game smashed across his opponent's head. Former co-Tag Champion The Hurricane (who defeated Steven Richards in a *Sunday Night Heat* match leading into the PPV) rushed down to Kane's aid and handled Flair on the outside, until Triple H took him out of the equation with a Pedigree.

The referee soon became a casualty again after a big boot missed Hunter, though Kane would find his mark outside and Chokeslam him through the announce table. Back inside, Kane snatched a sledgehammer from the Nature Boy and used it on him, while Hunter avoided being its next victim after low-blowing the Big Red Machine. Amazingly, Kane survived a sledgehammer to the solar plexus and delivered another Chokeslam to the Cerebral Assassin, but once again the Nature Boy interfered, preventing the new referee from completing a three-count. Flair earned himself a Chokeslam for his efforts, though it bought Triple H time to catch the Intercontinental Champion off guard with the Pedigree for the one-two-three.

Earlier that evening, Tracy told Coach backstage that her "accusations" about being the "other woman" in Undertaker's life were true, "and I can't wait for that scumbag to get what he deserves inside Hell in the Cell." Yet Stephanie uncovered the truth in her office when she played Tracy into admitting that it was all a setup by Paul Heyman, and the relationship they had was long in the past. Suddenly, the Dead Man appeared, having heard everything and calling Tracy a lying bitch before leaving to get ready for his match. Stephanie added to his sentiments, telling the vixen she'd told her last lie around *SmackDown!* and to get out of her office.

Edge, Rey Mysterio, Kurt Angle and Chris Benoit did justice to the exciting WWE Tag Team tournament that played out on *SmackDown!* over the past several weeks, delivering a five-star final match to determine the champions of the WWE's first Tag title created in thirty-one years. Being forced to work together by Stephanie McMahon had transformed Angle and Benoit into a well-oiled machine that would need every bit of ring expertise to fend off the luchador high-flier and the eight-time co-Tag Champion. Both teams pulled out all the stops with high-risk maneuvers for over twenty minutes, with neither side able to finish off the other. After launching Mysterio onto Angle for a Hurracanrana, Edge dodged a flying headbutt from Benoit that nailed his own partner. The Rabid Wolverine recovered and locked the Crippler Crossface on Edge, until Mysterio made the save with a 619 through the ropes that nailed Benoit head-on. Edge sent his partner flying over the top rope to moonsault Benoit on the outside floor, then traded ankle locks with Angle until the gold medalist finally cinched his submission move in the center of the ring. Edge was forced to tap out, while Angle and Benoit earned the distinction of becoming the first-ever WWE Tag Team Champions.

Women's Champion Trish Stratus faced sheer brutality in the ring with newcomer Victoria, whose increasingly aggressive nature dominated the contest. Rolling Trish back in the ring after dumping her onto the security barrier, the challenger somersaulted over the ropes and landed a massive legdrop. Fighting back with an Electric Chair that dropped Victoria out of the corner, Trish's mat skills would soon emerge the difference-maker, in which she'd reverse her opponent's pinfall attempt with a rollup for the win. Victoria ruined Trish's short-lived celebration, however, by nailing her with a ferocious kick to the jaw, and sending a message to the Women's Champion that their feud was far from over.

Before entering Hell in the Cell, Undertaker coerced his unwilling trainer to administer a shot that would enable him to keep fighting without the pain from his broken hand becoming unbearable. The shot would prove necessary—'Taker used the hand cast early and often to cut open the forehead of Brock Lesnar. After grinding and driving the WWE Champion's head into the steel cage walls, the Dead Man exacted some vengeance against Paul Heyman, kicking the fence against the agent, then grab-

bing his tie through a mesh opening and pulling him into the Cell wall repeatedly, making him a crimsoned mess.

The assault on Heyman allowed Lesnar to recover and concentrate a steel-chaired attack on the Phenom's injured appendage and eventually removed his hand cast. 'Taker's high-risk lunge through the ropes missed Brock, who twice slammed the steel ring steps into the American Badass, causing the blood to pour from his head. Lesnar next used the Cell to his advantage, running Big Evil's face across the wall like a grater. The extremely bloodied Undertaker regained the upper hand back in the ring, using the top rope to go old school on Lesnar before Chokeslamming him to the canvas. Yet Brock refused to stay down, kicking out of several near-pinfalls even after 'Taker delivered a Last Ride out of the corner. But as the Dead Man prepared to finish him off with the Tombstone, Lesnar reversed the move into the F-5, driving Undertaker to the mat and getting the three-count for the victory. The battered and bloodied Next Big Thing slowly emerged from Hell in the Cell, having bested another ring legend at his own signature match, and he climbed the top of the cage to hold the WWE Championship he retained up high. ■

Brock Lesnar survives Hell in the Cell.

to escape backstage, it looked like Matt had nowhere left to run when Brock suddenly blindsided Undertaker, giving him an F-5 that sent him crashing to the concrete floor. Matt took advantage of 'Taker's prone body, picking up an easy three-count for the upset. The Next Big Thing, however, had one more order of business to take care of; seeing the Dead Man struggle to his feet, he picked up a propane tank and rammed it into Undertaker's right hand! 'Taker screamed in agony as he clutched his hand, while Lesnar, Matt Hardy and Paul Heyman left the scene of the crime.

Inside Brock's locker room, Heyman lauded his client. On top of ending Hulk Hogan's career and taking the WWE title from The Rock, now he'd taken out the "unstoppable" Undertaker. Matt stopped by and cut in again; beating the American Badass wasn't some unfortunate Twist of Fate. "It was sheer *Mattitude!*" And since he'd just pinned the No. 1 Contender, who was probably out of the picture at *No Mercy*, that meant Version 1 was probably the man to face Brock for the WWE Championship at the Pay-Per-View. Heyman humored Matt and said he'd talk with Stephanie about making it happen, but the *SmackDown!* GM had other topics to address. She confirmed that Undertaker's hand was indeed broken, but he insisted on competing at *No Mercy* for the WWE Championship. And after discussions with the Phenom, she decided to name the stipulation: *Hell in the Cell!*

The Dead Man's right hand was in a cast with the words "No Pain" written on it as he waited for Brock

Undertaker prepares a Chokehold for Version 1.

Lesnar in the parking lot of the America West Center on October 10. Which meant that Matt Hardy, Version 1, saw it as the best possible time to kick off *SmackDown!* in the ring and talk trash about all the fan mail he'd received since beating Undertaker, "yet *again*," in last week's Falls Count Anywhere match. "Everyone knows that it wasn't a Twist of Fate that led to my victory," he stated. "It was a defining moment in the era of Mattitude. It was a moment in time where Matt Hardy single-handedly proved his dominance over Undertaker."

Matt decided to relive the moment on the TitanTron, conveniently leaving out the F-5 Brock Lesnar gave Undertaker, then had the audacity to suggest Deadman, Inc., was in the parking lot because he didn't want another dose of Mattitude. His bravado plummeted, however, as he saw 'Taker heading to the ring, during which he warned, "I don't want to maim a crippled man!" Matt would hurt Undertaker, sort of, but only because Big Evil used his hand cast to bust Mattitude open! Matt tried fighting back with a steel chair, only to open himself up more when 'Taker's right hand smacked the steel into his face. He'd barely escape to the back after Undertaker missed with the broken hand and caught the outside ring post, resulting in him having to go for more X-rays.

'Taker's night was about to get more painful. Lesnar and Heyman showed up and brought a special guest with them to the ring—a voluptuous brunette named Tracy. Paul acknowledged that the Dead Man clamored for Brock at *No Mercy*, but he asked the Phoenix

Here Comes The Pain, Lesnar punishes Chuck.

audience, "What kind of a man wants to enter Hell in the Cell with the WWE Champion?" Realizing 'Taker had shortened careers and taken years off men's lives inside Hell in the Cell, Heyman redirected his query, "What kind of a *man* is Undertaker?" The agent admitted he wasn't qualified to answer the question, "but *Tracy*, on the other hand...is *very* qualified to tell us all just what kind of a man Undertaker happens to be."

Before Tracy could speak, Undertaker's entrance music cut her off. Brock and Heyman bailed out of the ring as the Phenom entered, fists raised and ready to fight. Surprisingly, Tracy stood her ground. "What, are you going to *hit* me now?" she asked, then addressed him by his first name. "How *could* you, Mark? For three months, you have *lied* to me and *slept* with me. And now I find out you're married, and your wife is pregnant? You're a *bastard!*" Undertaker stared at Tracy in shock as she continued her diatribe; now she understood why he allegedly never wanted their relationship made public, and she appealed to his wife at home. "Sara, I hope you're watching. I'm sorry that you had to find

out about me like this. I didn't know, and your husband lied to me just like he's lying to you. I wonder how many *other* women you sleep with, Mark?"

"Listen, lady," replied the Dead Man, trying to restrain himself, "I have *no idea* who you are!" Tracy slapped him across the face and headed back up the ramp with Lesnar and Heyman. Undertaker didn't follow after her, proof enough that her accusations had left him utterly stunned.

Lesnar and Heyman started to leave, thinking their night was over and their mission was accomplished. But Stephanie McMahon begged to differ; since Jamie Noble hadn't returned for his upcoming WWE Tag tournament match, Tajiri needed a partner, and Brock just volunteered. The agent protested over the "unsafe working environment" Undertaker posed, but the GM stood firm, and assured that the American Badass was banned from ringside; if he interfered in the match, there would be no Hell in the Cell at *No Mercy*. Backstage, 'Taker seemed too preoccupied to intervene in anything; he was on his cell phone trying to convince his wife that the "other woman" was a setup by Heyman and Lesnar, though she left him eating dial tone. Brock also made a call just before heading out for his Tag match. "Just calling to see if you're OK. I mean, the stress you must be under right now, to witness that on live television." He was offended that the person on the line didn't recognize his voice, but added, "I'm so glad that we could spend another moment like this together...*Sara.*"

Was Tracy just another part of Heyman's and Lesnar's mind games?

Despite losing the bout, The Next Big Thing dominated the ring afterwards, tossing Edge to the outside and F-5'ing both Mysterio and Tajiri. Suddenly, Undertaker charged in and plastered Brock with his hand cast, sending the WWE Champ out of the ring. Making their way backstage, Lesnar and Heyman looked at the American Badass standing tall in the ring, realizing that the cast on his broken hand might give him a much-needed edge at the Pay-Per-View.

With three days to go before *No Mercy*, Undertaker requested air time at October 17 *SmackDown!* to set the record straight—he admitted lying about not knowing Tracy. But he hadn't seen her in seven years, long before he met his wife. "To say I was surprised last week when I got to *SmackDown!* and hear this woman accusing me of being a cheater...would be an *understatement*," he explained. He didn't know what Tracy wanted, or if she'd been paid off; all he knew

Undertaker gives Brock a taste of things to come.

was that his life had become a living hell over the past week. But he made a guarantee for the WWE Champion and his agent: "The hell that I've been through is nothing—*nothing*—compared to the hell I'm going to put you through this Sunday in the Cell."

Inside the *SmackDown!* General Manager's office, Tracy called Undertaker a liar; they'd slept together only ten days ago! Stephanie didn't care, and since Tracy didn't seem to have any respect for anyone on *SmackDown!* she told her to leave. Paul Heyman escorted her out the door, since he had another matter to discuss with the boss. He was concerned that his client, "the future of *SmackDown!*", had to enter Hell in the Cell with "a crazed lunatic" who used the cast on his hand like a lethal weapon. "I'm appealing to you, Stephanie," he begged, "make him take that cast off." Stephanie would confront Undertaker about the request; although Lesnar broke his hand in the first place, Heyman made a strong case that he'd been using the cast as an offensive weapon. The Dead Man was furious. "You think the things that I've done have been 'offensive'?" he asked. "Well, let me show you how 'offensive' I can be!" Undertaker scared the hell out of Stephanie, using his cast to demolish a lamp sitting next to her desk, and walked out of the room.

Brock had just taken his aggression out in a hard-fought F-5-powered victory over a crimsoned Chuck Palumbo (now working solo after Michael Cole and Tazz announced Billy Gunn was out for the foreseeable future with a serious shoulder injury) when Undertaker charged the ring and made good on his threat to Stephanie. Catching Brock with a big boot, he stomped the hell out of him in a corner, then busted him open with the hand cast. Security also felt Big Evil's wrath as they tried restraining him, though they bought time for Heyman to drag Lesnar from the ring.

The agent was irate as he marched into Stephanie's office, telling her that the WWE Champion's blood on his jacket would be on the GM's hands if she didn't order Undertaker's cast removed. But both he and Brock became outraged when she later asked them to the ring and announced she'd decided to allow Undertaker to wear the cast for Hell in the Cell! Lesnar stalked the *SmackDown!* GM into a corner, getting uncomfortably close until Deadman, Inc., made the save. Brock caught him with a spinebuster and put the boots to the broken hand, then left the ring while 'Taker writhed in agony. Heyman screamed in his face, "You want hell?! *You've got hell!*" Yet when he foolishly tried to kick him, Undertaker grabbed the leg and busted Heyman's forehead open. Brock tried to rush back in, but Big Evil caught him with a shot that knocked him off the ring apron. Undertaker's cast was a blood-soaked mess as his adversaries took off, yet it was only a sample of the blood he'd spill at *No Mercy*.

[**"Let me show you how 'offensive' I can be!"**]

NOVEMBER

survive (sur viv) v. 1. To exist in spite of adversity: come through, last, persist, pull through, ride out, weather. 2. To live, exist or remain longer than: outlast, outlive, outwear.
—*Roget's II: The New Thesaurus*, 3rd Ed.

"If thou canst believe, all things are possible to him that believeth."
—*King James Bible*, New Testament, Mark 9:23

"Survivor" of the Fittest

Since its inception back on November 26, 1987, the annual *Survivor Series* has been about not only survival, but beginnings and endings. It's a Pay-Per-View that not only introduced the world to icons like Undertaker and The Rock, but gave both of them their first taste as WWE Champion. It's an event that started the legendary rivalry between then-WWE Champion Bret Hart and Shawn Michaels in 1992, then ended it five years later with HBK winning sports entertainment's most controversial decision ever. It's a venue that in 2001 served as the defining moment in the WWE's existence, when double agent Kurt Angle helped The Rock put World Championship Wrestling forever out of business in a winner-take-all contest. And in 2002, *Survivor Series* was all about elimination—eliminating title reigns, eliminating doubts...and perhaps eliminating careers.

For the *SmackDown!* brand, it started with a big, nasty giant...on October 21 *Raw* in Nashville, Tennessee's Gaylord Entertainment Center. Big Show wanted to do more than "survive" in WWE; after reaching the top of the mountain by defeating The Rock and Triple H for the WWE Championship at *Survivor Series* in 1999, his star had since fallen, and General Manager Eric Bischoff offered no plans to change its trajectory. Twenty-four hours after the seven-foot-two, five hundred-pounder got his attention with a not-so-

veiled threat to improve his personal stock within the company, Bischoff invited Show to his office, to tell him their heated exchange at *No Mercy* was "...water under the bridge." That, plus he wanted to inform him of his *Raw* match that evening against Rico...and Jamal...*and* Rosey.

Bischoff expected a three-on-one Handicap match to teach Big Show not to lay his 13 1/4-inch hands on him, but it was 3 Minute Warning and Rico learning an embarrassing lesson; Show dominated them with frightening ease, Chokeslamming Rosey for a convincing win. Humiliated and outraged, Bischoff ordered Jonathan Coachman *not* to interview a "piece of garbage" like Show—"He's just been traded!" The big man told the stunned Coach not to feel sorry for him, pointing out, *"You* still have to work for that asshole."

For his first day as part of the *SmackDown!* roster, Big Show opted to make a bigger impact in Memphis than even Rikishi's sit-out piledriver of Matt Hardy on October 24. Cutting short the Phat Man's victory dance with a Chokeslam that drove the three hundred fifty-pound Superstar's frame to the canvas, the self-professed "biggest, baddest man in the universe" issued a challenge to WWE Champion Brock Lesnar. "If I know Brock Lesnar, he's like every other coward on *SmackDown!,"* he yelled. "He won't have the *guts* to face me!"

The weary Lesnar and his bruised, battered agent Paul Heyman, both still hurting several days after their excruciating Hell in the Cell experience with Undertaker at *No Mercy,* arrived in The Pyramid shortly after Show made his challenge. But The Next Big Thing had no problem facing a limping, equally exhausted Dead Man who called him out to the ring later that night. 'Taker admitted his broken right hand was no excuse for losing in the Cell, adding the slight caveat that the match result would have ended differently five years ago. As for bringing 'Taker's personal life into the conflict, "Hell, there ain't nobody that appreciates head games more than me. For the past twelve years, I've taken people out of the game before they ever got *in* it." Having seen, fought and beaten the best, Undertaker was man enough to concede to Brock that at *No Mercy, "You* were the best." For the first time since they'd met, Lesnar reciprocated the respect, looking at Heyman almost disdain-

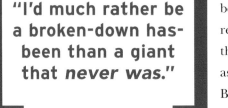

"I'd much rather be a broken-down has-been than a giant that *never was.*"

fully while he assured the personal attacks were "all about business," and give him an edge over the Phenom.

After Brock exited the ring, Undertaker started announcing what sounded like his retirement when Big Show came down and cut him off. *"Brock Lesnar's* the best?" he said, looking sickened by 'Taker's comments. After two years of supposedly busting up the Dead Man, Show demanded the credit for 'Taker's loss at Hell in the Cell, and for making him "a *broken-down has-been."* 'Taker retorted, "I'd much rather be a 'broken-down has-been' than a giant that *never was,"* then made his way up the *SmackDown!* ramp. Noticing Big Show coming up behind him, the American Badass readied himself for a fight, of which the giant seemingly wanted no part as he continued his way backstage. But when Undertaker acknowledged the crowd at the top of the stage, Show attacked, press-slamming him all the way down onto storage equipment on the arena floor! *SmackDown!* officials, Superstars and General Manager Stephanie McMahon came out to aid paramedics with the fallen Phenom, who slowly struggled to his feet. Despite being badly injured, Undertaker refused to let himself be carried out; slowly leaving to a chorus of cheers, 'Taker left his final appearance of 2002.

Outside his locker room, The Next Big Thing responded to Show's challenge, telling Marc Loyd, "I'm

Big Show demands Undertaker's respect.

On The Record:

WWE ANTHOLOGY

The history of the WWE never sounded better than when *SmackDown!* Records, a division of World Wrestling Entertainment, Inc., and KOCH Entertainment released *WWE Anthology* on November 12. The three-CD deluxe collector's edition scored a decisive victory with fans, debuting at No. 13 on *Billboard* magazine's Top 200 chart in its first week, and being certified platinum only ten days after shipping.

Containing eighty-six Superstar theme songs, including seventeen brand-new and twenty-five never-before-released tracks, the CD collection covers nearly three decades' worth of WWE theme music, including Hulk Hogan's "Real American," Bret Hart's "Hitman" in *The Federation Years*, to D-Generation X's "Break It Down" and The Rock's "If You Smell . . ." in *The Attitude Era*. The third CD, *Now*, features more diverse music that's identified with today's Superstars, including Brock Lesnar's "Next Big Thing"; Trish Stratus's "Time To Rock & Roll," performed by Lil' Kim; Saliva's "King of My World"; and *Raw* announcer Lilian Garcia singing Torrie Wilson's "Need a Little Time." A complete list of songs for each CD, plus an added bonus track, is available at www.wweanthology.com. ∎

not too hard to find. After all, *you* found me, Sherlock." It wasn't long afterwards when Show entered the room where Heyman tried to head off a hostile situation. But then Brock shoved his agent aside, got in Show's grill and did the talking. "You want a shot at my title? You've *got* it." With a WWE Championship match scheduled to take place at *Survivor Series* on November 17, Heyman voiced his concerns to Lesnar backstage at Grand Rapids, Michigan's Van Andel Arena on October 31. While most everyone else enjoyed a *Smack-Down!* Halloween party catered by the bewitchingly costumed Stephanie McMahon, the agent couldn't disguise his fears that Hell in the Cell might have caused more damage to Lesnar than they realized. He also assessed the champion's *Survivor Series* opponent— "You can't manhandle the Big Show. You can't suplex him; he's too big. And I don't think you can get him up for an F-5." Simply put, Heyman said, "Brock...you *can't beat* the Big Show."

The evaluation appeared alarmingly on target during Big Show's match with Rikishi; he withstood everything the Phat Man dished out, then dominated him with a devastating powerslam and Chokeslam for the win. After the match, Show called out Brock again, bragging that what he did to Rikishi was "only a taste" of what a "little man" like Lesnar could expect at the Pay-Per-View.

"You think you can do anything you want to, but take it from somebody who knows about being The Next Big Thing," Show cautioned. "When you least suspect it, reality will walk up and slap you in the face. And *your* reality is a seven-foot-tall, five hundred-pound giant." Ignoring his agent's urgings backstage, Brock made his way to ringside and confronted Show, admitting, "You *are* a giant. You're a giant *piece of shit!*"

Instead of striking Lesnar, the big man walked away, but not before promising to do something never before done to Brock before the end of the night. Big Show made good on the threat during Lesnar's nontitle contest against Rey Mysterio, whose uncanny agility and speed often kept Brock disoriented throughout the match. Without warning, Big Show arrived to catch Rey in the middle of a 619 on the ropes, then *threw* him several rows into the Van Andel crowd! Brock tried going toe-to-toe with the behemoth on the outside floor, only to get Chokeslammed through the *SmackDown!* announcers' table! Never having been so easily brutalized before, the WWE Champion lay decimated at the massive size twenty-twos of the giant, who roared, "I will destroy you! Give me the belt! It's mine! *It's mine!*"

Upon his arrival for the November 4 *SmackDown!* at the Verizon Wireless Arena in Manchester, New Hampshire, Big Show resumed his intimidation

Big Show is not impressed by Lesnar.

unleash the animal. Those things are better left to *my* judgment."

Version 1's judgment to face Big Show proved an unfortunate "twist of fate" on his part; the giant easily dispensed with him after catching Matt's legdrop off the ropes and Chokeslamming him to the canvas. Knowing Lesnar was watching from the back, Show goaded him on—"Let's get one thing straight: *I* was The Next Big Thing long before Brock Lesnar *ever* was. And at *Survivor Series,* I *will* be the next WWE Champion!" The comment drove Lesnar ballistic inside his locker room, forcing Heyman to cower in one corner while he smashed a large television to the ground.

Eddie and Chavo Guerrero soon added fuel to the inferno outside Brock's locker room, telling Heyman they not only thought the WWE Champion would lose to Big Show at the PPV, but that he couldn't even beat Latino Heat in a few minutes. Los Guerreros ran off as Lesnar came out to feed them their words, but it was Heyman who lost his cool this time. Having been with his client since day one of his climb to the top, Heyman was sick of Brock not listening to him about Big Show, adding that if he wanted to waste his time chasing Eddie Guerrero, he could do it *without* his agent at ringside. "See if you like being the brawn without the brains!" he yelled, walking off.

Despite outside assistance from nephew Chavo and a solid game plan to take down Lesnar's vertical base, Eddie was still no match for The Next Big Thing, who powered his way out of the Lasso from El Paso and F-5'd Latino Heat for the victory. But Heyman's words came back to haunt the WWE Champion when Big Show, in eerily similar fashion as he'd done with Undertaker, blindsided and press-slammed Lesnar off the top of the *SmackDown!* platform. The angry giant stood taller than ever on the stage, while the once-seemingly invincible Brock Lesnar looked like a broken toy lying at the bottom of the arena floor.

With only three days remaining until *Survivor Series,* Marc Loyd cautiously approached Paul Heyman backstage at Columbus, Ohio's Nationwide Arena at

games, ordering a guard to tell Brock Lesnar he was around. Matt Hardy cut short his instructional session with newly converted "M.F.'er" ("Mattitude Follower") Shannon Moore to discuss "some very serious issues" with Paul Heyman. Reminding the agent how he already "softened" Undertaker up for Brock to destroy him at Hell in the Cell, Matt was sure that he'd take care of Big Show that night. An insincere Heyman expressed his appreciation. His client wasn't quite so grateful; he wanted Show for himself. Again, Heyman appealed to the champion, telling him to just focus on his nontitle match with Eddie Guerrero. "Brock, I understand you," he said. "I'm not just your agent. I'm your *friend.* I know you're like a caged animal, ready to explode. Let me do my job, and my job is to decide when to

November 14 *SmackDown!* and asked about the WWE Champion's condition. Heyman defensively answered that despite having a broken rib and coughing up blood all week, his client would defend his title at the PPV. But he wouldn't show up for *SmackDown!* as per *his* orders. Big Show interrupted and issued Heyman a warning: if by some chance his client decided to show up, "I'm calling Brock Lesnar out." Like a true WWE Champion, The Next Big Thing would show up at the arena, earning himself another uninspiring rant from the disapproving agent. "If you don't get away from this guy right now, I can't protect you," Heyman exhorted. "I'm *pleading* with you…put your pride aside! Enough is enough! He is going to rip you limb from limb!"

Unable to get through to Lesnar, the agent decided to visit Big Show's locker room and beseech the giant. Heyman understood what kind of competitor Show was; he'd beaten WWE icons like The Rock, Undertaker and Hulk Hogan ("In Hogan's *prime,*" he pointed out), and Brock's injuries were a testament of what the giant could do. "All I'm asking for is a little professional courtesy here, just to back off until *Survivor Series.*" Show paused a moment before replying, "You know, the best thing Brock Lesnar has going for him is *you,* Paul. You are the brains behind the brawn." Convincing Show to consider his request, the agent was delighted with himself as he informed Brock of his achievement, crediting his own intelligence for "intimidating" the giant in some small way. But Brock quickly deflated Heyman; he wasn't leaving. "If the Big Show isn't calling me out," he said, "then I'm going to the ring, and *I'm* calling *him* out."

The Next Big Thing did exactly that, despite Heyman screeching in his ear every step of the way down to the ring. Dropping his WWE Championship belt to the mat and facing towards the *SmackDown!* stage, Lesnar threatened to drag Big Show out if he didn't come out and face him. Show's music hit, but the giant wouldn't even get in the ring; Brock met him at the foot of the ramp and whipped him into the steel corner steps, causing a large bloody gash on Show's right arm. Lesnar followed up with several massive chair shots, bending the seat area in half as it impacted against the big man's skull. The crimsoned Show barely got to his feet when Lesnar put him down and out with his WWE belt. The Columbus fans cheered as the WWE Champion silenced Big Show, Paul Heyman and anyone else who claimed he had no chance of bringing down the giant. And Brock Lesnar was determined to make sure his bigger adversary took a harder fall at *Survivor Series.*

For Stephanie McMahon, establishing the new WWE Tag Team Division was a large enough headache on its own. The headache quickly became a migraine when she forced Chris Benoit and Kurt Angle to work together as a team in the tournament. Perhaps Stephanie thought the pain would subside when the Canadian Crippler and the

BIG SHOW

HEIGHT: **7'2"**
WEIGHT: **500 lbs.**
FINISHING MOVE: **Chokeslam**
CAREER HIGHLIGHTS: **WWE Champion (2); Tag Team Champion (2); Hardcore Champion (2); WCW World Champion (2); WCW Tag Team Champion (2)**
2002 HIGHLIGHTS: **Joining the nWo on April 22 *Raw;* being traded to *SmackDown!* by Eric Bischoff on October 21 *Raw;* hurling Undertaker off the *SmackDown!* stage on October 24; becoming the first man ever to pin Brock Lesnar and winning the WWE Championship at *Survivor Series.***

Superstar ★ profile

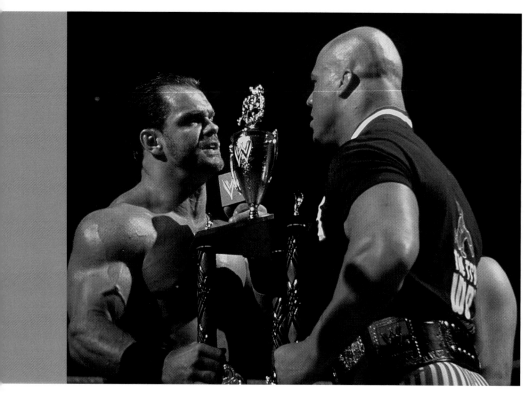

Unwilling partners Benoit and Angle.

SmackDown! GM decreed they'd settle their differences "the old-fashioned way": one-on-one, inside the ring. "And the winner of that match," she added, "will be able to keep this stupid, broken trophy!"

Before Benoit and Angle locked up, there was also the matter of securing a No. 1 Contender for the WWE Tag Team Championship. That meant a match between tournament finalists Rey Mysterio and Edge against Los Guerreros, who saw an opportunity to further the champions' rift. Approaching Angle backstage, Chavo acted like a parrot, repeating everything Eddie told

gold medalist became the first-ever WWE Tag Champions at *No Mercy,* and she could commemorate their historic win on October 24 *SmackDown!* with a majestic-sized trophy.

Perhaps even more than before they entered the tournament, the champs hated each other's guts. And Stephanie made the mistake of presenting them with only *one* trophy, which "team captain" Angle took upon himself to accept, assuring his partner he'd set it aside with the Olympic memorabilia in his home's "Wall of Fame." Taking hold of the prize, the Rabid Wolverine told Kurt to leave his Olympic-sized ego in the locker room. "We wouldn't have won these titles if it wasn't for *me,*" he stated. "You're damn lucky Stephanie made that stipulation between us, because if she hadn't, I'd have kicked the hell out of your Olympic ass." Angle ordered "Mr. Toothless Aggression" to let go of *his* trophy, while Benoit threatened to make him eat it, resulting in a struggle that ended only after they broke the trophy and accidentally knocked Stephanie to the canvas. Almost slapping the faces off her "petulant children," the angered

the medalist of rumors that Benoit planned to break his neck once the tournament ended. Too bad the Guerreros didn't devote as much attention to their work *inside* the ring. Eddie foolishly thought he'd sewn up the match when he scored a hilo on Edge. But while the official instructed Latino Heat to return to his corner, Rey springboard-legdropped Chavo off the ropes, allowing Edge to pick up the one-two-three for the victory.

Despite the huge loss, the Guerreros continued their backstage treachery afterwards. Benoit laughed while Latino Heat explained he'd messed up with Angle and just wanted to be friends again, then admitted, "What you told Kurt Angle earlier...you may be *right.*" In what developed into another great wrestling clinic hosted by the Tag Champs, Benoit looked like he'd settle for Angle's arm as a trophy when he latched on the Crippler Crossface. Kurt countered the hold and soon gained the match advantage with a top-rope suplex. Suddenly, Eddie raced down and distracted the *SmackDown!* official, while Chavo entered the other side of the ring and smacked Angle with one of the Tag belts, enabling Benoit to cover him for the win. The irate Kurt Angle Slammed Benoit while Los Guerreros high-tailed it into the crowd. Kurt demolished the trophy against the steel steps; if he couldn't have it, then neither could his partner.

Unable to mask their contempt for one another, Benoit and Angle were better suited for singles competition. At October 31 *SmackDown!*, the Rabid Wolverine was on the verge of winning a tough opening contest with a Crossface on Edge when Angle's sudden ringside arrival drove him to distraction. As the partners argued outside the ring, Edge capitalized with a baseball slide to the arena floor that bumped Benoit into Angle. Ducking a top-rope clothesline that almost took Kurt's head off on the outside, Benoit rolled Edge into the ring, only to catch a spear to the midsection that gave the Superstar a huge win. Benoit fumed while Angle laughed all the way to the back, though Angle was

nowhere to be found when Benoit looked for him at the Halloween party minutes later. Benoit might indeed have cried murder, however, had he known Kurt was standing right in front of him, wearing the killer mask made famous in the *Scream* films.

Brandishing the sword of the masked swashbuckler Zorro at the party, Eddie Guerrero talked trash about carving his "L.H." initials into Kurt Angle when they locked up later that night. But neither he nor nephew Chavo joked when they asked Stephanie for a shot at the WWE Tag titles. Although Rey and Edge already defeated them to become the No. 1 Contenders, the *SmackDown!* GM told them she'd think about it. The possibility fired up Latino Heat, who kept Angle off-balance in their match with high-impact moves till he "felt froggy." Kurt crotched Eddie by shoving the referee into the ropes, then averted an outside assist from Chavo. But as the medalist went up top to suplex his adversary,

THE VOTE IS IN WITH SMACKDOWN!

Cast no pregnant chads about it—"*SmackDown!* Your Vote!" was a clear and decisive winner again in 2002, with more than 185,000 new voters across the United States electing to register with the partnership led by The Participate America Foundation and Rock the Vote. Since the partnership began in 2000, "*SmackDown!* Your Vote!" has registered more than 400,000 new balloters.

The partnership's campaign began with "National High School Voter Registration Month" in May, in which a scholarship competition and voter program toolkits were offered to juniors and seniors in 12,000 high schools across the United States. Among the thirteen states to hold "*SmackDown!* Your Vote!" registration days that month, WWE Superstars and secretaries of states visited high schools in Arizona, Alabama, Connecticut, Minnesota and Rhode Island. The campaign efforts doubled throughout the summer via a national promotion in Sam Goody music stores, with over 300,000 WWE-related voter materials distributed to promote registration, as well as through more than fifteen registration drives at WWE live events held by Youth Vote Coalition and Project Vote Smart.

More than a thousand people attended the launch of the "*SmackDown!* Your Vote! Pledge to Participate Tour" in New York City on August 26. The first leg of the tour, co-sponsored by WWE, *Weekly Reader* and The Participate America Foundation, was supported greatly by the attendance of Governor George Pataki, WWE CEO Linda McMahon, "*SmackDown!* Your Vote!" Honorary Chairman Kurt Angle, The Rock, Edge, Bradshaw, Stacy Keibler, Mark Henry and WWE announcers Jonathan Coachman and Lilian Garcia. Subsequent tour destinations included Minneapolis, Washington, D.C., Denver, Los Angeles and Houston, during which over 104,000 people signed replicas of the U.S. Constitution both through local registration events and on the Internet at WWE.com. The highly successful tour made its final stop at Boston's Northeastern University on Election Day, November 4, during which former Massachusetts Governor Michael Dukakis joined Kane, The Hurricane, Al Snow and Spike Dudley in encouraging one and all to make themselves heard in the ballot booths. The WWE looks forward to beginning another triumphant "*SmackDown!* Your Vote!" campaign in the spring of 2003, and plans to score another victory in achieving voter awareness. ■

Chris Benoit tagged him with his own belt from the outside. Eddie frog splashed Angle for the one-two-three, though his ring celebration with Chavo was cut short when the Crippler came in and nailed them with the belt as well.

It was Angle's turn to crash the party minutes later, throwing Shannon Moore over a nearby table and warning no one to leave until he found Benoit. Kurt thought his search was over when he saw someone in the same *Scream* outfit he wore earlier, though he almost screamed himself upon discovering longtime WWE personality Brother Love under the mask! Benoit suddenly jumped the gold medalist, forcing him to bob for apples in a tub of water before slapping on the Crossface. Angle countered with the ankle lock, but just as he put Benoit up in the Angle Slam, the Crippler smashed a bottle in his face, in the process sending both men crashing through a table. Needless to say, the WWE Tag Team Champions, sprawled unconscious on the floor, had brought the *SmackDown!* Halloween party to an abrupt end.

One had to wonder if Angle and Benoit were on the same *book*, let alone the same page, when they met Edge and Rey Mysterio for a Two-Out-of-Three Falls Championship match at November 7 *SmackDown!;* they couldn't even start the competition without arguing over who'd wrestle first. The challengers, on the other hand, worked on all cylinders, nabbing the vital first fall when Edge propelled his one-hundred-sixty-five-pound partner into a West Coast Pop on the Crippler. The Tag Champs wouldn't easily relinquish the belts; Benoit used one of the belts to clobber Edge, who soon tapped out to Angle's ankle lock.

With the match tied at a fall apiece, the Rabid Wolverine and gold medalist's clashing egos again delayed them from building any immediate momentum they gained on Edge. However, they'd soon direct their quarrels at referee Brian Hebner, who counted three on a Mysterio power sunset flip despite Angle's hand holding the ring rope. Upon further review, Hebner ordered the match to continue, and the champions turned on the offense. Angle slapped another ankle lock on Edge, who broke the hold by sending Kurt into the turnbuckle. From the outside floor, Rey delivered an amazing 619 around the steel corner post, setting Angle up for a spear inside the ring. Benoit tried making the save with a flying headbutt off the top rope, only to catch his own partner. There was no mistake when the referee's hand hit the mat a third time—Edge and Rey Mysterio were the new WWE Tag Team Champions!

Stephanie McMahon followed what many considered a strong candidate for "match of the year" with a major announcement at *Super Tuesday,* a November 12 joint production between *Raw* and *SmackDown!.* "Due to the incredibly high level of competition," she said, "I've decided that at *Survivor Series,* it will be a Triple-Threat match for the Tag Team titles, featuring Kurt Angle and Chris Benoit vs. the Guerreros vs. Edge and Rey Mysterio." Furthermore, as a preview to the Pay-Per-View matchup, she'd kick off *Super Tuesday* with a

Edge and Rey Mysterio celebrate their win.

Triple-Threat match between Benoit, Eddie and Edge. The contest was fierce from the opening bell—Benoit broke up Eddie's Lasso from El Paso on Edge, but when Eddie tried returning the favor and breaking up a Crossface, the Crippler put him in the submission hold instead. Spearing Benoit to the outside, Edge scored an Edgecution on Eddie, only for Chavo to interfere with the three-count by pulling the referee out of the ring. Rey Mysterio ran down and handled Chavo on the outside, while Benoit's Crossface on Latino Heat was broken up after Kurt Angle made his way down and rolled the official into him. As the Crippler chewed out Kurt, Eddie seized the moment, schoolboying Benoit for the three-count.

At the final *SmackDown!* before *Survivor Series*, the Triple-Threat Tag combatants would face each other in singles competition—Edge against Chavo Guerrero, Mysterio against Eddie Guerrero and, of course, Angle against Benoit. Chavo gave Edge a run for his money, surprising the nine-time Tag Team title holder with a spear of his own for a near-fall. But as he attempted a tornado DDT out of the corner, Edge countered with the Edgecution for the three-count.

The loss wouldn't stop Chavo and Eddie from talking trash to the champions backstage as Latino Heat prepared to square off against Mysterio. The way Eddie saw it, they were "blind squirrels finding nuts," but their luck was running out, and at *Survivor Series*, "there's *nothing* in the way of Los Guerreros having the gold around our waist!" Eddie tried backing his words in the ring, but the luchador was in control until a 619 attempt caught the referee's midsection instead. With the official down, Chavo raced in and nailed Rey with a Gory special. Edge made the save, spearing Eddie and hammering away at Chavo on the outside before the recovered referee ordered officials to escort them to the back. Rey built momentum with a top-rope moonsault on Eddie, then a hilo to the outside. But Latino Heat would ultimately roll through a West Coast Pop and slap on the Lasso from El Paso for the submission victory.

Earlier that night, Angle and Benoit's "blame game" over losing the WWE Tag titles had deteriorated into a "who's better" argument: the gold medalist with more teeth and claimed he was ten times better, or the Rabid Wolverine with more hair and asserted he was *eleven* times better. Angle would make his way out before the match and argue his case to the Nationwide Arena fans, to whom he'd apologize "for being too predictable." He'd beaten Chris Benoit, Edge, Rey Mysterio and Los

> [**"Get your freakin' gap-toothed butt out here right now!"**]

Guerreros so many times "it's become one big blur." Angle not only considered himself a better athlete than the Crippler, but also far better looking than Edge and the Guerreros. "I can actually speak *English*, for goodness sakes!" he noted, and *he'd* been through puberty, unlike Rey Mysterio. "Come *Survivor Series*," he added, "there's no doubt in my mind who's going to wind up with the Tag Team titles, *if* Chris Benoit doesn't screw up again!"

Los Guerreros interrupted Angle, as Eddie reminded Kurt who pinned him "one-two-*tres*" two weeks ago. Edge and Mysterio came out next, with Edge telling "chrome-dome" he'd lost his mind as well his hair. "If memory serves me correctly...*we* beat *you* for these Tag Team Championships." Angle started losing it, rationalizing they were all out there just to scout him. "You're all scared of me!" he yelled, then invited them to have a seat, "because you're about to see your Olympic Hero in rare form. So, Benoit! Get your freakin' gap-toothed butt out here right now! So I can prove to you, to these idiots here and to all these people tonight who the very best wrestler is in this business today! Oh, it's true! It's *damn* true!"

Benoit didn't need to be called out twice, and took it right to his tag team partner. But when neither

ROAD TO REBELLION

World Wrestling Entertainment made its second trip over to Europe in 2002 with the "Road to *Rebellion* Tour" on October 24-27. The WWE Superstars covered Finland, Northern Ireland and England during the four-day tour, which was highlighted by the WWE's second U.K. Pay-Per-View *Rebellion* October 26. A sellout crowd of 10,840 attended Helsinki's Hartwell Arena to witness Finland's first-ever live WWE event October 24, during which WWE Champion Brock Lesnar picked up a hard-fought victory over Booker T (substituting for the injured Undertaker) and Crusier-weight Champion Jamie Noble retained his title against Tajiri. Less than twenty-four hours later, the Superstars performed for a sold-out Odyssey Arena in Belfast, where 8,680 fans were treated to their first live house show in a decade. Kurt Angle and Chris Benoit stopped arguing long enough to successfully defend the WWE Tag Titles against Chavo and Eddie Guerrero, while Ron Simmons helped D-Von pull out a victory over Rikishi, who had native son Fit Finlay in his corner. Following the *Rebellion* PPV event, England's sold-out Sheffield Arena hosted the tour's final leg on October 27, during which 10,365 spectators enjoyed watching Torrie Wilson come out on top over Dawn Marie in a Bra and Panties match, and Rikishi and Booker T grab an upset win over Brock Lesnar and Matt Hardy. Although all parties were sad to see another highly successful tour come to an end, both the Superstars and their fans eagerly anticipate WWE's two European trips planned for 2003, including its next U.K. PPV *Insurrextion*, to be held in Newcastle, England, on June 7. ∎

Superstar could make the other tap out to their respective finishers, Kurt surprised the Canadian Crippler with the Lasso from El Paso. Seeing Angle use his specialty move boiled Latino Heat to the point where he charged into the ring, only to have Angle eject him onto Edge and Mysterio on the outside. A six-man slobberknocker quickly erupted inside the ring, giving the referee no choice but to call the match. Rey and Edge put Angle and Benoit in their own submission moves respectively, but within moments Kurt had Eddie in the ankle lock, while the Rabid Wolverine countered the Edgecution with the Crossface.

By the time officials restored order in the ring, only Benoit and Angle remained, and they immediately went nose-to-nose. Angle surprised everyone, however, especially Benoit, when he offered his hand in friendship. Benoit paused for a moment…then accepted it. From there, things got downright *weird*—Kurt motioned for a hug! Benoit looked at the gold medalist like he was nuts, but Angle insisted, and took it upon himself to hug the Crippler. Although genuinely disturbed by the turn of events, Chris Benoit went along with it, especially if it meant he and Kurt Angle could recapture the WWE Tag titles at *Survivor Series*.

He may be a redneck, but Jamie Noble was also a survivor. He accomplished one of the more overlooked achievements of 2002— since winning the Cruiserweight Championship at *King of the Ring* on June 23, Noble held onto a WWE title longer than anyone else on either *Raw* or *SmackDown!* But whether he liked it or not—and he didn't— nothing lasts forever. That included his championship, which wasn't so much a question of "if" he'd lose it, but *"when"* and "to *whom.*"

Noble didn't realize it yet, but "when" started on October 24 *SmackDown!* in the Bluff City of the mighty Mississippi. The Memphis Pyramid crowd likened the Cruiserweight Champion's Elvis impersonation to something they'd scrape off the bottom of their "blue suede shoes." Fortunately, Noble's personal groupie

Rey Mysterio flies into Kurt Angle.

Nidia helped him make it through the night, plus his match against Tajiri, literally handing her boyfriend the leverage he needed to pin the Japanese Buzzsaw and retain the title. Fellow cruiserweight Billy Kidman, meanwhile, relied on his own hands to avenge last week's loss to John Cena, grabbing the ropes to secure a counter-pinfall on the rookie.

Noble had already bested Kidman in competition several times, most notably during last July's *Vengeance*, but for the next three weeks Kidman had the Cruiserweight Champ's number. A top-rope Shooting-Star Press on Noble's partner Crash Holly lifted the cruiserweight and Funaki to a *Velocity* Tag victory on November 2, with the same move finishing off the redneck himself when Kidman and Torrie Wilson faced Noble and Nidia in a *SmackDown!* Mixed Tag match five nights later. The two losses prompted Noble to challenge Kidman to a one-on-one non-title bout at November 14 *SmackDown!*, where it looked like he might pick up the "W" with Nidia's ringside assistance and a super-

plex off the top rope. But Kidman was as resourceful as he was agile, altering the jolt to the mat into a small package for the three-count. As a result of the win, the challenger had catapulted himself back into top contention for the Cruiserweight title, with the match to occur at *Survivor Series*.

Even though he'd come up short against Kidman in recent weeks, Noble pointed out to the *Velocity* crowd on November 16, "Month after month, I've beaten every cruiserweight that's had the nerve to step up and challenge Jamie Noble!" He also guaranteed the result of his *Survivor Series* contest would be the same as every other one. "Jamie Noble goes in champion. Jamie Noble comes *out* champion. And you ain't gonna be able to do nothin' 'bout it, Kidman! The only thing you're gonna be able to do is respect the Cruiserweight Champion—*me!*"

Like Jamie Noble, John Cena was a survivor, demonstrating an ability to adapt that's required of any WWE Superstars. Cena needed an edge to partner his well-known ruthless aggression, and he started finding it when he blamed Billy Kidman for their first-round loss in the WWE Tag tournament. He used his growing edge to score a cheap win over Kidman in a *SmackDown!* one-on-one on October 17, then unleashed his aggression after Kidman beat him in similar fashion a week later. Cena bullied the referee, then surprised the cruiserweight with a vicious attack both in and outside the ring.

"When the match is over he'll taste *my* cheeks' cheeses."

It was at the *SmackDown!* Halloween party when Cena, garbed like a Vanilla Ice wannabe, found a way to channel both elements: through *rap*. No one could decipher his freestyle phraseology, however, including "Number One *SmackDown!* Announcer" Funaki, who looked hopelessly lost on November 7 while listening to Cena's jive about his match with Rikishi. "Kish wants to release pieces of his *feces*? / When the match is over he'll taste *my* cheeks' cheeses." The Phat Man irritated the rookie when he entered the room and displayed his skills at busting a rhyme. "This ain't the time, / This ain't the place, / Get a piece of the Kish / Right in *yo' face*." He then backed up both his words and his ass in the ring with a Stinkface and rump-shaker on Cena. But the novice would juice himself into a better *SmackDown!* rhythm on November 14, when he and Version 1 hooked up for a duet and took down Rikishi and his tag partner Tajiri. In the weeks to follow, Cena's lyrics would make a much bigger impact in the *SmackDown!* roster, regardless of whether anyone understood them.

If predators are considered among the greatest survivors, then Dawn Marie should be around the WWE for a very long time to come. After losing her match to Torrie Wilson at *No Mercy*, it appeared she'd learned her lesson by October 24 *SmackDown!*, telling the blonde Diva backstage that she was the better woman, and that she intended to break off her romance with Torrie's father, Al. Instead, Dawn played Al like a fiddle, telling him she didn't want to come between him and his daughter, then saying goodbye to "...the most passionate man I have ever experienced." The fire suddenly burned in Al, who grabbed and kissed Dawn passionately; now more than ever, he belonged to her.

Torrie, meanwhile, continued to dominate inside the ring, particularly when it came to wearing sexy outfits. She sparkled during a *Velocity* Bikini match against Nidia on October 26, both in her two-piece gold swimsuit and with her ring work, vaulting over the trashy Diva and her discount swimsuit to roll her up for the victory. Torrie next hooked up against Dawn Marie in a special Trick or Treat match for the *SmackDown!* Halloween party on October 31, a contest sweetened by the stipulation that the Divas would wrestle in a pool of chocolate. But there was no sugar-coating the girls' dislike for one another; the Valkyrie-garbed Torrie smacked sexy police officer Dawn Marie with a pie before the two even

John Cena busts a move on Rikishi.

Torrie Wilson flips Dawn Marie in a Chocolate match.

Tuesday on November 12. Although a run-in by Nidia ruined the competition between Torrie and *Raw*'s Trish Stratus, fans cheered as the two Divas joined forces to send the trailer trash running back up the ramp, and Tazz declared both ladies the winners of the contest.

As for Al, it had become increasingly obvious to Torrie who was winning the bigger role in his life. At the November 14 *SmackDown!*, Dawn Marie once again manipulated her fiancé perfectly, encouraging him to give his daughter an invitation to their wedding when she knew how Torrie would respond. "You're being used," she told her father. "Why can't you see it? Dawn Marie is a manipulative *bitch*!" Knowing she was upsetting her father greatly, Torrie apologized, but she refused to attend the wedding. "I'm sorry if there's no nice way to say this, and I'm sorry if you get offended," she explained, "but, Dad...there is no fool like an *old* fool." Al took comfort in Dawn's arms afterwards, as she told him the wedding was right for them, regardless of what his daughter thought. "Everything's going to be fine," she said, her consoling words dripping with contempt. "I promise."

hit the pool, where Torrie would ultimately taste victory following a vicious chop and pinfall.

Unfortunately for Torrie, that taste had turned bitter by the following week's *SmackDown!*, when her father visited her backstage and asked her to understand what he was going to do that evening. The Diva learned with the rest of the New Hampshire crowd what Al meant when he asked Dawn to come down to the ring. Since he'd met Dawn, he'd felt "strong...sexy...and *virile!*" And because she made him feel like a man, Al got down on one knee and popped the question, "Dawn...will you marry me?" The vixen paused a moment, making the lovesick Al nervous enough to threaten to kill himself if she didn't accept his proposal. As the crowd chanted "Just Say No!"—a sentiment shared by *SmackDown!* commentators Tazz and Michael Cole—Dawn walked up to Al and answered, "*Yes,*" prompting a chorus of boos from the Verizon Wireless Arena. A visibly upset Torrie left the venue in tears.

The distressing news wouldn't stop the blonde bombshell from fulfilling her *SmackDown!* obligations, which included participating in an Interpromotional Bikini Challenge between the two WWE brands at *Super*

Without question, Dawn Marie and Al Wilson had the strangest relationship going in the WWE...that is, until World Wrestling Entertainment announced the signing of "Big Poppa Pump" Scott Steiner. A six-foot-one, two-hundred-seventy-six-pound genetic freak if ever there was one, the former WCW Champion was considered one of the hottest free agents on the market. Which meant both *Raw* and *SmackDown!* wanted him.

Eric Bischoff immediately made known his intentions of bringing Steiner to *Raw;* the Big Show trade was to

Manchester Evening News (M.E.N.) Arena Manchester, England

WWE CHAMPIONSHIP HANDICAP MATCH

Brock Lesnar (w/Paul Heyman) defeated *Edge* via pinfall; Lesnar retains the WWE title

WWE TAG TEAM CHAMPIONSHIP MATCH

Kurt Angle & Chris Benoit defeated *Eddie & Chavo Guerrero* via pinfall to retain the WWE Tag Team titles

KISS MY ASS MATCH

Rikishi defeated *Albert* via pinfall

Ron Simmons & D-Von defeated *Chuck Palumbo & Big Valbowski* via pinfall

CRUISERWEIGHT CHAMPIONSHIP TRIPLE-THREAT ELIMINATION MATCH

Jamie Noble (w/Nidia) defeated *Tajiri* and *Rey Mysterio* via pinfall to retain the WWE Cruiserweight title

Funaki defeated *Crash Holly* via pinfall

INTERGENDER TAG TEAM MATCH

Torrie Wilson & Billy Kidman defeated *Dawn Marie & John Cena* via pinfall

Booker T defeated *Matt Hardy* via pinfall

Rebellion broke out inside England's Manchester Evening News Arena, and the 13,416 fans in attendance rose to their feet as the opening pyro kicked off the WWE's second U.K. Pay-Per-View for 2002!

Coming out on stage and welcoming the sellout crowd was *SmackDown!* General Manager Stephanie McMahon, who had an unfortunate announcement: due to the injuries suffered by Undertaker over the past week, the Phenom was unable to appear. The good news was that in addition to Big Show joining the *SmackDown!* roster, Stephanie had one *Raw* member sign up specifically for *Rebellion:* Booker T, who came out to a huge pop from the crowd as he squared off against Matt Hardy. The philosophies of Mattitude were lost on the Book, who kicked out of a pinfall after Version 1 delivered the Twist of Fate, then countered a second attempt and landed the scissors kick. Picking up the one-two-three, Booker celebrated the win with a special Spin-a-Roonie for the U.K. fans!

Backstage, Paul Heyman wasn't reveling inside Stephanie McMahon's office. The agent thought it was unfair having to be in the evening's Handicap match with Edge; he could just pin Heyman and take the title from his client, Brock Lesnar! Besides, he didn't have any wrestling gear. Stephanie asked if it was fair that Lesnar broke the Dead Man's hand before Hell in the Cell, and it didn't matter about not having any gear—Paul could just wrestle in his twenty-five hundred dollar suit!

The fans would undoubtedly have preferred the WWE Divas *not* wearing any wrestling attire in an Intergender Tag Team match that pitted Dawn Marie and John Cena against Torrie Wilson and Billy Kidman, but no such luck. The ruthlessly aggressive Cena dominated Kidman early in the match until Dawn Marie tagged herself in. Kidman easily overcame her and tagged Torrie, who proceeded to spank the Diva inside the ring! Cena soon tried asserting himself over Torrie, but a low blow enabled her to make the tag to Kidman. Billy followed an Enziguri to the rookie's head with a Shooting-Star Press off the top rope, giving him and Torrie the victory, and earning himself a passionate kiss from the blonde beauty!

Speaking from backstage to Michael Cole at the *Rebellion* announcer's table, Edge told his "Edge Army" that even though he hoped to see Undertaker back as soon as possible, one man's loss was his gain, and he intended to make the most of his WWE Championship opportunity later that night. Crash Holly, meanwhile, decided to make little of Funaki and Japan when they hooked up in the ring, putting on a karate headband with a U.K. flag on it and mocking martial arts moves. The "Number One *SmackDown!* Announcer" answered with a kick to Crash's face, followed soon by a swinging DDT off the ropes. A series of rollups and counter-rollups resulted in several near-falls until Funaki was able to keep his opponent secure long enough for a three-count and the win.

Hearing trailer trash like Jamie Noble and Nidia's disdain for the British sounded real paradoxical, but there was nothing contradictory about the WWE Cruiserweight Champion's ability in the ring against opponents Tajiri and Rey Mysterio. As he and Tajiri battled to the outside floor, the luchador struck them down with a corkscrew plancha over the top ropes. The Japanese Buzzsaw soon kept Rey tied up in the ropes with the Tarantula, until Noble broke it up and quickly Tiger Bombed Tajiri to eliminate him. On the outside, Nidia rammed Mysterio's left arm, priming it for further punishment by Noble. Rey battled back, countering an Electric Chair into a swinging DDT, then almost scoring the West Coast Pop for the win. Nidia's outside assistance again proved instrumental by holding Noble's hands to help him secure the pinfall, but as the happy couple celebrated, Tajiri returned to the ring and sent them into the ropes, setting Rey up to leave both of them with a 619 parting shot.

Chuck Palumbo and Big Valbowski paired up for tag action against the newly aligned Ron Simmons and D-Von. Chuck and Valbowski opened strong until Simmons

dominated Val with a vicious spinebuster, allowing him and D-Von to control the match. Chuck eventually got the tag and cleaned house against the tandem, catching D-Von with a superkick. But when Simmons broke up the near-fall and prompted Chuck to chase him out of the ring, D-Von seized the moment to schoolboy Chuck from behind and hook the tights for the one-two-three.

Coming out to the ring for his Kiss My Ass match with Rikishi, the hairier-than-ever Albert told the crowd he knew what they were thinking—that he was "*wicked sexy*." While rubbing his chest hair, he also assured the ladies in the audience that everything on him was "*Al Natural*." Mercifully, Rikishi headed to the ring and put Albert out of the fans' misery, landing the superkick and Banzai drop for the three-count. Albert took off before the butt-smooching could commence, but was forced to return when the referee warned he would be suspended indefinitely without pay. Returning to the ring and puckering up, Albert surprised the Phat Man with a low blow and Baldo Bomb. But as he went for his own Stinkface, Rikishi returned the cheap shot and made sure he felt the real deal, then had Michael Cole, Tazz and ring announcer Tony Chimel celebrate in the ring with a dance that got the crowd on its feet.

Earlier backstage, the WWE Tag Champions weren't dancing around over who was in charge of their title defense that night. Kurt Angle insisted he was team captain because of the United States' alliance with England, while the not quite-as-good Canadian Commonwealth's Benoit warned Angle to just follow his lead. Opponents Eddie and Chavo Guerrero just wanted to win the WWE Tag titles in Germany, or Ireland, or whatever country with funny-talking people they were visiting that night, and head back home to Grandma's home cooking in Mexico.

The two teams hooked up for a great physical confrontation, one which saw Angle and Benoit again engage in their ongoing one-upsmanship competition until Eddie countered an Angle Slam and shoved Kurt into the Crippler, which also knocked the referee to the outside floor. Latino Heat capitalized on the feuding partners with the Lasso from El Paso, until Kurt reversed the submission move into the ankle lock. Chavo nailed the medalist with one of

Brock Lesnar puts the pressure on Edge.

the WWE Tag belts, then rolled the official back in for the cover. Angle somehow kicked out at two, then hit Eddie with the Angle Slam while Benoit pushed Chavo off the top rope to the outside floor. Benoit and Angle still couldn't see eye-to-eye despite the victory, though they quickly got back on the same page to stop Los Guerreros from running off with their WWE Tag Team belts!

WWE Champion Brock Lesnar laid it all on the line for his agent backstage; he would bust Paul Heyman in half if he screwed up the evening's Handicap match with Edge. Not surprisingly, the agent was nervous as he and The Next Big Thing entered the ring. Edge looked confident as ever, mocking Lesnar into recklessly ramming his shoulder into the corner post, then spearing Heyman to the outside floor. The WWE Champion recovered and battered the challenger down with a series of power moves and a bearhug to the mat, but the "Edge Army" in attendance rallied their Superstar to fight back. Edge hit a facebuster and sent Brock to the outside, then dragged Heyman into the ring and clobbered him with a double-axe handle off the top rope.

From the outside, Lesnar broke up the pinfall, only to get covered himself after Edge hit with a missile dropkick. Brock kicked out, then dodged a top-rope crossbody that nailed the referee. The fallen official would cost Edge WWE Championship gold after an Edgecution on Lesnar obtained more than a three-count. Heyman tossed in a chair to his client, but Edge speared Lesnar before he could connect. But The Next Big Thing would find his mark moments later, nailing Edge with the chair and the F-5 just as the referee recovered, and getting the easy three-count. Lesnar headed back up the ramp while his agent scared off the ref with the chair. But as Heyman talked trash and prepared to hit Edge with the steel, Edge countered and planted him to the canvas with the Edgecution. Edge might not have walked away from *Rebellion* as the WWE Champion, but he did himself and the fans a huge favor by shutting Heyman up for the rest of the night. ∎

compensate his show with an assortment of "incredible talent" Eric was certain would help lure the "Big Bad Booty Daddy" over to his show. In fact, Bischoff was so confident Steiner would sign with *Raw*, he had "Vince McMahon" visit Stephanie at her *SmackDown!* Halloween party on October 31 and tell her so. Appalled that Bischoff would infiltrate her show, costumed as her father, Stephanie tried to slap the *Raw* General Manager. Bischoff caught her hand…then *kissed* her! Stephanie resisted, but only for a moment; in fact, she became as passionate as Bischoff. But when the two came up for air, they looked completely confused over what had transpired between them. For once, Bischoff was at a loss for words, and left the room.

The *Raw-SmackDown!* war for Scott Steiner would continue over the next several weeks, with both sides claiming to have the inside track on signing the Genetic Freak. As for "The Kiss," both Stephanie and Bischoff would later watch the moment on tape from their respective offices, though the incident would remain undiscussed. During the *Sunday Night Heat* preceding *Survivor Series* on November 17, it looked like Bischoff might crack as he prepared to knock on the door to Stephanie's office. But he withdrew his hand and walked away; for now at least, it was business before pleasure, and the business was Big Poppa Pump.

Not so long ago, asking a Dudley and a Hardy to coexist in the ring would have been akin to asking a Hatfield and a McCoy to share livestock. Like the famous rivalry between those two families, there was simply too much history between the long-standing tag teams, including then-WCW Tag Champs Bubba Ray and D-Von Dudley unifying the WWE Tag titles with a Cage match win over Matt and Jeff Hardy at *Survivor Series 2001*. But what a difference a year, a shot at World Tag Team gold and a 3 Minute Warning can make.

After the way Big Show embarrassed them in a three-on-one Handicap match only seven days before, Rosey, Jamal and Rico were in Eric Bischoff's *Raw* doghouse on October 28. And because they didn't get the job done, the giant—Bischoff traded Show to *SmackDown!* immediately after their match—was now poised to make the *Raw* GM look like "the biggest fool in the business," by competing for the WWE title at *Survivor Series*. Eric felt the threesome had disrespected him as badly as Spike Dudley, who told Bischoff to go bite two weeks ago. He didn't want to hear any excuses from them; he just wanted results. "Go out there, make some impact," he warned, "or *your* three minutes are *up*."

3 Minute Warning and Rico would honor "The Bisch"'s demands when Bubba Ray and Spike Dudley came out to face Christian and Chris Jericho for the World Tag Team titles that evening. The Dudleyz earned a shot at the belts at *Raw* a week before with a victory over William Regal and Lance Storm for the No. 1 Contenders spot. Spike's Dudley Dog on Regal powered the win, though the runt of the Dudley litter paid for it with a series of brass knux shots to his ribs. And it was that injury 3 Minute Warning further exploited when they raced into the ring and attacked Spike and Bubba before the Tag Title match even started. With Spike hurt so badly he was unable to compete, Bubba brought his grievance to an unsympathetic Bischoff, who suggested he just "...find another partner. I don't care." Bubba thought about it, then a look appeared on his face like a giant lightbulb had gone off over his head.

From the reaction on Jericho and Christian's faces, Bubba Ray couldn't have picked a more Xtreme tag partner than Jeff Hardy. Although the makeshift tandem had no time to prepare for the match, they'd battled so often in the past they anticipated each other's moves beautifully. Bubba provided back support for a Poetry in Motion that sent the daredevil sailing onto Christian and Jericho on the outside, while Jeff contributed his variation of the "Wassup?!" top-rope groin shot, substituting a double legdrop in place of D-Von's flying headbutt. The duo even fended off another 3 Minute Warning attack, with Bubba crashing down onto Y2J, Jamal and Rosey on the arena floor. But as Jeff and Bubba had the World Tag Champs reeling, Rico, Jamal and Rosey reappeared on the *Raw* stage, this time hanging Spike upside-down like a broken wind chime. Bubba headed up the ramp to help his injured brother, which unfortunately left Jeff unguarded against Jericho's cheap shot with one of the Tag belts. Y2J then followed up with the Lionsault, getting the one-two-three to retain the titles.

Since 3 Minute Warning cost them the World Tag titles, Bubba and Jeff decided to pair up again and put Jamal and Rosey on notice when *Raw* opened in Boston on November 4. The match quickly developed into a slobberknocker, with Jeff again taking his

Bubba tosses Spike into 3 Minute Warning.

Poetry in Motion outside the ring and onto the Samoan tandem and Rico. Spike Dudley stormed to his brother's rescue with a Dudley Dog on Rico, though paid for it when Jamal sent his still injured midsection crashing down on top of the security barrier. Jeff soon climbed up top to finish Jamal with the Swanton Bomb, only to be forced down prematurely by Rosey, then practically press-slammed by Jamal into a Samoan drop for the victory.

With the wood almost broken out during their last confrontation, it was all but made a certainty when a Six-Man Tag Team Tables match was announced for *Survivor Series* between 3 Minute Warning and Rico against Jeff Hardy, Bubba Ray and Spike Dudley. Spike, who'd returned to ring action on November 10 with a *Sunday Night Heat* win over D'Lo Brown, partnered with his brother for some early retribution against Jamal and Rosey at the following night's *Raw*. Once again, 3 Minute Warning would know they were in a fight, but a hard Samoan drop on Bubba eventually provided them with another "W" in the column. Jeff, who'd accompanied Spike and Bubba to their corner following his singles win over Lance Storm earlier, cleaned house of the titanic twosome and Rico, until he and Spike were placed on a table that Jamal's top-rope splash splintered moments later, nearly breaking the pair in half! And with an almost certain brutal Tag Tables match only days away, Jeff and the Dudleyz' now battered bodies might very easily become broken.

Understandably, most wrestlers are interested in taking their opponents down. Yet in recent weeks, a number of *Raw* Superstars focused more on building themselves *up*. Among those included was a Harvard graduate deeming himself smarter than his teacher, a young stud who became a pain in the neck while on the injured list, a *SmackDown!* rookie that promised pure *Raw* power, two former Un-Americans whose belief systems kept them unified...and a third whose Diva guidance erected a Test-icle movement!

Despite Christopher Nowinski's total disrespect for him, *Tough Enough* head trainer Al Snow still saw the smarmy scholar as one of his kids. But a week after his paternal instincts cost Tommy Dreamer a loss to Nowinski, Snow wasn't going to provide his former student another cheap *Raw* win over Jeff Hardy on October 21. From the outside floor, Al tried halting the Harvard grad from using a steel chair, but the struggle resulted in the chair remaining inside the ring even longer, with Jeff crashing on top of it moments after his Swanton Bomb missed Nowinski. To make matters worse, a still upset Dreamer later decided to take his pound of flesh out of Snow in a Singapore Cane match, during which Nowinski ran down to hit the Innovator of Violence with a kendo stick. Instead, he laid out his former teacher by mistake, giving Dreamer the three-count.

There was no mistaking which match Stacy Keibler wanted to guest referee that evening; after getting Eric Bischoff's blessing, she officiated a one-on-one between D'Lo Brown and Test, which soon became more like a *two*-on-one. After holding the ropes open for the former Un-American, the obviously partial Diva went over the rules with both men before slapping D'Lo's face. Throughout the match, Stacy sabotaged several pinfall attempts made by D'Lo, including a probable win when he hit the Sky High, yet she was right there for the quick three-count when Test caught him with the big boot. From there, one can safely assume that Earl Hebner or any other *Raw* official would

Tommy Dreamer in a Cane match against Al Snow.

never jump into Test's arms after calling the victory, nor would they leave the ring with the Superstar arm-in-arm.

After lending a helping hand in each other's matches over the past few weeks, William Regal and Lance Storm entered the ring as a tag team for a match against Bubba Ray and Spike Dudley. Before the bout started, the always-dour Storm wanted to be serious with the Nashville fans for a minute, and confirmed that even though the Un-Americans were finished, he and Regal were "...very much together, because we share one common view. And that's that this country

> **"This country is nothing more than a zoo filled with *crazed savages.*"**

is nothing more than a zoo filled with *crazed savages."* Taking the mic, the brash Brit added his twopence and pronounced the United States a cesspool. "How far does this country have to deteriorate before you people listen to us, and realize we know what we're bloody well talking about?!" he yelled. "You people should all be thoroughly ashamed of yourselves!"

Despite losing the match, Storm and Regal demonstrated their commitment to remain a united front with a post-match beatdown on the Dudleyz. Their

teamwork would pay off *Raw* dividends against Tommy Dreamer and Rob Van Dam on October 28, especially after Storm nailed Dreamer with the Canadian flag, allowing Regal to pick up an easy one-two-three.

Test picked up more than a victory last week; he now had a drop-dead gorgeous image consultant with plenty of ideas to beef up his visage, one of which included getting him to make a statement in front of the Motor City crowd before locking up against Goldust. Test's face suggested he was totally against the idea as he halfheartedly declared, "I just want to say hi to *all my Test-icles*!" yet his trepidation gave way to excitement when he heard the audience's reaction. Stacy was on to something here. Goldust, on the other hand, tried dampening the duo's mood with a pair of Golden Globes for both her and Test. The official vetoed the Bizarre One's attempt at Stacy, though he wouldn't see the Diva go low on Goldust, ruining his Curtain Call and elevating Test to another victory.

While things were definitely looking up for Test, Randy Orton's fast track since moving from *Smack-Down!* to *Raw* was forced into some down time after he'd torn his right shoulder earlier in the month. Unfortunately, the swelling in his arm had extended to his head—two weeks after promising the Bell Centre fans in Montreal he'd return, "unlike Bret Hart" after *Survivor Series 1997*, Orton cut into the October 28 *Raw* broadcast with a special "RNN" news update. His "news" was to assure everyone he was still all right and on the mend, and to ask the fans—"especially the ladies out there"—to send their get well wishes to GetWell Randy@WWE.com. "With your support," he affirmed, "I know I'll be back in no time."

Christopher Nowinski, meanwhile, continued to hurt Al Snow with his behavior, which only reaffirmed that Al had made the right decision in choosing Maven over "a pompous, arrogant ass" like him to win the first *Tough Enough* competition. The Harvard grad asserted he'd be successful in the WWE regardless of *Tough Enough*'s existence, adding, "The fact that I *am* is a testament to *me*, and it has *nothing* to do with *you.*" Nowinski then invited Al to pick his next opponent and witness personally how he'd beat them, a challenge Snow answered that evening with Booker T, who called

[

"[Bring your] punk ass, Harvard ass out here so I can *kick* it, Motor City-style!"

]

for Nowinski to bring his "…punkass, Harvard ass out here so I can *kick* it, Motor City-style!" Al cringed at ringside while Nowinski took his lumps, never once planning to contribute some until the arrogant rookie rolled outside and sucker-punched him. The cheap shot riled Snow into the ring to pummel Nowinski, who picked up a DQ win over Booker as a result of outside interference.

The November 4 *Raw* didn't start out much better for Snow, despite making amends and partnering Tommy Dreamer in a Tag match against Lance Storm and William Regal. A melee had broken out involving all four wrestlers just before Dreamer's Death Valley Driver put Storm in Slumberland. Regal, seeing the official still preoccupied with ordering Snow back to his corner, seized the moment and delivered a vicious kick to the extreme Superstar's face. The Canadian

regained enough of his wits to cover Dreamer, giving himself and Regal another victory.

Nowinski was also disheartened later that night, seeing how Boston had gone "completely down the gutter" since he graduated Harvard. The town obviously needed degree-bearers like him. "Your combined brain power couldn't generate enough heat to melt Ted Williams' frozen corpse!" he mocked. He then directed his insults towards the ramp, where Snow made his way down. "Are you going to teach me a lesson? Why don't you just *ground* me… *'Dad'*? Or perhaps you'd like to do some *'grappling'*?

"Chris, I didn't come down here to 'grapple' you," Al replied, pointing behind Nowinski. "I think somebody else wants to do that." Turning around, Nowinski was horrified to see the first *Tough Enough* Champion, Maven, in the ring for the first time since breaking his fibula at May 30 *SmackDown!*. Maven put a resounding *Raw* beating on his one-time classmate before dropkicking him to the outside floor, where his mentor delivered shots worthy of the earlier-disparaged Sultan of Swat. Nowinski either started training for the Boston Marathon or demonstrated genuine intelligence, escaping through the crowd and beating feet out of the Fleet Center.

Nowinski may have turned the fans off, but the Test-icles were *surging*…according to the hordes of fan mail an ecstatic Stacy Keibler read backstage. Test wasn't feeling quite so elated; he was getting his hair cut short, a big step the Diva was certain would attract more Test-icles. The new 'do certainly didn't hurt as he entered the ring, nor did his ensuing match performance against The Hurricane, whom he left spinning with a front-twisting reverse neck-breaker. After Test picked up the one-two-three, Stacy's motivational liplock drove him to the mic and shout, "I *love* my Test-icles!" a proclamation the crowd wholeheartedly supported.

Equally as impressive was the *Raw* debut of David Batista, who renounced Reverend D-Von's ministry just prior to *SmackDown!*'s WWE Tag tournament last month. The six-foot-five, two-hundred-seventy-five-pound powerhouse was the classic "strong but silent" type, his intensity in the ring expressed itself with a crushing sit-down powerbomb for a speedy and decisive win over Justin Credible. Batista wouldn't have much to say when even former sixteen-time World Champion Ric Flair introduced himself backstage at November 11 *Raw,* though he had no problem silencing D'Lo Brown. He sent the veteran Superstar spinning almost 360 degrees with a clothesline off the ropes, then 'bombed him to the mat for another definitive three-count.

For a moment, the Cincinnati fans thought the book-carrying Christopher Nowinski had smartened up. He won their approval after telling them Pete Rose

Test slams Hurricane.

should be in the Baseball Hall of Fame, then laughed himself silly; the U.S. Bank Arena crowd deserved to be in the "Hall of Fame of *Stupidity*" for letting him manipulate them as easily as he was about to handle Al Snow in the ring. The Harvard alumnus stopped chuckling when Al came down and schooled him hard on the canvas, but he'd have the last laugh after rolling through a solid crossbody and using his feet on the ropes to pin Snow. In even poorer fashion, the spineless graduate literally started beating the Dickens out of Al with his book, until Maven ran in and made the save. But once again, the student had outsmarted his teacher.

Seeing how smart Test was to put himself in Stacy Keibler's hands, Steven Richards approached the Diva in the locker room and asked if she could do the same

for him. When Stacy turned him down, Richards asked her to motivate him with a Singapore cane before his Tag match against Hurricane and Goldust. He was unpleasantly surprised when his tag partner Test arrived and whaled his backside with the cane, though Stacy thought it looked like fun and bent over. What happened next was left to the imagination, since Randy Orton thought it more important to interrupt the broadcast with an important "RNN" update: the chafing problems caused by his arm sling had been resolved, and his sling was now fitted with padding. Richards probably would have liked some cushioning as he limped to the ring with Test, though he soon forgot about the pain after Test withstood the Eye of the Hurricane and finished him off with his spinning reverse neckbreaker. Steven put his hands all over a turned-off Stacy until Test dropped him with a big boot, then shouted into the mic, "Don't you *ever* touch one of my Test-icles!"

Few Superstars better established themselves as survivors in the WWE than Trish Stratus did in 2002. She'd enter this year's *Survivor Series* the same way she left 2001's Pay-Per-View; on top as the Women's Champion. But even though she defeated a fierce competitor in Victoria at *No Mercy,* Trish would quickly discover the Diva was every bit as persistent as her, and more than a little disturbed.

Victoria maintained that Trish was a close friend who dumped her when an opportunity in the WWE came knocking. Few people believed her, however; even *Goldust* considered her crazy! But the demented Diva didn't care what anyone thought; she fixated herself only on Trish, who successfully defended her Women's title with dual Stratusfaction Bulldogs to Molly Holly and Jacqueline in a *Raw* Triple-Threat match on October 28. Watching every moment of it from backstage, the stalker-like Victoria appeared on *Sunday Night Heat* the following week and openly challenged Trish for the Women's Championship at *Survivor Series*. Unlike their *No Mercy* affair, this contest would be fought under Hardcore rules, which favored the more power-ful and unstable challenger who promised, "I'm going to show you the true feeling of pain."

[**"I'm going to show you the true feeling of pain."**]

Hearing Trish had accepted her challenge thrilled the Diva to no end at November 4 *Raw*. She confided to Ivory, who came over from *SmackDown!* as part of the Big Show trade, that she'd take Trish's soul as well as her title, though the *Tough Enough* instructor cautioned there wouldn't be much left of Trish if things went her way in their non-title match that evening. It was no surprise to anyone that a ring veteran like Ivory could dominate early in the match, yet Victoria's actions bewildered everyone as she came out and joined Jim Ross and Jerry "the King" Lawler at the *Raw* commentary table. Even stranger was the fact that she'd say nothing throughout the match, which Trish eventually won with a modified Bulldog out of the corner. Unfortunately, the Women's Champ's usual good nature following a win disappeared when she noticed Victoria at the announcer's table. The two Divas quickly traded blows, with Victoria getting the better of the exchange when she rammed Trish into the *Raw* stage.

Minutes later, a hidden camera caught the outraged Victoria storming into a room backstage where Terri was getting a beverage. Terri made the unfortunate mistake of asking to interview Victoria after she got herself together, which the ultra-sensitive Diva took entirely the wrong way. "What's *that* supposed to mean? Am I not *pretty* enough for you, Terri?" The *Raw* inter-viewer's endeavor to appease Victoria only made things worse, until she lashed out and beat the hell out of Terri, tearing away at her clothes while doing so. If not for Randy Orton's special "RNN" update of a two percent improvement in his shoulder's mobility, the footage could very well have turned *Raw* literally.

Always looking out for his *Raw* Superstars' best interests, Eric Bischoff gave Terri a chance to get some pay-back on November 11, booking her in a one-on-one against Victoria. Frightened, Terri pleaded with Bischoff; she wasn't a wrestler, and a "psycho wack-job" like Victoria would rip her apart. Watching from Bischoff's office television, that outcome grew even more likely as Victoria entered the ring. Her face was twisted as she called for Terri to bring out the "pretty little eyes and pretty little puppies" that reminded her of the Women's Champion she planned to destroy at *Survivor Series*. "Since Trish and you have so many pretty little things in common," she yelled, "I'm going to start tonight by annihilating *you*, Terri!" Seeing how things were shaping up, the sadistic Bischoff offered Terri two choices: she could go to the ring and try to talk Victoria out of the match, or she could head home and tell her daughter Dakota that there would be no Christmas presents this year "because *Mommy got fired.*"

Between a rock and a hard-hitting Diva, the petite Terri cautiously entered the ring and told Victoria she was big enough to admit she was the better woman. Victoria allowed Terri a sigh of relief when she agreed to call off the match, then grabbed her arm and said, "That doesn't mean I won't rip your head off." She smashed Terri's face with the microphone, then tore the shirt off her back and began beating her mercilessly. Terri tried fending off the vicious attack, but neither she nor the intervening referee were a match for the powerhouse, who turned Hardcore and pulled a ladder out from under the ring. Trish Stratus raced down to make the save, smacking the ladder into Victoria's face and knocking her to the outside floor. But although it appeared Trish got some personal Stratusfaction in their physical exchange this time around, Victoria still couldn't help but smile; she was just six days away from proving herself as the dominant female, and the next Women's Champion.

In what could have been misconstrued as a sign of the Apocalypse, Eric Bischoff publicly gave Stephanie McMahon credit on October 21 *Raw*—*No Mercy*'s Hell in the Cell match between Brock Lesnar and Undertaker was "…a spectacle. No…it was a *bloodbath*." Not one to be out-promoted, however, the GM promised it would pale in comparison to the "ingenious creation" he had in mind for *Survivor Series*. With that, Bischoff's ever-smug look suddenly gave way to a cold, icy stare as he announced, "At *Survivor Series*, you *will* bear witness to the *Elimination Chamber*."

Having successfully defended the World Championship from Kane at *No Mercy* less than twenty-four hours before, a very confident Triple H opened that evening's *Raw* with two words for the fans, for the boys in the back, and for the writers that argued he didn't deserve to have the World title handed to him, "*Screw you!*" Having beaten all challengers since then, plus ending twenty-three years of Intercontinental title history in last night's "Winner Take All" match, Hunter not only found himself deserving to be the World Champion, "but I damn well might be the *greatest* World Champion of all time." He joked with Ric Flair that defeating Kane was like "one more nail in Katie Vick's coffin," and hoped the absent Big Red Machine "hasn't gotten into a car accident and *killed* somebody."

Triple H and Flair wouldn't blame Kane if he chose not to face them in his Tag match with Rob Van Dam,

especially since Hunter planned to show "graphic and salacious" videotape footage that would answer whether Kane had intercourse with his friend while still alive or dead. Neither Hunter nor the Nature Boy expected an attack from The Hurricane, who gained possession of the tape after surprising Triple H with a neckbreaker. The tandem quickly pounded Kane's ally to the outside floor and recovered the tape, with Triple H yelling it wouldn't matter what he or Kane did. "I'm going to show this videotape, and when I do, this issue with Kane is going to be just like Katie Vick—*dead!*"

Meanwhile, World Tag Champions Chris Jericho and Christian had reason to feel good about themselves after their *No Mercy* victory over Booker T and Goldust. Jericho felt he'd proved he wasn't a "sucka," and he wanted Women's Champion Trish Stratus to pass that message along to her intergender tag partners before their match. Also thinking his partner Victoria's allegations regarding Trish's promiscuity were true, Y2J

"[I'll give him] a dose of Vitamin *T*—straight up his punk ass like a largemouth bass!"

suggested the Women's Champ come to his dressing room afterwards for an injection of "Vitamin C." Just before the contest, the Book promised Terri he'd give the King of the World "a dose of Vitamin *T*—straight up his punk ass like a largemouth bass!" Throughout the match, Booker and his partners often exploited their opponents' deficiencies, until Jericho ultimately prescribed Trish his painful Liontamer maneuver, forcing the Diva to submit.

As Triple H prepared to air the videotape, he assured Jonathan Coachman that it would establish Kane was not only a murderer, but "some kind of sick freak." The footage depicted a sexual encounter in a funeral parlor between "Kane" (who was obviously The Game wearing a Kane mask) and a mannequin in a coffin that was supposed to be the late Katie Vick, with the grotesque punchline of the "Big Red Machine" slinging some slop to the floor afterwards and yelling, "Oh, my God...*I screwed your brains out!*" The segment had Hunter—and admittedly much of the crowd watching—in stitches, though the joke was lost on the real Kane, who arrived for the upcoming Tag match shortly beforehand. Terri tried entering Kane's locker room afterwards to have a word with her friend, but his emphatic slam of the door strongly indicated he had no wish to be disturbed.

Triple H could enjoy himself, but things were about to turn serious, beginning with Jim Ross and Jerry "the King" Lawler's satellite interview with Shawn Michaels. Hosting *Raw* from the World in Times Square that evening, a wheelchair-bound Heartbreak Kid reported his back still wasn't one hundred percent after Hunter's vicious sledgehammer shots at *SummerSlam.* He'd thought about giving up and letting his career stand on its own, but realized that his former best friend needed to be reminded, "Don't hunt what you can't kill." For a moment, Shawn struggled to lift himself out of his wheelchair, then got the World crowd jumping as he rose to his feet easily and put the Cerebral Assassin on notice. "HBK is coming back," he warned, "and somewhere down the line, HBK is gonna *get'cha!*"

Michaels would have to get in line; Kane had first dibs on Triple H, and collected during that evening's tag contest. Rob Van Dam would deliver the Five-Star Frog Splash on Ric Flair for the win, while the Big Red Machine picked the Cerebral Assassin apart backstage,

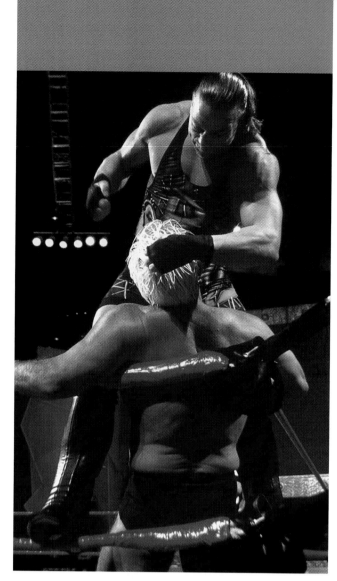

Van Dam traps Flair in the corner.

throwing him into a Pepsi machine before Chokeslamming him onto the hood of a car. With an assist from Hurricane, Kane trapped Hunter inside the car trunk and told him, "Now I'm going to screw *you.* The only question is . . .will you still be alive, or will I just wait until you're *dead*?!" Kane then entered the vehicle and drove out of the Gaylord Entertainment Center.

"Now I'm going to screw *you*. The only question is...will you still be alive, or will I just wait until you're *dead*?!"

Fans entering the Joe Louis Arena or just tuning into October 28 *Raw* might have wondered momentarily if Kane had carried out his threat when they saw a closed coffin on the arena floor. Even more of a surprise, however, was seeing The Game come out and explain his escape from the car trunk last week. "You should try to make sure the trunk doesn't have one of those child safety latches," he advised Kane, "where you can just pull it and *jump out* of the trunk before the person even drives off."

Hunter next agreed with the numerous complaints WWE had received regarding the footage he aired last week. "The things Kane did in that funeral parlor to that poor girl's dead body were absolutely disgusting, and quite frankly, sick." But there was really only *one* opinion that mattered on the subject, so The Game opened the coffin and asked fans to "give a warm welcome to a cold body"—a cheerleading-garbed mannequin he introduced as "Katie Vick." Like a third-rate ventriloquist, Hunter sat "dead-heavy" Katie on his lap and mouthed her memories of the experience. He joked how "Kane's chestnuts were roasting on an open fire a long time ago," then compared the Big Red Machine's "burnt little wiener" to his attempts to take the World title from him. "He just always seems to come up...a little bit *short.*" And for those who were seriously offended last week, he responded, "I seriously don't give a damn. If you didn't like it, you can *kiss my ass*! I will do *what* I want to do, *when* I want to do it!"

The Hurricane's entrance music cut into Hunter's rant; after what happened to the Cerebral Assassin last week, the hero wanted to know how he could be all smiles and giggles, asking, "*Whassup wit dat*?!" Though Hunter told the "comic book freak" nothing happened, Hurricane asked him to explain a tape he acquired from a local hospital last week—operating room footage of someone wearing Triple H cutout faces with varying expressions while "doctors" removed items from his posterior, including a sledgehammer, a long strand of handkerchiefs, a rubber hand, a squirrel, a gear shift, a steering wheel and a mannequin head of The Game himself! Cringing and holding his own backside as he watched the footage, Hunter didn't appreciate being the butt of the joke this time, and took his anger out on "Katie," smashing the dummy to pieces. Suddenly, the Big Red Machine's music sounded, and Kane made a

beeline to the ring, pounding away at Triple H until Eric Bischoff and a team of *Raw* officials broke up the fight. Since Kane and Hunter were so eager to beat the hell out of each other, Bischoff decided, "You're going to do it here tonight, in this ring...in a Casket match!"

A nervous Coach soon informed Kane backstage that Bischoff declared the Casket match a non-title event. The Big Freak'n Machine responded that the match wasn't about the World title, anyway. "This is about sealing Triple H in an airtight casket," he said. "What happened to Katie Vick was an accident, but what I do to Triple H tonight...that *won't* be." Triple H, meanwhile, later admitted to Coachman that he was scared; Kane became "highly aroused" the last time he was in a coffin, and the big red freak might develop "special feelings" for Hunter like he had with Katie Vick! "Kane, I am not your type," he mocked. "I am interested in purely *kicking* your ass, and nothing else." Coach also asked for a reaction regarding Shawn Michaels's comments last week, but The Game dismissed it as "a lot of hot air"; there was no way Michaels could be at one hundred percent after the sledgehammer shots he took at *SummerSlam*. As The Game adjourned to his dressing room, a hidden camera revealed he was more concerned about things than he let on. Speaking to Ric Flair over the phone, he was annoyed bad weather had prevented his mentor from getting to the arena, especially since he was in a Casket match with a man looking to bury him once and for all.

Hunter was about to receive even more bad news when Eric Bischoff addressed the *Raw* crowd about expecting to sign Scott Steiner. Eric described the show as "the place to be," especially since its General Manager continued to fire off "the most innovative ideas in the history of this business." He also took credit for being the brains behind the hidden cameras backstage, and if his Superstars didn't like it, "Well...that's why I like to call it '*F-View TV.*' " As for *Survivor Series*' Elimination Chamber match, Bischoff would only reveal that it was for the World Championship, and included elements of *Survivor*

Madison Square Garden
New York, NY

WORLD CHAMPIONSHIP ELIMINATION CHAMBER MATCH

Shawn Michaels defeated **Triple H** via pinfall to become the new World Heavyweight Champion

WWE TAG TEAM CHAMPIONSHIP TRIPLE THREAT ELIMINATION MATCH

Eddie & Chavo Guerrero defeated **Edge & Rey Mysterio** and **Kurt Angle & Chris Benoit** to become the new WWE Tag Team Champions

WWE CHAMPIONSHIP MATCH

Big Show defeated **Brock Lesnar** (w/**Paul Heyman**) via pinfall to become the new WWE Champion

WOMEN'S CHAMPIONSHIP HARDCORE RULES MATCH

Victoria defeated **Trish Stratus** via pinfall to become the new Women's Champion

CRUISERWEIGHT CHAMPIONSHIP MATCH

Billy Kidman defeated **Jamie Noble** (w/ **Nidia**) via pinfall to become the new Cruiserweight Champion

Booker T defeated **Matt Hardy** via pinfall

SIX-MAN TAG TEAM TABLES MATCH

Bubba Ray Dudley, Spike Dudley & Jeff Hardy defeated **3 Minute Warning & Rico**

Perhaps more than ever before in its sixteen-year history, this year's *Survivor Series* was precisely a matter of survival inside New York City's Madison Square Garden on November 17, in which a rabid sellout crowd of 17,930 witnessed an unprecedented five title changes, The Next Big Thing's first pinfall loss and a Showstopper reborn from the Elimination Chamber.

Jeff Hardy, Bubba Ray Dudley and Spike Dudley got the tables and raised the roof in an exciting Six-Man Tag match against 3 Minute Warning and Rico. Spike's Dudley Dog attempt on Rico resulted in Rosey and Jamal eliminating him with a face-first double powerbomb through a table. Jeff's daredevil antics shortly evened the sides with a Swanton Bomb onto Rosey from a second-floor entranceway. Slamming a table into Mr. Xtreme's skull as he came off the ring barrier, Jamal eliminated Jeff with a top-rope splash through some wood on the arena floor. Jamal went up top again, only to be powered through a table courtesy of a Bubbabomb. 3 Minute Warning stuck around and helped Rico work over Bubba, but neither they nor the MSG crowd expected the sudden arrival of D-Von Dudley! The reunited Dudley Boyz hit Rico with the 3-D through the table, giving them the victory!

Following Saliva's live performance of the *Survivor Series* theme song "Always" from the World, Cruiserweight Champion Jamie Noble tried to rebound from his recent non-title losses to Billy Kidman. Nidia rescued her redneck boyfriend from an early Shooting-Star Press, though Kidman vaulted himself onto Noble on the outside. Kidman battled his way back from the trailer trash champion's Tiger Bomb and DDT, then fought off both Nidia and Noble from up top and nailed the Shooting-Star Press, making him the new Cruiserweight Champion!

Backstage, Kurt Angle pointed out to Chris Benoit that if Billy Kidman could win the Cruiserweight title, then they should have no problem regaining the WWE Tag Team titles...provided Benoit didn't trip up the team's captain. The Rabid Wolverine snarled at the gold medalist's comment, but Kurt wasn't falling for it; they were "friends to the end." Benoit maintained his composure and extended his hand for his "buddy," but Kurt corrected him again; tag team partners *hug*, an act that weirded out the Crippler to no end.

The *Raw* F-View camera snuck a peek at Victoria's unique last-minute match preparations, which included arguing with her mirror over who was prettier, then trashing a cardboard cutout of Trish Stratus. But the demented Diva saved the rough stuff for the Hardcore rules contest against the Women's Champ, choking Trish with her own ring coat and a broomstick. Trish battled back, smacking Victoria with a garbage can before working her over with a Singapore cane. Yet Victoria proved as durable as she was dangerous; she withstood the Stratusfaction, then snap-suplexed Trish after spraying her face with a fire extinguisher to end her arch-enemy's title reign.

Backstage, Eric Bischoff told Jonathan Coachman that with the eagerly awaited Elimination Chamber, he'd not only outdone Stephanie McMahon, but himself as well, and once again he'd laid the groundwork for history in the making. Big Show approached the *Raw* GM and soured his mood, telling him he'd show just how big a mistake he made trading him by winning the WWE title. Thinking that might be the case was Brock Lesnar's agent, Paul Heyman, who voiced his concerns to the champion who was working despite a broken rib. He also promised he'd do everything humanly possible to ensure his client left *Survivor Series* as the WWE Champion.

Heyman would be true to his word soon after The Next Big Thing hooked up against Big Show. The two fought to a standstill, though Brock's back- and German suplexes on the five hundred-pound giant impressed even the staunchest of naysayers. The referee went flying out to the arena floor after a charging Lesnar missed his target, an opportunity Heyman used to throw in a steel chair. Brock battled his way out of a Chokeslam and caught the big man with the steel, then again displayed his awesome power with an F-5 to Big Show. A guaranteed victory was denied the champion, however, when Heyman interrupted the new referee's three-count! Lesnar chased after his traitorous agent, only to get nailed by several chair shots from Big Show. Chokeslamming Brock onto the steel chair and picking up the one-two-three, the giant stood taller than ever, with Heyman by his side and the WWE Championship belt over his shoulder.

Things didn't get any calmer when Edge and Rey Mysterio put their WWE Tag titles up against Los Guerreros and Angle and Benoit in a Three-Way Elimination match that offered all kinds of high-risk moves from each Superstar. As had been the case

since being forced to team together last October, the gold medalist and the Rabid Wolverine caused their own downfall. Benoit put Edge in the Crippler Crossface while Angle made Eddie scream from the ankle lock, but Chavo nailed Benoit with one of the Tag belts and tossed it to Kurt, who instinctively caught it. Rey took advantage of Benoit and Angle's ensuing argument, knocking Kurt out of the ring while Edge speared Benoit for the one-two-three. The tandem would continue their argument in the back, but only after putting a beating on the other match participants.

From there, Eddie and Chavo dominated over Edge until he made the tag to Mysterio, who went to town on the pair and hit Eddie with the 619. Once again Chavo relied on one of the Tag belts, this time nailing Mysterio and setting him up for his uncle's Lasso from El Paso. While Chavo kept Edge distracted, Eddie soon made Rey tap out to the painful submission move, giving Los Guerreros the WWE Tag Team titles.

An unscheduled interpromotional war of words next took place in the ring between *Raw*'s Christopher Nowinski and *SmackDown!*'s Matt Hardy. The Harvard grad insisted the "street smart" New York crowd was Number One in stupidity, while Version 1 contended they weren't stupid, just losers who were sucking the Mattitude right out of him. Nowinski and Matt debated until meeting halfway and calling New Yorkers "lupid," but by then it didn't matter; the MSG crowd hollered when they heard the music of the Genetic Freak—the WWE's new and highly sought-after free agent, Scott Steiner. The Big Bad Booty Daddy flexed the largest arms in the world as he slowly made his way to the ring, then decimated both Matt and Nowinski. After tossing the Harvard grad to

MSG witnesses the Elimination Chamber.

the outside, Steiner sent Matt promptly behind him, press-slamming Version 1 on top of Nowinski. Grabbing a mic, Steiner said, "This goes to all my freaks in New York City: Big Poppa Pump is your hookup! *Holla if you hear me!*"

While the Elimination Chamber was prepared at ringside, Terri asked Shawn Michaels backstage what made him think he'd win the World title. But the Showstopper's answer gave way to another "RNN Breaking News" report from Randy Orton, who just wanted to assure his fans he sustained no further damage to his injured arm while making the trip to *Survivor Series*. After the "big scoop," the Coach asked World Champion Triple H, accompanied by Ric Flair, for his thoughts on perhaps "the most inhumane, vile match in WWE history." The Game's response was direct: he'd beaten all challengers to the title given to him three months ago, and even though he was facing five of the best Superstars ever in the Elimination Chamber, "I will walk out of Madison Square Garden still the best, still The Game and *still* the World's Champion, because I am that damn good. But for right now, I've got a first-class ticket to hell, and I just want to know who's going with me."

It appeared the Cerebral Assassin would be in good company that night, as *Raw* General Manager Eric Bischoff introduced the audience to the intimidating structure that was the Elimination Chamber—over two miles of chain, wrapped around more than ten tons of solid steel. Two Superstars would start the contest inside the ring with the other four competitors isolated within individual bulletproof-tough plexiglass chambers, one of which would be randomly unlocked every five minutes. Victory could be achieved either via pinfall or submission, until only one Superstar emerged as the sole victor.

Triple H and Rob Van Dam kicked off the match while Chris Jericho, Booker T, Kane and Shawn Michaels were placed inside their oppressive chambers. Van Dam quickly busted The Game open by ramming him into the steel surroundings repeatedly, then used the steel outside floor (which was level with the ring floor) for the Rolling Thunder. But as Mr. Pay-Per-View went up top onto Jericho's chamber, Y2J pulled his legs through the steel mesh, holding them while Triple H pounded away at Van Dam. RVD recovered and flipped onto Hunter on the steel outside floor, regaining the advantage as Jericho's chamber opened. Van Dam landed a moonsault and crossbody from the cage wall on the King of the World, but a double-team effort soon found him slammed into the steel several times.

Next in was Booker T, whose housecleaning of Triple H and Y2J sent him into a Spin-a-Roonie before exchanging blows with RVD. With Booker and Jericho knocked

to the outside floor, Van Dam climbed above the ropes and on top of Jericho's empty chamber, then blew the crowd away with an astonishing Five-Star Frog Splash onto Triple H! The high-risk move proved detrimental to both men—Van Dam's knee went straight across The Game's throat, making even breathing difficult, while Van Dam's banged-up knee made it impossible for him to avoid Booker T's top-rope missile dropkick, resulting in a pinfall and eliminating him. The next chamber unlocked, and Jericho quickly felt the Big Red Machine's presence, especially when Kane threw him right through a plexiglass chamber wall! Miraculously, the crimson-faced Y2J recovered and capitalized on a freshly Chokeslammed Booker T, hitting the Lionsault to get the one-two-three.

Shawn Michaels was raring to go as the final chamber unlocked, and took the fight right to Y2J and the Big Red Machine. Kane then Chokeslammed his opponents before attempting to finish off a clearly injured Triple H with a piledriver. The Cerebral Assassin somehow countered and directed Kane straight into Michaels's Sweet Chin Music, while another Jericho Lionsault gave him his second three-count of the match. Triple H and Jericho joined forces against Michaels, making him a bloody mess but unable to end the Heartbreak Kid's comeback story. Hitting a moonsault on Y2J, Michaels next put his own Walls of Jericho on him, until The Game broke it up with a vicious DDT. Hunter then went for a Pedigree on Y2J, who countered with the Walls of Jericho, only to leave himself wide open to HBK's Sweet Chin Music. The superkick put Jericho down and out, leaving only Michaels and Triple H as the last survivors.

The World Champion went to work on the Showstopper's surgically repaired back, but couldn't finish him off with a spinebuster. The two battled their way out to the steel floor, where Triple H countered Michaels' attempted Pedigree and launched him straight through a plexiglass chamber wall, which shattered on impact. Shawn refused to be covered, however, and soon battled back with an elbow from the top of his own chamber. Amazingly, the Cerebral Assassin still had the wits to counter Michaels's superkick and hit the Pedigree, but again was denied victory when Shawn kicked out at two. Triple H went for another Pedigree, but HBK back-bodydropped him and connected with the Sweet Chin Music to get the three-count. The jubilant fans inside Madison Square Garden erupted as confetti and streamers dropped from everywhere. The Showstopper Shawn Michaels had completed his phenomenal comeback story in one of the grizzliest, most brutal matches ever seen, and became the new World Champion! ∎

Series, Royal Rumble and his all-time personal favorite, the defunct *WCW War Games.* And the participants would include Triple H, Chris Jericho, Booker T, Rob Van Dam, Kane…and *Shawn Michaels.* Eric explained that Michaels had one week to decide if he wanted to exact revenge against the World Champion "…on *my* terms, *not* yours. None of this sneaking-around, surprise-attack crap. All you have to do is show up in the Elimination Chamber, and I'm going to give you a shot at Triple H and the World title, all in one night."

For the moment, Triple H was concerned more for his well-being than his Championship belt when he locked up with Kane in the non-title Casket match. The two struggled early to place each other in the funerary box outside the ring, with referees standing by to close the lid and signal the end of the match. At one point The Game rolled the Big Red Machine all the way in, until Kane came back to life (so to speak) and grabbed Hunter by the throat to fight his way out. It appeared there was no putting Kane to rest until the Cerebral Assassin nailed him with a low blow and steel chair. But as Hunter motioned for the officials to open the lid, Shawn Michaels emerged from the casket, assaulting Hunter with a flurry of rights and a forearm off the ropes. HBK then tuned up the band and nailed The Game with his Sweet Chin Music, while a revived Kane rolled his adversary into the coffin once and for all. As Kane left the ring victorious, the Showstopper celebrated with the crowd, dancing on top of what might soon represent the final resting place for Triple H's career.

Perhaps Triple H remembered not having the greatest of luck at previous *Survivor Series.* He orchestrated a hit-and-run to knock Stone Cold Steve Austin out of a Triple-Threat match for the WWE Championship in 1999, only to lose to his replacement, the Big Show. A year later, the returning Texas Rattlesnake almost ended The Game when he forklifted a car with him

inside, then demolished the vehicle by letting it freefall several stories to the ground. Perhaps he also remembered the most controversial decision in sports entertainment history, when Shawn Michaels allegedly "screwed" Bret

Triple H tries to close the coffin on Kane.

"Hitman" Hart out of the WWE title at the 1997 PPV. Regardless, The Game, accompanied by Ric Flair, addressed his concerns at the November 4 *Raw* with Eric Bischoff, a man with whom he also had problems.

"Ever since Vince McMahon froze these rosters on *Raw* and *SmackDown!,* Eric, you've been treating me like a piece of crap," Hunter said, citing as evidence last week's Casket match, "F-View TV" in his locker room, being booked with Chris Jericho for a contest against Kane and Booker T while Michaels lurked

[
"I put on a mask to dress up like Kane and screw a mannequin. *You* put on a mask to look like Vince McMahon and make out with my ex-wife. Who's screwing *who*?"
]

around the Fleet Center that evening, and facing five other Superstars in a *Survivor Series* match without even knowing what an Elimination Chamber was. Eric told him to think, "You're Triple H. You're *The Game*. You deserve to be a part of history." Winning that match would not only prove to the world Hunter was "that damn good," he could also avenge his *SummerSlam* loss should Michaels accept the match. "I've been doing a lot of thinking, Eric," Triple H replied. "Either you're screwing me...or maybe somebody's influencing you." With that, Flair played a videotape with footage of Bischoff kissing Stephanie at the *SmackDown!* Halloween party. Eric looked completely busted as The Game reviewed. "*I* put on a mask to dress up like Kane and screw a mannequin. *You* put on a mask to look like Vince McMahon and make out with my ex-wife. Who's screwing *who*?"

Shortly following his tête-a-tête with Bischoff, the Cerebral Assassin called HBK out to the ring; he wanted to see if he could "make lightning strike twice in the same place," referring to Michaels's then last match in Boston at *WrestleMania XIV*. When Shawn didn't come out, Hunter warned him not to accept the *Survivor Series* match, for if he did step in the ring that night, there would be no next time. The fact was, The Game would walk out of *Survivor Series* the same way he'd enter: as the World Champion. "And there's not a damn thing that you or anybody else can do about it!" he promised.

Booker T came out on stage to take issue with Triple H's claim, though Hunter told him he couldn't even hold his jock. The Book saw things differently, stating as he entered the ring, "You think you run this show, right? Well, you *don't* run Booker T! At *Survivor Series*, Elimination Chamber match, I'm gonna be thinking of one thing and one thing only: *Don't hate the playa, hate The Game!* Now can you dig that, *suckaaaaaa!*"

The tension grew as Chris Jericho started walking down the *Raw* ramp, not the least bit concerned whether

his entrance music upset Booker for interrupting him. "I'm sick of hearing you say 'sucka,'" he yelled, "and I'm sick and tired of you calling *me* a 'sucka,' because Chris Jericho is *not* a sucka!" Y2J guaranteed to prove it at *Survivor Series*, when he'd not only beat Triple H for the World Championship, but eliminate Booker from the Elimination Chamber himself. And although he and Hunter didn't like each other, they were tag partners for their match later that evening. "And the way *I* see it," he told Booker, "*you're* the sucka now... *sucka!* Because right now, Booker T, the 'T' stands for *'trapped'!*" Triple H jumped Booker from behind, with Jericho quickly joining The Game in putting the boots to him. But their attack was cut short when the fire of Kane suddenly exploded, and the Big Red Machine stormed the ring, scaring off his own tag partner's assailants.

Backstage, Jericho enjoyed the latest "WWE Desire" video, one that spotlighted him to the tune of Saliva's "King of My World." He also loved Christian's idea to beat Rob Van Dam so badly in their upcoming singles bout that Eric Bischoff would have to replace "Mr. Monday Night" with *him* at the Elimination Chamber match. Unfortunately for Y2J, Christian hadn't really planned on being his *ally* inside the chamber; he wanted the chance to become World Champion as

> **"Don't hate the playa, hate The Game!
> Now can you dig that, *suckaaaaaa!*"**

well! An F-View TV camera caught the disgruntled Jericho exiting the room and running into Triple H and Flair, who warned Shawn Michaels might try to interfere in their match. Jericho didn't seem worried about the "Has-Been Kid," especially since the Nature Boy assured he'd deal with him, though none of them noticed that Shawn was hanging by a nearby doorway listening to every word.

Christian would have to come up with another plan if he wanted to involve himself in the *Raw* main event at *Survivor Series*. Despite working over Van Dam's legs on the outside and coming up with several near-falls, he'd eventually fall victim to a Five-Star Frog Splash for the loss. Meanwhile, in the back, Goldust almost became a casualty after trying to help Kane "get his freak on" for his Tag match. Reminding the Big Red Machine they were partners for the match, Booker needed Kane not to let Triple H get to him; besides, he asked, who in their right mind would have sex with a dead body? Goldust slowly raised his arm and answered, "What? I was young and stupid. Gimme a break." Booker got back to his point—"I need you focused. Can you dig that?" Kane replied, "Yeah. I can dig that," and left, only to return moments later and shout, "*Suckaaaa!*"

Both the Big Freak'n Machine and the Book came out to the ring focused for their match, with Booker delivering a Spin-a-Roonie and twin clotheslines on Jericho and Triple H. His scissors kick soon clipped The Game for a two-count, while Kane saved his partner with the top-rope clothesline to break the Walls of Jericho. But when the referee went down to the outside floor, Shawn Michaels charged the ring and nailed Hunter with the Sweet Chin Music, then rolled the referee back in so that Booker could collect the three-count. Before leaving the *Raw* stage, Shawn remembered he had a question to answer for Eric Bischoff: "Let's see… HBK. *Survivor Series*. First-ever Elimination Chamber match. Main event. Madison Square Garden. For the World Championship. My goodness…well, the answer is…*yes!*"

The fans cheered as the Showstopper had one last thing to say to The Game, who was still on his knees inside the ring: "Triple H, I can assure you, I'm walking out of that chamber match the *new World Champion!*"

With just six days remaining before *Survivor Series*, tempers ran hotter than the opening pyro effects that kicked off November 11 *Raw*. Although Rob Van Dam and Kane would oppose each other in the Elimination Chamber match, they planned to do so as the new World Tag Team Champions. But current title holders Jericho and Christian weren't so quick to part with their belts; after Kane delivered a massive chokeslam on Christian, Jericho went unnoticed by the referee as he smashed the Big Red Machine with one of the Championship belts. Van Dam quickly dispensed Y2J to the outside with his educated feet, then went up top and hit the Five-Star Frog Splash on Christian. Jericho re-entered the ring in time, breaking up a certain three-count with numerous chair shots that floored both challengers. Kane and RVD won the match via DQ, yet Jericho and Christian remained the Champions.

Jericho's explanation for the chair attack was twofold. "I'm single-handedly softening up every single ass-clown who's in the Elimination Chamber with me!" he yelled. "No one is winning that match but me!" As Y2J moved on, Christian told Terri what he thought was the best news: "If someone can't make it to the Elimination Chamber, Eric Bischoff told me *I'll* get their spot! Me! I don't care if I have to beat my own tag team partner…I'll do anything!" Christian suddenly went down as Jericho blindsided him and beat him to the ground. Looking down at his fallen partner, he emphasized his earlier statement. "*No one* is winning that match but *me!*"

Believe it or not, Shawn Michaels later told the Cincinnati audience he had no problem with Y2J coming away with the World title. He was also fine with the notion of RVD, Booker T or Kane having the honor of wearing the belt. Michaels just didn't want *Triple H* leaving *Survivor Series* as World Champion. For that matter, he certainly wasn't counting himself out. He may not know what an Elimination Chamber match was, but HBK didn't know what a Ladder match, a Hell in the Cell match or a Marathon match was when he became the first WWE Superstar to compete in each of those contests.

"How tough can it be?" Michaels joked with the fans. "It's only been four years. It was only a career-ending back injury. It was only partial paralysis. I mean, what's to keep *me* from becoming the new World Champion?" Citing the word of God as saying all things are possible to those who believe, Michaels added, "Quite honestly, I believe that [at *Survivor Series*], the new World Champion will be *me*." Triple H suddenly came out on stage and disputed Shawn's belief. "Let me tell you this," he said, heading down the ramp, "In this arena...*I'm* God. And *I* believe I'm going to come to that ring and *kick your ass*."

No surprise attacks nor foreign objects came into play as Hunter went toe-to-toe with Michaels; The Game simply caught Shawn with a brutal clothesline, then planted him to the mat with the Pedigree. The Cerebral Assassin went under the ring and produced his trademark sledgehammer to finish the Heartbreak Kid off once and for all, until a slew of WWE officials raced down and stopped him from committing what would most definitely have been the end of Shawn's career. Nevertheless, he felt he'd driven home his point—that no power in heaven nor on Earth could help Shawn Michaels at *Survivor Series*.

Shortly after Michaels' assault, Eric Bischoff came out on stage and decided now was as good a time to inform everyone about the Elimination Chamber, a ten-ton "steel hell" of structural grade steel, consisting of two miles of chain and measuring thirty-six feet in diameter and sixteen feet from the roof to the floor. Upon airing promo footage of the chamber itself, Bischoff went over the rules of the match. "Two men will be chosen at random to start the match," he explained. "The other four, locked in individual chambers. Every five minutes, one of those chambers will be opened *at random*, and that Superstar will enter the match. Once defeated, that man is eliminated, and the match will continue until there is one...*one* sole survivor. That man will become the World Champion, and once

"In this arena...*I'm* God. And *I* believe I'm going to come to that ring and *kick your ass*."

again, Eric Bischoff will prove that he is *the* most dynamic force in sports entertainment today!"

Moments before heading ringside for a non-title match against Triple H, Booker T caught up with The Game backstage to let him know his chances of walking out of the Elimination Chamber in six days, "slim and none. And slim just left the damn building." Booker didn't think winning the match mattered to him as much as it did to the Cerebral Assassin, who'd have more than the five-time WCW Champion to worry about. "You've got five guys, five guys, five guys, five guys, *five guys* whooping your punk ass!" he yelled. Ric Flair cautiously held back Triple H, who told Booker he'd beat those opponents one by one, "until it comes down to just *you* and *me*. Now can you dig *that*?"

The comments only seemed to fire both men up more as they locked up in the ring. Momentum shifted several times throughout the match until Booker caught Hunter with a scissors kick, then brought the interfering Flair in the hard way by throwing him off the top rope. A low blow shut the Book's offense down long enough for the Cerebral Assassin to hit the Pedigree and score the pinfall, but no sooner had the referee's hand slammed on the canvas a third time when Shawn Michaels charged the ring. The Heartbreak Kid pounded away on pretty much anything that moved, though he was soon overpowered after Chris Jericho joined Triple H and Flair in the attack.

With Rob Van Dam and Kane entering the fray moments later, all six Elimination Chamber combatants were in the ring, and any alliances that might have existed quickly disintegrated. RVD Five-Starred Triple H, only to get scissors kicked by Booker T. Y2J felt the Chokeslam from Kane, who in turn fell to HBK's Sweet Chin Music. Triple H tried to Pedigree his former best friend, but Michaels reversed it into finishing The Game with his own move. Yet any victory Shawn might have felt became fleeting when Jericho scrambled his brains with a steel chair. As fallen bodies littered the ring area, the King of the World stood above them all as the sole survivor. And if things went his way, the result would be exactly the same at *Survivor Series.*

The following night, the *Raw* portion of *Super Tuesday* offered an intense Ten-Man Tag match in which Triple H, Chris Jericho, Christian and 3 Minute Warning went up against Booker T, Bubba Ray Dudley, Jeff Hardy, Kane and Rob Van Dam. Virtually all ten participants hit their finishing moves during the match, with RVD and the Big Red Machine dominating

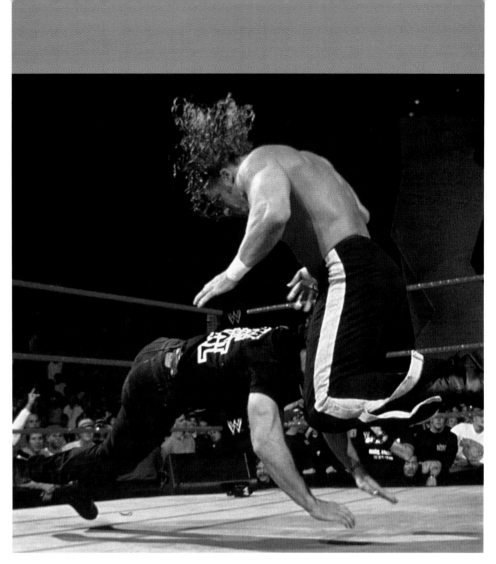

Triple H drives Shawn Michaels to the mat.

the ring late in the game. Kane hit Chokeslams on Jamal and Triple H, while Van Dam rode the Five-Star on Jamal, then deflected Jericho's attempted chair shot by kicking the steel back in his face. But as Kane came off the ropes to follow up Van Dam's plancha to the outside floor, Ric Flair caught the big man with a chair to the back, dazing him long enough for The Game to hit the Pedigree for the victory.

As exciting as a contest of that magnitude was, the overall feeling was that it would easily give way to Sunday's Elimination Chamber match, which Shawn Michaels, from his home in San Antonio, Texas, described to Jim Ross and Jerry Lawler as "wild, crazy, chaotic," especially since it was every man for himself fighting for the World title. Shawn's game plan, however, wouldn't be complicated. "Triple H bases every ounce

of his being, his reason for existence, on being the World Champion," he explained. "After everything Triple H has put me and my family through the last couple of months, I figure the least I can do is ruin *his* life. It's not nice. It's not moral. But that's my goal. Take that Championship title from around his waist, you take away his reason for living." And if by some miracle HBK were to walk out of *Survivor Series* as World Champion, Shawn Michaels guaranteed, "You better believe there's gonna be a *new* sheriff in town."

12

The End

The end was near. The end of 2002. The end of another unbelievable year in World Wrestling Entertainment. The end of several championship reigns. And come *Armageddon*, the end of several championship reigns.

Raw General Manager Eric Bischoff wasn't expecting the end to start in the parking lot of Bridgeport's HarborYard Arena November 18. He envisioned a beginning with impending guest Scott Steiner, over whom he waged a signing war with *SmackDown!*'s Stephanie McMahon. But a warm welcome for the limousine that pulled in cooled off when Ric Flair emerged from it with bad news: Triple H was a probable no-show. Eric didn't want to hear about some severe trachea injury The Game suffered during the Elimination Chamber match at *Survivor Series*. "All I do care about is *Eric Bischoff*, and what you, Triple H and everybody else can do for *Raw*," Bischoff said, which included putting the Nature Boy in a match against Kane. Flair wasn't worried about Kane; he suggested that his boss had a bigger concern: "You should be worried that *Raw* will be minus Triple H tonight. Let's see you produce *Raw* without The Game."

Twenty-four hours after one of the most brutal contests in WWE history, new World Champion Shawn Michaels had one question for the "HBK" supporters in Connecticut: "Where do we go from here?" It was a fact his body could no longer handle the strain of weekly *Raw* competition, and relinquishing the belt would be the sensible move, however, "I figure we'll see how much more this ol' body has got left in him. And I say that this belt is staying *right here*, in the possession of yours truly."

With that, fellow Elimination Chamber survivor Rob Van Dam came out to shake Michaels's hand. As someone who found HBK "quite inspiring...as a *kid*," RVD was glad "a *fighting* Champion" had won the title. He also had an idea: "How about for your first title defense, the Showstopper goes one-on-one with The Whole Dam Show?" Before Michaels could accept, Eric Bischoff interrupted. He reminded Shawn who called the shots on *Raw*, and declared Van Dam would have to earn his No. 1 Contender spot in a No-Disqualification Triple-Threat match against Chris Jericho and Booker T with the winner facing Michaels next week. He also concurred with RVD. "You *will* be a fighting champion," he told Shawn, "because you're a *Raw* champion. You're *my* champion."

Hearing rumors the Cerebral Assassin might arrive in the HarborYard parking lot any moment, Bischoff expected Triple H to rush out of the approaching limo and *beg* to be included in the three-way dance. When Scott Steiner exited the vehicle instead, the GM shifted into immediate suck-up mode; the sky was the limit for Big Poppa Pump, provided he signed on the *Raw* dotted line. Steiner would save his words for the ring, telling everyone he'd been busy with the two things he cared about most, "my *freaks,* and my *peaks,*" before signing with the WWE. But when the Big Bad Booty Daddy wasn't helping women nationwide "find Nirvana" on the mountaintop, he was watching *Raw* and *SmackDown!* wrestlers call themselves huge stars, which "made me want to *puke!*" Regardless of which brand he'd join, Steiner put everyone on notice: "I'm not here to make friends, and I'm gonna prove that *nothing* and *nobody* can compare to the power of the Genetic Freak!"

Interrupting him from the *Raw* stage, Chris Jericho wanted Big Poppa Pump to realize his so-called largest arms in the world were no match against a "gorgeous piece of meat" like the "larger-than-life *King* of the World." Besides, when Y2J beat HBK—"the *Has-Been* Kid!"—for the World title next week, he'd have bigger things to worry about "than a jive-talking moron who dresses like he thinks he's King Arthur!" Jericho declined the chainmail-coifed Superstar's invitation to a medieval ass-kicking in the ring so he could prepare for his Triple-Threat match, for which Steiner warned he might stick around and see if the "little man" was as good as he believed. "My freaks here in Bridgeport know who's the best. So this goes to all my freaks out there—Big Poppa Pump is your hookup! *Holla if you hear me!*"

Backstage, Eric Bischoff was cut down by the newest *Raw* member Val Venis. "Don't you *ever* call me that again," Val admonished, then apologized to his new employer. He preferred to go by his real name, Sean Morley, and considered himself a changed man, with a new job and new responsibilities. The locker-room F-View TV camera showed Jericho, still apologizing to Christian over last week's steel chair attack. He'd been caught up in the Elimination Chamber match then, but with Michaels, Steiner and possibly Triple H hanging around the arena now, Y2J needed his partner's help to win the Triple-Threat match and become No. 1 Contender. "Maybe you should have thought about that *last* week," Christian responded, then stormed off.

Booker T gets Jericho's respect.

Booker T was also upset as he came out for the main event. Everyone was talking about Triple H, HBK, Y2J and RVD, yet there was *no* mention of the five-time WCW Champion, who guaranteed victory. Booker's chances looked good until late in the match, when Christian nailed him with a steel chair to save his partner. But as Y2J went for the Walls of Jericho, Big Poppa Pump steamrolled his way to the ring, demolishing Christian with a press-slam before nearly powerbombing Jericho through the canvas. With Y2J down and out, Van Dam climbed up top and rode the Five-Star Frog Splash for the one-two-three!

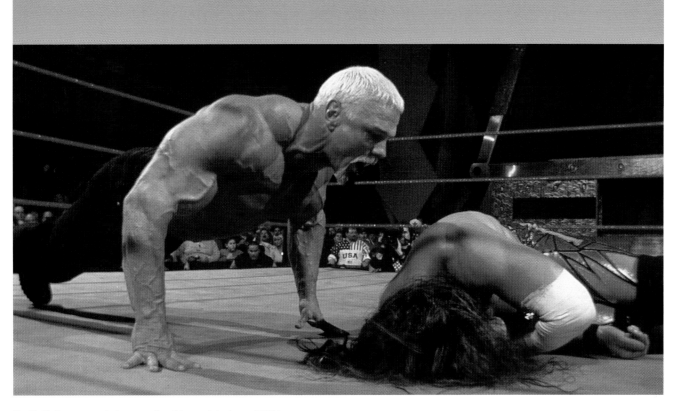

Scott Steiner proves he's as good as his word, laying out Y2J.

Sheer *Raw* excitement had built up within the North Charleston Coliseum on November 25, seven days after Shawn Michaels personally congratulated Rob Van Dam for earning the No. 1 Contendership. The South Carolina fans in attendance had plenty to be thankful for, and not just because it was Thanksgiving week. Michaels' first *Raw* match in nearly five years was a title defense against a challenger whose style mirrored a young HBK in his prime. Shawn himself made the comparison to RVD backstage before their match, yet noticed he lacked "*one* very important thing." Humoring the World Champion to "enlighten" him, RVD's illumination came as a hard slap across the face. Furious, Van Dam returned the strike to Michaels, who only smiled. "*Now* you're speakin' my language, kid," Shawn said, and left the room.

If Michaels wanted to light a fire under Van Dam's educated feet for their contest, he succeeded. Mr. Monday Night's moonsault to the outside floor demonstrated the same reckless abandon that made Michaels famous. Meanwhile, the former Showstopper had become a *smarter* wrestler, wearing down Van Dam's left knee to keep him grounded. But The Whole Dam Show was a quick study—surviving Michaels's elbow off the top rope, he exploited the champion's primary weakness with a Rolling Thunder and Five-Star Frog Splash to his lower back. Van Dam covered for an almost-certain three-count when Triple H suddenly pulled him to the outside floor and gave him the Pedigree! Entering the ring with something far worse in mind than drawing a DQ for HBK, the Cerebral Assassin unfolded a chair and used it for a shattering backbreaker onto Michaels's surgically repaired spine! The Game was on again!

Having taken care of HBK, Triple H confronted another problem backstage when *Raw* rolled into the Frank Erwin Center in Austin, Texas, on December 2. It was Eric Bischoff's Elimination Chamber that cost Hunter his title and nearly his career, so being forced into a No. 1 Contender's match with Rob Van Dam that evening was "a damn insult" on top of his injuries. Pointing out who handed the belt to Hunter in the first place, Bischoff argued that if he wanted the title he'd have to deliver "great TV" in the main event against RVD for the right to face Shawn Michaels at *Armageddon.* Seething, Triple H promised more than great TV—"I'll give you a *friggin' train wreck!*"

Shawn Michaels confessed to Terri how much he needed to get his hands on Triple H after last week's assault. Van Dam empathized with HBK, but it didn't change the fact that without Triple H's help, "I had you beat." Barging into their conversation, Eric Bischoff saw Shawn was in a tight spot, trapped between one man who almost destroyed his career, and another who nearly ended his title reign. Therefore, he decided to make the No. 1 Contender's match "all the more interesting...with Shawn Michaels as the *special guest referee!*" And should Michaels abuse his position to unjustly determine his opponent at *Armageddon,* Bischoff promised, "I will *strip* you of the title, right in the middle of the ring."

Minutes before the match, Triple H warned the guest referee that last week's chair shot was just the beginning. "You've got something I want. Something that belongs to *me,*" he explained, and Hunter was taking it back at *Armageddon.* HBK didn't flinch; having already beaten The Game at *SummerSlam* and *Survivor Series,* he realized "...that as long as I'm wearing that championship

around my waist, it's *your* life that'll remain a living hell." He also offered his own warning: Triple H wouldn't have to submit, or even be pinned in the upcoming bout. "All you have to do is cross the referee, just *one* time," he stated, "and you get disqualified. And then it's 'Game Over.'"

While it wasn't the nWo attire he'd worn earlier in the year, the black and white on his officiating shirt made HBK a tough SOB in the ring. Besides making deliberately slow counts on several pinfall attempts by Triple H, Michaels's positioning kept The Game from finding sanctuary in the ropes to escape Van Dam's sleeper hold. Yet Shawn's officiating ultimately backfired when he stopped Triple H from using a steel chair on Van Dam, whose educated foot missed its target and caught Michaels instead. The Cerebral Assassin took advantage of the miscue, landing a chair shot that put RVD out for a very reluctant three-count by the revived referee. Forced to raise Triple H's hand in victory, Michaels hesitantly obliged...then followed with rights and

Triple H finds the "impartial official" seems to be helping his opponent.

lefts before laying him out with the Sweet Chin Music. Poised over the sprawled-out No. 1 Contender to his title, the World Champion's superkick sent a hard message: *Armageddon* was Triple H's third strike, and this time Michaels would make certain *he* was *out*.

Accompanied to the ring by new Chief of Staff Sean Morley, Eric Bischoff opened December 9 *Raw* at the University of Tennessee by addressing his *Armageddon* main-eventers on the TitanTron. Since no regular match could encapsulate Sean Michaels and Triple H's history together, Bischoff announced their World title match was now two out of three falls! "The first fall," he explained, "just like your match at *SummerSlam*, is going to be a Street Fight." That made The Game smile, particularly when "Chief Morley" added, "The second fall, just like your match at *Survivor Series*, will take place inside a steel cage." And if it went to a third fall, the GM informed the pair, "You're going to have a chance to compete in a match that Shawn Michaels made famous—a *Ladder match*." The smile on Triple H's face suddenly looked like it fell off a ladder as Bischoff concluded, "This issue between you two *is* coming to an end at *Armageddon*. And with *Armageddon* less than a week a way…Shawn, Hunter…*the end is near*."

Superstars like Jeff Hardy might have believed Michaels already met his end when he retired four

"I'll give you a *friggin' train wreck!*"

years ago. Jeff told Terri he felt honored that Triple H challenged him to a match because his high-risk style resembled the Heartbreak Kid of years past. "HBK was *untouchable*," he remembered, "and if I could capture a little bit of that tonight, I'm good to go." The comment struck a nerve in the "untouchable" Michaels, who pointed out, "You're talking about the Heartbreak Kid as if Shawn Michaels were *dead. Nothing* could be further from the truth." Shawn provided Jeff with advice on how to beat Triple H, while the daredevil offered his services should Michaels want any counseling for the Ladder match portion of his *Armageddon* contest, prompting a strained grin on the face of the insulted innovator of Ladder matches.

Jeff wouldn't get much of an opportunity to utilize Shawn's wisdom. He was barely in the ring when the Cerebral Assassin struck, relentlessly beating the Xtreme Superstar down as if he were HBK and held the World title in his hands. Decisively ending the match with a pair of Pedigrees, The Game took hold of a steel chair while Ric Flair kicked away at Jeff on the outside floor, until the crowd's cheers suddenly focused their attention towards the *Raw* stage, where the World Champion now stood.

The Nature Boy invited Michaels to the ring, where he related to him his days as WCW Champion, and the moment a fan told him he was no longer "The Man." He recalled that title had become so synonymous with a young Showstopper, "that I had to go home one day, and I had to look in the mirror and say, 'Nature Boy, you've had the ride of a lifetime…but you're not The Man anymore. *Shawn Michaels* is.' " No longer seeing the heart or head of a "Showstopper," Flair urged Michaels to find his own mirror and admit it to himself, then "pass the torch" at *Armageddon* to "*The* Man," Triple H. "If you don't," he warned, "he'll *kill* you, taking the most coveted trophy in our life from you."

Shawn Michaels's silence hushed the "HBK" chorus in Knoxville, as he simply exited the ring and returned up the ramp. That didn't mean *a* response wasn't forthcoming backstage, when Shawn gave Flair a message for his protégé. "The *Heartbreak Kid*, and his heart, will be in the parking lot, waiting on him." The duo showed up ready to fight, but when they saw only a dumpster, a WWE equipment truck and some garbage men, Hunter told Flair he knew Michaels wouldn't have the heart to face them. He was right; it was the *Showstopper* who smacked him with a shovel, then laid out Flair with the Sweet Chin Music! Michaels asked if he had enough heart while he tossed The Game in the dumpster, then took notice of a ladder braced against the parked eighteen-wheeler. Climbing to the top of the semi, HBK paused as he stood over his target below… then leaped off the edge, plummeting down into the dumpster! Debris flew upwards from the impact, followed by several long moments of stillness before Michaels slowly made his way out.

"How *dare* you mistake my humility for *weakness*?!" Michaels yelled at an unconscious Triple H amid the waste and rubbage. "Come Sunday night at *Armageddon*, Hunter, you're going to find out that the Heartbreak Kid is *alive* and *well*! You're going to see the *Showstopper*, and I'm going to prove, once and for all, that *I* am The Man! And you want to know why?

Because I *can*. Oh, yeah…I *still can*. Triple H, at *Armageddon*, the end is *indeed* near!"

The paths of several tag teams were converging in a Fatal Four-Way, a sure sign *Armageddon* was upon them. One reunited tandem sought to re-establish their legendary dominance. Another duo that hadn't been paired together all that long used a consecutive string of victories as stepping stones to the top. A third team threatened to buckle under the weight of self-doubt. And they all wanted to adorn the World Tag Team gold currently held by a nine-time Co-Tag Champion and the King of the World.

As one of the Superstars traded from *SmackDown!* to *Raw* in exchange for Big Show (the others officially being Ivory, Maven and Chief Morley), D-Von Dudley made a triumphant return to his tag team roots at *Survivor Series*. For the first time in over a year, all three Dudley Boyz partnered together for a *Raw* Six-Man Tag match against 3 Minute Warning and Rico on November 18. D-Von and Bubba Ray helped Spike take care of Jamal and Rosey, then acquainted Rico's groin with a signature "Wassup?!" headbutt off the top rope. Planting Rico to the canvas with a resounding 3-D for the win, it took less than twenty-four hours for Bubba and D-Von to mend any rifts caused by the WWE draft eight months ago, and put themselves in contention for the World Tag Team titles.

Although not an experienced team like the Dudleyz, William Regal and Lance Storm continued piling up their share of "W's." That included a November 18 win over Tommy Dreamer and Jeff Hardy, who never even got a chance to tag into the match. From the outside floor, Regal knocked the daredevil off the ring apron, then followed with a sharp kick to Dreamer's head, providing Storm an easy three-count. The loss became extremely painful for Dreamer

> "How *dare* you mistake my humility for *weakness*?!"

Jericho and Christian con*chair*to misses the Bubba-Tough target.

moments later, when Storm's drop-toehold sent his jaw impacting against a steel chair that Regal placed in the ring. Jeff tried sharing Dreamer's pain with the tandem in another *Raw* tag bout on November 25, this time Jeff partnering himself with The Hurricane. Unfortunately, the outcome didn't change much; despite getting some licks in after Storm's sharpshooter forced Hurricane to tap out, a missed Whisper in the Wind left the risk-taker open to a double-team beatdown.

One possible consolation for Jeff is that he wasn't the only one who'd left himself exposed in the North Charleston Coliseum that evening. The Dudley Boyz became embroiled in *several* attempts to strip Chris Jericho and Christian of their World Tag titles, thanks to new Chief of Staff Sean Morley, who overruled match decisions for each team to rectify rule infractions. Unfortunately, Chief Morley was nowhere to be found

when an equally violating low blow to Bubba Ray enabled Y2J to latch on the Walls of Jericho for the submission win. But the Dudleyz had a suitable revenge in mind, one that became apparent when Jericho and Christian came out of the locker-room showers and discovered the luggage holding their clothes were missing. Christian blew his shower-capped stack at Hurricane for not being a good crimefighter and preventing the thefts; until D-Von poked his head in the doorway and showed them their bags. The towel-wrapped twosome gave chase before realizing they weren't exactly dressed for a fight, a situation that grew more problematic after Bubba suddenly yelled *"Wassup?!"* from *inside* the locker room, then locked the door behind them!

The prospect of spending *Raw in* the raw, cold South Carolina air had Christian seriously fretting over shrinkage. "The little general's about to go into

Office Depot Center
Fort Lauderdale, Florida

ARMAGEDDON

**WORLD CHAMPIONSHIP
TWO OUT OF THREE FALLS MATCH**

Triple H (w/Ric Flair) defeated *Shawn Michaels* two out of three falls to become the new World Champion

WWE CHAMPIONSHIP MATCH

Kurt Angle defeated *Big Show (w/ Paul Heyman)* via pinfall to become the new WWE Champion

TRIPLE-THREAT WOMEN'S CHAMPIONSHIP MATCH

Victoria defeated *Trish Stratus & Jacqueline*, pinning Jacqueline to retain the Women's title

Batista (w/Ric Flair) defeated *Kane* via pinfall

Chris Benoit defeated *Eddie Guerrero* via submission

Edge defeated *A-Train* via disqualification

FATAL FOUR-WAY ELIMINATION WORLD TAG TEAM CHAMPIONSHIP MATCH

Lance Storm & William Regal eliminated *Dudley Boyz*; *Booker T & Goldust* eliminated *Lance Storm & William Regal*; *Booker T & Goldust* eliminated *Chris Jericho & Christian* to become the new World Tag Team Champions

Like the song said, "The end is here." And with that, *Armageddon* had arrived in the Sunshine State's Office Depot Center, putting four championships on the line and bringing the WWE's 2002 Pay-Per-View slate to an end.

World Tag Team Champions Chris Jericho and Christian hoped the end didn't begin with a title defense against Bubba Ray and D-Von Dudley, William Regal and Lance Storm, and Booker T and Goldust. Eliminating each team was the order of the Fatal Four-Way contest, which saw the Dudleyz' "Wassup?!" and 3-D on Christian erased by a blind tag to Regal and a hook of Bubba's tights for the pin. Regal and Storm joined the Dudleyz moments later, however, when Goldust caught the brash Brit off guard for the three-count. The Bizarre One stood out in the match, Bulldogging Y2J before Booker submitted to the Walls of Jericho, then halting Christian's Tag belt assault off the top rope. But despite being nailed with one of the straps by Jericho, the five-time WCW Champion rebounded, driving Jericho to the mat with the Book End for the one-two-three. Celebrating the moment with the crowd and Jonathan Coachman at ringside, an elated Booker reaffirmed to Goldust that he wasn't the weak link he believed himself to be; he was now one half of the new World Tag Team Champions! "Now can you dig that, *suckaaa!*"

Looking to derail the newly dubbed A-Train as payback for putting Rey Mysterio on the shelf recently, Edge soon had his hands full with the former Albert who'd been riding high and railroading the competition of late. Unable to secure the pinfall with an A-Bomb that powered Edge down to the canvas, A-Train tried offering his opponent a steel seat across the skull. But while the referee took the chair before it could reach its destination, Edge stopped the big man with a spear to the midsection. A-Train surprised Edge and the crowd when he kicked out of a probable three-count, then drew himself the disqualification after grabbing the steel chair again and connecting across Edge's knee. Intent on hurting the young Superstar, A-Train went to inflict more punishment until Edge kicked the seat back in his face, then scared off the official and unleashed a barrage of chair shots until the big man stayed down.

WWE Tag Champ Eddie Guerrero's one-on-one against Chris Benoit was a great showcase of mat wrestling and high-impact moves, with neither Superstar claiming a clear advantage until Eddie went up top and crossbodied Benoit on the outside floor. Eddie worked over the left leg of the Crippler, who soon cooled off Latino Heat with five successive German suplexes. Retaliating with the Frog Splash for a near fall, Eddie sent himself and Benoit sailing to the outside, where Chavo raced down and whacked the Rabid Wolverine with the Tag belt while his uncle distracted the official. Benoit again fought back, powerbombing Eddie and fending off separate attacks from both Guerreros as he went up top and hit the flying headbutt. Latino Heat cinched on his Lasso from El Paso, but Benoit countered into the Crippler Crossface, then switched arms as Eddie tried reaching the rope. Unable to break the hold, Guerrero had no choice but to tap out.

Earlier, Brock Lesnar wouldn't confirm for Josh Matthews whether or not he'd be in Kurt Angle's corner when he took on Big Show for the WWE Championship. Yet The Next Big Thing's guarantee to make an impact concerned Show enough to head towards Stephanie McMahon's office and make his grievance known to the *SmackDown!* GM. Paul Heyman suggested the intimidation tactics were what prompted Stephanie to lift Lesnar's suspension in the first place; he urged his giant client to return to the locker room and let him take care of business. The agent quickly learned that his polite appeals had no sway with Stephanie, either, and that Brock had the option of appearing in Angle's corner. Heyman's courteous facade faded as he warned the General Manager that there'd be no Mr. Nice Guy should Lesnar appear; Big Show would break his neck.

Dawn Marie next headed to the ring with her betrothed, Al Wilson, to answer all of the questions surrounding her recent rendezvous in Room 357 with Al's daughter, Torrie. Implying Torrie's absence from *Armageddon* was due to being embarrassed and ashamed over their *SmackDown!* encounter, Dawn presented video footage that provided a steamy "kiss-and-tell" account of the scantily clad Divas. Although the crowd seemed to enjoy it, Al insisted that his fiancée stop the tape, with Dawn finally consenting only after she felt she'd proven her point, that Torrie was nothing but "a sexual predator." Dawn suggested that she and her "little Bobo" head back to the hotel and make some footage of their own, and they took their leave.

Neither *Raw* newcomer Batista, accompanied ringside by Ric Flair, nor Kane masked any feelings as they faced off inside the squared circle; they just didn't like each other. To everyone's surprise, the rookie powerhouse showed no fear going toe-to-toe with the Big Red Machine, matching him blow for blow throughout the contest. But the Nature Boy's repeated distraction of the official would prove the difference-maker, particularly after Kane caught Batista with the Chokeslam. Dragging Flair into the ring, Kane dropped him with the big boot, only to fall moments later to a kick to the midsection and sit-down powerbomb, giving Batista a major upset in his first Pay-Per-View match.

Accompanied by his boy, B-2, Rappin' Rigoletto John Cena came out freestyling a message for everyone at *Armageddon*: anyone messing with him or "Bling-Bling" Buchanan and thought they could throw blows, "You'll end up like Marcia Brady—'Oh, no, *my nose!*' " Ironically, Trish Stratus would suffer a broken nose during an intense Triple-Threat match against Jacqueline and Women's Champion Victoria. It was every Diva for herself, with Victoria spending much of the match either on the outside floor or disrupting numerous pinfall attempts between Jacqueline and Trish. Jacqueline's aggressiveness often kept both opponents off-balance, until a roundhouse kick and forearm in the corner primed Trish for the win. But while the referee made the count, Victoria nailed Trish's head with the Women's title, then entered the ring and covered Jacqueline for the one-two-three. Retaining her title, the demented Diva added to the insult by walking off with Trish's hat.

Inside his locker room, Brock Lesnar told Kurt Angle that he wouldn't regret his role in lifting The Next Big Thing's suspension last week, though he still wouldn't confirm whether he'd be in Angle's corner. Before heading out for his match with Big Show, Kurt played a video of Paul Heyman screwing Lesnar out of his WWE title at *Survivor Series*, to remind Brock that retribution on the agent could be only twenty feet away. Still, there was no sign of Lesnar when Angle locked up with the five hundred-pound WWE Champion. Using his amateur background and ring smarts, the gold medalist elbowed out of a fireman's carry that forced Show to drop him on top of Paul Heyman on the outside floor, then snuck around the ring and came up behind Show, dumping him to the outside. From there, Show's awesome strength took over, catching Angle's flying crossbody from the apron and dropping him on the outer ring barrier.

The WWE Champ continued manhandling Angle, nearly finishing him with a sidewalk slam and bone-crushing bearhug until Kurt mounted an offense from the top rope, hitting a tornado DDT, moonsault and missile dropkick before dropping Show with the Angle Slam. Unable to secure the pin, the medalist cinched the ankle lock, but the struggling giant's kickout sent Angle crashing into the referee. Heyman worsened matters after throwing in a steel chair that Angle intercepted and used to scramble Show's brains, but with the referee still down as the big man tapped out to the ankle lock, A-Train raced in and blindsided Angle with a backbreaker. But moments after A-Train departed the ring and Big Show Chokeslammed Angle to the canvas, in came Brock Lesnar. The Ft. Lauderdale crowd erupted as The Next Big Thing slayed the giant with an F-5, then exited the ring just as Angle crawled on top of Show and the official recovered to make the three-count. With Lesnar's help, Kurt Angle had climbed over his biggest hurdle ever to capture the WWE Championship for the third time!

From the World in New York City's Times Square, Rob Van Dam predicted the Two-Out-of-Three Falls match between World Champion Shawn Michaels and Triple H would be a classic. That was an understatement. Halfway through the first contest, a vicious Street Fight exploded that saw the Heartbreak Kid and The Game beat the hell out of each other with a garbage can, a steel chair and whatever else they could get their hands on. The Cerebral Assassin, his right leg taped (it was discovered later that he'd partially torn his right quadriceps muscle), blocked HBK's Sweet Chin Music and worked his knee into a figure-four leglock. Escaping the hold, Shawn took the battle down the aisle, where Triple H broke out and ignited a barbwired two-by-four using the incendiary *Armageddon* set. Michaels stopped him with a kick to the midsection, then smacked the torched weapon into The Game's face, making him a burned and bloody mess. Back inside the ring, HBK continued pressing the advantage until his already-hurting knee gave out long enough for Triple H to hit the Pedigree and score the first pinfall.

The second contest, a Steel Cage match, proved just as violent. Although busted open after being slingshot into the unforgiving steel, Michaels still had plenty of fight left, exchanging blows as he and The Game were perched on top of the cage. Ignoring the official's ringside ban prior to the first match, Ric Flair came down and set up four tables, two on top each other around the aisle walkway, then entered the cage with a steel chair moments after

Michaels nailed Hunter with a flying elbow off the top rope. Intercepting the chair, HBK laid out both men, then kept them down with the Sweet Chin Music. Placing the Cerebral Assassin onto a table, Michaels climbed the top of the cage, from where he delivered a devastating splash that broke the wood—and nearly Triple H—in half. Hunter didn't budge as the referee counted to three, and awarded the second fall to the Showstopper.

Officials assisted a crimson-masked Flair from ringside as the battered and bloodied Triple H and Michaels squared off for the World title that dangled high in the air above them. Long hailed as the wrestler who set the standard in Ladder matches, the World Champion wasted no time exploiting his advantage over The Game, suplexing him onto the ladder before setting it up for an attempted splash. Hunter avoided the high-risk maneuver and Pedigreed his adversary, but there was no quit in Michaels, who threw the Cerebral Assassin off the ladder before he could take possession of the belt. Shawn sent Hunter to the outside with the Sweet Chin Music, but as he made his way up top to grab his prize, a desperate Triple H tipped the ladder over, sending Michaels out of the ring and crashing through the tables Flair set up earlier! All eyes in the Office Depot Center focused on Michaels's limp body while Hunter forced himself to climb the ladder and reclaim the World title. In many ways, neither man looked like a winner after *Armageddon*. Though they'd both close 2002 having accomplished their goals: Shawn Michaels was still the Showstopper, and Triple H was still The Game! ∎

Shawn Michaels shows why he is called the Showstopper.

retreat!" He and Jericho noticed the suitcase-carrying Dudleyz headed ringside on a nearby video wall. By the time they made their way out to the *Raw* stage, Bubba and D-Von were already offering the crowd a shirt, pants...and a jar of *ass cream*. Jericho didn't see anything funny about displaying his...that is, *Christian's* ass cream, but neither man would accept D-Von's invitation to come down and reclaim their belongings. The duo blanched as the Dudleyz threw their bags into the crowd, not even noticing that Spike was standing behind them on the ramp. "If you're going to rob us of our Tag Team titles," Bubba roared, "then *we're* going to rob you of your *dignity*! Spike—*get the towels*!" Before they could react, Jericho and Christian suddenly had a twofold problem—they were buck naked in the middle of the ramp, and *everyone* was *laughing*. The panicked pair raced backstage, while the silhouette of Christian behind the *Raw* screen suggested his "little general" had become a casualty of this particular war.

Wearing a larger than life grudge, Jericho and Christian exacted retribution at December 2 *Raw*, moments after a 3-D on Rosey gave the Dudleyz the three-count over 3 Minute Warning. They tossed Spike (who earlier held Rico at bay on the outside floor) off the *Raw* stage and onto the announce table. Then Jericho and Christian joined Jamal, Rosey and Rico for a vicious beatdown of Bubba and D-Von, who took a heinous one-man conchairto shot by Christian. Like they'd done to so many opponents throughout their career, the Dudleyz were left completely decimated in the ring, motionless and in need of medical attention.

With the Dudleyz out of the picture for the rest of the night, Jericho focused on his singles match with Booker T, determined to teach him that he wasn't a "sucka." Before squaring off, Booker suggested the "huge rock star" should consider a movie career based

> **"If you're going to rob us of our Tag Team titles, then *we're* going to rob you of your *dignity*!"**

on last week's *Raw* performance. "Chris Jericho, starring in his first feature film: *Stuart* **Little**!" As for himself, Book thought another title summed his parts up best: *8 Mile*. Jericho charged the ring, only to run into more problems than he bargained for. Unable to finish him with the Lionsault, he put the Walls of Jericho on Booker, who roll-reversed it into a near-fall. Christian came down to provide an outside assist while Jericho got the referee's attention, though Goldust's sudden intervention allowed his partner to retaliate with the scissors kick.

Booker would have had the win, but Chief Morley came out and stopped the referee from finishing the three-count. Declaring their bout officially over, Morley decided to involve Christian and Goldust and restart the contest as a World Tag title match. Coming off a Curtain Call performance that powered his singles victory against Rico last week, Goldust opened strong with an inverted atomic kneedrop, priming Christian's groin for a Golden Globes kick and surprise drop-toehold of Jericho moments later. Tag Team gold was within Booker's reach when he hit Y2J with the Book End, but Christian pulling the official to the outside allowed Jericho to tag him with one of the belts, then land the Lionsault to retain the titles.

Despite the loss, Booker and Goldust learned they would get another shot at the title at *Armageddon*, in a Fatal Four-Way Elimination match that also included December 9 *Raw* opponents William Regal and Lance Storm. Using an exposed turnbuckle on Tommy Dreamer's still-hurting jaw to defeat him and Jeff Hardy a week ago gave the former Un-Americans their sixth consecutive victory, a momentum they'd struggle to keep six days before the PPV. Booker landed the scissors kick on Storm while Goldust's boot offered the Golden Globes to Regal's groin, yet neither man could pick up the elusive three-count. But as Regal and Booker took their battle to the arena floor, Storm surprised Goldust by rolling through into a sharpshooter, and forcing the Bizarre One to tap out.

From ringside, a visibly frustrated Booker threatened to find Jonathan Coachman a new place for his microphone when the interviewer pointed out how often he and Goldust had come up short in their quest for Tag Team gold. The disheartened Goldust offered Coach a reason: "I'm the weak link." He added, "and, Book...I'm going to ask Eric Bischoff to give you another partner at *Armageddon*." Before Goldust knocked on Bischoff's door, however, Booker spoke from his heart. Yes, Goldust was a "sick, weirdo gold freak," but Booker realized "Goldie" was there whenever his back was against the wall. "You're the best Tag Team partner I've ever had, as well as my friend," Booker said. He gave Goldust a choice: he could go to Bischoff and quit, "or you can walk into *Armageddon* with me, Tag Team partners, and become Tag Team *Champions* of the World." Letting the words sink in, Goldust answered, "Let's *do* it," then roared in his best Booker T voice, "*Now can you dig that, suckaaaa!*"

Chris Jericho wasn't concerned with any of the Fatal Four-Way opponents he and Christian were facing at the PPV, including the Dudley Boyz, who they and Victoria were scheduled to compete against later in a Six-Person Tag Table match. Instead, he was more interested in offering the Dudleyz' partner Trish Stratus a backstage dose of "Vitamin C." Trish teased that it sounded, "very nutritious, especially if it's...*freshly squeezed*," yet thought his supplement two weeks ago looked more like "Vitamin *Wee*." Jericho laughed it up, until he thought of something even funnier: "Me looking at your *motionless, unconscious, bruised body* lying in the center of the ring after I put you through a table."

Jericho tried getting that last laugh as the no-DQ Tag Table match turned into a chaotic preview of *Armageddon*'s Fatal Four-Way, during which all four teams, Steven Richards and Spike Dudley ran interference from all sides. Booker T's scissors kick dropped Y2J before he could send Trish through a table, only to fall from a kick by Lance Storm, who got planted by a Dudley 3-D. Helping Trish pick up the win with a top-rope powerbomb of Victoria through some wood, Bubba and D-Von remained the last team inside the ring, and they were prepared to keep it that way when the referee awarded the Tag Team titles at *Armageddon*.

RAW PASSAGE TO INDIA

World Wrestling Entertainment completed its most ambitious international tour ever with a three-city live event tour of India in November 2002. Marking the organization's first visit to the country since 1996, the "WWE *Raw* Tour of India" was a long overdue happening that curried overwhelming favor from both fans and Superstars alike.

Over 20,000 fans packed New Delhi's I.G. Indoor Stadium for the first show, held on November 21, during which Bubba Ray and Spike Dudley defeated William Regal and Lance Storm in tag action, Rob Van Dam rode the Five-Star Frog Splash against Rico, and Chris Jericho and Christian retained the World Tag titles against Booker T and Goldust. The Superstars next traveled to Mumbai on November 22, where the 20,000 spectators within the MMRDA Grounds saw Test best Goldust, Y2J and Christian defeat RVD and Jeff Hardy in an Xtreme Tag title contest, and Kane Chokeslam William Regal to the delight of everyone in attendance. The final leg of the brief trip concluded in Bangalore's Palace Grounds on November 23, where the capacity crowd on hand witnessed The Hurricane's heroic win over Raven, and Tommy Dreamer emerge victorious in a Triple Threat match against Al Snow and D'Lo Brown. The Big Red Machine's overthrow of "King of the World" Jericho appropriately capped off not just an evening of exciting WWE action, but a successful tour within the world's largest democracy. ■

Suplexing Stacy is a snap for Victoria.

For *Raw* Superstars Test, Victoria, Christopher Nowinski and Batista, the end of 2002 came down to brains and brawn. In some instances, the two clashed; in others, they conjoined. In Test's case, there was no doubt who was the brawn; his successful new image firmly established consultant Stacy Keibler as the gorgeous brains behind his Test-icles. Test was overseas while Stacy juiced the *Raw* Test-icles with her latest marketing creation on November 18: a new T-shirt that declared, "I love my Test-icles!" Firing off free samples to the crowd with her "Test-icular cannon," the Diva saved one last blast for the groin of Steven Richards, who came out seeking payback after being humiliated by her a week ago. Stacy's laughter quickly subsided, however, when the new Women's Champion Victoria attacked her with a viselike armbar. She then savagely bit off a fingernail from her hand and screamed, "These people didn't come to see you! They came to see *me*!"

Filing a grievance with Eric Bischoff wasn't the smartest move on Stacy's part; the brains behind *Raw* loved watching someone as clearly out of their mind as Victoria. "The Bisch" decided the Women's Champ should have her first title defense against Stacy. The battle was short, and not at all sweet; Victoria locked her hands under Stacy's chin, stretched her on her back, and dropped to the canvas, forcing the Diva's skull and neck into hers. The new move, called the Widow's Peak, made for a painfully effective win. However, when Victoria decided to keep battering Stacy, former Women's Champion Trish Stratus raced in for the save. Unfortunately, Trish suffered a fate similar to Stacy when Richards planted her on the mat with his "Stevie T" DDT.

Carrying a backpack and chalkboard, Harvard grad Christopher Nowinski hoped "teacher's pet" Maven was taking time out from greeting fans inside the World in Times Square to watch his Hardcore rules-styled "School of Hard Knocks" match with *Tough Enough* mentor Al Snow. After "out-wrestling" Snow a week ago, Nowinski now guaranteed to out-*think* him, "...because in the end, brains *always* wins over brawn." Quickly putting Nowinski to the test, Snow used the chalkboard to break a few points off the Harvard grad's I.Q., then schooled him in the bloody, painful art of chair shots. Though fitted with a dunce cap, Nowinski was smart enough to dodge a moonsault that sent Snow crashing through several chairs, and picked up the three-count to earn another "W."

Ric Flair didn't get to be known as the dirtiest player in the game without being one of the smartest. Still fully dressed while Kane headed down the *Raw* ramp for the match Eric Bischoff had imposed earlier, Flair insisted he was only kidding when he told Bischoff he didn't sweat the Big Red Machine. Kane wasn't laughing as Flair provoked him into a chase around and into the ring, where the big man was nearly decapitated by a rock-hard clothesline from Batista. The Connecticut Kanenites watched in awe as the rookie powerhouse manhandled Kane like a seven-foot rag doll, then laid him down and out with the sit-down powerbomb. With a *Raw* bronco like Batista in his stable, the Nature Boy wouldn't have to worry about not having The Game around to watch his back.

Steven Richards could have used some of that muscle against Test on November 25. Richards crashed and burned after several high-impact slams and the "Test Drive" reverse neckbreaker that would make any Test-icle wince. Backstage, Stacy loved the taste of victory as her No. 1 Test-icle went to get dressed, until Victoria grabbed her from behind and told her that during her upcoming match against Trish Stratus, "...maybe I'll be thinking of *you*." Licking Stacy's ear, Victoria relished what only she could give her—"I love the taste of *fear*." Despite taking a "chick

Test powerslams Steven Richards.

[**"I love the taste of *fear*."**]

kick" to the face that drew blood, the psychotic Diva and her Widow's Peak fended off Trish's efforts to capture the Women's title a fourth time. She'd then celebrate her victory with some "tough love" for Richards on the *Raw* stage, pulling his hair and biting his ear. Truly, the perfect couple.

Before stepping into the ring with Maven, the book-carrying Christopher Nowinski wanted to savor the moment, since it would be the last time anyone could say the first *Tough Enough* Champion was better than him. "We all know the only reason you won *Tough Enough* was because of politics," he said, accusing Maven of using his mother's cancer to play "the sympathy card" with the judges. Maven dove through the ropes and pummeled the unbearable degree-bearer, who'd save himself when he broke out the heavy reading material and used it to dim Maven's lights out. Batista, meanwhile, needed more than book smarts to disorient Kane after a top-rope clothesline took out both him and the referee. Fortunately, the Nature Boy intervened with a chair shot that left the Big Red Machine defenseless against Batista's powerbomb, and unable to kick out before the shocking three-count.

For reasons known only to her, Victoria decided to add some personal items to her emotionally unstable baggage at December 2 *Raw*. Backstage, she wore what looked like one of Trish's hats while watching her hated arch-rival deliver Stratusfaction on Ivory for the one-two-three, then got busted while rifling through Jacqueline's locker-room belongings. Victoria didn't regard Jacqueline's resultant challenge to a match worthy of a Women's title shot. Then again, she also wasn't prepared for her response—"Who said anything about your title, you *psycho-bitch?*" Jacqueline was the one Diva who could match Victoria in sheer muscle, and did so to fight her way out of the Widow's Peak delivering a spin kick for a huge non-title victory in front of her hometown Dallas fans. Not even the ringside presence of batty boy-toy Steven Richards could calm Victoria as she screamed for her opponent to return to the ring.

Despite losing her match, Victoria exhibited an intensity that Ric Flair wanted to exploit in his young stud. That meant Batista needed to channel the rage built by a lifetime of foster homes and fighting, and channel it in the ring. The Hurricane became the first to bear witness to "the *real* Dave Batista," who knocked the wind out of him with a spinebuster, then emphatically picked up the victory with his sit-down powerbomb. But before Batista could display his pent-up rage with another powerbomb, Kane ran down and unleashed his fury, clotheslining the six-foot-five strongman from the ring and eyeing his every step back up the *Raw* ramp.

Inside the *Heat* locker room on December 8, Christopher Nowinski appealed to the educated man in D'Lo Brown, who split a pair of *Heat* decisions with Johnny "The Bull" Stamboli over the past two weeks. According to the Harvard grad, the University of Maine alumnus—a former European and Intercontinental Champion—was struggling to get airtime because guys like Maven played up their sick mother to acquire sympathy and a WWE contract. Damned if he'd let some rookie steal away his time, D'Lo paired with Nowinski against Al Snow and Maven, demonstrating his vicious streak by assaulting Snow from behind and going Sky High on Maven. The outcome was ultimately decided by the two former *Tough Enough* students, with Nowinski's ironic schoolboy of Maven leveraged by his feet on the ropes for the one-two-three. D'Lo would also get his time in the spotlight when the four

Superstar ★ profile

SCOTT STEINER

HEIGHT: **6'2"**
WEIGHT: **255 lbs.**
NICKNAMES: **Big Poppa Pump; Big Bad Booty Daddy; Genetic Freak; Freakzilla**
FINISHING MOVES: **Steiner Recliner; Frankensteiner**
CAREER HIGHLIGHTS: **Tag Team Champion (w/Rick Steiner) (2); WCW Television Champion (2); WCW Tag Team Champion (7); WCW U.S. Heavyweight Champion (3); WCW Heavyweight Champion**
2002 HIGHLIGHTS: **Making his first WWE appearance in nine years at *Survivor Series*; beating up Chris Jericho on November 18 *Raw*; walking out on Stephanie McMahon at December 12 *SmackDown!*; officially signing with Eric Bischoff and *Raw* on December 16.**

Batista celebrates the holidays his way with season's beatings.

men squared off again on *Raw* the following night; he'd catch Snow off guard with the Sky High, powering himself and Nowinski to another victory.

Hearing that *everything* was bigger in Texas, Stacy generated *Heat* for the Test-icles on December 8, while Test cooled off Justin Credible with a big boot for the three-count. Though they didn't have a match on *Raw* the next evening, bikini-clad "Stacy Claus" was busy producing holiday cheer with the perfect ornament for Test-icles to celebrate in style: Test's Christmas balls! Seeing his image on a pair of blue ornaments unnerved Test, though Stacy assured him they came in all colors, and looked perfect whether hung on a tree or held in her hands! The season for giving wasn't lost on Batista, who decided to bestow a *Raw* pounding on Rob Van Dam. But when Mr. Monday Night's top-rope kick to the chest prepped the strongman for a Five-Star Frog Splash, Ric Flair's apron assist distracted

him long enough for Batista to hurl him off the top turnbuckle. Before he could finish RVD with the powerbomb, Kane stormed the ring and delivered a big boot that sent Batista to the outside floor, while Van Dam followed suit with a spinning heel kick to the Nature Boy.

Although RVD wasn't upset that Kane's interference in the match drew him a DQ, Chief Morley voiced huge disapproval backstage. Acting like he didn't recognize the man formerly known as Val Venis, Kane gyrated his hips and offered two words when Morley reminded him, "*Hel-llooo, Morley*!" The outraged chief asked Kane what he thought about now having to face 3 Minute Warning in a Handicap match, to which the Big Red Machine replied, "I think it *sucks*...to be *3 Minute Warning*." He was right about that—Rico provided Jamal and Rosey with outside assistance throughout the match, yet it didn't stop Kane from taking out all three men, or from chokeslamming Jamal for the three-count. Their attempted triple-teaming after the contest also fell apart when RVD helped Kane clear the ring, then flew corner to corner for a steel-chaired Van Terminator on Jamal! The Big Red Machine wouldn't have Van Dam's aid when he and Batista squared off at *Armageddon* in six days, but the momentum Kane built on *Raw* that evening strongly suggested he might not need it.

Kane only needed a little time to take down 3 Minute Warning.

Steven Richards was also displaying extra bite in the squared circle, probably because of the literal scratching and clawing he and Victoria enjoyed *outside* the ring. She gnawed on him after his Stevie T win over Johnny "The Bull" on *Heat* the previous night, then gave him a good luck bite on the ear for his *Raw* Intergender match with Jacqueline, whose win over Victoria earned her a spot in a Triple-Threat Women's title match at *Armageddon*. Despite learning firsthand from her powerful forearm shots and tornado DDT that Jacqueline was no pushover, Richards eventually hooked her in his

specialized DDT for the victory. But when Victoria chimed in afterwards with the Widow's Peak, Trish Stratus dashed into the ring and put a beating on the Women's Champ. Though she was the other challenger in the Triple-Threat match, Trish respected her fellow Diva, who was less than appreciative; pushing Trish away, Jacqueline wanted it to be every Diva for herself come Sunday.

That kind of thinking suited Victoria, though if she had her way in that night's Six-Person Tag Table match, Trish wasn't going to make it to *Armageddon*. Before the bout, Victoria warned partners Chris Jericho and Christian, "Nobody puts that bitch through a table but *me!*" She might have been more successful, however, had her loathing for the Diva not detracted her from just winning the match. It was Trish's Dudley-propelled powerbomb putting Victoria through the wood that cost her team the match. Victoria may have been the strongest Diva in the WWE, but she was going to have to plan a better strategy if she wanted to keep that Women's title.

The *Raw-SmackDown!* war over Scott Steiner would be resolved before 2002 ended, though it couldn't happen soon enough for either general manager; until Big Poppa Pump declared his allegiance, no WWE Superstar was safe. Chris Jericho could attest to that, as would Steiner's next victim, Jamie Noble, who was already in a rut that cost him the Cruiserweight title at *Survivor Series*, and a *SmackDown!* loss to Rey Mysterio on November 21. Backstage at Columbia's Carolina Center for November 28 *SmackDown!*, the Genetic Freak made a bad first impression with Noble after handing a particularly strong one to Nidia's derriere! Heading ringside to defend his girl's honor, the livid

Noble flexes his "peak."

at least from the ring, after treating Richards to a press-slam, pushups and trash talk. Eric Bischoff personally welcomed the coveted free agent with a present backstage: an assortment of ladies he referred to as "Texas' finest." Though suitably impressed, the Big Bad Booty Daddy had to decline; he had a *superfreak* waiting in the limousine. "She's got the potential to be my favorite of *all time*," he told the GM as they headed to the vehicle. Bischoff's curiosity immediately turned to dismay when out came *Smack-Down!*'s GM, Stephanie McMahon! "What's the matter, Eric?" she asked, smiling. "Are you jealous because *I* can offer Big Poppa Pump something *you* just *can't?*" As Steiner entered the limo, Stephanie had one more thing to tell Eric before driving off, "*Holla, if you hear me."

Stephanie's "personal sacrifice" seemed to do the trick. It was announced that Steiner would sign with *SmackDown!* in the former WCW stomping grounds of Atlanta's Philips Arena on December 12. Yet when Freakzilla entered the ring that night and reviewed the contract sitting on a table, he refused to sign. It seems Stephanie never delivered on the

cruiserweight called out Steiner, who obliged him with a hellacious clothesline, press-slam and suplex that jettisoned Noble to the outside floor.

Giving Nidia another smack on the backside before she could exit the ring, Freakzilla took center stage. He hadn't decided between *Raw* or *SmackDown!*, but his assaults on Jericho last week and "the redneck" moments before showed he wasn't just sitting at home and wasting away. For now, his priority remained flexing his peaks and pleasing his freaks. "And when they screamed, 'Boom Shaka Laka,'" he said, "that's when they call me the daddy...the Big Bad Booty Daddy! So this goes to all my freaks in South Carolina: Big Poppa Pump is your hookup! *Holla if you hear me!*"

The Genetic Freak returned for December 2 *Raw*, only moments after Victoria dropped her non-title match to Jacqueline. Steiner showed the psychotic Women's Champ how to dump her "wacko" boyfriend,

"Holla if you hear me!"

"suggestive promises" she made during their *Raw* ride ten days ago. Stephanie tried explaining that her offer was "a *signing bonus.* All you have to do is sign on the dotted line, and then we can...*seal the deal.*" Steiner propped her up on the table and asked, "*Why wait?* My freaks are watching! They *like* watching!" Shocked and embarrassed, the GM pushed him away, prompting the Big Bad Booty Daddy to ask his freaks if he could trust his career to such a "tease." The audience cheered in unison, "*Hell, no!*" Steiner gave Stephanie his decision: "*SmackDown!* is a great show, and I'd love to be on it, but *you're* the reason why I'm not signing. So this goes to all my freaks in Atlanta: Big Poppa Pump is your hookup…on *Raw*! *Holla if you hear me*!"

As Steiner made his way back up the ramp, Stephanie begged him to reconsider; she'd even seal the deal on the table! Coming out on stage to meet his new acquisition, Eric Bischoff smiled towards his fellow general manager, now tossing everything around the ring in frustration. Whatever feelings he had for Stephanie, victory seemed much more enjoyable.

For *SmackDown!*'s Dawn Marie, John Cena and Bill DeMott, the name of the game was dominance, whether it was in the ring, the bedroom or "thugonomics." Before Cena mixed it up against Rikishi in the Hartford Civic Center on November 21, Dawn and Al Wilson came out on stage and invited every *SmackDown!* fan to be part of their impending blessed union. The two-hundred-forty-pound Cena made a futile attempt to "out-Kish" his three-hundred-fifty-pound opponent's chest. Taking Cena belly-to-belly for an easy win, the Phat Man climbed up for the corner rump-shaker. Suddenly, returning WWE Superstar Bull Buchanan raced under him and dropped backwards with an Electric Chair that practically dented the center of the ring. Adding the "Ice" to Cena's new "Vanilla" personality, "Bling-Bling" Buchanan, a.k.a. "B-2," made his bad self known when Cena and Matt Hardy hooked up against Rey Mysterio and Edge on November 28.

Stopping Mysterio's digits from going 619 on Matt's head, his outside interference bought Version 1 time to recover with a powerbomb and grab the ropes to secure the pin on Rey.

Between Cena, B-2 and the entrants of the upcoming "Pilgrim Fashion Show," the Thanksgiving edition of *SmackDown!* resembled the show's *Halloween* party. Even with the Turkey Day feast inside the ring, guest announcer (and current *Velocity* co-host) Ernest "The Cat" Miller just couldn't swallow "*SmackDown!*'s favorite turkey," Al Wilson, wearing a fowl-feathered costume and extolling the virtues of Thanksgiving for bringing his "little angel" Torrie together with his "little pookins" Dawn Marie. Torrie wowed the crowd of judges with her two-piece "Poca*hot*ness" outfit, though her thoughts were of burying her toy tomahawk into Dawn's back, especially when the provocative pilgrim flaunted a Plymouth-sized engagement rock in her face. Torrie made Dawn taste some pie, tore the clothes off her back, served a bowl of punch over her and then dumped a giant pumpkin on her head. And since her father was acting like a birdbrain over Dawn, she made sure he looked the part, placing the turkey head back on Al before leaving.

Life in the ring was no laughing matter for Bill DeMott, who made his return at December 5 *SmackDown!* after completing his trainer stint on *Tough Enough 3*. After picking up *Velocity* wins against up-and-comers, DeMott gave "Number One *SmackDown!*

GIVING THANKS, TIMES TEN

Families attending or tuning in to the annual Macy's Thanksgiving Day Parade were in for a *Raw* morning on November 28, and not just because of the freezing temperatures in New York City. World Wrestling Entertainment gave thanks to its loyal supporters everywhere with a *Raw* tenth anniversary float in the world-famous parade. The float was well represented with a ring, a TitanTron and announce booth, tables, ladders, chairs and of course, the Superstars of the WWE. In attendance was Triple H, The Hurricane, Victoria, Sgt. Slaughter, Jonathan Coachman, Lilian Garcia, WWE owner Vince McMahon, and *Raw* commentators Jim Ross and Jerry "the *Ring*" Lawler, according to NBC's Al Roker. Perhaps he didn't realize that it's good to be the *King…sometimes*. ■

B-2 lays the beat down on the Phat Man.

Announcer" and "big fan" Funaki an even bigger ass-whooping. DeMott moonsaulting his large frame on top of Funaki. Meanwhile, John Cena came out to bust a rhyme against Rikishi in *SmackDown!*'s first-ever Hip-Hop Challenge. Cena's "fresh" street duds drew more laughs than his freestyle. "Me and B-2 is *way* too nice for this place. / Yo, Kish, how's it feel to get the verbal *Stinkface*?" Rikishi, on the other hand, got the Dallas crowd in the groove with his lyrics: "See, we old-school thugs. / This game ain't new to me. / Boy, I ain't scared / O' no Eminem *wannabe*!" The Phat Man also showed Cena and B-2 he was versed in fighting off double-team efforts, though contest host Tazz pitched in and made Cena "just another victim" with his Tazzmission.

With Al Wilson away overseas, Dawn Marie decided to do a number on Torrie—specifically, Room 357, her hotel room, when she revealed, "He's not the *only* Wilson in your family that I'm interested in." Despite confessing her admiration for the Diva had grown into so much more, Dawn insisted, "I love your father so much. The question is…how much do *you* love your father?" With that, the vixen handed Torrie a room key, and an indecent proposal: she wouldn't marry Al, provided Torrie saw her later that evening. Though she appeared repulsed by the notion, a *SmackDown!* camera stationed in the hotel later caught the Diva entering the room. Dawn Marie, wearing a sultry black robe and holding a glass of champagne, walked over and caressed Torrie's blonde hair. When Torrie rejected her advances and headed for the door, Dawn commented, "I guess you *don't* love your father, after all." Slowly, she returned to the dominating vamp, who smiled and said, "That's better."

What happened between the Divas remained a mystery when the December 12 *SmackDown!* kicked off with a match between Rikishi and B-2, who demonstrated some slick moves inside the ring, including a springboard off the middle turnbuckle that brought the Phat Man down. A savage kick set B-2 up for a "piece of the Kish," until a low blow and distraction of the referee allowed John Cena to nail the big man with a steel chain between the eyes. Bill DeMott, meanwhile, didn't have need of foreign objects; he was a formidable weapon without them, and he didn't waste time demolishing his competition. Mattitude follower Shannon Moore couldn't even mount an offense before DeMott moonsaulted him so hard the "M.F.-er" practically needed to be scraped off the mat.

Torrie Wilson prepared to dish out more than gossip that evening when she learned Dawn Marie was making their secret rendezvous the talk of the *SmackDown!* locker room. Dawn feigned hurt feelings over the Diva's threats, "…especially after the night we spent together. Wasn't it as special to you as it was to me?" Torrie demanded that she live up to her end of the agreement and publicly call off the wedding. Dawn brought Al to the ring and confessed to spending the night with his daughter. She stressed, "Every time I looked into Torrie's eyes, I saw yours. And every time I kissed Torrie's lips, I felt like I was kissing yours." With Dawn twisting the events of the tryst like a pretzel, Al's reaction wasn't surprising—he still wanted to get hitched. Ecstatic, Dawn hugged Al and said, "Despite what that *bitch* Torrie wanted me to do, I'm *still* going to marry you on *SmackDown!*, and *no one* is going to tell me I can't be your wife!"

Jumping into the ring, Torrie started beating the

> **"*Everyone's* going to see exactly what you are! They're going to see that you enjoyed it, and that you're nothing but a *sexual predator!*"**

hell out of her future stepmom, even knocking her father down as he tried to separate them. Torrie took the fight to the outside floor, ramming Dawn into the steel steps before officials could restrain her. From the top of the ramp, a furious Dawn announced she'd get even in three days, when everyone watching *Armageddon* would learn exactly what happened in Room 357. "I'm going to show the whole world how much you *enjoyed* what happened in that hotel room!" she screamed. "*Everyone's* going to see exactly what you are! They're going to see that you enjoyed it, and that you're nothing but a *sexual predator!*"

To hear Paul Heyman tell it, the end came for Brock Lesnar at *Survivor Series*, when the seven-foot-two Big Show accomplished what no other Superstar in World Wrestling Entertainment could do: pin The Next Big Thing and win the WWE Championship. But as Heyman, Show, General Manager Stephanie McMahon and the *SmackDown!* Superstars vying for No. 1 Contendership would discover in the final weeks of 2002, Lesnar was anything but done. And *Armageddon* was just the beginning.

Stalking the backstage area of the Hartford Civic Center, Brock Lesnar wanted to personally welcome Paul Heyman and Big Show to November 21 *SmackDown!*. No one dared look in his direction while he was in the locker room. No one, that is, but Matt Hardy, who was impressed with his "buddy's" F-5 of Big Show at *Survivor Series*. "Too bad your agent had to screw you out of the title," he lamented, suggesting if Brock had a few more Mattributes and a touch more Mattitude, "then you probably wouldn't have suffered such an unfortunate Twist of Fate." Lesnar nodded, patted Matt on his shoulder…and threw him through a wall!

The unconscious Version 1 was certainly in no condition to report Lesnar's assault to Stephanie McMahon. It didn't stop Eddie Guerrero and his personal parrot Chavo, who complained that Brock was turning *SmackDown!* into "a *very* unsafe work environment!" Approaching him in the parking garage, the GM empathized with the still-stewing Lesnar, promising that even though Edge had a title shot against Big Show later that night, he'd soon get his rematch. But she wouldn't tolerate his actions in the locker room, or put her Superstars' lives in jeopardy. "If you so much as lay a hand on Paul Heyman, the Big Show or any other *SmackDown!* Superstar tonight," she cautioned, "then I'll be forced to suspend you." Brock shot his boss a look, then walked off, obviously none too pleased.

Regardless of whether Stephanie's edict made him feel safer in his work environment, Eddie Guerrero accompanied nephew and WWE Tag Team Co-Champion Chavo to the ring for his one-on-one against Chris Benoit. But he wouldn't get to stay at ringside; the referee ordered him backstage. While Chavo mounted a solid offense without having his uncle to watch his back, the Rabid Wolverine locked Chavo into the Crippler Crossface for the submission.

Brock Lesnar's quarry arrived within minutes of Stephanie's warning, and they'd heard the good news. Stephanie invited Lesnar to her office to warn him that Big Show and Paul Heyman were headed to the ring. She had to give the new WWE Champion airtime, and in Brock's current state of mind, she was afraid he'd fall for the agent's likely attempts to provoke him. Refusing to let "a viable commodity to *SmackDown!*" hurt himself like that, Stephanie restated her earlier warning. Brock replied, "That's *bullshit.*"

When Lesnar's music hit the arena, it appeared to all that Brock was calling Stephanie on her threat. The crowd was unpleasantly surprised, however, when Paul Heyman came out on stage, wearing the WWE title around his waist and bouncing back and forth as if *he* were The Next Big Thing. The agent urged fans everywhere to credit his "extraordinary greatness" that led Brock to *King of the Ring*, plotted the end of Hollywood Hulk Hogan, provided the necessary tools to defeat The Rock at *SummerSlam* and ensured Brock's Hell in the Cell victory over Undertaker at *No Mercy*. But when the monster stopped listening to his Dr. Frankenstein, "I had to show Brock Lesnar *who was boss.*" That's when the colossus of mind teamed with the giant of body, and "…single-handedly engineered the greatest inside job in the history of sports entertainment," costing Lesnar the WWE title at *Survivor Series.*

Introduced as Heyman's new client, Big Show fought back a crocodile tear as he thanked The Next Big Thing for giving him the title shot, and "…for being so hotheaded and leaving the door wide open so that I could walk in and take everything that you had." Now that he was "a focused, determined and defending champion, with the most brilliant mind in our business today behind me." Show wasn't giving up his title to Lesnar, Edge or anyone. That reminded Heyman of one other matter: he officially dumped Brock as his client, but not before he negotiated one extra clause in his *Survivor Series* contract. "And that clause," he revealed, "is called '*no rematch.*'"

The sense of triumph Heyman felt carrying the belt back up the *SmackDown!* ramp quickly turned to fear when he saw The Next Big Thing charging fast behind them and wielding a chair. The agent barely escaped

[**"You *will* listen to me, Brock! If you do anything else tonight, you *will* be suspended, I guarantee it! *Try* me!"**]

Edge tries cutting down Big Show with a spear.

as Brock leveled the new champion with a massive chair shot across his back. Officials could barely contain him as he pursued Big Show all the way backstage, though Stephanie McMahon showed no fear as she got in Lesnar's face. "You *will* listen to me, Brock!" She promised, "If you do anything else tonight, you *will* be suspended, I guarantee it! *Try* me!"

To say order was restored when *SmackDown!* resumed would be untrue, since Kurt Angle and Eddie Guerrero were squaring off in the ring. Latino

"King Kong *always* kicks Godzilla's ass!"

Heat took control of the contest after conning the referee into taking a chair from him and returning it to the outside, while he used another one positioned nearby to smash the gold medalist's lower back. Like his uncle earlier, Chavo had been ordered backstage, though he'd slowly inch his way down to the *SmackDown!* ramp, never realizing that Chris Benoit also came out and stood on the stage behind him. Not that it made a difference; Benoit was of no help to his partner when Chavo ran down and cheap-shotted

Angle on the outside floor. Angle crotched Latino Heat as he climbed up for the Frog Splash, then fought off another attack from Chavo before nailing Eddie with a top-rope Angle Slam. Picking up the three-count and ankle-locking Chavo for good measure, Angle glared towards the stage, from where his tag partner smugly clapped away.

While interviewing Edge about his title shot against Big Show, "Number One *SmackDown!* Announcer" Funaki compared the WWE Champion to Godzilla. If that were the case, Edge suggested he consider himself "…a big, hairy ape named King Kong, and like everyone knows, King Kong *always* kicks Godzilla's ass!" Inside his locker room, an agonized Big Show looked not-so-monstrous after Lesnar's chair shot almost broke his spine. "There's no way I can compete tonight!" he argued, and directed his agent to give Stephanie the bad news. Unfortunately, her news was worse. Whatever shape he was in, "…make no doubt about it, the Big Show *will* be defending his title against Edge, *tonight.*" Her promise to suspend Brock Lesnar if he interfered didn't hold much weight with Heyman, who offered his own guarantee to Stephanie; if the "ruthless animal" attacked either his client or himself, "I will sue you. I'll sue your father. I'll sue your whole freakin' family. And I'll sue *SmackDown! right into the ground*!"

> **"I will sue you. I'll sue your father. I'll sue your whole freakin' family. And I'll sue SmackDown! right into the ground!"**

Whether or not the giant was injured, Edge still had his hands full with him when the match started. Though he couldn't budge his near-immovable frame for an Edgecution, he would find success with a drop-toehold into an exposed turnbuckle, followed by a low blow and tornado DDT from the corner. Finally taking Show off his feet with three consecutive spears to the midsection, Edge was on the verge of making his life-long dream reality when the frantic Heyman pulled him to the outside floor before the referee counted three. Before Edge could dish out payback, Show suddenly pulled him onto the apron, then Chokeslammed him back into the ring.

Edge was finished, but Heyman wasn't. He ordered his giant client to "treat him like he's *Brock Lesnar*!" Show delivered a second Chokeslam, then a *third*, and would surely have continued had the real Lesnar not showed up. Hammering away at the WWE Champion, The Next Big Thing hoisted him onto his back and delivered an F-5 in the center of the ring! Heyman ran for his life, bolting to the backstage area with Brock hot in pursuit. Unfortunately, he just missed the agent as he jumped into the back of a limousine that speeded off.

While Paul Heyman had escaped an untimely demise that evening, The Next Big Thing's fate remained uncertain as Stephanie McMahon opened November 28 *SmackDown!* with a major announcement for the Carolina Center crowd. With her responsibilities divided between the fans and the well-being of her Superstars, Brock Lesnar had placed her in an awkward position. She explained, "*I* am the boss. I don't speak just to hear myself talk, and what I say *goes.*" Before Stephanie could say much else, Lesnar made his way to the ring; since it was *his* career the GM was discussing, "you can tell me face-to-face exactly *what* you're going to do with it." Brock's imposing presence spooked Stephanie out of the ring and up the *SmackDown!* ramp, where several police officers suddenly lined up as a barrier. "I'm not stupid," she told Brock. "I know you can snap at any minute, and these officers are here for your protection." Hearing the upset fans boo her, Stephanie urged them to understand, "I didn't screw Brock Lesnar. *Brock Lesnar* screwed Brock Lesnar. Brock…you're *suspended. Indefinitely.*"

"Brock...you're *suspended. Indefinitely.*"

Having police escort Lesnar from the building only further destroyed the respect Stephanie had built with fans since becoming *SmackDown!*'s General Manager last July. She also seemed unwilling to accept her part in drawing their boos, complaining to Kurt Angle backstage that she'd never again bring *SmackDown!* to a disrespective "hellhole" like Columbia, South Carolina. Angle tried to relate, but couldn't understand why a recent visit from "Aunt Flo" put her in a bad mood. He thought it was "awesome" that she visited, even more so after Stephanie pointed out Aunt Flo's visit was a *monthly* call. The GM finally gave up and spelled it out. "I had *PMS*. You *do* know what PMS is, don't you?" Kurt halfheartedly mumbled, "Yeah...pretty much," but as Stephanie left, he wondered aloud, "What the heck does PMS have to do with her Aunt Flo?"

At least the gold medalist wasn't so ingenuous when it came to matters inside the ring. If anything, he and Chris Benoit understood all too well what they were doing when they engaged in their usual round of one-upsmanship, this time exchanging dueling German suplexes on WWE Tag Champs Chavo and Eddie Guerrero. Not appreciating being their personal whipping boys, the champs grabbed their belts and started to leave, until the referee ordered them to continue the match or forfeit the titles. Angle and Benoit's self-destruction as a team continued as both men competed over which submission move Latino Heat would tap out to first. The referee pulled Kurt off, missing Eddie tap out, while Chavo broke Benoit's hold with a Frog Splash. Eddie tried following up with one of his own until Angle took him belly-to-belly off

the top rope, but as Kurt and the official argued, Chavo clobbered Benoit with his Tag belt, allowing his still-groggy uncle to pick up the pinfall.

While Tajiri spit his trademark green mist into the face of Chuck Palumbo knocking the stuffing out of him for a Thanksgiving Day win, Marc Loyd pursued a growing cloud of controversy that Brock Lesnar had returned to the arena parking lot. Instead, Loyd came across Scott Steiner, whose only comment was to flex his peaks for the *SmackDown!* camera. Inside her office, Stephanie prepared to greet her special guest, only to be paid a visit by the Fabulous Moolah instead. She'd forgotten her appointment with the ring legend, who became upset with the GM's continued barbs about her hometown of Columbia. Stephanie didn't seem to care for Moolah's tone, either, though she apologized and offered to make amends with a match against an opponent to be determined later. Always ready for a fight, Moolah accepted, while a smiling Stephanie encouraged her to "give 'em hell" in the ring.

Despite Loyd's efforts to get a scalper to admit he sold a *SmackDown!* ticket to someone fitting Lesnar's description, Paul Heyman was so convinced The Next Big Thing had left the Carolina Center that he informed Stephanie that Big Show would waive his "no-rematch" clause against Brock for that evening. Not wanting to disappoint the agent or his client, Stephanie declared Show would defend his title that night "against an opponent of championship status." To everyone's surprise, that opponent was a twenty-five-year holder of the Women's title! Moolah was so frightened by the approaching giant she couldn't move, while the pompous Heyman mockingly assured that Big Show merely wanted to wish a "Happy Thanksgiving" to someone of her accomplishments. "Then again," he realized, "maybe the Big Show *doesn't* look at you like you're the Fabulous Moolah. Maybe the Big Show looks at you...like *you're Brock Lesnar*...and maybe 'Brock Lesnar' needs to be *Chokeslammed right through that mat!*"

Thankfully, Big Show never got his hands on the seventy-nine-year-old Superstar; Brock Lesnar raced in and beat him all the way to the outside floor. Lifting the giant up over his shoulders, Brock brought the crowd to its feet as well, delivering an F-5 that obliterated the *SmackDown!* announce table! Looking to offer the same to the terrified agent heading up the ramp, Brock charged towards Heyman, only to be stopped at the last moment by the police and Stephanie McMahon, who stood out on stage and yelled, *"Get him out of here! He's suspended!"*

With any possibility of Brock Lesnar obtaining a rematch with Big Show at *Armageddon* completely removed by his suspension, a Fatal Four-Way Elimination match was announced at December 5 *SmackDown!*. Edge, Eddie Guerrero, Kurt Angle and Chris Benoit would compete for the coveted No. 1 Contender's spot, with the winner advancing to the PPV and facing the giant for the WWE Championship.

Though Albert could run with any *SmackDown!* heavyweight, he vented his frustrations against guys like Crash Holly. After losing on November 23 *Velocity* Holly continued goading Albert with a razor and shaving cream inciting "Shave your back" chants. Although Rey Mysterio was hardly the same size or weight, Albert saw a chance to make his mark against a major *SmackDown!* Superstar. He'd succeed on December 5, though not because he countered Rey's West Coast Pop rollup into a backbreaker victory. Instead, Albert ambushed and hung him upside-down in the corner, then smashed away at his left leg with a steel chair. Edge raced down for the save, but the damage was done. Stretchered out of the ring by paramedics, Mysterio would require surgery on his left knee, putting him out of action for the next several months.

On stage, Stephanie McMahon tried making the ludicrous comparison of Rey's tragic sacrifice to one she was making for the American Airlines Arena crowd that evening: letting Brock Lesnar tell his version of the past few weeks, live…but via *satellite*. Appearing on the *SmackDown!* TitanTron from his home in Minneapolis, Minnesota, The Next Big Thing would offer announcers Michael Cole and Tazz no excuses; he got what he deserved for associating himself with a slimeball like Heyman. He also stressed that he'd since learned from his mistakes, and now sought to punish the agent and his giant puppet "…in the most brutal fashion imaginable." Suddenly, Heyman and Big Show came out for a "face-to-face" at ringside, where the now-fearless agent wanted to correct a comment Stephanie made. "Brock Lesnar did *not* screw Brock Lesnar," he insisted. "*We* screwed Brock Lesnar!" We *enjoyed* screwing you! If we could turn back the clock a week before *Survivor Series*, when Big Show and I came up with this whole plan, we would screw you *all over again*!"

Letting Heyman rub in the fact that other Superstars were about to compete for the No. 1 Contendership, Brock conceded that the idea of Angle, Edge, Benoit or Guerrero facing Big Show at *Armageddon* sounded like "one hell of a title match. I can't wait to see it…*in person*." With that, Lesnar stood up, removed his microphone and left the screen, giving a very upset Big Show and Heyman a new problem to worry about.

> **"We *enjoyed* screwing you! If we could turn back the clock…we would screw you *all over again*!"**

As for the evening's Fatal Four-Way participants, each of them realized what was at stake. Benoit saw it as the end result from a lifetime of sacrifices, which included a broken neck, a divorce and rarely seeing his family "…to become what I want to be, what I've always dreamed of being since I was three years old: a

Heyman realizes that he'd better
deliver on his promises.

The Canadian Crippler German
suplexes Latino Heat.

champion. *The* champion. The *WWE Champion*." In the locker room, Latino Heat believed Chavo's upcoming Cruiserweight title match against Champion Billy Kidman, joined by the prospect of him becoming "El Numero Uno," was a chance to show what the Guerreros were all about. "If we are the Tag Team Champions, Cruiserweight Champion *and* the WWE Champion," he said, "there is *no* stopping Los Guerreros from taking over!"

Edge admitted to Marc Loyd that his focus to become WWE Champion may have shifted after witnessing the assault on Rey Mysterio, but it wasn't lost. "If anything, this match is going to be an outlet for the aggression that I'm going to take out on Albert when I get my hands on him!" That came moments later, when Edge saw Mysterio's assailant and charged him, prompting officials to break them apart. Kurt Angle flashed more intensity than usual when Loyd approached him for his last-minute thoughts before the match. "My thoughts are on winning the title for the third time," he said. "My thoughts are proving my superiority over Chris Benoit, *again*. My thoughts are showing Eddie Guerrero why I won these little bad boys [in the Olympics]. My thoughts are proving to Edge, and everyone else for that matter, why I'm not just the greatest Superstar ever in the history of *SmackDown!* Why I'm not just your hero, but also your next WWE Champion. Oh, it's true. It's damn true. And I'm about to prove it, right now."

Before the match officially started, it appeared Edge had been eliminated after Albert ran in and nailed him in the leg with a steel chair. Taken backstage for medical attention, the young Superstar showed his intestinal fortitude as he limped his way back to the ring. The injured leg became a focal point from the onset, with Angle and Benoit taking to it like a shark smelling blood. Yet it was Edge who'd set Latino Heat up to tap out first, after a spear left him helpless against Benoit's Crossface. Eddie's revenge against the Rabid Wolverine was equally swift—he'd knock Benoit senseless with his WWE Tag belt, allowing Edge to spear the Crippler and pick up the three-count.

With the match down to Angle and Edge, the medalist slapped the ankle lock on his opponent's injured leg. Escaping the hold, Edge soon battled back, yet couldn't finish Angle even after planting him with an Edgecution and his own Angle Slam. Kurt's refusal to stay pinned prompted Edge to climb the ropes once more for the killing blow, but it was the gold medalist who delivered it, leaping up and catching Edge with a tremendous Angle Slam off the top rope. Whether they liked or hated him as he picked up the one-two-three, Kurt Angle earned the appreciative Dallas audience's respect, as well as the No. 1 Contendership for the WWE title at *Armageddon*. He also merited the ire of the Big Show, who stormed to the ring within moments of Angle's victory and laid him out with a vicious Chokeslam to the canvas.

> **"I'm not just the greatest Superstar ever in the history of *SmackDown!*...I'm not just your hero, but also your next WWE Champion. Oh, it's true. It's damn true."**

Kurt Angle may have won the battle, but he realized he needed an ally for the war that lay ahead. Before *SmackDown!* kicked off on December 12, Kurt stood on line for Brock Lesnar's autograph, and his attention: he'd help get his suspension lifted if Brock helped him beat the Big Show "by being in my corner this Sunday, at *Armageddon*." Lesnar remained wary until the gold medalist pointed out that even he couldn't beat the giant with Heyman in his corner. Not only could Brock now get his hands on the agent who screwed him, but he'd be first in line for a title shot should Kurt walk away with the belt. "Don't tell me for a second you haven't thought what it would be like to face an Olympic Champion. To perhaps *beat* an Olympic Champion," Angle said. "It's right here, Brock: Angle versus Lesnar. The greatest match in WWE history. If you help me out, *I'll* help *you* out." Brock paused for a moment, then answered, "If...*if* you can get my suspension lifted...I'll think about it."

Inside the *SmackDown!* locker room, Paul Heyman was in a good mood. Not only was his "favorite client ever," the Big Show, scheduled for tag action later against Angle and Edge, but he was teaming up with a run-away locomotive he dubbed "A-Train," the sound of which Albert loved. But Heyman's thoughts of WWE Tag Team gold took a back seat when new *SmackDown!* interviewer and *Velocity* co-host (as well as runner-up in the first *Tough Enough*) Josh Matthews informed them of Brock Lesnar's possible reinstatement and subsequent appearance in Kurt Angle's corner at *Armageddon*. Big Show also erupted at the news, urging his agent to take care of the problem, but when neither man could keep themselves composed inside Stephanie McMahon's office, they only helped make her decision. "As of *Armageddon*," she declared, "Brock Lesnar's suspension will be *lifted*."

Since Eddie Guerrero had cheated Chris Benoit of his chance at the WWE title, the Rabid Wolverine had no problem taking on Latino Heat at *Armageddon*, and he hoped to do so with the WWE Tag title around his waist. He faced Los Guerreros with Cruiserweight Champion Billy Kidman, whose gravity-defying Shooting-Star Press stayed true since he won the title at *Survivor Series*, landing three consecutive *SmackDown!* wins over Tajiri (November 21), Crash Holly (November 28) and Chavo (December 5). Eddie would halt Kidman from

Big Show makes it clear he's keeping the WWE title.

delivering one on him and end his streak with a rollup for the three-count, while the referee failed to notice that Benoit's Crossface already had Chavo tapping out in the other corner.

Backstage with Josh Matthews, Edge was a roller-coaster of emotions; last week's steel chair assaults resulted in knee surgery for Rey Mysterio and a torn medial collateral ligament which hampered his own performance in the Fatal Four-Way match. Edge guaranteed that between their Tag match now and their one-on-one at the Pay-Per-View in three days, "Albert, or A-Train, or Big Baldy Hairy Ape or whatever the hell he's calling himself, is in for one severe *beat-down* for what he did to Rey, and for what he did to me." Suddenly distracted by Kurt Angle's arrival, Edge acknowledged him as his partner, but their past history forced him to ask, "Do you have my back?" Kurt's only response was, "I'm *confident* that I'll have your back tonight, just as I'm confident that *Brock Lesnar* will have *my* back this Sunday at *Armageddon*."

> "I'm *confident* that I'll have your back tonight, just as I'm confident that *Brock Lesnar* will have *my* back this Sunday at *Armageddon*."

Perhaps it was Angle's prior relationship with Chris Benoit that familiarized him to working with animosity in his own corner, but he and Edge functioned extremely well as a unit, until the giant's diversion of the referee allowed A-Train to take out Edge with another chair shot. Still, Kurt fought off the two-to-one odds, delivering Angle Slams to both men before slapping the ankle lock on Big Show. Suddenly, Paul Heyman's presence on the apron distracted Kurt into breaking the submission hold, and bought time for his giant to recover and Chokeslam Angle for the victory. Big Show and Heyman stood over their fallen adversary, whose fears were painfully confirmed; without The Next Big Thing in his corner, there was no way Kurt Angle was leaving *Armageddon*, or entering the New Year, with the WWE Championship.

Acknowledgments

I'd like to thank all the people who made this book a reality. First and foremost, the WWE Superstars who took the bumps while giving us fans a wonderful year, and all the people who support their work behind the scenes. For this book, I'd like to thank Donna Goldsmith, Stacey Pascarella, Frank Vitucci, and John Spooner at WWE for all the help they gave me, from the words to the photos. At Red Herring, I'd like to thank Deb and Carol, whose design brought the static words and pictures to life. For all the production folks at Pocket Books—Linda Dingler, Joann Foster and John Paul Jones, who once again pulled a rabbit out of the hat by getting this book out in record time. I'm also grateful to Dan Abnett, Eddie Berganza, Fearghal Brennan, Fletcher Chu-Fong, Michael Jan Friedman, Bob Greenberger, Charles Kochman, Andy Lanning, Dave McDonnell, Kilian Plunkett, Stuart Schreck, Rob Simpson, and Connor Stanton—family, friends, and colleagues who provided invaluable advice, the occasional videotape of WWE programming, and many ears for me to bend while producing these pages. Finally, I express endless gratitude to my editor, Margaret Clark, whose leadership and efforts make her the undisputed champion of this book. Thank you, one and all.